WITHDRAWN

HARVARD LIBRARY

WITHDRAWN

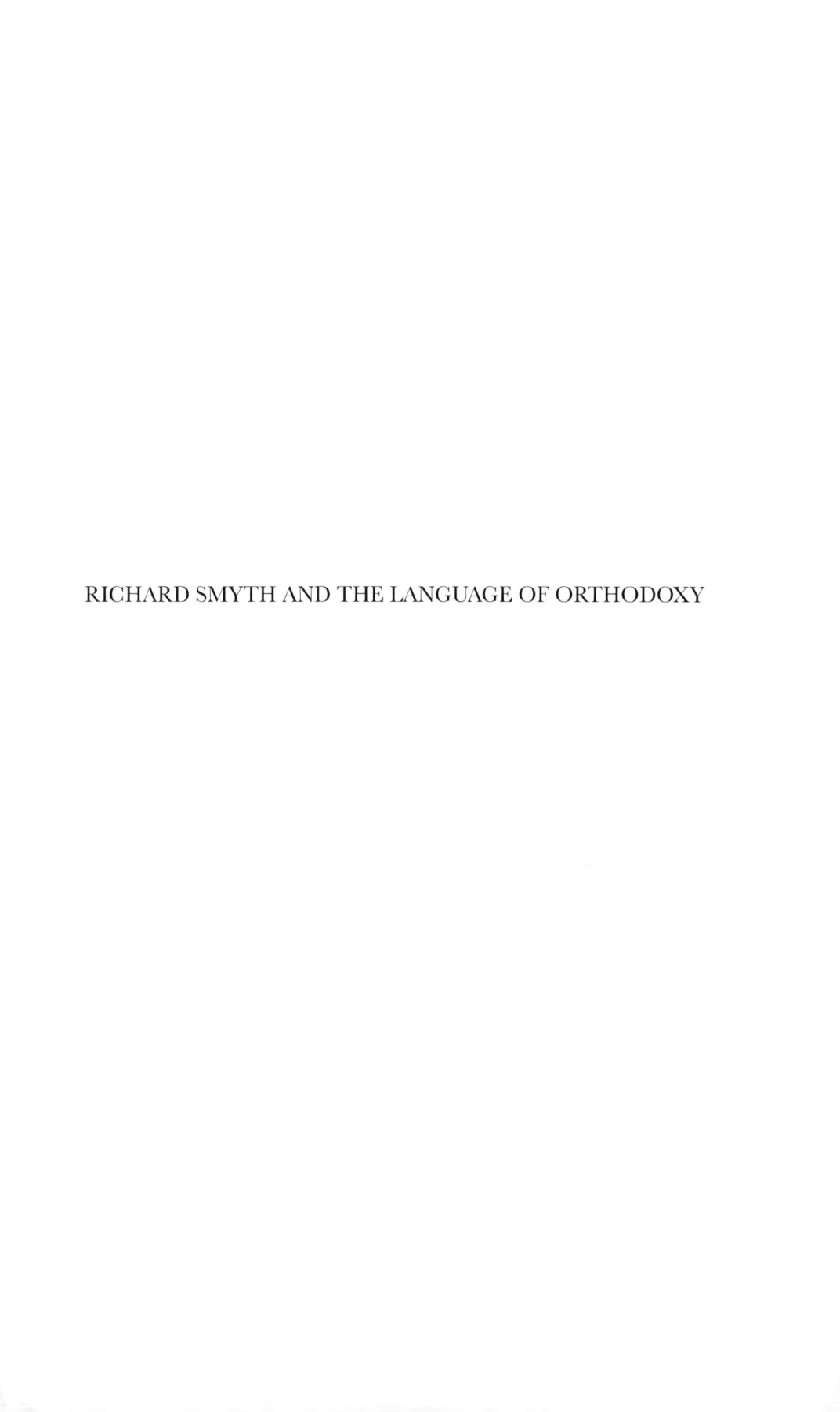

RICHARD SMYTH AND THE LANGUAGE OF ORTHODOXY

STUDIES IN MEDIEVAL AND REFORMATION THOUGHT

FOUNDED BY HEIKO A. OBERMAN †

EDITED BY

ANDREW COLIN GOW, Edmonton, Alberta

IN COOPERATION WITH

THOMAS A. BRADY, Jr., Berkeley, California
JOHANNES FRIED, Frankfurt
BRAD GREGORY, Stanford, California
BERNDT HAMM, Erlangen
SUSAN C. KARANT-NUNN, Tucson, Arizona
JÜRGEN MIETHKE, Heidelberg
M. E. H. NICOLETTE MOUT, Leiden

VOLUME XCVI

J. ANDREAS LÖWE

RICHARD SMYTH AND THE LANGUAGE OF ORTHODOXY

RICHARD SMYTH AND THE LANGUAGE OF ORTHODOXY

RE-IMAGINING TUDOR CATHOLIC POLEMICISM

BY

J. ANDREAS LÖWE

BRILL
LEIDEN · BOSTON
2003

This book is printed on acid-free paper.

Library of Congress Cataloging-in-Publication Data

Löwe, J. Andreas, 1973-
 Richard Smyth and the language or orthodoxy : re-imagining Tudor Catholic polemicism / by J. Andreas Löwe.
   p. cm. -- (Studies in medieval and Reformation thought, ISSN 0585-6914 ; v. 96)
 Includes bibliographical references and index.
 ISBN 90-04-12927-8

 1. Smith, Richard, 1500-1563. 2. Catholic Church--Apologetic works--History and criticism. 3. Reformation--England. I. Title. II. Series.

BX1752.L69 2003
203'.2'092--dc21

2002033026

ISSN 0585-6914
ISBN 90 04 12927 8

© Copyright 2003 by Koninklijke Brill NV, Leiden, The Netherlands

All rights reserved. No part of this publication may be reproduced, translated, stored in a retrieval system, or transmitted in any form or by any means, electronic, mechanical, photocopying, recording or otherwise, without prior written permission from the publisher.

Authorization to photocopy items for internal or personal use is granted by Brill provided that the appropriate fees are paid directly to The Copyright Clearance Center, 222 Rosewood Drive, Suite 910 Danvers, MA 01923, USA.
Fees are subject to change

PRINTED IN THE NETHERLAND

DUOBUS MAGISTRIS EGREGIIS
MEMORIA DIGNISSIMIS

RICHARD SMYTH (1500-1563)
BERND ROLAND LÖWE (1943-1993)

CONTENTS

List of Illustrations x

Acknowledgements xi

Introduction 1
   1.   Mid-Tudor Reforms.. 2
   2.   International Catholicism 7
   3.   The Language of Orthodoxy 9

Chapter One   Biography 13
   1.1.   Early Education (c. 1510-1536) 17
   1.2.   Oxford and London 22
   2.1.   Recantations (1547) 34
   2.2.   Peter Martyr Vermigli (1547-1549) 40
   3.1.   Smyth's First Continental Exile (1549-1551) 44
   3.2.   St Andrews (1551-1553) 49
   4.1.   Restitution (1553-1559) 51
   4.2.   Heresy trials: Latimer, Ridley and Cranmer (1555) 53
   4.3.   Arrest and Escape (1559) 57
   5.1.   The Foundation of the University of Douai 60
   5.2.   Evangelical Polemicists... 75

Chapter Two   Exegetical Lectures 78
   1.   The Evidence from François de Bar's Studies 79
   2.   De Bar's Lecture Notes 81
   3.   Smyth's Introductory Lectures on Romans (1562-1563) . 83
   4.1.   Smyth's Hermeneutical Method...................................... 92
   4.2.   Smyth's Exegesis of 1 Cor 10 and 11 96
   5.   'La vraye Religion et Foy catholique' 105

Chapter Three   Justification 108
    1.1.   The Medieval Understanding of Justification 110
    1.2.   Objections to the Late Medieval Understanding of Satisfaction and Merit 114
    2.1.   Smyth's 'Diatriba de Hominis Iustificatione' (1550) 120
    2.2.   Smyth's 'Bouclier' (1555) and 'Refvtatio' (1563): Works of Supererogation 138
    2.3.   'Stipendium Iustitiae Vita Aeterna' 142

Chapter Four   Monastic Vows 145
    1.   Early Reformation Debates (1521-1541) 147
    2.   Smyth's 'De Votis Monasticis' (1550) 151
    3.   Smyth and Vermigli Irreconcilable 171

Chapter Five   Eucharistic Theology 175
    1.   The Late Medieval Understanding of the Eucharistic Sacrifice 177
    1.1.   Gabriel Biel (c. 1420-1495) 179
    1.2.   Luther and his Early Opponents 181
    2.   Smyth's 1546 Publications and their Sources—Eck and Fisher 185
    2.1.   Eck's 'De Sacrificio Missae' and Smyth's 'Defence of the Sacrifice of the Mass' 186
    2.2.   Fisher's 'De Veritate Corporis et Sanguinis Christi in Eucharistia' and Smyth's 'Assertion and Defence of the Sacrament of the Aulter' 200
    2.3.   'Priest and Prophet'—Smyth's 'A Defence of the Blessed Masse' and his 'Assertion and Defence of the Sacrament of the Aulter' 209
    3.   1550 and 1562—The 'Manducatio Impiorum' and the Sacrifice for the Dead 210
    3.1.   The 'Manducatio Impiorum' 212
    3.2.   The Sacrifice for the Dead 216
    4.   Seeking to Restore the Eucharistic Life 218

Conclusion   'A Bouclier of the Catholike Fayth' 221
    1.   Smyth as a Polemicist 222
    2.   Smyth's Polemical Achievement 228
    3.   The Purpose of Sixteenth-Century Polemicism 235

Bibliography 239
   1. Manuscript Sources 239
   2. Primary Sources and Contemporary Sources in Print 239
   3.1. Secondary Literature 249
   3.2. Secondary Literature: Articles 257

Indices 263
   Name Index 263
   Place Name Index 269
   Subject Index 271

LIST OF ILLUSTRATIONS

Figure 1   Smyth preaching at the burning of Bishops Latimer and Ridley in Oxford 55

Figure 2   Manuscript page, *Epistolae Virorum Illustrorum* 59

Figure 3   François de Bar, *Obscurity in Romans* 89

Figure 4   Parallel use of Old Testament evidence in Johannes Eck's *De Sacrificio Missae* and Richard Smyth's *Defence of the Sacrifice of the Mass* 190

ACKNOWLEDGEMENTS

It is a great pleasure to thank the institutions that have made this study possible, and the many colleagues and friends who have given so generously of their time, friendship and support to help complete it.

I owe a great debt of gratitude to my former supervisor at the university of Cambridge, Richard Rex. Richard has scrutinised every sentence in this book at least twice, he has motivated me to keep on searching beyond the established evidence, and given his stalwart support to my requests to take the research of Smyth's life further afield. I am privileged to have been his first research student.

I am particularly thankful for the help of my colleagues in this country and abroad: in the Netherlands, Wim Janse, at the university of Leiden, and Mgr Joris Vercammen, at the university of Utrecht, have not only been a tremendous help during my biographical research there but have become personal friends. In Switzerland, my sincere thanks go to Emidio Campi and Michael Baumann at the Schweizerisches Institut für Reformationsgeschichte, Zürich. In Belgium I have enjoyed the help and hospitality of Guido Marnef at the Universitaire Faculteiten Sint Ignatius, Antwerpen. Nearer to home, my work has profited greatly from the critical comments and good ideas of Colin Armstrong, Caroline Barron, Lavinia Byrne, Owen Chadwick, Eamon Duffy, Andrew Ryder, Anne Sutton, Ian Thompson, and the Medieval and Tudor London Seminars at the Institute for Historical Research, London.

I have been able to make use of some of the most remarkable libraries in Europe. My particular thanks go to the friendly staff of the rare books room of the Cambridge University Library and of Duke Humfrey's Library Oxford. I have been helped by the librarians at the Bibliothèque Municipale in Douai, the university libraries of Amsterdam, Heidelberg, Leiden, Leuven, Utrecht, as well as at the British Library and the Zentralbibliothek Zürich. In particular I should like to extend my gratitude to Catherine Butler, archivist of Corpus Christi College Oxford, to Gill Cannell, assistant librarian of the Parker Collection at Corpus Christi College Cambridge, to the archivists of Merton College and Christ Church College Oxford, of the former Hereford and Worcester County Council, at Lambeth Palace Library, and the city of Douai.

I should like to thank Max Engammare of Librairie Droz and Paul Ayris of the *Reformation and Renaissance Review* for allowing me to make use of previously published material for this study, and Professor Mark Greengrass of the Sheffield University John Foxe project and the Master and Fellows of Corpus Christi College Cambridge for permitting me to reproduce the two illustrations.

This study would not have been possible without the help of my friends: Katherine Firth gave freely of her generous friendship. Anne Marie Koper, her father Fons, and Helga Beer gave me a home during my time in the Netherlands. Joy and John Bithell, and Julian Littlewood have been a constant support. Hugh Houghton has assisted with translations from Latin and proof-read the book. Many other friends stood by my side during the past years: Sylvia Pokorny, Bernd Scherzinger, Wolfgang Stoll and William Watkins; at Utrecht university, Mattijs Ploeger, Peter Ben Smit, Bernd and Elly Wallet; in Oxford, Henriette van Eijl, Anasuya Sengupta, Dom Henry Wansbrough OSB and Sr. Benedicta Ward SLG; in Cambridge, Tanya Houghton, Ben King, Sara Mohr-Pietsch, Edmund Newey, Eleanor O'Keeffe, Suzana Ograješek, Yazeed Said, David Smith and James Sparks. Finally, this project would have been inconceivable without the love of my family, Brigitte and Christina.

Slough, Berkshire,
Advent Sunday 2002.

INTRODUCTION

This book sets out to examine the catholic polemical writings of the mid-Tudor period in the light of their encounter with evangelicalism. In their attacks on progressive theologians English catholic polemicists made use of the whole arsenal of debate. They tailored the use of their language to their audiences and thought nothing strange in composing their works both in scholarly Latin and the vernacular alike in order to disseminate their ideas as widely as possible. They looked far beyond the shores of the British Isles for support of their course and made good use of the works of their fellow-conservatives in Germany, France and the Low Countries. Their writings were imbued with a 'language of orthodoxy'—a structural meta-language based on late scholastic methodology—that provided an intellectual backbone linking mid-Tudor conservatives with the heroes of scholasticism and the early church Fathers.

This 'language of orthodoxy' pulsates in the works of the subject of this study. The polemicist Richard Smyth (c. 1500-1563) was one of the most prolific conservative writers of the mid-Tudor period. His affinity to the nominalist school characterise his works far beyond the actual language that make up his sentences. Equally at home in his mother tongue as in scholastic Latin, the language that is at the heart of Smyth's writings is the language that speaks 'in defense of the true doctryne of Christ and his churche'—the language of orthodoxy.[1] Just as for many of his contemporaries, for writers like Smyth concepts such as heresy and orthodoxy remained absolutes that could not be negotiated, directly associated with the eternal salvation or condemnation of a Christian believer. In an age whose theological views were just as fluid as those of our own, Smyth and his fellow-polemicists sought to define the values of salvation in a lasting language that pointed

---

[1] R. Smyth, *A defence of the blessed Masse and the sacrifice thereof, prouynge that it is aualable bothe for the quycke and the dead*, London, 1546.

beyond the personal tastes of the ruling monarchs and their theological advisors. Smyth found his language in the rigorous theology of late-scholasticism, the writings of the church Fathers, and the teaching of the Apostles. Anything that went beyond these fixed points was fanciful innovation—alleged 'truthe that ... is false in deede'—and as such truly perilous.[2] In the course of four successive English reformations Smyth composed his defence of catholicism in the only language he thought worthy to speak of the eternal values he sought to uphold—the language of orthodoxy.

1. MID-TUDOR REFORMS

The reformation in England has never been a homogeneous process. Where Martin Luther and Huldrych Zwingli personally led extensive reform movements on the continent, in England such reforms were entirely dependent on the religious convictions of the reigning monarch. Where continental reformers developed new doctrines from the pulpit in front of ordinary churchgoers, English reformation doctrine was hammered out by learned men and promulgated by royal authority. In many continental cities and principalities the reformation was able to develop progressively. In England the very nature of the mid-Tudor succession prevented any such continuity. Only weeks after Henry VIII established a chantry at Windsor and was buried there with full catholic privileges, for instance, his own archbishop Thomas Cranmer along with his son's advisors initiated significant doctrinal reforms on the theological lines of Zürich and Strassburg.[3] Thirteen years later, Edward's catholic sister and her Cardinal–legate Reginald Pole put an end to reformed teaching, prescribing instead catholic beliefs.[4] Another seven years on, and all notions of

---

[2] Smyth (1546), xxviii r.

[3] For Henry VIII's funeral, see J. Loach, *Past and Present* 142 (1994), 43-68: 'The function of ceremonial in the reign of Henry VIII', 56-68; for the sudden shift to reformed doctrine among Edward VI's councillors, see for instance D. MacCulloch, *Tudor Church Militant: Edward VI and the Protestant Reformation*, London, 1999, 57-104.

[4] For the restoration of Catholicism, see E. Duffy, *The Stripping of the Altars: Traditional Religion in England 1400-1580*, New Haven and London, 1992, 524-564, and D. M. Loades, *Mary Tudor: A Life*, Oxford, 1992; for Reginald Pole's role, see T. F. Mayer, *Reginald Pole: Prince and Prophet*, Cambridge, 2000, 252-302.

catholicism were once more replaced by evangelical teaching.[5] On the continent religious settlements like the *Augsburg Religious Peace* brought about a permanent segregation of nations into Lutheran and catholic principalities. England, on the other hand, experienced a succession of reforms that were shaped almost entirely by the sovereign's religious views.[6]

All four mid-Tudor monarchs shared a desire to implement church reforms. Their various reformations were more haphazard than their continental counterparts and, on the whole, did not follow any overarching doctrinal structure.[7] This holds true for Henry's endeavours to gain control of the English church, as for Mary's frantic scramble to reconcile that church with Rome. It is reflected in the struggle to introduce reformed doctrines in the Edwardian church, as it is in the attempts to create a uniform protestant state-religion under Elizabeth. Motivated as much by the personal aspirations of the monarch as by some genuine desire to bring about religious change, English reformations can, at best, be described as piecemeal.[8]

The Henrician reformation reflects this process particularly well. Unlike the catholic church on the continent, the church in England had become neither corrupt nor removed from its members. Henry's initial reforms were chiefly concerned with the 'king's great matter': the divorce of his union with Katherine of Aragon.[9] Consequently, it was the question of authority rather than far-reaching doctrinal changes that remained at the heart of his attempts to reform the church. Even when in 1538 the king found it politically beneficial to liaise at some length with Lutheran

---

[5] Though slightly dated, P. Collinson, *The Birthpangs of Protestant England*, 1988, and N. L. Jones, *Faith by Statute: Parliament and the Settlement of Religion, 1559*, 1982, still provide important background information.

[6] For the Augsburg Settlement, see for instance E. Cameron, *The European Reformation*, Oxford, 1991, 348-350; H. Rabe, *Reichsbund und Interim: Die Verfassungs– und Religionspolitik Karls V. und der Reichstag zu Augsburg 1546/47*, Köln, 1971, is still 'maßgebend'; P. Warmbrunn, *Zwei Konfessionen in einer Stadt*, Wiesbaden, 1983, gives fascinating insights into the practical adaptation of the Ausgburg Settlement.

[7] For an introduction to the concept of 'English reformations', see C. Haigh, *English Reformations: Religion, Politics and Society under the Tudors*, Oxford, 1995, 12-13.

[8] Haigh (1995), 13.

[9] See principally G. Bédouelle and P. le Gal, edd. et al., *Le 'Divorce' du Roi Henry VIII: Etudes et Documents*, Genève, 1987.

princes and their theologians, ultimately any such flirtations with the idea of genuine doctrinal reform came to a resolute end.[10] On the whole Henry sought to retain traditional catholic doctrines while asserting the authority of the crown over the church. This principle can be detected throughout his entire reign: in 1536 the affirmation of royal supremacy went hand in hand with the defence of the doctrine of the real presence; three years later, the final dissolution of monastic communities in England was followed by the promulgation of the *Six Articles of Religion*, a document that upheld monastic vows and celibacy.[11]

For the implementation of his tentative reforms, Henry relied as much on his new archbishop as on a small group of conservative theologians, many of whom were recruited from the king's divorce 'think-tank'—those high-powered intellectuals who were prepared to argue the 'king's great matter' in Rome and at home.[12] Rewarded with lucrative livings and therefore dependent on the king's patronage, the conservative elements among them sought to adopt traditional catholicism for Henry's English church while fighting to retain essential catholic doctrines of the church. So in 1535 bishop Stephen Gardiner of Winchester was able to argue at length for the royal supremacy over the church, while adamantly maintaining that the doctrine of the real presence should not be

---

[10] For a Lutheran perspective on Henry's negotiations, see N. S. Tjernagel, *Henry VIII and the Lutherans: A Study in Anglo-Lutheran Relations from 1521-1547*, Saint Louis MO, 1965; for an English view, see D. MacCulloch, *Thomas Cranmer: A Life*, New Haven and London, 1996, 214-224; for Henry's early campaigns against Luther, cf. R. Rex, *Transactions of the Royal Historical Society 5th series* 39 (1989), 85-106: 'The English campaign against Luther in the 1520's'.

[11] Both R. Rex, *Henry VIII and the English Reformation*, London, 1993, and D. MacCulloch, ed., *The Reign of Henry VIII: politics, policy and piety*, Basingstoke, 1995, offer good introductions. For the Six Articles of Religion, cf. G. Redworth, *Journal of Ecclesiastical History* 37 (1986), 42-67: 'A Study in the Formulation of Policy: The Genesis and Evolution of the Acts of Six Articles'; for the practical implications of Henry's reforms, cf. M. Bowker, *The Henrician Reformation: The Diocese of Lincoln under John Longland 1521-1547*, Cambridge, 1981.

[12] Bédouelle and Le Gal list some 160 theologians and canon lawyers at 23 universities throughout Europe who were in some way involved in arguing for the king's 'great matter', Bédouelle and Le Gal (1987): Répertoire Bio–Bibliographique, and 464-472. Of these a smaller 'home' team consisted of theological high-flyers such as Thomas Cranmer, Edward Foxe, provost of King's College Cambridge, and Stephen Gardiner, who would contribute to the *Collectanea satis copiosa*, reproduced in E. Surtz and V. Murphy, edd., *The Divorce Tracts of Henry VIII*, Angers, 1988.

tampered with.[13] In like vein Edmund Bonner (another royal protégé who had furnished Gardiner's fulsome defence of the royal supremacy with a resounding introduction) maintained traditional doctrines with such ferocity that he found himself the subject of countless evangelical attacks as bishop of London.[14] Throughout the Henrician reign conservative theologians showed a profound loyalty to their monarch and sought to accommodate his claim of supremacy over the church. At the same time, however, they made good use of their key positions in the English hierarchy to defend the central tenets of the catholic faith.

A recent commentator argues that to 'maintain that the reformist elements within Catholicism were little more than window dressing for the sake of political advantage ... to earn ... Henry VIII's approval' fails to appreciate that both English conservatives and evangelicals shared in a significant 'common humanist foundation'.[15] Both evangelical and catholic scholars, Lucy Wooding suggests, shared in the same education which, in turn, led to a certain convergence of scholarship. The implementation of humanist thought, both by catholics and evangelicals, 'blurred' the lines between 'Protestants' and 'Catholics'. This (rather than, say, the need to appease a royal patron) was the reason why catholics were able to argue for the royal supremacy. Wooding suggests:

---

[13] As a result of his involvement in the king's divorce think-tank, Gardiner was appointed bishop in 1531 of Winchester after Wolsey's fall. For a good summary of his preferments, see A. B. Emden, *A Biographical Register of the University of Oxford A.D. 1501 to 1540*, Oxford, 1974, 227. Gardiner's ambivalent theological position is summed up well by two of his Henrician publications, S. Gardiner, *Stephani Vuintoniensis episcopi De vera obedientia, oratio: Vna cum praefatione Edmundi Boneri archidiaconi Leycestrensis ... in qua etiam ostenditur caussam controuersiae quae inter ... Regiam Maiestatem & Episcopum Romanum existit, longe aliter ac diuersius se habere*, London, 1535; idem, *A detection of the Deuils sophistrie: wherwith he robbeth the vnlearned people, of the true byleef, in the Most Blessed Sacrament of the Aulter*, London, 1546.

[14] For instance, J. Bale, *Yet a course at the Romyshe foxe, a dysclosynge of the manne of synne cotayned in the late declaratyon of the popes olde faythe made by Edmonde Boner, compyled by Johan Harryson*, Zürich, 1543.

[15] L. Wooding, *Rethinking Catholicism in Reformation England*, Oxford, 2000, 14; for an introduction to the concept of *Kontroverskatholiken*, see D. Bagchi, *Luther's earliest Opponents: Catholic Controversialists*, Minneapolis MN, 1991, 2n.

> Catholic and Protestant traditions existed side by side in England during the formative years of the reformation, and to see them as polarities in a single conflict is to parody their relationship.[16]

It is, however, misleading to suggest that a 'common humanist foundation' for conservative and evangelical scholars alike—that is, a shared interest in humanist principles and their return to the source texts of theology (*ad fontes*)—led to an English 'rapprochement' between evangelicals and catholics.[17] The unreconstructed fervour shown by a significant part of the conservative hierarchy only reinforces a perception of entrenched and somewhat frustrated opponents: Henry VIII neither fulfilled the evangelical desire for far-reaching theological reforms on the lines of Wittenberg, Zürich or Geneva, nor did he live up to his title as a defender of the—catholic—faith. Consequently, Henrician churchmen had to resort to a considerable amount of theological 'window dressing' in order to square allegiance to their royal patron with their own beliefs. Conservative thinkers in royal employ had to be seen to be upholding the royal supremacy. After all, it was their position in the English church that furnished them with an opportunity to uphold their conservative theological views in the first place.

For one such churchman, any thought of a common understanding between conservatives and evangelicals remained utterly implausible. The subject of this study, Richard Smyth, is best remembered for his biting polemics, which he composed with the fervour of someone engaged in a battle of eschatological urgency with his evangelical opposition. An outstanding exponent of English conservative theology, Smyth was one of the most prolific defenders of catholic orthodoxy in the mid-Tudor period. His printed output exceeded that of his colleagues Gardiner and Bonner by far, and extended through the reigns of three successive Tudor monarchs. His first works, composed in defence of the doctrine of the real presence and the sacrifice of the mass, were circulated in the closing years of Henry VIII's reign. His last, a resounding refutation of Melanchthon's *Loci Communes*, left a Douai printing press in the fourth year of the reign of Queen

---

[16] Wooding (2000), 13.
[17] For instance, Wooding (2000), 51-52.

Elizabeth.[18] For almost two decades Smyth ceaselessly sought to respond to 'the new preachers euil sermons, and wicked bookes' by amassing evidence in support of controverted catholic doctrines.[19] Ardent defences of catholicism such as his works lend themselves well to an examination of English catholicism in the mid-Tudor period. Although Smyth (like many of the king's protégés) sought to accommodate a number of Henrician church reforms, following the death of his royal patron he swiftly resorted to his papist roots. At the time of his own death in 1563, he had propagated his conservative theology from the lecterns of four major European universities, and defended catholic orthodoxy in eighteen polemical works.[20] These are a fine example of how a significant part of the English catholic community sought to resist religious innovations by drawing not on humanist teaching, but its own traditional roots—roots that extended far beyond the shores of the British Isles and reflected a rich, late-scholastic heritage.

2. INTERNATIONAL CATHOLICISM

During the formative years of the Henrician reformation, English catholicism was never insular. Nothing less than the 'king's great matter' itself bears witness to this fact. As seen above, the compilers of Henry VIII's *Collectanea satis copiosa* thought nothing strange in approaching twenty-three European universities to act as theological advisors in the king's divorce case. While the universities of Oxford and Cambridge obviously played a central part in this undertaking, Henry's theological aides were able to rely on a much larger theological network beyond the English channel, and did not hesitate to make use of this theological expertise.[21] Such readiness to draw on the work of other European theologians is mirrored by the English defenders of catholic orthodoxy. In the course of Henry's tentative church reforms conservative theologi-

---

[18] Smyth (1546) and R. Smyth, *Assertion and Defence of the Sacrament of the Aulter*, London, 1546².

[19] R. Smyth, *The second parte of the booke called a Buckler of the Catholyke fayeth ... made by Richard Smith*, London, 1555, ¶ vi v.

[20] See below, chapter 1.

[21] Bédouelle and Le Gal (1987); G. B. Skelly, 'Henry VIII consults the Universities of Oxford and Cambridge', 59-75.

ans did not suddenly cease to look to the continent for support in their struggle against evangelicalism. On the contrary, even books that may have been deemed unsuitable by the crown due to their ardent support of the papal primacy were still consulted by conservative theologians in England. After all, whatever one's views on the supremacy of sovereign or pope over the church in England, books like these still provided useful resources in the defence of the real presence or the sacrifice of the mass.

This readiness to embrace the work of his continental colleagues can be traced particularly well in the compilation of Richard Smyth's first work—*The Assertion and Defence of the Sacrament of the Aulter* (1546). In preparing his own defence Smyth drew extensively on the works of German theologians Johan Eck and Johannes Cochlaeus (both of whom had upheld the papal supremacy over the church in their debates with Martin Luther and would therefore have been regarded as *personae non gratae* by the English king).[22] Omitting any references to his German sources and their views on the papal supremacy, however, Smyth was able to use the works as a valuable resource that contained useful material for his own struggle against evangelicalism. It is no surprise that Smyth's arguments parallel the works of his continental counterparts closely: their fundamental standpoint was essentially the same. Cochlaeus and Eck as well as their English counterpart shared a common predilection for nominalist theology and principally drew on the scholarship of Gabriel Biel and John Fisher. They spoke a common meta-language: all modelled their methodology on late scholastic lines and made use of acerbic polemicism in their common struggle against the dilution of orthodox doctrine by evangelical scholars and preachers.[23]

Rather than draw on the work of the humanist school, as commentators like Wooding might suggest, English conservative scholars like Smyth looked towards the continent for support in their struggle with evangelicalism, making use of the international

---

[22] J. Cochlaeus, *De gratia sacramentorum liber unus aduersus assertionem M. Lutheri*, Strassburg, 1522; J. Eck, E. Iserloh, ed. et al., *De sacrificio missae libri tres (1526)*, Corpus Catholicorum 34, Münster, 1982; Smyth's use of these works is discussed extensively below, chapter V, 2.1.

[23] For a thorough comparison of Smyth's works with those of Eck and Cochlaeus, see below chapter V, 2.1, 184-199.

nominalist school for their own writings.[24] The fact that they were equally at home in the vernacular as in scholarly Latin shows that they wrote for specific audiences—it does not represent a debt to Erasmus. Accordingly Smyth crafted Latin refutations in order to oppose particular fellow scholars, and made good use of the vernacular for more general polemical works.[25] Like many of his fellow conservatives, Smyth made use of the English language to reach as wide an audience as possible. He would later explain that he primarily sought

> to teach the vnlearned, to stay and establish the waueryng, to assure and certify the doubtfull of the trouth, to bryng them agayne vnto the trouth of the catholyke churche[26]

and, in doing so, frequently used the vernacular as a polemical tool. Smyth's use of his native tongue in his defence of catholic doctrine reflects the language both of popular religion, and of a skilled polemicist who, when addressing his theological peers resorted to the *lingua franca* of international scholarship—Latin—yet, when teaching the 'vnlearned' and convincing the 'doubtfull of the trouth', consistently wrote in English. The work of English polemicists, therefore, was not unlike that of translators: rendering the theological ideas of their international colleagues intelligible to their audience by summing up and applying their arguments to their own context. Smyth and his fellow conservatives crafted polarised accounts of the current international debate for their own purposes—the defence of English catholicism against any doctrinal innovation.

3. The Language of Orthodoxy

It becomes increasingly clear that the basic element in the defence of conservative doctrine against the influence of evangelicalism was its language. English conservative writers made good use both of Latin and the vernacular in their writings. The 'language' that

---

[24] Wooding (2000), 9.
[25] It is unlikely that the use of the vernacular by catholic polemicists like Smyth betrayed the influence of Erasmus, as is suggested by Wooding (2000), 9-11.
[26] R. Smyth, *The second parte of the booke called a Buckler of the Catholyke fayeth ... made by Richard Smith*, London, 1555, ¶ vii r.

distinguishes conservative writings from progressive humanist works, therefore, was neither English nor Latin but rather a methodological language. The backbone of conservative writings was made up of late scholastic logical principles. Where conservative writers made skilful use of the vernacular to disseminate their ideas widely, the segregation of writings along the lines of the use of Latin over and above the use of the vernacular makes no sense at all. The claim that 'to write in English was to declare an interest in the work of the religious regeneration' (and therefore by implication to write in Latin was to oppose this process) is equally difficult to maintain.[27] As authors like Smyth matched their use of language to their prospective audiences it is rash to segregate conservative writers in England along linguistic lines. A balanced analysis of catholic theology in the mid-Tudor period, therefore, needs to draw both on Latin and English writings alike and clearly stands in need of another means of distinction: a meta-language of orthodoxy that reflects on structure and ideas, rather than words.

While it can be difficult to distinguish between conservative and humanist writings on the basis of their use of actual language, it is certainly possible to discern a certain methodological meta-language. The use of late scholastic methodology (frequently characterised by the structure and ideas of a specific line of argument) is a much more helpful tool in distinguishing conservative writers from progressives. True, at times even leading evangelical theologians such as Peter Martyr Vermigli and Martin Bucer would resort to scholastic methodology in their encounters with conservative polemicists. However, their use of scholastic logic was on the whole restricted to the context of formal oral debates, and did not find its way into their doctrinal writings. During the first Oxford debate on the real presence (1549), for instance, Vermigli defended the newly defined Edwardian eucharistic doctrine within the context of a strictly scholastic debate.[28] Yet

---

[27] Wooding (2000), 2; cf. E. Macek, *The Loyal Opposition: Tudor Traditional Polemics, 1535-1558*, Peter Lang Studies in Church History 7, New York, 1996, xv.

[28] P. M. Vermigli, *Tractatio de Sacramento Eucharistiae habita in celeberissima Universitate Oxoniensi in Anglia per D. Petrum Martyrem Vermilium Florentinum, Regium ibidem Theologiae professorem, cum iam absoluisset interpretationem 11 capitis prioris epistola D. Pauli Apostoli ad Corinthios*, London, 1549, see below, chapter I, 2.2, 39-43.

INTRODUCTION

Vermigli merely emulated in practical terms the Pauline dictum to be 'all things to all men' (1 Cor 9.19-23) by meeting his opponents on their own terms.[29] Even though evangelicals like Bucer and Vermigli had themselves been steeped in nominalist methodology during the course of their own training, neither of them made any use of late scholastic reasoning as a vehicle of genuine theological advancement.

Smyth's outstanding polemic aptitude, on the other hand, was thoroughly rooted in the rhetoric of late scholasticism. His literary works—just like his lectures—frequently followed on the lines of a late scholastic disputation.[30] *Quaestiones* were matched with *defensiones*, allowing for a meticulous analysis of the subject matter. No doubt his natural ability for the oral academic disputation contributed to the use of similar scholastic principles in his writings.[31] But conservative theologians like Smyth did not make use of scholastic logic merely because they had excelled in the discipline at university. The rigid architecture of the scholastic debate provided more than an instant logical framework: it was in itself a language of orthodoxy that linked the writer with the scholastic 'Fathers' such as Thomas Aquinas, and more recent exponents of catholic orthodoxy such as Gabriel Biel and John Fisher. For those seeking to defend and restore traditional catholic doctrines this language of orthodoxy was both a methodological tool and a testimony to the author's doctrinal rectitude.

This book seeks to examine the use of this meta-language of orthodoxy in Smyth's polemical writings. An extensive biography tells the fascinating story of his life. It aims to provide an accurate background for the ensuing evaluation of four aspects central to his theological work. The discovery at the municipal library in Douai, France, of a volume of lecture notes taken at Smyth's introductory lecture series on the Pauline corpus and his exegesis of the first epistle to the Corinthians inspired the examination of Smyth's hermeneutic and methodological technique. It is followed by an assessment of Smyth's deep conviction that human justifica-

---

[29] And protested against the use of scholastic method.
[30] For a thorough analysis of Smyth's hermeneutics, see below, chapter II, 4.1, 91-95; for a good example of the use of late scholastic methodology in his writings, see below, chapter IV, 2, 150-153.
[31] See below, chapter I, 1.1., n. 38.

tion was primarily based on God's grace, the catholic faith, and human works. The four central works of his impressive overall output of six studies on the eucharist are at the heart of a reflection on Smyth's views on the sacrifice of the mass and the real presence. An intriguing direct polemical debate with Smyth's principal opponent, Peter Martyr Vermigli, on the validity of monastic vows and priestly celibacy rounds off the examination of Smyth's main theological concerns.

A brief note on conventions: the term 'man' is used generically to include both women and men. Quotations are cited in their original spelling and, where appropriate, have been translated. Place names and personal names are also given in their vernacular spelling. So for instance the Flemish university town of Louvain is referred to as 'Leuven', and the cities of Brussels and Cologne as 'Brussel' and 'Köln'. The city of Strasbourg, in the sixteenth century a place of overwhelmingly German character, is referred to as 'Strassburg'. Richard Smyth signed his letters 'Smyth' or 'Smythaeus'. This work follows him in the spelling of his surname.

CHAPTER ONE

BIOGRAPHY

The story of the life and work of the sixteenth-century conservative polemicist Richard Smyth (c. 1500-1563) has not been told for more than 400 years following his death in exile. While reasonably accurate lists of Smyth's work still reappeared frequently in the bibliographical publications of the seventeenth and eighteenth centuries,[1] by the mid-eighteenth century details of his life had been consigned to a few lengthy footnotes in the histories of Oxford or Leuven universities.[2] By the end of the eighteenth century Smyth had become just another entry in the registers of four European universities.[3] Modern research into Richard Smyth's *vita* commenced again with Thompson Cooper's 1897 contribution to the *Dictionary of National Biography*.[4] While Cooper assembled successfully a large number of valuable bibliographical sources and some contemporary evangelical polemical writings

---

[1] For instance, J. Bale, *Illustrium majoris Britanniae scriptorum summarium*, Wesel, 1548; J. F. Foppens, *Bibliotheca Belgica, sive virorum in Belgio vita, scriptisque illustrium catalogus, librorumque nomenclatura, continens scriptores a Valerio Andrea aliisque, recensitos usque ad anno M.D.C.L.XXX*, Brussels, 1739; idem, Bibliothèque Nationale de Paris, MS Fasti doctorales universitatis Lovaniensis; J. B. Gramaye, *Rerum Duacensium libri tres ex archivis publicis collecti*, Douai, 1618; A. Sanderus, *Bibliotheca Belgica manuscripta, siue, Elenchus vniuersalis mss in celeberrimis Belgij coenobijs, ecclesij, vrbium, ac priuatorum nominum bibliothecis adhuc latentium*, Lille, 1641-1644; idem, *Valerii Andreae ... Bibliotheca Belgica: in quae Belgicae seu Germaniae inferioris provinciae urbesque viri item in Belgio vita scriptisque clari et librorum nomenclatura*, Leuven, 1623.

[2] A. à Wood, P. Bliss, ed., *Athenae Oxonienses: An exact History of all the Writers and Bishops who have had their Education in the University of Oxford*, London, 1813-1820; idem, *Fasti Oxonienses*, London, 1815-1820; D. Valerius Andreas, *Fasti academici Lovaniensis*, Leuven, 1650.

[3] Oxford, Leuven, St Andrews and Douai; see for instance, J. M. Anderson, *Early Records of the University of St Andrews. The Graduation Roll, 1413-1579, and the Matriculation Roll, 1473-1579*, Scottish Historical Society, Edinburgh, 1926; H. E. Salters, *Registrum Annalium Collegii Mertonensis, 1483-1521*, Oxford Historical Society (cited as: OHS), Oxford, 1921; E. Reusens, A. Schillings, ed. et al., *Matricule de l'Université de Louvain (IV: Février 1528-Février 1569)*, Brussel, 1903-1961; J. Sylvius (Dubois), *Nascentis Academiae Duacensis eiusdemque illustrium Professorum Encomium*, Douai, 1653.

[4] T. Cooper, *Dictionary of National Biography*, Oxford, 1897, 53.101: 'Smith, Richard, DD. 1500-1563'.

against Smyth, his work contains some obvious biographical inaccuracies.[5] However, late nineteenth-century research on this catholic exile was not restricted to Britain. Canon Théodore Leuridan commenced his own research in Douai. Later published as an article in the series *Les Théologiens de Douai*, Leuridan's account makes good use of local source-material, but where Cooper had a tendency to attribute too much credence to evangelical polemics Leuridan chose to canonise the subject of his study.[6]

Although a growing number of Catholic Historical Society publications, such as Thomas Knox's *The first and second diaries of the English College, Douay*, contained passing references to the English exile, mainstream research centring on Smyth lay once more dormant until 1970, and the completion of a doctoral dissertation by Fr. Andrew Ryder on some aspects of his eucharistic doctrine.[7] Ryder's work has its roots in a 1960s debate about recurring Anglican claims considering the reformation 'to have been nothing more than an attempt to purify the true Catholic doctrine from its late mediaeval accretions and corruptions'.[8] Unaware of Leuridan's previous work, Ryder made use of Smyth's work as an example of catholic orthodoxy during the Edwardian reformation to counter these claims.[9] He concludes that 'there can be no doubt whatsoever that [Smyth's] thought on the eucharist is completely sound', and he therefore rejected the Anglican assertion that the reformation primarily intended to purge late medieval catholic

---

[5] For instance his erroneous claim that Smyth 'had a famous disputation with Peter Martyr at Oxford', ibid.

[6] For instance when attributing the later stream of catholic underground clergy to England to the strength of Richard Smyth's teaching at Douai; see Th. H. J. Leuridan, *Les Théologiens de Douai* 11 (1904), Extrait de la Revue des Sciences ecclésiastiques: 'Richard Smith', 25: 'A Smith revient incontestablement le mérite d'avoir inauguré et même provoqué en partie ce mouvement de salut'.

[7] Th. F. Knox, *The first and second diaries of the English College, Douay, and an appendix of unpublished documents edited by the Fathers of the Congregation of the London Oratory*, Records of the English Catholics under the Penal Laws, London, 1878, I.XXVII; A. Ryder, SCJ, *The Eucharistic Doctrine of Richard Smith*, Excerpta ex dissertatione ad Lauream in Facultate Theologiae Pontificiae Universitatis Gregorianae, Roma, 1970.

[8] Ryder (1970), 6.

[9] Ryder (1970), 7: 'no previous analysis has been made of Dr Smith's theological writings'.

doctrine from its scholastic framework.[10] Ryder's brief biographical sketch made reliable use of the sources first assembled in Cooper's work, supplementing them at times with more general modern Roman Catholic evaluations of the period.[11]

Initially fully independent of Ryder's work, Ellen Macek contributed an article on the life and work of Richard Smyth in 1986.[12] In a more recent monograph on Tudor religious conservatives (1996) she combines her earlier work with her doctoral research and incorporates some brief references to Ryder's thesis.[13] In both cases much of her biographical research derives from Cooper and her close reading of John Strype's *Ecclesiastical Memoirs*.[14] In her theological evaluation she explicitly restricts herself largely to Smyth's printed English work.[15]

While both Cooper and Leuridan derived a number of useful biographical details from Smyth's Latin writings, the later two expositors made use of the works only for their theological content.[16] In addition to treating Smyth's writings essentially as an illustration of his theological views, both modern commentators also relied almost exclusively on Smyth's English work for their evidence. In the case of the North American Ellen Macek this is almost certainly due to the fact that, while Smyth's English oeuvre

---

[10] Ryder (1970), 99.

[11] See for instance Ryder (1970), 22, n. 8.

[12] E. A. Macek, *Catholic Historical Review* 72 (1986), 383-402: 'Richard Smith: Tudor Cleric in Defense of Traditional Belief and Practice'.

[13] E. A. Macek, *The Loyal Opposition: Tudor Traditional Polemics, 1535-1558*, Peter Lang Studies in Church History 7, New York, 1996; making extensive use of idem, *The Nature of English Catholicism 1535-1558: A Study of the Intellectual and Theological Basis of the Catholic Position on the Sacrament and Justification*, unpublished doctoral dissertation, University of Nebraska, Lincoln NE, 1980.

[14] J. Strype, *Ecclesiastical memorials; relating chiefly to religion, and the reformation of it: shewing the various emergencies of the Church of England, under king Henry the eighth (Historical memorials, chiefly ecclesiastical, and such as concern religion and the reformation of it under king Edward vi; Historical memorials, ecclesiastical and civil, of events under the reign of queen Mary i)*, Oxford, 1822.

[15] See Macek (1996), xv, 254-255, although she does refer to one of his Latin publications, the *Diatriba de hominis ivstificatione aedita Oxoniae in Anglia, anno à natiuitate Domini nostri Iesu Christi. 1550. Mense Februario aduersus Petrum Martyrem Vermelium, olim Cartusianum Lucensem in Italia, nunc apostata in Anglia Oxoniae, acerrimum improborum dogmatum assertorem, sed imperitum, & impudentem cum primis. Per Ricardum Smythaeum Anglum Mygorniensem* [sic], Leuven, 1550²; her bibliography only covered Smyth's English work.

[16] So for instance Leuridan (1904), 25, 28.

has already been released in *Short Title Catalogue Microfilm* editions, his Latin works are only available in early printings. Andrew Ryder also spoke of the difficulty 'of obtaining copies of his work'.[17] This would explain why in his analysis of Smyth's eucharistic doctrine he supplemented Smyth's three English works on the subject with only one relevant Latin counterpart and proved unable to trace the exile's two other contemporary Latin works on the subject.[18]

The fact that Ryder and Macek did not incorporate much of Smyth's Latin works in their studies does not detract much from their conclusions in general. Still, their picture of the English polemicist remains more unpolished and rough than that emerging from his later Latin publications. In the two languages Smyth addressed, respectively, the needs of two different audiences. His vernacular works, 'rudely, & grossely set fourth, for the easier vnderstandynge of it',[19] were not intended for the use of theologians 'whiche nede not much my teachyng, but to teach the vnlearned'.[20] His Latin works, on the other hand, were composed to display his theological finesse and orthodox erudition to impress both potential patrons and the circle of catholic academics on whose kindness and support he had come to rely during his

---

[17] Ryder (1970), 7. This difficulty does not pertain in Cambridge, where most of Smyth's writings are lodged in the University Library or college libraries.

[18] In his analysis Ryder (1970), made some use of R. Smyth, *Confutatio eorum, quae Philippvs Melanchthon obijcit contra Missae sacrificium propitiatorium. Autore Ricardo Smythaeo Wigorniensi, Anglo, Sacrae Theologiae Professore, Lovanii. Cui accessit & repulsio calumniarum Ioannes Caluini, & Musculi, & Ioannes Iuelli, contra Missam, eius canonem, & Purgatorium, denuò excusa*, Paris, 1562; but neither incorporated idem, *De Missae Sacrificio succincta quaedam enarratio, ac brevis repulsio praecipuorum argumentorum, quae Philippus Melanchthon, Ioannes Caluinus, & alii sectarii obiecerunt aduersus illud, & Purgatorium. Quae iam denuò excusa prodeunt, longè peniora, & locupletiora. Accessit epistola ad lectorem, docens quae Ecclesia sit nobis tuto sequenda, hoc infoerici seculo. Autore Ricardo Smythaeo, Wigorniensi, Anglo, sacrae Theologiae Professor*, Leuven, 1562; nor idem, *Defensio comprehendaria, et orthodoxa, sacri externi, et visibili Iesu Christi sacerdotii. Cui addita est sacratorum catholicae Ecclesiae altarium propugnatio, ac Calvinia altarium propugnatio, ac Calvina communionis succincta refutatio*, Leuven, 1562.

[19] R. Smyth, *A Defence of the sacrifice of the masse. Made and set furth by mayster Rycharde Smyth doctour in diuinitie, and reader of the kynges hyghnes lesson of diuinitie in his maiesties vniuersitie of Oxforde. Wherin are diuerse doubtes openede, ouer and aboue the principall matter*, London, 1546¹, x v.

[20] R. Smyth, *A bouclier of the catholic fayth of Christes church, conteynyng diuers matters now of late called into controuersy, by the newe gospellers. Made by Richard Smith, doctour of diuinitee, & the Quenes hyghnes Reader of the same in her graces vniuersite of Oxford*, London, 1554, C vii r.

two exiles in the Low Countries. Just as neither the hard-hitting vernacular polemics, nor the sophisticated scholarship of his Latin works can ever truly characterise Smyth's theological work, so only a combination of the one with the other can ever do justice to his ambiguous and complex personality.

The present work, therefore, endeavours to present as broad a range of manuscript and printed sources as possible. Biographical research is based on extensive archival and bibliographical study in England, the Low Countries and Northern France which, among others, brought to light lecture notes taken at Smyth's last lectures in Douai, and a number of his letters.[21] The ensuing theological evaluation of the most contended of Smyth's works made use of both his English and Latin publications. Both form the basis for a newly-commissioned article on the English polemicist for the *New Dictionary of National Biography*, bringing to a close a circle of a hundred years' research initiated, after all, by Thompson Cooper's contribution to the original version of this invaluable reference work.[22]

1.1. EARLY EDUCATION (C. 1510-1536)

Richard Smyth was born in Worcestershire in the early sixteenth century. On the basis of his epitaph (no longer extant) in the Collégiale Saint-Pierre Douai, his seventeenth-century biographers established his year of birth as 1500.[23] There is no reason to doubt their observation. James Ussher believed him to be of Irish extraction, yet colophons and official registers consistently listed him as

---

[21] Bibliothèque municipale de Douai, MS 57: Pauli Apostoli Epistolae; Corpus Christi College Cambridge, MS 119: Epistolas Virorum Illustrorum.

[22] See J. A. Löwe, *New Dictionary of National Biography*, Oxford University Press: 'Smyth (Smythaeus, Smythus), Richard (1499-1563)' [forthcoming].

[23] See for instance J. Foppens (1739), 2.1069; J. Pits, *Relationum historicarum de rebus Anglicis tomus primus*, Paris, 1619, 761; for a plan of the gothic building of the Collégiale Saint-Pierre, Douai, see M. Rouche, ed., *Histoire de Douai*, Lille, 1998, 64; for its demolition and rebuilding in 1734, see P. Héliot, *Revue Belge d'archéologie et d'histoire* 28 (1959), 129-173 'Quelque moments disparus de la Flandre wallonne: L'abbaye d'Anchin, les collégiales Saint-Pierre et Saint-Amé de Douai', H. R. Duthillœul, *Histoire ecclésiastique et monastique de Douai*, Douai, 1861 and G. Rausch, *Douai: Kultur– und kunstgeschichtliche Studien in Nordfrankreich*, Heidelberg, 1917.

'Vigorniensis' or 'Worcestriae'.[24] Neither friends nor enemies ever spoke of him as an Irishman. Similarly, when he required letters dimissory from his home diocese to secure leave for his ordination in Lincoln diocese (1533), these were issued by bishop Geronimo Ghinucci of Worcester, not bishop John Purcell of Ferns.[25] Little is known about his family background or his early education. Speculation about Smyth's surname led Ussher to believe his father to have been an artisan 'who was an iron-working craftsman (the English call it Smith)'.[26] While, in a rare personal reflection, Smyth himself later styled himself a 'poor man's child', he gave no further clues as to his father's profession.[27]

Smyth received his earliest education at a Worcestershire abbey school, most probably in Evesham.[28] His only recorded preaching engagement outside London and Oxford took place in the parish of St Lawrence's Evesham, which suggests an earlier link.[29] The fact that the abbey-school modernised its teaching in the humanities during the early decades of the sixteenth century makes this more

---

[24] J. Ussher, *Ignatii, Polycarpi, et Barnabae, epistolae atque martyria. Quibus praefixa est de Polycarpi & Ignatii scriptis J. Usserii dissertatio*, Oxford, 1643, cxxii-cxxiii: 'Either I am completely mistaken, or Richard Smith is [Irish]; who was first professor of Theology ... in the university of Douai. ... Nor was he born in England, although from his ancestors he may say that he is a native of Worcestershire, but rather he is from Rosslare, a small town in Ireland, about three miles from Wexford, as ... Richard Stanihurst told me' (Aut me fallunt omnia, aut Richardus Smithaeus [Hibernus] est; qui in Academiam Duacenam ... primus Theologiam professus est. ... Nec in Anglia natus ille, licet à patris ... patriam Wigorniensem ipse se indigitet; sed in Racmacneiano Hiberniae oppidulo, tribus passuum milibus à Weisefordiam distante: quemadmodum me docuit ... Richardus Stanishurstus).

[25] Worcester and Hereford County Archives, Registrum Ghinucci (cited as: Registrum Ghinucci), II, f. 70, and Worcestershire Record Office, Worcester Register 9 (i), 106, 129; for Ghinucci see for instance, M. Dowling, *Fisher of Men: A life of John Fisher, 1469-1535*, Basingstoke, 1999, 159-160 and J. J. Scarisbrick, *The conservative Episcopate in England, 1529-1535*, unpublished doctoral dissertation, University of Cambridge.

[26] Ussher (1643), cxxiii: 'Qui faber fuit ferravius (Angli *Smith* appellant)'.

[27] Smyth (1555), C iii v: 'For where the abbeys nourished many poore mens chyldren at schole (emongst the whiche I was one, or els I shoulde neuer haue bene lerned) ... now is found a shepearde, and hys dogge only';

[28] For Evesham abbey, see W. Tindale, ed., *The history and antiquities of the abbey and borough of Evesham: Compiled chiefly from MSS. in the British Museum*, London, 1794.

[29] *Letters and Papers Foreign and Domestic Henry VIII*, 12/2.534. For his sermon at St Lawrence's, see E. J. Carlson, ed., *Religion and the English People, 1500-1640*, Kirksville MO, 1998, 49-74: S. Wabuda, 'Fruitful preaching in the diocese of Worcester: Bishop Hugh Latimer and his influence, 1535-1539', 70-71.

probable.[30] From Worcestershire Smyth came up to Merton College Oxford in 1520 where he was elected to a junior fellowship in the last year of his undergraduate studies and graduated Bachelor of Arts soon after.[31] Barely fifteen months later, he was confirmed a full fellow.[32] Following his election to the fifteen-strong fellowship of Merton, his academic career proceeded swiftly.[33] He completed the prescribed general studies leading up to the degree of Master of Arts within three years and, after a statutory academic disputation 'apud scholares Augustinorum', was admitted to read for a bachelor's degree in theology in 1533.[34]

His formal theological studies formed the prescribed basis for his doctoral course, which he completed in 1536.[35] While no particular records of his doctoral work have survived, the intricate principles by which students and tutors defended their different theological positions have been documented well. They formed the basis for much of Smyth's later dialectic work.[36] Both students and masters underwent the rigours of regular formal debates, following a narrowly defined system of discourses *de quaestionibus* by which they expounded 'the text and the questions arising from it', a teaching method practised at Oxford since at least the mid-

---

[30] For an insight into the rapid growth of humanities at Evesham abbey-school in the 1520s and 1530s, see J. C. H. Aveling, W. A. Pantin, edd., *The letter book of Robert Joseph, monk-scholar of Evesham and Gloucester College, Oxford, 1530-1533*, OHS New Series 19, Oxford, 1967.

[31] For his election to a junior fellowship on 25 February 1525, see Merton College Archives, Collegium Mertonensis Registrum Vetus (cited as: Registrum Vetus), I, f. 269 r; for his graduation on 5 April 1527, see C. W. Boase, ed., *Register of the University of Oxford, 1449-63, 1505-1571*, OHS 1, Oxford, 1885, 1.146.

[32] 1 August 1528, cf. Registrum Vetus, I, f. 272 v.

[33] For Smyth's early career at Merton, see G. C. Brodrick, *Memorials of Merton College*, Oxford, 1885, 254f.

[34] 27 February 1533, cf. Registrum Vetus, f. 279 v; for his graduation as MA on 18 July 1530, see Boase (1885), 1.146.

[35] Boase (1885), 1.146.

[36] He frequently scolded his opposition for not adhering to a systematic logical framework, for instance, R. Smyth, *Eivsdem D. Richardi Smythei confvtatio qvorundam articulorum de votis Monasticis Petri Martyris Itali, Oxoniae in Anglia Theologiam profientis. De votis haec incogitanter, indocte, & impie effutiuit, obnixe contendas illa nuncupare Deo nefas esse homini Christiano, saltem vt sint perpetuo necessaria*, Leuven, 1550[1], F 4 v: 'Colliquescit itaque ex his, quam crasse hallucinatus sit Petrus Martyr, quando hunc tam futilem, & neruorum exortem contra vota syllogismum contexuerit'; for Peter Martyr Vermigli, see K. Sturm, *Die Theologie Peter Martyr Vermiglis während seines ersten Aufenthalts in Straßburg 1542-1547*, Neukirchen, 1971 and J. C. McLelland, *The Visible Words of God*, Edinburgh and London, 1957.

thirteenth century.[37] Contemporary characterisations of Richard Smyth confirm that he had mastered the art of disputation to the fullest extent. Even his greatest opponents acknowledged his innate talent for academic debate. While an evangelical opponent saw him as 'Sophista magis cum Theologus', a later historian of Oxford described him as 'the best school man of his time, a subtle disputant, and admirably well read in the Fathers and councils'.[38] Smyth was a strong-minded character who pursued what he took to be true with great determination. However, those who smugly dismissed his theological aptitude as mere sophistry had chosen to overlook that he was an integral part of an academic system that valued the skill and finesse of the debater more than his personal convictions.[39]

During his studies towards the doctorate, Smyth pursued an administrative career at Merton and in the university. In 1531 he had been elected junior dean of his college, and six months later he was made scribe to the university.[40] As scribe, he was responsible for the official correspondence between the university congregation and state officials or institutions. Smyth's official letters assumed a diplomatic and subservient tone that was paralleled in some later personal supplications. The fine, humanist Latin of his letters is echoed in some later dedications.[41] While serving as a university officer, he continued to pursue his theological studies

---

[37] See for instance S. Gibson, ed., *Statuta antiqua universitatis Oxoniensis*, Oxford, 1931, 32-33, and 128.

[38] L. Humphrey, *J. Juelli Episcopi Sarisb. vita et mors, ejusque verae doctrinae defensio*, London, 1573, 43; Wood (1813-1820), 1.143; cf. for instance P. M. Vermigli, *D. Petri Martyris Vermilii Florentini divinarum Literarum in Schola Tigurina Professoris Oxoniensis duos Libellos de Caelibatu Sacerdotum, & Votis Monasticis, Nunc Primum in lucé edita. Basileae apud Petrum Pernam M. D. L. IX*, Basel, 1559, 643-644.

[39] Cf. J. I. Catto, ed., *The History of the University of Oxford: The Early Oxford Schools*, Oxford, 1984, 367-399; J. M. Fletcher, 'The Faculty of Arts', 374ff.

[40] Registrum Vetus, I, f. 279 r-280 v; Oxford University Archives, Register H, f. 261.

[41] W. T. Mitchell, ed., *Epistolae Academicae 1508-1596*, OHS New Series 26, Oxford, 1980, 212-214; for Smyth's private supplications see for instance, Corpus Christi College Cambridge, MS 119: Epistolae Virorum Illustrorum, f. 113, for Vermigli's comments on the same see op. cit., f. 106 ξ r.

and was granted leave to be ordained in Lincoln diocese.[42] Soon after his ordination, probably at Thame abbey, he was installed to his first ecclesiastical living—the rectory of Cuxham (Oxfordshire).[43] He continued to live at Merton, where he became an integral part of college life. Made senior dean in 1533, the fellowship came in great numbers to hear him preach the university sermon in Hilary Term 1534, as both college and university registers recorded at length.[44] The fellowship of Merton was renowned for its religious conservatism, and included for instance William Tresham and Willam Chedsey, two theologians who would later take his place in a 1549 disputation on the eucharist against his evangelical opponent Peter Martyr Vermigli.[45]

Some aspects of the evangelical caricature on the other hand do hold true: Smyth never suffered financial hardship, even in exile. His income as a newly-ordained clergyman and fellow of Merton was in excess of £14 12s 3p per annum, and was augmented by further 'perpetuall annuall chargys' from his college.[46] Supplemented by a theology lectureship at Magdalen College, and a position as warden of a university hall of residence he was a

---

[42] On 19 April 1533, see Registrum Ghinucci, II, f. 70 and Worcester Register 9 (i), 129, an earlier set of general letters dimissory was granted on 6 December 1530, idem, 106.; for a historical view of Lincoln Diocese in the 1530s, see particularly, M. Bowker, *The Henrician Reformation: The Diocese of Lincoln under John Longland, 1521-1547*, Cambridge, 1981.

[43] The parish of the Holy Rood Cuxham was a Merton College living, see Registrum Vetus, I, f. 284 r.

[44] For his appointment as senior dean on 1 August 1533, see Registrum Vetus, I, f. 279 r; for the university sermon on 8 March 1534, see Oxford University Archives, Registrum Cancellarii ᴴ: Registrum Curiae Cancellarii, Ab Anno 1527 ad anno 1543, f. 366 v, and Registrum Vetus, I, f. 281 v: 'On the eighth day of March ... on the fourth Sunday [of Lent] Master Richard Smyth preached in the Church of St Peter-in-the-East in the presence of the University' (8 die martij omnes in media dominica 4° praedicavit magister richardus Smythus in ecclesia sancti petri in oriente coram universitatem).

[45] Later published by P. M. Vermigli, *Disputatio de sacrosanctae Eucharistiae habita in celeberissimae universitate Oxoniense in Anglia*, London, 1549; cf. Tresham's account, British Library, Harleian MS 422, ff. 4-31 and Chedsey's account, Corpus Christi College Oxford, MS cclv. For Tresham and Chedsey, see J. McConica, ed., *The History of the University of Oxford: The Collegiate University*, Oxford, 1986, 363-396: J. Loach, 'Reformation Controversies', 375.

[46] Registrum Vetus, I, f. 281 v; *Valor Ecclesiasticus Tempore Henrici VIII[i] auctoritate Regia institutus, printed by command of His Majesty George III*, London, 1814, 2.227.

comparatively well-off academic.[47] Indeed, by summer 1536 he had every reason to celebrate the end of his doctoral studies at Oxford with an 'actus solemnis' in the company of conservative celebrities: The engaging scholar had just been appointed regius *praelector* in theology.[48]

1.2. Oxford and London

In 1536 Henry VIII had created a lectureship at the universities of Cambridge and Oxford, 'whiche lecture shal be called perpetually Kyng Henry the eight his lecture'.[49] In return for a complete exemption 'from payment of there fyrst frutes & tenthe', the universities were instructed

> to fynde in everye of the said Univeristies one discrete and larned personage to reade one opyn and publique lectour in every of the said universities in any such science or tonge as the Kings Majestie shall assigne or appoynte to be mooste profitable for the studentes.[50]

In Oxford, the newly-created post was assigned to the openly conservative Richard Smyth, who transferred his lodgings from Merton to King Henry VIII's College (later Christ Church), where

---

[47] *Letters and Papers Foreign and Domestic Henry VIII*, 12/2.308; see also Wood (1813-1820), 1.143: 'principal of St Alban's Hall, Divinity Reader of Magdalen College'; see idem, *The History and Antiquity of the Colleges and halls in the University of Oxford*, Oxford, 1786, Appendix, 93, and Brodrick (1885), 254.

[48] 10 July 1536; cf. Oxford University Archives, Registrum Actae Congregationis, f. 17 v: 'On the tenth day of July a solemn act of worship took place in the Church of the Blessed Virgin, at which these most learned men took over theology in practice: Master Owen Oglethorpe, Master John Hastyngs, Master Nicholas Cartwryght, Master John Hurnsey, Master Thomas Raynoldes, Master Matthew Wyttaff, Master George Cotes, Master Richard Smyth' (Decimo die Julij celebratus est actus solemnis in aede diuae virginis in quo his litteratißimi viri realiter inceperunt theologia. Mr Owen Oglethorpe, Mr Johannes Hastyngs, Mr Nicholaus Cartwryght, Mr Johannes Hurnonsey, Mr Thomas Raynoldes, Mr Matthaeus Wyttaff, Mr Georgius Cotes, Mr Richardus Smyth). For Cartwright and Oglethorpe, see Loach (1986), 375f.

[49] *The statutes of the realm 1235-1713: printed by command of His Majesty King George the Third ... from original records and authentic manuscripts* (cited as: *Statutes of the Realm*) London, 1810-1822, 1.599: 'An Acte concernyng the exoneracyon of Oxford and Cambrydg from payment of there fyrst frutes & tenthe'.

[50] *Statutes of the Realm*, 1.599.

he remained on the payroll until his flight to Flanders.[51] In an even handed appointment, the Scotsman Alexander Allan (Alesius) was called to Cambridge at about the same time.[52] Alesius' theological views could not have been further from Smyth's conservatism. Following his studies in Wittenberg under Luther and Melanchthon, he proved to be a champion of unadulterated Lutheran doctrine in Cambridge until his resignation of the royal lectureship in 1537.[53]

Smyth's appointment to the post was probably a royal reward for his previous support in the king's divorce case. When Henry had requested various European universities in spring 1530 to examine the grounds for an annulment of his failed marriage to Katherine of Aragon, the faculty of Divinity at Oxford promptly set up a commission to contribute theological reasons in preparation for the divorce.[54] Any support Smyth might have rendered in the Oxford examination of the case would account for his sudden appointment to the newly-created royal lectureship.[55] It would also have made up for his fervent conservatism when, only months before his appointment, in a formal sermon 'Master Smyth, of Martyn College' condemned justification by faith alone and

---

[51] For Smyth's appointment, see Oxford University Archives, *Registrum Actae Congregationis*, f. 17 v; for his move to Christ Church, see Christ Church College Oxford Archives, Battels Books, MS x (1) c.6, f. 2 v, etc.

[52] For Alesius' career, see G. Wiedermann, *Der Reformator Alexander Alesius als Ausleger der Psalmen*. Dissertation, Universität Erlangen-Nürnberg, Erlangen, 1988, 37-55, and R. A. W. Rex, *Reformation and Renaissance Review* 2 (1999): 'The Early Impact of Reformation Theology at Cambridge University', 64-65; for Henry's balanced appointments, see D. MacCulloch, ed., *The reign of Henry VIII: politics, policy and piety*, Basingstoke, 1995, 159-180: 'Henry VIII and the reform of the Church', 174-175.

[53] Wiedermann (1988), 41.

[54] Smyth had most presumably been part of that commission; cf. W. B. Turnbull, ed., *State Papers preserved in the Public Record Office*, London, 1830, 1.377: 'the Faculte of Dyvynyte ... [was found] very desirous to fulfill our sayde desire'; for a thorough account of the consultations at Oxford, see G. Bédouelle, P. le Gal, edd. et al., *Le 'Divorce' du Roi Henry VIII: Etudes et Documents*, Genève, 1987; G. B. Skelly, 'Henry VIII consults the Universities of Oxford and Cambridge', 59-75, particularly 68-69.

[55] For the university's *Acta ... circa divortium regis Henrici VIII*, see D. Wilkins, ed., *Concilia Magnae Britanniae et Hiberniae: a Synodo Verolamiensi A.D. CCCC XLVI. ad Londinensem A.D. M DCCXVII. Accedunt constitutiones et alia ad historiam Ecclesiae Anglicanae spectantia*, London, 1737, 2.726-727.

instead propagated the efficacy of good works and the existence of purgatory.[56]

1.2.1. *Whittington College (1537)*

In 1537 Smyth's star was still rising. A little over a year after his appointment as the King's reader at Oxford, the London Livery Company of Mercers had to elect a new master for their college of priest-scholars, Whittington College, following the death of Edward Field.[57] The college was first endowed generously in February 1425 as a chantry for Richard Whittington, former mayor of London, and his wife Alice. Its statutes provided for a chapter of five academically trained men 'without benefice or other means of support' who took turns in saying offices and a daily mass for the repose of their benefactors' souls.[58] Much of the college's additional revenue was generated by the parish living of St Michael's-Paternoster Royal in London's Vintry Ward, and private benefactions further supplemented the initial endowment.[59] What had

---

[56] In March 1536, see *Letters and Papers Foreign and Domestic Henry VIII*, 10.396; for Henry's attempted rapprochement with Lutheranism, see for instance J. J. Scarisbrick, *Henry VIII*, New Haven CT, ²1997, 336-337.

[57] 9 September 1537; for Whittington College, see J. Imray, *The Charity of Richard Whittington*, London, 1968; L. Lyell, ed., *Acts of Court of the Mercers' Company, 1453-1527*, Cambridge, 1936; G. L. Hennessey, *Novum Repertorium Parochiale Londinense*, London, 1889, 334: 'Richard Smyth, Professor of Sacred Theology, was admitted to the Church of St Michael Paternoster-Royal, London, on 9 September 1537, [vacated] by the death of Edward Field, through the nomination of the wardens of the worshipful company of Mercers in the city of London' (Ric. Smith STP admiss. ad eccl. S. Mich. Ryal, Lond. 9 Sept 1537, per mort. Edw'di Feld, ad nominat. custodum communitatis misteriae merceriorum civit. Lond.).

[58] R. Newcourt, *Repertorium ecclesiasticum parochiale Londinense: An ecclesiastical parochial history of the diocese of London*, London, 1709-1710, 2.492: daily prayers were offered for the repose of the souls of Richard and Alice Whittington and their parents, of king Richard II and the Duke of Gloucester (both patrons of Richard Whittington), as well as of king Henry VI. An annual obit was made for king Edward III, the London citizens Walter and Joan de Waldeshef and Philip and Sabina de Taylour. In return, the college received an annual payment of £63 from the estate of the former mayor until its dissolution in 1548, see C. J. Kitching, ed., *London and Middlesex Chantry Certificate, 1548*, London Record Society, London, 1980, No. 96.

[59] For St Michael's Pasternoster-Royal, see H. Morley, ed., *A Survey of London written in the year 1598 by John Stow, citizen of London*, Stoud, 1999, 242-243; for benefactions to Whittington College, see particularly R. Sharpe, ed., *Calendar of Wills proved and enrolled in the Court of Husting London, 1258-1688*, London, 1889, 2.457.

initially been little more than a residential college of secular priests serving the parish church of St Michael's was subsequently enlarged by the acquisition of various buildings in the neighbourhood, most notably Whittington's own property, purchased by his livery company in 1468.[60] The foundation was augmented by two clerks and four choristers, all of whom came under the supervision of a master chosen by the five chaplains 'from among their own number'.[61] By 1478, however, the right of appointment had fallen exclusively to the wardens of the livery company:

> Where as of olde used for & uppon the nominacion of a newe Maister electe & chosen at Whytyngdon College that we to afferme and the said nominacion ... unto the Prior & Chapitour of Crychurch in Canterbury presented &c.; this so shewede tofore the felyshyppe &c. they haue remytted alle things vnto the discrecion of the Wardens.[62]

Since the college fell under the joint patronage of the company of Mercers as trustees of Whittington's charity, and the Prior and Chapter of Canterbury Cathedral as patrons of St Michael's, the newly-elected master was first formally presented to the two wardens of the company and subsequently to the Prior and Chapter of Canterbury.

In 1495, the college forged its initial link with the university of Oxford when Hugh Clopton, alderman and master Mercer, left considerable property to the foundation with the stipulation that henceforth 'whenever there is a vacancy by reason of death or resignation of the master of the collegiate church ... preference may be given ... to a member of the university of Oxford before all other universities'.[63] The preference for Oxford graduates was later extended to members of the fellowship.[64] In the late fifteenth century, the college began to further its reputation as an academic

---

[60] Lyell (1936), 50: 'That as for the Purchas of Whytingtons howse by his Colage, if it can be had for the Summe of iij c marcs and so surely made by acte of Parlement ... shall bye it.'
[61] Imray (1968), 31.
[62] 23 March 1478, cf. Lyell (1936), 109; 110: Three days later this right was exercised for the first time 'at sent pancras Churche'.
[63] 8 March 1495, Sharpe (1889), 2.595.
[64] Cf. Lyell (1936), 245: 'The Maister of Wytyngton Collage came before us & shewed us that the roume of oon of the Felawes of his place was voyde, ... saying that he hath written for oon to Oxenford'.

institution. In 1481 Gilbert Heydok left the college 600 marks for the employment of two further chaplains 'which were to be Doctors or Bachelors of Divinity, at least Masters of Art, not only to pray for his soul but also to preach and instruct the people'.[65] The establishment of a *Fraternitas Sanctae Sophiae* eight years later 'for the reading of a Divinity-lecture' at the instigation of the college's master Edward Underwood formalised the college's academic function.[66]

In October 1537, then, Richard Smyth was elected master of this intriguing institution.[67] He undoubtedly benefited from the college's lasting links with Oxford university, but it is impossible to determine whether he had formerly been a fellow of the London college or not.[68] Since no previous links with the London company of Mercers can be confirmed, he may have been selected on the strength of his recent academic appointments as an Oxford lecturer in theology and regius *praelector*. Smyth held office until the first dissolution of the college in 1548, when the chapter of academic priests was dismissed and the almshouses formally run by a 'tutor' on behalf of the chaplains took on the name of Whittington's foundation.[69] He was re-appointed master at the restoration of the college, in 1553.[70] The college provided Smyth not only with an additional annual income in excess of £15, but also with a much sought-after London base, giving him access to his future patron, bishop Edmund Bonner, and to various city pulpits.[71]

---

[65] Newcourt (1709-1710), 2.492.

[66] Cf. Lambeth Palace Library, Registrum Cantuar Liber Moreton, 28; for Underwood, see Newcourt (1709-1710), 2.492.

[67] *Letters and Papers Foreign and Domestic Henry VIII*, 12/2.621; Registrum Vetus, I, 285 r.

[68] No records for the appointment of fellows are extant.

[69] Imray (1968), 31. The set of almshouses providing a living for twelve 'brothers' had been run concurrently with the chapter of secular clergy from 1538, cf. Company of Mercers Archives, Renterwardens Accounts Book 1501-1538, f. 337 v.

[70] Hennessy (1889), 334.

[71] 1537; Company of Mercers Archives, Renterwardens Accounts Book 1501-1538, f. 337 r: 'Salary of prestes & almesmen of Whytyngton Coledge payd. To the master of Whytyngton College for a yere xiii £'; f. 337 v: 'payd to the master of whytyngton colledge for a full yere £ xiii. Payd to the tutor and xii brethren for a yere £ xxxii iiii s. xxii d. Payd for the obyte of master whytyngton ... ii £ ii s. iii d'; *Letters and Papers Foreign and Domestic Henry VIII*, 4/1.964; see Kitching (1980), No. 96.

Smyth did not take up permanent residence at Whittington College, but remained at Christ Church, Oxford. While the chantry statutes specified that ordinary chapter members of St Michael's were obliged to live at the college 340 days a year, the master was either granted dispensation or not bound by these residency requirements.[72] As *praelector* at Oxford, Smyth was bound by statute to moderate regular university disputations and was frequently called upon to represent the university at the convocation of Canterbury, where he added his signature to those of the bishops of England and Wales on a declaration on holy orders.[73] He entertained members of the royal commission to Oxford on behalf of the university and endorsed the publication of the 'bishops' book', *The Institution of a Christian Man*, as a member of the lower house of convocation.[74] By 1537 the 'poor man's child' had clearly assumed a central role in the theological debates of the national church.[75]

1.2.2. *Consolidating Conservatism (1536-1546)*

Smyth's humble social background had brought with it an early dependence on influential patrons. The newly-appointed *praelector* certainly was burdened by obligation towards his patrons and sought to repay them by loyal service. Two official investigations displayed his fierce allegiance to the conservative bishop of London and Henry VIII.[76] Following a sermon and bidding prayers in July 1538 at St Lawrence's Church, Evesham, he was reported to the crown by the county-sheriff, the bailiff of Worcester and Sir Richard Tracy, an influential evangelical associate of Thomas

---

[72] Imray (1968), 32.

[73] Gibson (1931), 346. Smyth was dispensed from his duties as a moderator twice, cf. Oxford University Archives, Registrum Actae Congregationis, f. 16 v; 17 v; for his duties at convocation, see Wilkins (1737), 3.834; and *Letters and Papers Foreign and Domestic Henry VIII*, 11.31.

[74] Wilkins (1737), 3.832; *Letters and Papers Foreign and Domestic Henry VIII*, 12/1.201, 264; 12/2.402ff.

[75] Smyth (1555), C iii v.

[76] For bishop John Stokesley, see for instance S. Brigden, *London and the Reformation*, Oxford, ²1991, 145, 109; also, A. A. Chiby, *Henry VIII's conservative scholar: Bishop John Stokesley and the divorce, royal supremacy and doctrinal reform*, Bern, 1997.

Cromwell and Hugh Latimer.[77] In Latimer's own diocese Smyth's bidding-prayers for king Henry and 'Lady Jane, past Queen' as well as 'our most holye father, bishop of London, a founder of the faith of Christ' were regarded as ostentatious and injudicious.[78] His prayers for former benefactors, such as the archbishop of York, the bishop of Lincoln and the abbot of Evesham obviously caused offence to local evangelicals. It is unlikely that Smyth prayed for 'souls in purgatory', as his accusers maintained. In the light of the royal attempt to achieve a rapprochement with Lutheranism such prayers could easily have proved to be a stumbling block.[79] Smyth's shrewdness in avoiding prosecution and newly-gained status is illustrated by the fact that a companion was 'committed to the common jail but Smythe is departed to Oxford'.[80]

A few months later, Smyth chaired a royal commission to Oxford and once more was reported to the crown.[81] Whereas he had previously been accused of religious conservatism, Thomas Bewliam now accused him of treason. He reported that when sitting as a vice-commissary Smyth had claimed to present 'the King's proper person'.[82] What may have been an attempt to

---

[77] 8 July 1538; *Letters and Papers Foreign and Domestic Henry VIII*, 12/2.534; Tracy was a local evangelical pamphleteer who, in the autumn of 1538, would confiscate the Blood of Hailes with bishop Hugh Latimer. In 1543, he published a work on justification by faith, R. Tracy, *The Profe and Declaration of thys Proposition: Faythe only Justifieth*, London, 1543?; see also C. J. Litzenberger, *The English Reformation and the Laity: Gloucestershire, 1540-1580*, Cambridge, 1997, 35, 53.

[78] *Letters and Papers Foreign and Domestic Henry VIII*, 12/2.534.

[79] A Lutheran party had arrived in London in May 1538 and agreed on thirteen articles of faith, cf. *A book containing Divers Articles de Unitate Dei et Trinitate Personarum, de Peccato Originali, &c.*, in: C. Hardwick, ed., *A History of the Articles of Religion*, London, 1851, 251-263; these were mostly derived from the *Wittenberg Articles*, and the *Confessio Augustana*, cf. E. Kinder and K. Haendler, edd., *Lutherisches Bekenntnis. Eine Auswahl aus den Bekenntnisschriften der evangelisch-lutherischen Kirche*, Berlin and Hamburg, 1962. English translation in: *Concordia Triglotta: Libri symbolici Ecclesiae Lutheranae Germanice, Latine, Anglice*, St Louis MO, 1921.

[80] *Letters and Papers Foreign and Domestic Henry VIII*, 12/2.534; D. MacCulloch, *Cranmer: A Life*, New Haven CT, 1996, 275, explained: 'Evangelicals listened out for any hint of conservative intrigue to return England to papal obedience, or to threaten the dynasty. ... Success was measured by convincing the King of the truth of their charges, and by how high up the social and political scale the charges could reach'.

[81] 8 September 1538; Oxford University Archives, Registrum Cancellarii Ǝ, f. 356 v.

[82] *Letters and Papers Foreign and Domestic Henry VIII*, 12/2.308.

establish his impeccable royalist loyalties was perceived by the audience as sheer hypocrisy. Since he still strongly maintained traditional theology in his lectures it was reported that

> he transgresses the statute for abolishing the Bishop of Rome's usurped power both in the hall of which he is principal and in the whole university.[83]

Smyth's lack of finesse was matched only by his unreformed conservatism. He continued to uphold in public the seven sacraments, the doctrine of sacrificing priests, the benefits of prayers for the dead, and apostolic tradition.[84] It is remarkable that even though Smyth had been accused of treason at a time when the crown imposed stringent punitive measures he once more was left completely unscathed. On the contrary, he extended his influence in Oxford to such an extent that John Foxe, then still an undergraduate at Brasenose, declared that

> doctor Smith and doctor Cotes gouerned the deuinitye scholes, who together with other deuines and doctors seemed not ... to shew the duety which the mooste meke Apostle requireth in deuines towarde suche as are fallen into anye error or lacke instruction or learning.[85]

He continued to proclaim his conservative doctrine in the Divinity School, although his evangelical successor suggested that he occasionally mitigated his views to suit his audience.[86]

---

[83] *Letters and Papers Foreign and Domestic Henry VIII*, 12/2.308.
[84] Oxford University Archives, Registrum Cancellarii Ǝ, f. 356 v-357 r.
[85] 1539, J. Foxe, *Actes and monuments &c.*, London, 1563, 570 [=J. Foxe, *The Acts and monuments of John Foxe. New and complete edition, with a preliminary dissertation by G. Townsend. Edited by S. R. Cattley*, London, 1837-1841, 5.252]; for Foxe's Oxford career, see C. B. Heberden, ed., *Brasenose College Register, 1509-1909*, OHS 55, Oxford, 1909, 1.6; for George Cotes, master of Balliol College, Oxford, see A. B. Emden, *A Biographical Register of the University of Oxford, 1501-1540*, Oxford, 1971, 140.
[86] 1539?; Vermigli (1559), 634, maintained that, during a visit of bishop Latimer to Oxford, 'a crowd gathered with the aim of seeing the bishop and, as almost all the university was waiting, Smyth, as he had promised, [spoke] about the fifth chapter of the Epistle to the Romans. These words discussed justification and taught how it is attained only by faith—he laboured his point many times, and imaginatively, "faith alone", "without any works", "without any deserts of our own", indeed, he said, "if Latin were able to express it thus, most solely and most uniquely, faith justifies us". And with such a contention he spoke on the truth of this proposition, as no-one could testify better than all those who were then studying at Oxford who are still alive' (Confluxit eodem studio videndi episcopi, & rei expectatione tota ferè Academia Smythaeus vt erat pollicitus è quinto capite ad

30   CHAPTER ONE

In London, Smyth's position as master of the collegiate church of St Michael's-Paternoster Royal also proved to be a useful platform to broadcast orthodox catholic views. The early 1540s saw a sudden loss of influence for the evangelical party within the English church. Following the publication of the *Act of Six Articles* in 1539, and the translation of bishop Edmund Bonner to the diocese of London a year later, Smyth was frequently called to the open-air pulpit of St Paul's Cross.[87] In 1541, his vociferous attack on Alexander Seton's evangelical doctrine of justification at the Grocers' church, St Anthony's Budge Row, earned him the Scotsman's condemnation for 'his doctrine of works and his interpretation of reconciliamini Deo'.[88] Smyth also made exceptional use of his polemical preaching in Oxford. He was specifically asked to speak at Thomas Malary's recantation in the university church of St Mary-the-Virgin since, as a later evangelical commentator suggested, 'that solemnity should not passe with out some effectu-

---

Romanos. Iustificationem, et sola fide docere aggreditur, haec verba disserè, et saepè, & asserueranter ingenians: sola fides, sine vllis operibus, sine vllis meritis nostris, imò, inquit, si latinè viceat ita dicere, solissima & vnissima fides nos iustificat: tantaque contentione de veritate huius propositionis disseruit, vt maiore nemo potuerit sicuti testati possunt, quotquot tum erant Oxonij studiosi, qui ad huc in viuis sunt). Vermigli claimed that, under pressure from his conservative colleagues, Smyth took back his 'evangelical' views. This account is not reproduced in Foxe, himself an undergraduate at Oxford at that time, and is therefore most probably a deliberate misrepresentation.

[87] For the renewal of his licence to preach in the diocese by bishop Bonner, see Guildhall Library, London, MS 9531/12, f. 13 v; for his sermons at St Paul's Cross, see M. Maclure, *Register of Sermons preached at St Paul's Cross, 1534-1642*, University of Toronto Occasional Publications VI, Ottawa ON, 1989, 24ff.; for a thorough introduction to Bonner's life, see G. Alexander, *The Life and career of Edmund Bonner, Bishop of London*, unpublished Ph.D. thesis, University of London, 1960; for a more recent evaluation of his later career, see her contribution in C. Haigh, ed. et al., *The English Reformation revised*, Cambridge, 1987, 157-175: G. Alexander, 'Bonner and the Marian persecutions'.

[88] 13 November 1541, J. Foxe, *Actes and Monumentes of these latter and perillous dayes ... newly recognised and inlarged by the Authour*, London, 1583, 2.1205-1206 [=Foxe (1837-1841), 5.448-450]. Seton was a private chaplain to the Duke of Suffolk; for the previous investigation of his heretical views by the doctrinal committee of the Convocation of Canterbury in April 1539, see MacCulloch (1996), 268; for his London preaching, see Brigden (²1991), 308-309; 335: 'Smith's insistence that "man, by his works, earns merit", Seton denounced. ... The man who, like Smith, preached that works might merit "preacheth a doctrine of the Devil"'.

all Sermon, for the holding vp of the mother Church of Rome'.[89] His sermon illustrated Smyth's skilful use of the dramatic well. Malary's eucharistic doctrine had been condemned as heretical and so, following the recantation,

> the preacher went vp into the pulpyt and began his Sermone, the argument wher of was vpon the Sacrament. He hadde also a cake or hoste tyed in a stryng for the greater confirmation and credit of his wordes.[90]

The *praelector* appears to have been a regular preacher at evangelical recantations. During at least two sermons in the university church he made use of the hanging pyx to demonstrate the real presence of the body of Christ in full view of the congregation.[91] At a 1541 recantation in St Mary-the-Virgin, however, even Smyth's acute sense for the dramatic must have been over-exerted.[92] Sudden shouts of 'fyre, the churche is set on fyre by heretics' caused great commotion among the 'great number of the chiefe doctors and deuines of the university'.[93] John Foxe left little doubt about Smyth's uncompromising treatment of evangelical dissidents, and commented how the false alarm affected the otherwise sanguine preacher:

> None cried out more earnestly then the doctor that preached ... who in a manner fyrst of all cried out in the pulpit: ... 'These are the traynes & subtilities of the heretykes against me, the Lorde haue mercy vpon me'. ... But myght not God as it hadde been out of the whyrle wynd haue answered 'Thou thyselfe shewest no mercy vnto thy fellowes and brethren ... wherefore synce you so lytle esteme the death of others, be now content that other men should also regard your death'.[94]

There was to be no voice out of the whirlwind, just as there had been no fire. The episode was nothing but an example to the catholic 'what it is to put other poore menne to the fyer', the

---

[89] Foxe (1583), 2.1208 [=Foxe (1837-1841), 5.455]; for Malary, see Emden (1971), 373; for his heretical views of the eucharist, see Wood (1786), 2.37.
[90] Foxe (1563), 621 [=Foxe (1837-1841), 5.455-456].
[91] Ibid.
[92] In the 1583 edition of his *Actes and Monumentes* Foxe conflated the two stories.
[93] Foxe (1563), 621 [=Foxe (1837-1841), 5.455-456].
[94] Foxe (1563), 622 [=Foxe (1837-1841), 5.456].

moral read.[95] The catholic, however, had no intention of heeding that moral.

Finally, in December 1542, Smyth was invited together with leading religious conservatives to preach a series of six sermons funded by the company of Mercers 'to be made in oure churche in the tyme of Lente'.[96] In return for 12 d. 13 s. per preacher 'for their paynes and labor', Dr John Standish (a contemporary of Smyth's from Corpus Christi College, Oxford, and fellow of Whittington College), Dr Nicholas Wilson (a long-standing associate of bishop John Fisher, confessor to Henry VIII and archdeacon of Oxford), John Hodgekynne (a former Dominican friar and a suffragan to the bishop of London), and the local vicar of St Lawrence Jewry, Christopher Worsely, each accepted to deliver a sermon alongside 'doctor Smythe, master of Whittington college'.[97] Smyth was now at the zenith of his influence in Oxford and London. The sermon series, conducted until the college's dissolution in 1548, were a clear manifestation of traditionalism in the livery company's chapel. For six years the notoriously conservative Nicholas Wilson delivered the entire sermon series,[98] until the Court of the Mercers decided in early summer 1549 that

> the compeny shall ... have the Communion in the stede of the sollen messe, and this to be confirmed to be continuously from yere to yere tyll further be knowne to the contraye.[99]

In 1546, Smyth not only confirmed his catholic credentials in print, but also sought to affirm his loyal submission to king

---

[95] Ibid.

[96] 20 December 1542, Company of Mercers Archives, Acts of Court 1527-1560, f. 161 r; based on a royal injunction connected with the purchase of the hospital and church of St Thomas Acon from the crown, 'the compeny have determined and agred that it shalbe performed accordynge unto their Indention'; cf. J. Imray, *The Mercers' Hall*, London, 1991, 380: 'The Lent preachers were provided under a covenant made by the company in 1542, when it bought the hospital of St Thomas Acon from Henry VIII'.

[97] For Standish, brother of Henry Standish, bishop of St Davids, see G. Hennessy, *Novum Repertorium Parochiale Londinense*, London, 1889, xxxii, c.95; for Wilson, op. cit., xxxvi, c.235 and Wilkins (1737), 3.737; for Hodgekynne, later bishop of Bedford, Hennessy (1889), xii, a.115; for Worsely, op. cit., cxix, p.65; for St Lawrence Jewry, see Stow (1999), 268.

[98] Company of Mercers Archives, Acts of Court, 1527-1560, f. 172 r, f. 185 r, f. 199 r, f. 223 r; for his friendship with bishop Fisher, see R. A. W. Rex, *The Theology of John Fisher*, Cambridge, 1991, 84-85.

[99] Company of Mercers Archives, Acts of Court, 1527-1560, f. 232 v.

Henry's supremacy, both of which he did in fine style by publishing two books in defence of the sacrament of the eucharist. 'The king's moost humble subiecte, chaplyne, beddysman, and seruant Richard Smythe' had dedicated both works to his patron, the 'mooste gratious soueraigne Lorde Henry the eughte ... in erth supreme head next vnder Christ'.[100] His *A defence of the blessed Masse and the sacrifice thereof, prouynge that it is aualable bothe for the quycke and the dead* proved so popular that it went through three print-runs within the year.[101] In early 1547, Smyth added a brief work on apostolic tradition numbering no less than 45 Church practices that 'Christe and hys apostles taught & lefte to the churche ... wythout wrytyinge, whyche we must both beleve stedfastly and also fulfyll obedientlye, under peyne of damnation ever to endure'.[102] In an injudicious attempt to buttress episcopal authority, Smyth also strongly maintained that English bishops had of old been entitled to pass legislation within their dioceses.

Presumably in recognition of his unwavering defence of traditional doctrine, Smyth was appointed one of the commissioners at the trial of the evangelical Anne Askew, in 1546.[103] The fact that the commission consisted of friends both old and new reflects on how central Smyth had become to the conservative cause. He sat in judgement alongside his diocesan and patron, bishop Edmund

---

[100] Smyth (1546[1]), colophon; idem, *The Assertion and Defence of the sacramente of the aulter. Compiled and made by mayster Richarde Smythe doctour of diuinitie, and reader of the kynges maiesties lesson in his graces vniuersitie of Oxforde, dedicate vnto his hyghnes, beynge the excellent and moost worthy defendour of Christes faythe*, London, 1546[2]; for a theological evaluation of the works, see below, chapter IV.

[101] Published at the printing presses of John Herforde, [1+2]1546, and William Myddylton, [2]1547.

[102] R. Smyth, *A brief treatyse settynge forth diuers truthes necessary both to be beleued of chrysten people, & kepte also, whiche are not expressed in the scripture but left to ye church by the apostles tradition*, London, 1547, D viii r. He argued for instance that traditions such as the Lenten fast, the reservation of the sacrament in a pyx, the blessing of chrism oils and other catholic practices had been passed on since apostolic times; see B. Gordon, ed., *Protestant History and Identity in Sixteenth-Century Europe: The Medieval Inheritance*, St Andrews Series in Reformation History, Aldershot, 1996, 1.60-77: P. Marshall, 'The Debate over "Unwritten Verities" in England', 73-74.

[103] For an evangelical hagiography of Anne Askew, see J. Bale, *The First Examinacyon of the worthy seruant of God, Mistress Anne Askewe, lately martyred in Smythfelde*, Marburg, 1546, and idem, *The Lattre Examinacyon of Anne Askewe*, Marburg, 1547; for a catholic defamation, see R. Parsons, *A treatise of three conuersions of England from Paganisme to Christian Religion*, St Omer, 1603-1604; Brigden ([2]1991), 371-377, has a balanced modern evaluation.

34   CHAPTER ONE

Bonner, as well as one of the preachers at his Lenten sermon series, bishop John Hodgekynne, and his long-standing Oxford friend and colleague Owen Oglethorpe at whose side he had graduated about ten years previously.[104] It is difficult to believe that within six months of Anne Askew's spectacular execution on 15 July 1546, the catholic party in council had been defeated. By spring 1547 the evangelicals, having regained the favour of the dying Henry VIII, had seized power under Edward and set out actively to overthrow their traditionalist rivals.[105]

2.1. Recantations (1547)

The numerous masses said for the repose of king Henry's soul, as well as the grandiose requiem celebrated by bishop Stephen Gardiner at Windsor Castle on 15 February 1547, were among the last manifestations of religious conservatism during the reign of Edward VI.[106] When Edward Seymour was appointed Lord Protector, he took over the reins of council and accelerated the previously hesitant and half-hearted attempts at ecclesiastical reform.[107] The council's reformation endeavours spared neither the two universities, nor the conservative Oxford *praelector*. In spring 1547 Richard Smyth was called to London for a ritual academic humiliation. King Edward's journal recorded: 'Dr Smith

---

[104] *Letters and Papers Foreign and Domestic Henry VIII*, 20/1.391. The court met 'to the intent the world may see what credence is now to be given unto the same woman, who in so short a time, hath so damnably altered and changed her opinion and belief; and therefore was rightly, in open court, arraigned and condemned'.

[105] See for instance D. R. Starkey, *The Reign of Henry VIII: Personalities and Politics*, London, 1985, chapter VIII.

[106] For Henry VIII's funeral, see Strype (1822), 2.289; for a recent account, see J. Loach, *Past and Present* 142 (1994), 43-68: 'The function of ceremonial in the reign of Henry VIII', 56-68.

[107] See MacCulloch (1996), 363: 'Power and profit were henceforth firmly in the hands of evangelicals. ... This evangelical establishment grouping knew from the start in 1547 exactly what Reformation it wanted: whatever hesitations occurred were primarily attributable to the need to disarm conservative opposition'.

of Oxford recanted at Pauls certain opinions of the Mess, and that Christ was not according to the order of Melchisedeck'.[108]

Edward's journal was ordinarily devoted to events of political or diplomatic significance, and his reference illustrates the importance of Smyth's recantation.[109] His public admission that his orthodox work was in fact corrupted by theological errors marked the weakening hold of the catholic establishment on political and ecclesiastical life in England and was an ominous foretaste of its imminent demise. In his chronicle Charles Wriothesley noted how Smyth was forced to observe the burning of his books and acknowledge the religious changes in public:

> The fifteenth daie of maie, 1547, Doctor Smyth of Wydyngton College ... recanted and burned two bookes ... and there professed another sincere doctrine, contrarie to his old papisticall ordre.[110]

Smyth's London recantation, published almost immediately, was in fact a masterpiece of equivocation.[111] As if to insult the evangelical establishment even in defeat, he had chosen as his text *omnis homo mendax*—words favoured in the Lutheran doctrine of justification.[112] In his ensuing interpretation, he declared that he was no worse than the church Fathers, since 'theldest & best writers in the Christen Church ... all haue erred in their bookes'.[113] His cynicism did not pass unnoticed by the authorities. Even former catholic

---

[108] Clarendon Historical Society, ed., *The Journal of King Edward's reign, written with his own hand* (cited as: *Journal of King Edward*), London, 1884, 5; cf. Maclure (1989), 28; Smyth in fact recanted that Christ was not a sacrificing priest according to the order of Aaron.

[109] The only other mention of religious change or correction was in 1549, when Edward reflected on the burning of Joan Boacher (Joan of Kent) for denying the Incarnation, see *Journal of King Edward*, 17; see also D. MacCulloch, *Tudor Church Militant: Edward VI and the Protestant Reformation*, London, 1999, 23: 'Edward's notebook on the sermons he heard ... would have complemented what the young king wrote in the Chronicle, so the loss accounts for the Chronicle's apparent lack of interest: ... Edward was too tidy-minded a boy to duplicate effort'.

[110] W. D. Hamilton, ed., *Charles Wriothesley: A Chronicle of the England during the reign of the Tudors, from AD 1485-1559*, London, 1875-1877, 184.

[111] R. Smyth, *A godly and faythfull Retraction made by R. Smyth. Reuokyng certeyn errors in some of hys books*, London, 1547¹.

[112] Smyth (1547¹), A iii r; for Luther's use of the term in his theology of justification, see for instance M. Luther, *Werke. Kritische Gesamtausgabe*, Weimar, 1883— (cited as: WA) 56.385.15-22; for Smyth's rejection of the same, see below, chapter III.

[113] Ibid.

allies disowned Smyth, since they felt they had been implicated by association.

Soon after the event Seymour wrote a lengthy letter to the conservative bishop of Winchester, praising Smyth's retraction. The credulous Lord Protector questioned Gardiner why he voiced dissatisfaction at Smyth's equivocal *omnis homo mendax*, yet did not condemn his previous 'furtheraunce of the Bishop of Rome's vsurped power'.[114] Gardiner's reply was swift. He had no good word for Smyth and rightly surmised that he had sought to mislead the evangelical establishment by humbly submitting to the king's authority. In particular Gardiner dismissed as absurd Smyth's view that 'bishops in this realm may make laws', and swiftly added that he was able to call on witnesses to testify to his own strong aversion to this particular point.[115] Finally, he endeavoured half-heartedly to disassociate himself from the troubled academic by the implausible claim that he had never known him:

> I neither liked his tractation ... ner yet hys retractation; and was gladde of my former Judgement that I neyuer had familiaryty with him ... for he that seketh for so much company in lieng as he did, hath smale humility; for he would hyde himself by the nomber, and this much as touching Smith, of whom, nor his booke, till he was in trouble, I neuer hard talking.[116]

Gardiner had assessed the spirit of the London recantation accurately. Only a very thin veil of humility disguised Smyth's distaste at the proceedings. Smyth primarily sought to pacify the evangelical establishment: he had not come to acknowledge his

---

[114] Foxe (1583), 753-736 [=Foxe (1837-1841), 6.35], Edward Seymour to Stephen Gardiner, 21 May 1547: 'And, as it apered, you be so angrye wyth hys retractions (whiche frankly without feare, dreade, compulsion or imprisonment, only with lerninge and truthe overcomed, he came vnto), that you cannot abide his beginning ... it appered vnto vs then of him taken but godly, ... we would haue wished your lordship to have written against his booke before, or now with it, if you thinke that to be defended whiche the author himself refuseth to averre. Your Lordship writeth so ernestly for lent, which we go not about to put awaye, no more then when Dr Smith wrote so ernestly that euery man should be obedient to the the bishops, the magistrates by and by went not about to bring kings and princes, and others, under their subjection'.

[115] Foxe (1563), 739 [=Foxe (1837-1841), 6.39]: 'And wher as in his vnwritten verities he was so mad to say, Byshops in this realm may make laws, I haue witness that I said at that word, we should then be dawes'.

[116] Foxe (1563), 739 [=Foxe (1837-1841), 6.39f], Stephen Gardiner to Edward Seymour, Winchester, 6 June 1547.

faults. On the contrary, he argued that while he may have strayed from the truth in some points, the corpus of his work still stood untouched. 'Shall I now be ashamed to acknowledge my self to haue ben deceyued? ... Wil ye not beleue S. Austen in other poyntes of our Religion because he erred?', he demanded of his audience.[117] Nonetheless, Smyth did have to withdraw some of his more extreme views. He was required to reconsider his views on episcopal authority, and had to accept that episcopal oversight consisted of the proclamation of the Gospel 'and not in makying laws'.[118] Furthermore, in line with recent council injunctions governing the restriction of catholic ceremonies, Smyth acknowledged that 'where [ceremonies] be receyued, and by disuse may be abrogate, or by contrary law made in any country by thauctority of the supreme powers many be clene taken away'.[119]

Lastly, he had been ordered to address the subject of the sacrifice of the mass. For once Smyth was not equivocating when he explained that in his *A Defence of the sacrifice of the masse* he had maintained a thorough distinction between Christ's redemptive sacrifice on the cross and the sacrifice re-enacted during the course of the mass.[120] While his statements that 'Christ was but once offered' and that 'neither Christ nor any other creature shuld at any tyme after, make any oblations for sin' undoubtedly pleased the evangelical authorities, it did not matter for his doctrine of the sacrifice of the mass.[121] On the contrary, catholic orthodoxy taught that the sacrifice on Calvary was sufficient for the remission of all sins, while the sacrifice of the mass was no new sacrifice but merely communicated the benefits of Christ's saving

---

[117] Smyth (1547¹), A ii v.
[118] Smyth (1547¹), B i r.
[119] Smyth (1547¹), C iii r; for the 1547 injunctions, see J. E. Cox, ed., *Miscellaneous Writings and Letters of Thomas Cranmer*, Parker Society, Cambridge, 1846, 498-504.
[120] See below, chapter IV.
[121] Smyth (1547¹), D i r; D iii r.

death to the believer.[122] The only theological concept Smyth genuinely recanted at St Paul's Cross, therefore, was his eccentric view that on the cross Christ acted as the last priest of the line of Aaron (who offered blood sacrifices), rather than a priest according to Melchizedek (who made a sacrifice of bread and wine).[123] As his views were contrary even to catholic teaching they were easily withdrawn.[124] While he continued to defend the sacrificial character of the mass in his later publications, Smyth no longer laboured this erroneous distinction.

After his recantation at St Paul's Cross, Smyth was obliged to retract his views once more, in Oxford. In his home-town, Smyth evidently permitted himself even greater evasions. John Strype recalled:

> A few days after he had pronounced his recantation, or (as rather he chose to call it) his retractation, at St Paul's Cross, he repaired to Oxford, and there, soon after, came up in public and recanted, as he had done in London. But, it seems, it was done by him by halves: for instead of declaring at length ... what he had said at St Paul's, he insisted much in shewing his auditory that what he then said was not

---

[122] See for instance the resolutions of Trent, Session 22, 17 September 1562, in: H. Denzinger, H. Holping, P. Hünermann, edd., *Enchiridion symbolorum et definitionum de rebus fidei et morum: Kompendium der Glaubensbekenntnisse und kirchlichen Lehrentscheidungen*, Freiburg im Breisgau and Rome, [38]1999, (cited as: DS) 1743: 'And since the same Christ who offered Himself bloodily on the altar of the cross is contained and bloodlessly sacrificed in the divine sacrifice carried out at mass, as holy Synod teaches, this sacrifice is indeed propitiatory, and happens through Himself, so that with a true heart and upright faith ... we will attain mercy and find grace for [our] time of need' (Et quoniam in divino hoc sacrificio, quod in Missa peragitur, idem ille Christus continetur et incruente immolatur, qui in ara crucis semel se ipsum cruente obtulit docet sancta Synodus, sacrificium istud vere propitiatorium esse, per ipsumque fieri, ut, si cum vero corde et recta fide ... misericordiam consequamur et gratiam inveniamus in auxilio opportuno) and DS 1754: 'If anyone should speak blasphemously about the most holy sacrifice of Christ offered on the cross through the sacrifice of the mass, or should criticise it: let him be anathema' (Si quis dixerit, blasphemiam irrogari sanctissimo Christi sacrificio in cruce peracto per Missae sacrificium, aut illi per hoc derogari: anathema sit).

[123] Smyth (1546[1]), xxvii r-v: 'No man can truely say that christe was a preest after this ordre of Melchizedech when he offred vp himselfe on the crosse to his father for our sinnes, for he did not offre his body vnder the forme of bread & wine [Gen 14.18], but vnder the forme of fleshe & blode, & therefore he was that time so offering sacrifice a priest after the ordre of Aaron & nat of Melchizedech, ... & the prophecy ... by Dauyd [Ps 110.4] was fulfilled by Christ at his maundy'; see the discussion below, chapter V, 185-186.

[124] Cf. DS 1740.

so much a recantation as a retractation. ... He wrote also letters to his friends, denying that he had made a recantation.[125]

Consequently, the authorities called once more on Smyth asking him to repeat his Oxford recantation. On 24 July 1547, he explained that 'my two books ... in those poyntes ... wher in they be not fully consonant with scripture, I forsake and announce as erroneous'.[126] In Oxford, Smyth was also forced to recant some aspects of his doctrine on justification. In a university sermon shortly before the second recantation he had upheld his conservative understanding of justification. He had argued that in order to attain justification, the believer not only had to rely on God's grace and the merits of Christ but also 'the worthiness of the person and the worthiness of the work', a position also maintained in his later work.[127] In his second Oxford recantation he suggested that he had been misunderstood and instead reluctantly subscribed to evangelical doctrine of justification *sola fide et gratia*: 'The truth is they dyd mistake me, applieng those wordes to our justification whiche I spake of the workes of a man that is already justified', Smyth concluded.[128]

His readiness to recant did not salvage Smyth's career. Some powerful catholic allies disassociated themselves from him, since they felt that he had included them in his sweeping confession. Most contemporaries saw the recantations as half-hearted statements to appease the state authorities. While Smyth maintained in public that he had erred, he continued to declare his innocence in private. He could not have expected much sympathy when he finally spoke up and acknowledged that his previous recantations had been disingenuous. Nonetheless he made one last appeal to the public to give credence to his new sincerity:

> Where as syns the tyme I declared my retraction at Pawlis crosse I wrote and sente abrode sondry letters for my excuse ... whiche I in my retractation wyllynglye did professe: In this and in al other my writinges, readynges and teachinges, what so euer I have written,

---

[125] Strype (1882), 1.61.
[126] R. Smyth, *A playne declaration made at Oxford the 24. Daye of July, by Mayster Richarde Smyth upon his Retraction*, London, 1547², D iiii r.
[127] Smyth (1547²), E iii r-v.
[128] Smyth (1547²), E iii v; cf. E iiii r.

read or taught heretofore, that that I now teache I know to be true.[129]

2.2. Peter Martyr Vermigli (1547-1549)

In the long term, Smyth's unreconstructed conservatism undermined his position as *praelector*. In autumn 1547 Archbishop Cranmer had invited the Italian evangelicals Peter Martyr Vermigli and Bernardino Ochino to leave their exile and teach in England.[130] Cranmer required 'the assistance of learned men' to further the introduction of reformed doctrine at Cambridge and Oxford.[131] Vermigli had responded to the archbishop's call gladly. By December 1547, he had left his Strassburg lectureship and was settled in Lambeth.[132] A few weeks later he moved on to Christ Church, Oxford.[133] Smyth was forced to vacate his Oxford post and was succeeded by Vermigli, the target of most his later polemics.[134]

Soon after his coming to England the new *praelector* complained that a large percentage of the university's fellowship and heads of houses was either unreformed or reluctant to change.[135] He confided to Martin Bucer, that 'those who possess any share of learning are either wholly opposed to religion ... or so cold altogether to shrink from the endurance of any labours or perils'.[136] He therefore decided to expound thoroughly on the first epistle to the Corinthians in an extended series of lectures, which

---

[129] Smyth (1547²), A iii r.

[130] M. W. Anderson, *Peter Martyr, A Reformer in Exile (1542-1562)*, Nieuwkoop, 1975, 89.

[131] H. Robinson, ed., *Original Letters relative to the English Reformation, written during the reigns of king Henry viii., king Edward vi., and queen Mary: chiefly from the archives of Zurich. With Epistolae Tigurinæ conscriptae A.D. 1531-1558*, Cambridge, 1846-1848, 17.

[132] Cf. Bodleian Library Oxford, MS Ashmole 826; and N. H. Nicolas, *Archaeologia* 21 (1827), 469-473: 'The Bill of the Expenses attending the Journey of Peter Martyr and Bernhardinus Ochin, from Basel to England, in 1547'.

[133] Christ Church Oxford Archives, Battels Book, MS x (1) c.1.

[134] Christ Church Oxford Archives, Battels Book, MS x (1) c.6, f. 9 v.

[135] See G. D. Duncan, *Oxoniensia* 45 (1980), 225ff: 'The Heads of Houses and Religious Change in Tudor Oxford, 1547-1558'.

[136] In a letter to Bucer, in: M. Young, *The Life and Times of Aonio Paleario*, London, 1860, 425.

he published later as a commentary.[137] The introduction sheds some light on the choice of text. In a dedication to king Edward, Martyr emphasised that his lecture series on the epistle

> was particularly set up for this sake, simply because there are no other works which consider so many different and numerous subjects that are at present disputed. ... In this letter we have found a φάρμακον ἀλεξίκακον [a cure for all evil] for all Papist abuses, in short: every sort of superstition, a form of panacea which, by its very name, promises a cure for all ills.[138]

Martyr and Smyth both independently asserted that Smyth had attended the Italian's controversial lecture-series habitually, and that he had been an attentive, if antagonistic, listener.[139] From Martyr's arrival in Oxford in January 1548 until Smyth's sudden departure to the Low Countries in late March 1549, Smyth not only took assiduous notes, but also interrupted lectures, proposed impromptu debates and successfully tried to cause much commotion.[140] In addition to disrupting the lecture-routine, Smyth also used his extensive notes for later polemical works directed against Martyr.

In a preface addressed to the chancellor of Oxford university, Richard Cox, Martyr described how his exposition of 1 Cor 7 had sparked off considerable debate: 'And when I had already reached the seventh chapter, where the Apostle writes at great length about

---

[137] P. M. Vermigli, *In selectissimam D. Pavli priorem ad Corinthios epistolam, D. Petri Martyris Vermilii Florentini, ad Serenissimum Regem Anglia, &c. Edvardum VI Commentarii doctissimi*, Zürich, 1551.

[138] Vermigli (1551), 5 r: 'uero fuit praecipua huius instituta causa, quod in nulla alia tractentur tam uaria & multiplicia capita, quae ad nostrorum temporum controuersias faciunt. ... Hinc omnium abusuum Papisticorum, & omnium fermè superstitionem *pharmakon alexikakon* petentum est, instar alicuius panacis, quae ipso nomine omnium morborum remedia promittit'.

[139] P. M. Vermigli, *D. Petri Martyris Vermilii Florentini divinarum Literarum in Schola Tiguriina Professoris ad Riccardi Smythaei Angli, olim Theologiae professoris Oxoniensis duos Libellos de Caelibatu Sacerdotum, & Votis Monasticis, Nunc Primum in lucé edita*, Basel, 1559, introduction 1: 'Smyth was often present in the Schools; indeed, he not only used to listen assiduously to what I said, but even took notes, so far as he could keep up' (Aderat in schola frequens, imo assidue Smythaeus. ... Is quae à me dicebantur, non solùm attentè audiebat, sed etiam quantum assequi poterat, literis consignebat); Smyth (1550[1]), A viij r.

[140] Smyth's departure from Oxford can be dated roughly from his matriculation date at Leuven, 9 April 1549, in: E. Reusens, ed. et al., *Matricule de l'Université de Louvain*, Brussel, 1903-1961, 4.612, and a letter sent by Johannes ab Ulmis to Heinrich Bullinger, in Robinson (1846-1848), 388.

virginity and marriage, I argued lavishly and widely, just as my thoughts were leading me'.[141] Martyr confirmed that while Smyth had not succeeded in confronting him in debate he did manage to elicit at least an oral *tractatio*, and spoke at length of the 'insistence and sophist methods' employed by his opponent to enforce this reply.[142]

In his lecture series on the first epistle to the Corinthians, Vermigli not only attacked clerical celibacy but also set out his reformed eucharistic doctrine in great detail.[143] Following a refutation of the sacerdotal sacrifice and transubstantiation, he presented his own views in a generally hostile academic environment.[144] Many traditionalists resented the presence of the foreign evangelical in their midst and even before Vermigli had commenced his lectures a large number of the heads of houses had refused their students permission to attend.[145] By March 1549 Vermigli was teaching a clear Zwinglian eucharistic doctrine and propagated the belief that only the faithful consume the body of Christ.[146]

Following this declaration, Smyth sought to extract more than just another *tractatio* from the Italian. He incited the townspeople by posting public notices, explained that Vermigli had mocked

---

[141] Vermigli (1559), introduction 1: 'Et quum ad septem capitem iam peruenissem, ubi Apostolus de uirginitate atque matrimonio permulta scribit, ibi de uotis, ut meae rationes ferebant, copiosè satis fuseque disputaui'.

[142] Vermigli (1551), 192 r: 'cauillis & sophisticis rationibus'.

[143] P. M. Vermigli, *Tractatio de Sacramento Eucharistiae habita in celeberissima Universitate Oxoniensi in Anglia per D. Petrum Martyrem Vermilium Florentinum, Regium ibidem Theologiae professorem, cum iam absoluisset interpretationem 11 capitis prioris epistolae D. Pauli Apostoli ad Corinthos*, London, 1549¹, 1 v.

[144] Vermigli (1549¹), 1 v-55 v, first presented Lombard's definition of transubstantiation, then traditional arguments in favour of transubstantiation, 2 v-26 v, and added his own rejection of the doctrine, 27 v-55 v.

[145] See Duncan (1980), 225ff.

[146] While catholics distinguished between the consumption of the body and blood of Christ and its benefits, Martyr's view is such that only the true believer, by his faith, partakes of both the sacrament and the benefits of Christ's saving death; for an evaluation of Vermigli's 1549 eucharistic doctrine, see A. Schindler, ed. et al., *Die Zürcher Reformation: Ausstrahlungen und Rückwirkungen*, Bern, 2000, 317-326: J. A. Löwe, 'The bodie and bloud of Christ is not carnallie and corporallie in the bread and wine: The Oxford Disputation revisited—Zwinglian traits in the Eucharistic Theology of Pietro Martire Vermigli'; cf. MacCulloch (1996), 415. For Zwingli's doctrine, see W. P. Stephens, *The Theology of Huldrych Zwingli*, Oxford, 1986, 250-255.

traditional beliefs and had now been challenged to defend himself in a public disputation.[147] Public opinion about the recent religious innovations in Oxford was generally hostile, and large crowds gathered at the Divinity School to hear the debate. Vermigli, caught entirely unawares, was advised to cancel the lecture but allegedly remarked that 'he had not feared the inquisition and would withstand the angry mob'.[148] On his way to Schools, the Italian was formally challenged by Smyth's footman to engage in an impromptu disputation.

Vermigli refused and began to lecture as usual. The crowds had expected a spectacular refutation of the evangelical and began to make their disappointment known vociferously.[149] The resulting clamour caused the vice-chancellor to interfere. The proctors extracted the Italian from the imbroglio and insisted that any future debate be conducted in orderly fashion.[150] Smyth proceeded to initiate a university disputation instead. Soon after, the two parties met the vice-chancellor to determine the *quaestiones* of the disputation.[151] A date was set granting both Vermigli's wish for royal moderators and Smyth's for the use of 'scholastic terminology'.[152]

However, by the time the king's visitors to the university had settled the final details of the debate, Smyth had left the country. It fell to his Merton friends William Tresham and William Chedsey to argue against Vermigli under the close scrutiny of a royal commission. The precise reasons for Smyth's sudden disappearance from Oxford cannot be established. Pursued by the English

---

[147] See for instance, F. C. Schlosser, *Leben des Theodore de Beza und des Peter Martyr Vermili*, Heidelberg, 1809, 423.

[148] Schlosser (1806), 424: 'Er, der die Inquisition nicht gefürchtet, werde auch die tobende Masse nicht fürchten'.

[149] J. Strype, *Memorials of Thomas Cranmer, sometime lord archbishop of Canterbury. With the appendix to the memorials*, Oxford, 1694, 2.203.

[150] Humphrey (1573), 44.

[151] Vermigli was supported by two Canons of Christ Church, Henry Syddall and James Courthop, who both renounced their evangelical views in 1553. In summer 1555, Syddall was instrumental in persuading Cranmer to recant and witnessed his fifth recantation, assuring the archbishop that he would be spared, cf. MacCulloch (1996), 595; Smyth brought with him two future presidents of Magdalen College, Owen Oglethorpe and Arthur Cole, cf. J. Le Neve, *Fasti Ecclesiae Anglicani*, London, 1716, 107, 142.

[152] Cf. Vermigli (1549^1), 2 r; Strype (1694), 2.200.

authorities, he fled across the border to St Andrews. An evangelical commentator offered a gleeful explanation:

> Yet this intemperate Achilles did not appear for the debate on the day appointed but fled to St Andrews in Scotland, clearly thinking that [only] the man who was well hidden at such a time would be alive and well.[153]

3.1. Smyth's First Continental Exile (1549-1551)

Smyth spent very little time in St Andrews and as English authorities were catching up with him, made his way to Flanders.[154] Barely a month after leaving Oxford in March 1549 he was entered in the registers of the university of Leuven.[155] Not much is known about his duties at the premier university of the Habsburg Low Countries. In his *Fasti Academici Lovaniensis* the Leuven historian Andreas merely numbered Smyth among other theologians, including Erasmus of Rotterdam, as a 'doctor of Sacred Theology and a professor who did not attain his title in Leuven'.[156] Anthony à Wood painted the romantic image of a spiritual homecoming, rather than a politically motivated escape:

> But being forced ... to leave his professorship in the reign of King Edward VI to make room for Peter Martyr, he went to Lovain in Brabant, where being received with solemnity, he became public professor of divinity there for a time, and read openly on the Apocalypse of St John.[157]

There is no evidence for Smyth's 'solemn reception' or his lecturing at the catholic university. However, the safety of his exile enabled Smyth to put pen to paper. Leuven possessed a large number of established printing presses and within the course of a year Smyth had launched three successful polemical salvos against

---

[153] Humphrey (1573), 44: 'Sed animosus iste Achilles, die ad disputandum constituo, cùm non compareret, sed ad Diuum Andream in Scotiam profugeret, ratus eum qui in hoc articulo benè lateret, benè viuere'.

[154] Historical Manuscript Commission, *Calendar of the Manuscripts of the Most Honourable the Marquis of Salisbury at Hatfield House*, London, 1883, 1.59.

[155] 4 April 1549; Reusens (1903-1961), 4.600: 'magister noster'.

[156] Andreas (1650), 85: 'doctor sacrae theologiae et professor qui titulum aliunde Lovanium attulerit'.

[157] Wood (1813-1820), 1.193.

Martyr.[158] On 10 June 1550, in a state of considerable agitation, Vermigli wrote to his Cambridge colleague Bucer about the latest calumnies directed against him:

> A certain adversary of mine, Dr Smith, who ... fled hence last year to Louvain (having conducted himself very turbulently here, by challenging me, with excessive petulance, to a public disputation with himself) has published two books, one 'On the Celibacy of Clerks' ... the other 'On Monastic Vows', professedly written against me, so stuffed full of with maledictions, accusations and the bitterest contempt, that I think I never have heard before of any tongue so unbridled in abuse. He does not even spare my wife, whom he most filthily traduces as my harlot.[159]

The book in question, *De Votis Monasticis*, had left the local press of Hugo Cornwels in March 1550.[160] Although Smyth's book was banned in England 'by order of the Magistrates, and chiefly ... of the Most Reverend of Canterbury', copies of the Latin treatise were circulated widely among scholars in the Habsburg Low Countries and neighbouring states.[161] Likewise, in order for Peter Martyr to respond to Smyth's writings, and council to ban the book, copies of the *Votis* must have been available in England. These were smuggled into England by loyal catholics, as the case of the second edition of the book demonstrates. In 1551, one of bishop Edmund Bonner's servants, William Seth, had been sent to France to collect 'two hundred of Dr Smiths books to bring back into England'.[162]

In the summer of 1550 Peter Martyr's English reputation was under threat unless he reacted swiftly to the fierce accusations made by Smyth. Cast in the role of the 'resident reformer' of Oxford, a city which in general would rather perpetuate accustomed traditions, severe criticism by an exiled fellow might easily

---

[158] For the Leuven printing presses, see particularly I. Cockx-Indestege, ed. et al., *Belgica Typographica 1540-1600. Catalogus Librorum impressorum ab Anno MDXLI ad annum MDC in regionibus quae nunc Regni Belgarum partes sunt*, Brussel, 1968; L. Antheunis, *Engelsche drukkers in de Spaansche Nederlanden*, Bijdragen tot de geschiedenis van Antwerpen 28, Antwerpen, 1937.

[159] P. M. Vermigli, to M. Bucer, in: G. C. Gorham, ed., *Gleanings of a few scattered Ears, during the period of the Reformation in England*, London, 1857, 154.

[160] R. Smyth (1550¹), colophon.

[161] Gorham (1857), 154.

[162] 8 March 1551; *Acts of the Privy Council, 1500-1552*, 232: A 'barrel of Dr Smith's most false and detestable books from Paris' was intercepted.

have tipped the delicate balance between public conformity and private religious conservatism. Any attack on the unpopular evangelical establishment would have filled many clandestine catholics with glee. Martyr frequently wrote about the substantial opposition Smyth had posed to his views while still at Oxford. Being a shrewd disputant backed at Leuven by a supportive catholic university, various established printing presses and means to distribute his writings in England, Smyth continued the debate from abroad. While Martyr might have expected polemical attacks from Leuven, the publication and actual distribution of the books still caused him acute embarrassment. On the one hand, he saw Smyth's works as poorly-researched pieces of polemic abounding in 'silly sophisms'. On the other he saw them as a threat to his academic integrity, both in Oxford and abroad.[163] He reflected on the dilemma:

> If I answer, I shall seem to do what has already been done: for it would be impossible to bring forward more than has been written ... by others in this controversy; or to add much to what I have taught in the schools, that fellow Smyth himself being a hearer and diligent annotator of all that was said. But if I take no notice, I shall be reminded of my duty by those who are on our side, and other nations, in which this book will generally be read, will easily lie imposed on.[164]

Smyth had based his polemical attacks on his punctilious lecture-notes. Confronted with 'sound-bites' from his own lectures, strategically assembled to back Smyth's line of argument Martyr could only correct this distorted image of his lectures by presenting his own account in writing. His letter to Bucer of 10 June 1550 shows that the printing of the *Votis* made Martyr feel persecuted. He spoke of Smyth as a contemptuous and resentful little man of dubious academic standing and a 'tongue ... unbridled in abuse', yet to be feared as his books 'will be universally circulated'.[165] Smyth's two books gained enough popularity among conservatives to confirm their doubts about the reformer. Martyr said that he

---

[163] Gorham (1857), 154.
[164] Gorham (1857), 154f.
[165] Ibid.

felt forced into a response from which his natural caution would have deterred him, lest his opponent interpret silence as victory.[166]

While Vermigli was still pondering how to answer Smyth's accusations on clerical celibacy, Smyth published another work against him. The *Diatriba de hominis justificatione adversum Petrum Martyrem Vermelium nunc apostatam* left the Flemish printing presses in October 1550.[167] The book is a sound exposition of the catholic teaching on justification. Nonetheless it formed a central part of Smyth's sustained attack on Martyr. By February 1551, Smyth had revised his *De Votis Monasticis*, 'now the second time coming forth, more correct and exact'.[168] Printed in Paris, a hundred copies of the book were intercepted on their way into England and attracted the attention of their intended recipient, Peter Martyr.[169] The printed version of his Oxford lectures therefore proved to be insufficient to refute Smyth's allegations. Martyr wrote to Bullinger: 'I hope to send you after the autumn, if I am not hindered, my book on Celibacy and Monastic Vows to be printed, in which I reply the calumnies of Smith'.[170] At the time the letter was sent the work had not yet been composed. It was not published until 1559.[171]

In the winter of 1550, Smyth had moved to Paris to supervise the second edition of the *Votis*.[172] He had been displeased about the Leuven edition of the work.[173] In addition to working on a revision of the text, he feverishly composed a refutation of archbishop Cranmer's latest book, *A defence of the true and catholike doctrine of the sacrament of the body and bloud of Christ.*[174] His *A confutation of a certen booke, called a defence of the true, and Catholike*

---

[166] Gorham (1857), 154: 'Should I leave him master of it, he will immediately ... proclaim triumph as gloriously having won the battle'.

[167] Smyth (1550²).

[168] R. Smyth, *Defensio sacri episcoporum et sacerdotum Coelibatus, contra impias et indoctas Petri Martyris Vermelii nugas*, Paris, 1551, colophon.

[169] *Acts of the Privy Council, 1500-1552*, 232.

[170] Gorham (1857), 283: Peter Martyr to Heinrich Bullinger, Oxford, 14 June 1552.

[171] Vermigli (1559).

[172] Cf. Strype (1822), 1.64: 'At Lovain he did not tarry long, but departed thence to Paris, where he professed Divinity'.

[173] Smyth (1550²), L 1 r.

[174] For a recent evaluation of Cranmer's *Defence*, see MacCulloch (1996), 460-469.

doctrine of the Sacrament was published in Paris in early 1551.[175] Smyth did realise that the work could have benefitted from further labour and asked his readers for lenience, 'consiyderynge hou that I am in à strange contry, without quitenes, bookes, helpe of learned men, sufficient loiser and tyme'.[176] On 10 January 1551, Martyr noted in a letter to Bucer:

> Doctor Smith, formerly professor at Oxford, who wrote so contemptuously against me last summer on Monastic Vows has now published a book in English against my Lord of Canterbury, on the Sacramentarian matter. Respecting which I can form no judgment, since I do not understand that language; however, I shall soon be made acquainted with its drift, and its follies. ... I can expect nothing but falsehoods from Satan and the slaves of the Pope.[177]

In Paris Smyth had made contact with David Haliburton, provost of Methven, to whom he dedicated his *Defensio sacri episcoporum et sacerdotum Coelibatus*.[178] Later commentators suggested that Haliburton 'had entertained him in some of his flights'.[179] Probably at Haliburton's instigation, Smyth left Paris for St Andrews, where he was incorporated Doctor of Divinity by the rector of St Mary's College on 7 July 1551.[180]

---

[175] R. Smyth, *A confutation of a certen booke, called a defence of the true, and Catholike doctrine of the Sacrament, &c., sette fourth in the name of Thomas Archebysshoppe of Canterburye*, Paris, no date (1551).

[176] Smyth (1551), colophon; a letter from Blois dated 30 December 1550 by Sir John Masone to the Council, in: W. R. Turnbull, ed., *Calendar of State Papers, Foreign Series of the Reign of Edward VI, 1547-1553*, London, 1861, 65, suggests that Smyth found himself in severe financial difficulties: 'Wavering Dr Smythe, who is presently reading at Paris, begs permission to return. ... States his own financial difficulties'. Three weeks later, in a letter to Masone from Greenwich dated 18 January 1551, in: Turnbull (1861), 67, the Council points out that 'Dr Smith has farthered his own suit by printing at Paris a slanderous book against the Bishop of Canterbury', adding that 'he has once deceived an ambassador in Flanders, and by likelihood wood deceive another in France; but indeed they know him too well to be deceived by him'. I am grateful to C. Armstrong for these two references.

[177] Gorham (1857), 229-230; MS in: Corpus Christi College Cambridge Archives, MS 119: Epistolas Virorum Illustrorum, f. 106 ξ r.

[178] For Haliburton, see D. E. R. Watt, ed., *Fasti Ecclesiae Scotianae Medii Aevi ad annum 1638*, Scottish Record Society, Edinburgh, 1969, 285, 368; and H. Scott, ed., *Fasti Ecclesiae Scotianae*, 11.

[179] Strype (1822), 1.65.

[180] J. M. Anderson, ed., *Early Records of the University of St Andrews. The Graduation Roll, 1413-1579, and the Matriculation Roll, 1473-1579*, Scottish Historical Society, Edinburgh, 1926, 254; 296.

3.2. St Andrews (1551-1553)

Smyth spent two years at the Scottish university and was closely involved in the life of the Scottish church. Margaret Sanderson notes that the presence of 'English priests such as Henry Bretton and Richard Smith ... provided the Cardinal [Beaton] with welcome orthodox ... propagandists, and he generously provided for them'.[181] In February 1552, Smyth took part in the deliberations of the catholic church in Scotland that eventually led to the drafting of archbishop John Hamilton's *Catechism*.[182] Still, his new patrons not only made use of Smyth's theological knowledge to provide a firm doctrinal basis for the new catechism. Two letters written to archbishop Cranmer at the time of the church 'Assemble at Candlemas' confirm that Smyth was under substantial pressure both to refute the archbishop's newly-published *An answere of Thomas, Archebyshop of Canterburye vnto a crafty and sophisticall cauillation devised by S. Gardiner, late Byshop of Winchester, agaynst the trewe and godly doctrine of the moste holye Sacrament wherin is also answered the booke of R. Smyth*, and the recently debated Forty Articles of Religion:[183]

> I do not write, most illustrious Archbishop, of the things that I lack and from which I could live magnificently, but what I shall argue again and again from these matters (on which I dwell on, if lengthily) is what is demanded of me. I will not be able to refuse to

---

[181] M. Sanderson, *Cardinal of Scotland, David Beaton*, Edinburgh, 1986, 123.

[182] S. Haynes, ed., *A Collection of of State Papers, relating to the affairs in the reigns of King Henry VIII, King Edward VI, Queen Mary, and Queen Elizabeth, from the year 1542 to 1570*, London, 1740, 130; for the 1552 council, see J. Robertson, *Concilia Scotiae*, Edinburgh, 1866, 1.147-182; for Hamilton's catechism, see A. F. Mitchell, ed., *Catechisms of the second Reformation, with introduction and biographical notices by A. F. Mitchell*, London, 1886.

[183] T. Cranmer, *An answere of Thomas, Archebyshop of Canterburye vnto a crafty and sophisticall cauillation devised by S. Gardiner, late Byshop of Winchester, agaynst the trewe and godly doctrine of the moste holye Sacrament wherin is also answered the booke of R. Smyth*, London, 1551; for the debate on the Forty Articles of Religion, see MacCulloch (1996), 503ff.

> write against the Forty Articles of Religion and against all your doctrines, both of which—in all conscience—I cannot do safely.[184]

Smyth also expressed his discomfort at the prospect of having to counter the archbishop's latest work on the eucharist and suggested that in return for a royal pardon he would remain silent. He spoke vividly of the demands made by his Scottish hosts:

> If I were to stay here three months longer, I would be required to write a reply against your book and the other book of Commonplaces, against all doctrines now prescribed in England by Royal authority: this I could not do with a clear conscience.[185]

It appears that the exertions of life in St Andrews seem to have shaken even Smyth's commitment to catholicism, who not only offered that 'less than half a year from my return I shall publish a book, in Latin, on clerical marriage' but concluded his desperate pleas by writing: 'For the love of God, see to the fact that I can return home as soon as possible. ... This you shall never regret'.[186] Smyth's central role at Cranmer's heresy trial in Oxford a few years later only emphasises his contempt for the prelate and the cynicism of these missives.

While Smyth kept his promise not to counter Cranmer's most recent defence of the evangelical eucharistic doctrine, it is unlikely that the archbishop petitioned the English privy council for a pardon on Smyth's behalf. Still Smyth continued to live in hope that his return home might no longer be delayed. In November 1552, he made contact with Sir Nicholas Strelley, 'Knight Capitayne of Berwicke', concerning the arrival of a pardon 'that your Maystreship had receaved from the King's Majestie ... for me'.[187] Smyth was ready to leave his exile at once:

---

[184] Vermigli (1559), 645: 'Non scribo isthaec, Archiepiscope ornatissime, quòd desit mihi, vnde viuam splendidè, sed quòd vrgear quotidie ab his quibus, si diutius, hîc perdurato, quod postulatur, nequeo denegare, vt ... scribam de thesibus quadraginta theologicis, contra omnia vestra dogmata: quid incolum procul dubiò conscientia facere non possum'.

[185] Vermigli (1559), 645-646: 'Mihi necesse sit, si tres menses longius hîc remansero responsionem scribere contra librum illum dominationis tuae, & librum alium locorum communorum contra omnia dogmata quae nunc in Anglia regiae maiestatis authoritate recepta sunt: quod salua conscientia facere non possim'.

[186] Vermigli (1559), 647: 'infra semi annum à reditu librum de Sacerdotum connubio latinè editurum'; 'Per amorem Dei effice vt redeam domum quam possis citissimè, ... nunquam te illius facti poenitebit'.

[187] Haynes (1740), 130.

> The which Tydings was to me very great Comfort and Joye, and I am much desyrous to se yt, the upon the Sight of yt, I maye dispatche my Besynes and Affayres that I have to do here, and prepare myselfe to returne in to my contrey agayne, as sone as I maye conveniently without Danger.[188]

While Sir Nicholas had received no such news, he proceeded to commend the case to his superiors nonetheless, and in December 1552 the request for a pardon was filed in London.[189] Smyth's supplication was met with approval, and at some stage during the winter of 1552-1553 he received a full pardon 'for treasons, heresies and all offences before 1 January last, and restitution of goods forfeited thereby'.[190]

4.1. Restitution (1553-1559)

Smyth probably did not make use of his pardon to return home that spring and instead waited until the accession of Mary Tudor to the throne before making his way back to Oxford. Following the death of his royal patron, Peter Martyr had already left the university and had made his way back to the continent.[191] On arrival in Oxford Smyth took up his preferments, and immediately began to work on his only catechetical book, *A Bouclier of the Catholike Fayth of Christes Church, conteynyng diuers matters now of late called into controversy, by the newe gospellers*.[192] The *Bouclier* set out to win back evangelicals by defining a number of disputed catholic beliefs (such as purgatory, rogation days and the sign of the cross) in simple form:

> Wherefore let them, which are gone out of this church, willingly deuidyng themselues from the vnitye of it, retourne home agayne to her, theyr louing mother, not forgeatyng that as no manne nor woman, whyche was out of Noes [Noah's] ship in the tyme of the floude, eschaped death, euen so no manne, nor woman whych is out of thys Saincte Peters shippe, the catholike Churche, as a

---

[188] Ibid.
[189] C. S. Knighton, ed., *Calendar of State Papers, Domestic Series, of the Reign of Edward VI., 1547-1553*, London, 1992, 280, SP 10/15, no. 68: 781.
[190] *Calendar of Patent Rolls 1550-1553*, 6 Edward VI, 3.844: 251.
[191] Bodleian Library Oxford, MS DD.
[192] All Souls' College Oxford Archives, MS c.282; Smyth (1554).

Schismatike, can be saued from the perill of that death both of body and soule which shall neuer haue ende.[193]

By the time of its publication, Smyth's fortunes had reverted to their former state. His stalwart orthodoxy during his exile was rewarded by Philip and Mary with a canonry at Christ Church cathedral.[194] A year later he was showered with ecclesiastical livings, supplementing the income he already drew from his Oxford canonry.

In January 1554, the queen granted Smyth the Buckinghamshire rectory of Aston Clinton and appointed him a chaplain extraordinary.[195] Earlier that month, he had been presented to the London living of St Dunstan's-in-the-East.[196] Following their complete turn from prayer-book evangelicalism, the company of Mercers once more needed to provide a full chapter of priests for Richard Whittington's collegiate foundation. In 1555, they reappointed the former master to lead the college and the church of St Michael's Paternoster-Royal.[197] Finally, as if to make up for the past defamations of their evangelical dean, Richard Cox, Christ Church added another living to Smyth's already impressive array of wealthy rectories, and made him rector of one of their Cheshire parishes, St Lawrence's, Frodsham.[198]

Smyth not only received financial rewards for his loyalty to the catholic faith. His theological exactitude was once more required by the national church. In 1555, he was called to assist at a number of heresy trials in the diocese of London. Bishop Bonner had been restored to the see of London in 1553. A year later the Papal legate, Cardinal Pole, had returned to England 'to reconcile and

---

[193] Smyth (1554), ¶¶ i r.
[194] *Calendar of Patent Rolls 1553-1554*, 2 Mary: 495.
[195] *Calendar of Patent Rolls 1554-1555*, 3 Mary: 149; Foppens (1739), 1.1069, suggested that Smyth was appointed 'confessor to that Queen' (hujus Reginae confessor), but this is not likely.
[196] C. W. Woodruff, I. J. Churchill, edd., *Calendar of Institutions by the Chapter of Canterbury 'sede vacante'*, Kent Archaeological Society (Records Branch), 8.75.
[197] Hennessey (1889), 334.
[198] 1 October 1557; G. Ormerod, *The History of the County Palatinate and City of Chester*, London, 1819, 2.54.

not condemn'.[199] For Bonner, however, reconciliation with the See of Rome presupposed the examination and conversion of those who still fervently maintained Edwardian religious doctrines. In February 1555, Smyth was requested to assist the diocesan consistory in the interrogation of two such evangelicals, Thomas Higbe and Thomas Cawson.[200] He joined bishop Bonner, his old London colleague Nicholas Harpsfield (the newly-appointed vicar general of London), and John Feckenham (Dean of St Paul's Cathedral and abbot of the recently restored monastery at Westminster) in their examination of two Essex sacramentarians. At the end of the interrogation 'there were seuerally required, by doctour Harpesfield and Doctor Smith ... to recant theyr forsayd doctrine, and specyally to acknowledge the veryty of Christes presence in the Sacrament of the altar'.[201] Since the two did not waver from their evangelical doctrine, the consistory condemned them to death by burning.

4.2. Heresy Trials: Latimer, Ridley and Cranmer (1555)

By the summer of 1555, Smyth had regained his former influence. He published a companion volume to his *Bouclier*, in which he considered pastoral issues such as divorce, alongside a number of controverted doctrines.[202] In turn, he devoted himself to a simple analysis of infant baptism, monastic vows, and 'a confutation of an abominable errour of Peter Martyrs setting furth ... whiche is that oure saluation consisteth onlye in God, and nothinge in vs'.[203] The

---

[199] For Bonner's restoration, see J. G. Nichols, ed., *Chronicle of the Grey Friars of London*, Camden Society First Series 53, London, 1852, 6-7; for Pole, see British Library London, Harleian MS 419, f. 132 r; W. Schenk, *Reginald Pole: Cardinal of England*, London, 1950, and Th. F. Mayer, *Reginald Pole: Prince to Prophet*, Cambridge, 2000.

[200] 17 February 1555; Foxe (1563), 1103-1104 [=Foxe (1837-1841), 6.729-737]; for Feckenham, see D. E. Knowles, *The Religious Orders in England*, Cambridge, 1949-1950, 3.423-424; 3.428-430, and J. Blair, ed., The Cloister and the World, Oxford, 1996, 302-322: P. Tudor, 'John Feckenham and Tudor religious controversies', 305-306.

[201] Foxe (1563), 1104 [=Foxe (1837-1841), 6.349].

[202] R. Smyth, *The seconde parte of the booke called a Bucklar of the Catholyke fayeth, conteyninge seuen chapiters: Made by Rychard Smyth doctoure of diuinitie of Oxforde, & reader of the same there*, London, 1555.

[203] Smyth (1555), contents page.

work is similar to Bonner's *An honestly godlye instruction* and addressed a comparable audience.[204] Rather than 'enstruct the learned in Diuinitie' it was directed towards lay-people, in particular 'the waueryng ... [and] the doubtfull of the trouth', who were in urgent need of catholic instruction.[205]

In Oxford, Smyth made use of his position as *praelector* of divinity to have himself elected vice-chancellor of the university for the duration of archbishop Cranmer's heresy trial there.[206] As vice-chancellor he chaired the commission that interrogated the deposed archbishop and ultimately consigned him to the flames.[207] During the trial Smyth not only took revenge for Cranmer's personal attack on his eucharistic works which he had been obliged to leave unanswered, but also for his enforced recantation. The archbishop's seven recantations, some of which were made in the presence of Smyth's London friends Bonner and Harpsfield, seemed to compensate Smyth's three recantations.[208]

---

[204] E. Bonner, *An honestly godlye instruction, and information for bringinge up of children*, London, 1555; cf. E. Duffy, *The Stripping of the Altars: Traditional Religion in England 1400-1580*, New Haven CT, 1992, 537-543, Haigh (1987), 386-388, and Brigden (^{2}1991), 578.

[205] Smyth (1555), ∀ vii r.

[206] Wood (1786), Appendix, 93.

[207] MacCulloch (1996), 579: 'Richard Smith was not able to do anything more interesting than take his own revenge on the man who had savaged him in the *Answer*, by confirming the authorship of Cranmer's eucharistic writings'.

[208] For Cranmer's recantations, see R. M. Milnes, ed., *Bishop Cranmer's Recantatcyons*, Philobiblion Society Miscellanies 15, London, 1877-1884; and MacCulloch (1996), 589-607.

Figure 1. Richard Smyth preaching at the burning of bishops Latimer and Ridley.

J. Foxe, *Actes and monuments &c. Newly reuised and recognised, partly also augmented, and now the fourth time agayne published. 8th time newly imprinted. Whereunto are annexed certaine additions (unto the time of king Charles. With the life of the author in Latin and English)*, London, 1641.

In the words of the monarch the disputation-cum-trial had been intended

> to hear in open disputation the said Cranmer, Ridley and Latimer; so as their erroneous opinions, being by the word of God justly and truly convinced, the residue of our subjects may thereby be better established in the true catholic faith.[209]

Foxe has a scanty account of the disputations.[210] Apparently Smyth did not once interrupt the archbishop's interrogation by Hugh Weston (the prolocutor of the lower house of convocation) and Henry Cole (the provost of Eton College).[211] Cranmer's interroga-

---

[209] Quoted in MacCulloch (1996), 563-564.
[210] Foxe (1563), 1471-1479 [=Foxe (1837-1841), 6.439-444].
[211] Foxe (1583), 2.1473 [=Foxe (1837-1841), 6.461]; cf. Strype (1694), 3.558-560.

tion effectively proved to be a repetition of the university debate on the eucharist Smyth had instigated in 1549. Since he had then been absent, one would have assumed that Smyth sought to take a central role in the debate. Yet he kept his conservative views to himself and let his writings speak instead. He must have observed the proceedings with some satisfaction, since his three works on the eucharist were used as a yardstick of orthodoxy.[212] Smyth did not break his icy silence throughout the trial. Even when invited by Weston to comment on the archbishop's views on the real presence, he chose not to reply to Cranmer's arguments, 'he only put off his cap, and kept silence'.[213]

In October 1555, Smyth was chosen to preach at the executions of bishops Latimer and Ridley. The sermon gave him a last opportunity to express his strong antipathies for his former London diocesan, Nicholas Ridley, and the deposed bishop of his home diocese, Hugh Latimer.[214] In the 'town ditch', near Balliol College Oxford, a pyre had been set up.[215] From the pulpit, Smyth launched a vicious attack on the two prisoners. As they were facing the flames, he expounded on words from 1 Cor 13.3: 'If I give away all my possessions, and if I hand over my body to be burnt, but do not have love, I gain nothing'. In a last attempt to bring about a conversion he pointed to the Fathers and argued that it was the cause which made martyrs, not their death. He emphasised strongly that by refusing to recant and to accept the queen's pardon they were in fact taking their own lives, and made one last appeal to return to the catholic church. Later evangelical commentators found only one praiseworthy fact—the sermon barely lasted fifteen minutes.[216]

---

[212] Ibid.

[213] Foxe (1583), 2.1473 [=Foxe (1837-1841), 6.461].

[214] For a modern account of the burning of Latimer and Ridley, see D. M. Loades, *The Oxford Martyrs*, London, 1970, 218-219.

[215] Foxe (1563), 1377 [=Foxe (1837-1841), 6.547].

[216] So for instance Loades (1970), 219, and C. H. Stuart, *Latimer: Apostle to the English*, Grand Rapids MI, 1986, 338.

4.3. Arrest and Escape (1559)

Four years later the tide had turned. Following the accession of Elizabeth I to the throne, Smyth lost all preferments and made moves to leave the country. After the expulsion from his Oxford lectureship in June 1559, he attempted to flee to Scotland.[217] Pursued by English authorities, he was apprehended in the borders and committed to custody at Lambeth Palace, together with his friend William Tresham. House-arrest was a common Elizabethan alternative to prison sentences.[218] At Lambeth, archbishop-elect Matthew Parker set about to convince his conservative charges to subscribe to the royal supremacy. Towards the end of August 1559, Parker wrote to members of council that Smyth was now ready to acknowledge Elizabeth's supremacy.[219] Soon after he reported a public recantation at Oxford.[220] Smyth cannot genuinely have believed that a second revocation of his life-time's work could revert the clock. Yet the archbishop reflected:

> Richard Smyth had raged most bitterly in public about clerical marriage in a book. By the persuasion of Matthew [Parker] he recanted and revoked this book alongside many other papist errors. He made his recantation at the Oxford Schools, where had taught theology, and affirmed that he had written the book too rashly, as an exercise and to show off his character and, if anyone should harbour any further doubts about the doctrines he was revoking, he asked them to come up to him: he was ready and prepared, giving excellent reasons to satisfy anyone—with some hesitation—that no-one should assault religion, by word or deed, in favour of the

---

[217] Christ Church Archives, Battels Books, MS x (1) c. 6, f. 98 r.
[218] Blair (1996), 312.
[219] J. Bruce, Th. Perowne, edd., *Correspondence of Matthew Parker: Comprising letters written by and to him, from A. D. 1535, to his death, A. D. 1575*, Parker Society Publications 33, Cambridge, 1853, 72; Lords of the Council to archbishop-elect Parker and bishop-elect Grindal, Hampton Court, 24 August 1559; cf. Corpus Christi College Cambridge Archives, MS 114, f. 53.
[220] 27 August 1559, Corpus Christi College Cambridge Archives, MS 119: Epistolae Virorum Illustrorum, f. 110; M. Parker, *De antiquitate Britannicae Ecclesiae & privilegiis ecclesiae Cantuariensis, cum archiepiscopis eiusdem 70*, Lambeth, 1572, 422: 'Quem librum permultosque alios errores Pontificios Matthaei suasionibus respiscus detestatus est. Quam detestationem Oxonij ... promulgauit'.

> Papists; and so he was sent from custody to his freedom and released.[221]

Smyth was released home on bail in autumn. On 2 December 1559, he wrote to the archbishop thanking him 'for your Grace's kindness toward my sureties; for the which you have (and shall whiles I live) my good Word and Prayer'.[222] He closed his letter with the diplomatic claim that he had never seriously upheld clerical celibacy and that he would be honoured to examine the works of his opposition on the matter:

> If it might please your Lordship, I would very gladly see some part of your Collection against my book, *De Coelibatu Sacerdotum*; which I wrote then to try the Truth out, not to the intent it should be printed, as it was, against my Will.[223]

By the time the letter reached Lambeth, however, Smyth was already planning his escape to the continent. In winter 1559-1560 he broke his assurances and made his way to Flanders.[224] Archbishop Parker wryly annotated his earlier correspondence with the fugitive with the words 'notwithstanding this ernest promise bond, yet this good father fled'.[225]

---

[221] Parker (1572), 422f.: 'Richardus Smythe in sacerdotum coniugia libro scripto, typisque, diuulgato acerrimè debacchatus est. Quem librum permultosque alios errores Pontificios Matthaei suasionibus resipiscus detestatur est. Quam detestationem Oxonij in eadem schole, in qua Theologiam publicè prius docuerat, promulgauit, eumqué librum a se temere exercendi atque ostentandi ingenij sui causa compositum affirmauit, & si quis de his dogmatibus, quae in ille reuocauit, dubitarent, petijt vt ad se accederent: paratum enim esse se & instructum optimis rationibus satisfacere singulis aliqua haesitatione datis ne quicquam dicto aut facto pro Pontificijs contra religionem attemptare, e custodia libertati suae permissus atque relaxatus est'.

[222] Corpus Christi College Cambridge Archives, MS 119: Epistolae Virorum Illustrorum, f. 114.

[223] Corpus Christi College Cambridge Archives, MS 119: Epistolae Virorum Illustrorum, f. 114.

[224] Smyth was registered at Leuven university on 15 February 1560; cf. Reusens (1903-1961), 4.612.

[225] Corpus Christi College Cambridge Archives, MS 119: Epistolae Virorum Illustrorum, f. 112, marginal note.

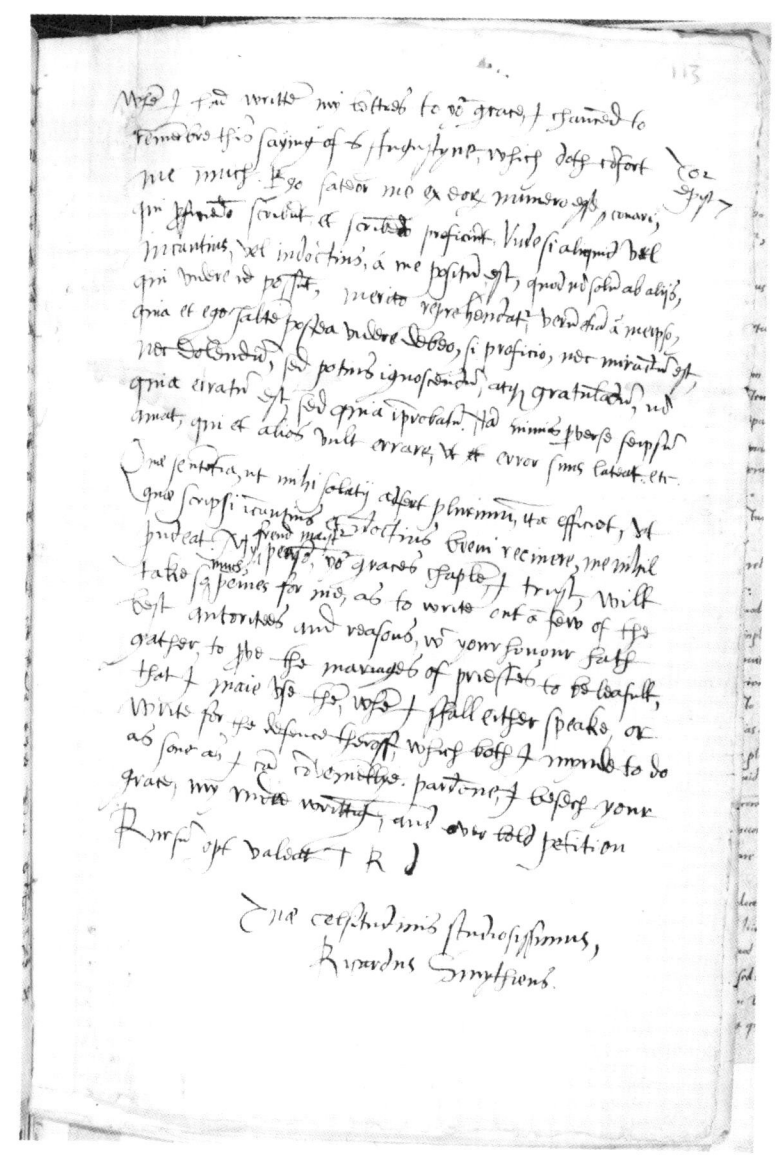

Figure 2. Smyth's letter to archbishop-elect Matthew Parker, assuring the prelate of his 'good Word and Prayer' for releasing him on bail.

Parker Library, Corpus Christi College Cambridge, MS 119: Epistolae Virorum Illustrorum, 113 r, reproduced by kind permission of the Master and Fellows.

Smyth made his way once more to Leuven. In February 1560 he joined the university's teaching staff.[226] He was never to return to his homeland and for the remainder of his life pioneered catholic education in the Low Countries. He was a founding professor of the university of Douai, a Flemish centre of learning established two years after his arrival in Leuven.[227] When the magistrates of Douai had to fill the chair in divinity, they appointed the English exile. The following overview of the events leading up to the establishment of Douai university provides some fundamental indications why such an appointment might have been more than putting past wrongs right, by giving an exiled theologian a second chance.

5.1. The Foundation of the University of Douai

Forming part of a centralised attempt to counter evangelical teaching, Douai was to house the second university of the Low Countries.[228] As early as 1530 emperor Charles V was considering requests by Lille, Maubeuge and Douai to establish a Francophone university in those cities.[229] A number of well-respected local colleges were already established in the vicinity.[230] The later university drew teachers and curricula from these institutions.[231] An undertaking as extensive as the foundation of a new university had not been contemplated since the establishment of the university of Leuven more than a century earlier.[232]

---

[226] Reusens (1903-61), 4.612; Andreas (1650), 85.

[227] For the foundation of the university of Douai, see for instance, J. A. Löwe, *Nederlands Archief voor Kerkgeschiedenis* 72/2 (1999), 142-169: 'Richard Smyth and the foundation of the university of Douai'.

[228] P. Beuzart, *Les hérésies pendant le moyen age et la réforme dans la région de Douai, d'Arras et au pays de l'Alleu*, Paris, 1912, 104ff.

[229] Archives Municipales de la Ville de Douai, Liasse 92; Andreas (1650), 359.

[230] For instance the *Collegium linguarum* at Tournai, and similar institutions at Valenciennes and Mons.

[231] A Tournai lecture schedule for the year 1562 survives in Archives de Douai, Layette 172.

[232] In 1425; for a history of the theology faculty at Leuven see H. De Jongh, *L'ancienne faculté de théologie de Louvain au premier siècle de son existence (1432-1540): ses debuts, son organisation, son ensignement, sa lutte contre Erasme et Luther, avec des documents inédits*, reprint Utrecht, 1980; E. J. M. Van Eijl, *Facultas S. Theologiae Lovaniensis 1432-1797: Bijdragen tot haar geschiedenis*, Leuven, 1977.

The fear of the further dissemination of evangelical teaching was the principal reason for setting up a university at the French border. Once the reformation had reached the South of the Habsburg provinces and, with Tournai, had laid claim on one of the centres of the Walloon Low Countries, this became a matter of urgency.[233] While Douai had also seen some evangelical teaching in the late 1530s, the authorities there reacted quickly enough to suppress the spread of evangelicalism.[234] According to a later French Reformed commentator, the local magistrates were

> very loyal to catholicism, they resist any new ideas with greater opposition than in any of the other centres of Walloon Flanders. ... Douai town council ... endeavours to suppress heresy both in town and county.[235]

On the basis of the town's open loyalty to the catholic cause, the governors of Flanders and Hainaut chose Douai as a home for their new university.[236]

In 1559, the Spanish king Philip II began to press the Holy See and the local government for the establishment of the new university. In an ever-increasing number of impatient letters to the regent of the Low Countries, Margaret of Parma, he urged her to devote herself wholeheartedly to the cause.[237] Philip was convinced that the rise of evangelical 'sectarians' among his French neighbours would result in their 'fishing on the site of their closest borders'.[238] His apprehension caused him to concern himself even with fine details such as the appointment of suitable bishops for

---

[233] G. Cardon, *La Fondation de l'Université de Douai*, Paris, 1892, 5; J. Crespin, *Histoire des Martyrs persecutez et mis à mort pour la verité de l'Evangile, depuis le temps des apostres jusques à present 1619*, Toulouse, 1885-1889, 1.428.

[234] Beuzart (1912), 117-123; orthodoxy was maintained in Artois by the suppression of evangelical cells, the burning of books and executions, cf. Archives de Douai, MS CC 258, f. 221; MS CC 261, f. 134.

[235] Beuzart (1912), 151: 'Très attachés au catholicisme, ils avaient opposé aux idées nouvelles une résistance plus grande que les autres centres de la Flandre wallonne. ... Le magistrat de Douai ... veillat réprimer l'hérésie dans la ville et dans la châtellenie'.

[236] H. J. Pilate-Prévost, *Table chronologique et analytique des archives de la Mairie de Douai, depuis le onzième siècle jusqu'au dix-huitième*, Douai 1842, numbers 1380-1389.

[237] 26 February 1560; L. P. Gachard, *Correspondence de Marguerite d'Autriche*, Brussel, 1881, 1.107.

[238] Gachard (1881), 2.22: 'pescher aux lieux de leurs frontières les plus prouches'.

the vulnerable border regions with France.[239] The newly appointed bishop of Arras, François Richardot, proved to be a valuable partner in Philip's personal campaign against the advance of French evangelicalism in Flanders.[240] He shared the king's fears: 'We run the risk of religion going the way it is in France, with the French doing all they can to corrupt those on our borders'.[241]

5.1.1. *The University of Douai (1559-1562)*

The new university received its letters patent in February 1562.[242] On 16 May, Douai magistrates authorised the constitution of a separate search-committee, which consisted of two city councillors and the *conseilleur pensionnaire* Jérôme de France.[243] Shortly after their appointment, they were sent to Brussel to pursue the selection of the five professors and their academic staff. There, the search committee requested the aid of the president of the privy council (*privé raad*), Viglius van Aytta,[244] for 'the selection of said professors and doctors, in order to locate the most excellent one could possibly find'.[245] A natural starting point to search for such highly-trained staff was the university of Leuven.

Fearing that they might be supporting consciously an institution which would cause them grave economic losses and deprive them of some of their best teaching staff, Leuven university authorities

---

[239] When a prelate had to be chosen for the see of Arras in 1561, François Richardot was the preferred candidate because of his 'good and learned sermons' (bonnes et doctes prédications).

[240] Gachard (1881), 2.94.

[241] Gachard (1881), 2.20, 2.419: 'Allant la religion comme elle va en France et faisant les Français ce qu'ils font pour corrompre noz frontières'.

[242] Gachard (1881), 2.156.

[243] Pierre Mallebranque and Jacques de Bonmarchiet; J. De France, Bibliothèque Municipale de Douai, MS 1304: 'Discovrs de la Povrsvite et Erection De L'Vniuersité de Doaui', f. 53ff, cf. Gachard (1881), 2.156: A magistrate at Douai, De France was himself closely involved in the process leading to the establishment of a university there. His detailed 'Discovrs' remains one of the most important records still available.

[244] Archives de Douai, Reg. aux Cons., MS BB 2, f. 134 r; for Viglius van Aytta, see F. Postma, *Viglius van Aytta als humanist en diplomaat 1507-1549*, Zutphen, 1983, and B. Sicken, ed., *Herrschafts- und Verfassungsstrukturen im Nordwesten des Reiches. Beiträge zum Zeitalter Karls V.*, Köln, 1994: F. Postma, 'Viglius van Ayttas kirchenpolitische Haltung unter Maria von Ungarn und in der Frühzeit Philipps II. bis 1566', 179-204, as well as B. H. D. Hermesdorf, *Wigle van Aytta van Zwichem. Hogeleraar en rechtsgeleerd schrijver*, Leiden, 1949.

[245] De France, Bibliothèque Municipale de Douai, MS 1304, f. 71.

did not permit the search committee to contact individual professors. Furthermore, by way of disdain, the Leuven academics sent the party to Antoine Granvelle, the newly-created Cardinal-archbishop of Mechelen, suggesting that they try their luck there.[246] The theology faculty in particular seemed to have regarded the establishment of a similar such faculty with great suspicion. Leuven, therefore, began to press Granvelle for the reimbursement of 'damages and interest'.[247] The regent of the Low Countries wrote to Leuven in the hope to bring about reconciliation:

> Likewise, for the preservation of true religion, and so that the new academy may conform to yours [in Leuven] and, furthermore, that harmonious links between the two may be maintained, we thought it would be fitting if particularly those first lecturers could set out from your university [as soon as possible].[248]

The subsequent offer of the university of Leuven to play an active role in the establishment of the new university must have been a final attempt to exercise at least some influence in the selection.[249]

When the search party finally succeeded in approaching academic staff directly, the Englishman Richard Smyth must have been a Leuven lecturer for over a year. He was then lodging at the College of the Crutched Friars (*Kruisheren*) where, as specified in the founder's statutes, three religious were able to make use of the facilities there to attend lectures in theology at Leuven. This institution, more a religious study house than a full-blown college, was set up by Philip Nicolai de Hondt (Volgaia) in 1491, as a gift to the Crutched Friars of Goes and Namur who subsequently estab-

---

[246] For Granvelle, see M. Van Durme, *Antoon Perrenot, Bisschop van Atrecht, Kardinaal van Granvelle, Minister van Karel V en van Filips II*, Brussel, 1953, for his relationship with Viglius van Aytta, see F. Postma, *Viglius van Aytta. De jaren met Granvelle 1549-1564*, Zutphen, 2000.

[247] 'Dommaiges et interestz'.

[248] 21 June 1562; *L'Annuaire de l'Université catholique de Louvain* (1846), 277: 'Tum ad rectae quoque Religionis conservationem, et novae hujus scholae ad vestram [Lovanium] conformationem perpetuamque inter vos necessitudinem et concordiam pertinere putavimus, si a vobis potissimum primi istii doctores proficiscantur'.

[249] De France, Bibliothèque Municipale de Douai, MS 1304, f. 71.

lished the Leuven study house.[250] In 1616 the house was left to the Greyfriars.[251] Smyth found refuge there and, in the colophon to his 1562 *Defensio compendiaria*, gives the reader a hint of the simplicity of his lodgings, when he states that the book had been completed in a monastic cell, his *cubiculum*, 'at the Crutched Friars'.[252]

5.1.2. *Four Publications (1562)*

Smyth had taken on some teaching to provide lectures for the other English exiles who were beginning to settle in Leuven.[253] A considerable number of later sources claim that he lectured in New Testament exegesis at the university.[254] While no contemporary accounts survive to shed some light on his precise activities from the time of his arrival at Leuven, this situation changed quite radically about the same time as the first arrangements were made to appoint new members of staff at the second university in the Low Countries.[255] On 3 and 5 February 1562 an impressive total of three of his polemical publications were presented to a Brussel censor, were granted imprimatur and received royal privilege.[256]

---

[250] In a personal communication G. Marnef pointed out that in a list of monastic houses of sixteenth-century Leuven the friars minors are not mentioned, see R. van Uytven, ed., *Leuven 'de beste stad van Brabant'. Geschiedenis van het stadsgewest Leuven tot omstreeks 1600*, Leuven, 1980, 1.246-247.

[251] *Analectes pour servir à l'histoire ecclesiastique de la Belgique*, 23.212.

[252] 'Apud Cruciferos', R. Smyth, *Defensio compendaria et orthodoxa, sacri, externi, et visibilis Iesu Christi Sacerdotii. Cui addita est sacratorum Catholicae Ecclesiae altarium propugnatio, ac Caluinianae Communionis succincta refutatio*, Leuven, 1562, colophon.

[253] R. Lechat, *Les Réfugiés Anglais dans les Pays-Bas durant le règne d'Elisabeth 1558-1603*, Leuven, 1914, 32.

[254] For Smyth's purported lecturing at Leuven, see Pits (1619), 761: 'He went to Belgium, to Leuven, where, as I mentioned, he taught Divinity' (Belgium petijt, Lovanij, ut dixi sacras litteras docuit); Foppens (1739), 2.1069; Wood (1813-1820), 1.193.

[255] The university library at Leuven was destroyed during the Great War. For the few remaining sixteenth-century Leuven records in Belgian archives, see Van Eijl (1977), 19-36.

[256] R. Smyth, *De Missae Sacrificio ... enarratio, ac brevis repulsio ... argumentum quae P. Maelanchthon, J. Calvinus, et alii sectarii objecerunt adversus illud, et purgatorium ... Acc. epistola ... docens quae Ecclesia sit nobis tuto sequenda*, Leuven, 1562¹; idem, *Confutatio eorum, quae P. Melanchthon objicit contra missae sacrificium propitiationem ... Cui acc. & repulsio calumniarum J. Calvini & Musculi, et J. Juelli, contra Missam, eius canonem et purgatorium, denuo excusa*; idem, *Refutatio luculenta crassae et exitiosae haeresis Johannis Calvini et Christop. Carlili Angli, qua astruunt Christum non descendisse ad inferos alios, quam ad infernum infirmum*, Leuven, 1562²; idem, *De infantium*

Smyth later made use of the same imprimatur to extend and update his arguments in the *De Missae Sacrificio* as well as the *Confutatio* to include a stern reply to Bishop John Jewel's 1562 *Apologia Anglicanae Ecclesiae*.[257] Barely three months later, in May 1562, the publication of his *Defensio compendiaria* followed. Both the urgency with which he put out four intricately argued polemical works and their recipients are intriguing.

After a lengthy pause of about six years it seems that Smyth had at last regained some of his former belligerent spirit. These books, most of them orthodox refutations of continental and English evangelical works, were highly successful since they ran to second, expanded editions within a few months.[258] The total output of 1562 amounts to no less than four printed works covering most aspects then called into controversy in contemporary theology. Four popular works in multiple editions, all bear the formal stamp of approval both of the Catholic hierarchy as well as the university of Leuven, whose censor Josse Ravesteyn (Tiletanus) approved the editions for use as textbooks within the university.[259]

As with his English publications, the dedications of Smyth's four works reveal a lot about the author's aspirations. In general, dedications served as an advertisement by which the writer commended his services to prospective patrons. Smyth was astute in bestowing dedications.[260] His first Leuven publication was dedi-

---

baptismo, contra J. Calvinum, ac de operibus supererogationis, et merito mortis Christi, adversus eundem Calvinum et eius discipulos, Leuven, 1562^3.

[257] Presumably in August 1562. That month also saw the second edition of 1562^2; cf. J. Jewel, *An Apologie or Aunswer in Defence of the Church of England*, London, 1562. A Latin edition was published simultaneously. J. Booty, *An Apology of the Church of England*, Charlottesville VA, 1974, has a general introduction.

[258] E.g. Smyth (1562^1), (1562^2).

[259] 'Cum vtilitate studiosorum', e.g. Smyth (1562^1), subscript.

[260] The 1546 *Defence of the blessed Masse and the sacrifice thereof, prouynge that it is aualable bothe for the quycke and the dead* was for instance dedicated to Henry VIII, by his 'mooste humble subiecte, chapleyne, beddysman, and seruant Richarde Smythe', while the 1550 Leuven *Diatriba de hominis justificatione aedita Oxoniae anno 1550 mense februario adversum Petrum Martyrem Vermelium ... nunc apostatam* was dedicated to a later Scottish patron. Both parts of the 1554/1555 *A Bouclier of the Catholike Fayth of Christes Church, conteynyng diuers matters now of late called into controversy, by the newe gospellers* were again dedicated to a royal patron, Mary Tudor. Similarly, Smyth dedicated almost his entire Douai oeuvre to the Spanish king, with the exception of his *De libero hominis arbitrio adversus Joannem Calvinum, et quotquod impie ... Lutherum imitati* which was dedicated to his diocesan bishop and later colleague, François Richardot.

cated to Guillaume de Poitiers (Pictavia), a French nobleman and an influential cleric in his own right. One of the patrons of the powerful chapter of St Lambert at Liège, he was provost of the Collégiale Sainte-Walburge at Furnes, a position he held in conjunction with the archdeaconry of Famenne and Campine in the diocese of Liège. One of Smyth's chosen allies, he rejected three episcopal sees (those of Thérouanne, Saint Omer and Brugge) in succession, thereby undermining any hopes of distributing lucrative livings Smyth might have cherished.

The recipient of Smyth's second work, *De Missae Sacrificio*, needs no lengthy introduction. The work is dedicated to Antoine de Granvelle, the most powerful clergyman of the Low Countries. In his dedicatory epistle Smyth enthused about the cardinal's magnanimity, himself expecting a share of Granvelle's liberality.[261] The remaining two works also had high-ranking clergymen as their recipients: Gerard Gruisbeck had been dean of St Lambert in Liège since 1548 and was later appointed coadjutor to the Prince-bishop of Liège, while Smyth's Leuven colleague Philip van Hosdein was the Abbot of St Gertrudis as well as 'warden of the school':[262] Considering the relatively short time of Smyth's Netherlandish exile, he showed superb instincts in his choice of potential patrons.

By means of his widely-approved output Smyth not only succeeded in presenting himself as a successful tutor (styling himself 'sacrae Theologiae Professor'), but also managed to dispel any possible doubts about his allegiance to the Holy See.[263] This self-styled image is echoed even by the highest authorities. In a letter to the king Margaret of Parma testified that the Englishman was 'a person of unblemished doctrine and good faith and highly recommended by those of the university of Leuven, where he has dwelt

---

[261] Smyth (1562²), 1 v.

[262] Smyth (1562³), 1 r; 1562⁴, 1 r: 'gymnasij ... Conseruatori'.

[263] Smyth (1562¹), colophon; e.g. op. cit., 6 r, 7 r: 'The pope is the successor of St Peter of Rome, instituted either by Peter or Christ Himself. ... The church of Christ—that is the Church of Rome—is erected on this See of Peter' (Romani Pontificem esse diui Petri successorem, illum vel Christo ipse authore ... Super eam Petri Christi ecclesiam fuisse extructam ... hoc est, Ecclesia Romana', etc.

for some time'.[264] Even the Holy See had heard of and appreciated the talents of the exiled theologian: 'His Holiness had called him to assist at the council [of Trent], but he was forced to make his excuses, so that he could serve this university'.[265] Apparently Smyth's devotion to academia had prevented him from attending the council, if indeed such an invitation was ever issued. The existence of an official summons could not be verified.[266] Still, even if a formal invitation to Trent should prove unfounded, the mere fact that contemporaries thought it a natural and likely possibility, speaks for Smyth's reputation in the Low Countries. As the exile had also succeeded in becoming the most-published author at Leuven in 1562, it is difficult to see how the search committee from Douai could have possibly failed to notice him in the late spring of that year.[267]

5.1.3. *Premier Lecteur (1562-1563)*

A bulwark of Catholicism on the borders with France, Douai university was particularly keen on employing an outstanding scholar to give a strong lead for their new faculty of theology. Magistrate de France stressed this intention repeatedly: 'As regards theology, to whose honour the said university was founded, the

---

[264] Gachard (1881), 2.419f.: 'ung personnaige de singulière doctrine et bonne vye et fort recommandé par ceulx de l'université de Louvain où il s'est tenu quelque temps'.

[265] Ibid.: 'Sa Sancteté avoit fait appeller pour assister au concile [de Trente], dont il s'est mieulx aymé d'excuser, affin de servir en ceste université'.

[266] Smyth's influence on the Leuven party at the council, however, can be inferred from the fact that among their chief contribution at Trent featured the formalisation of the sacrificial character of the Mass, a subject which Smyth had covered at great length in his 1562^1 and 1562^2; for Ruard Tapper's interpretation of the subject matter see H. Jedin, *Geschichte des Konzils von Trient*, Freiburg, Basel, Wien, 1940-75, 2.347f., P. F. X. de Ram, *Nouveaux Mémoires de l'Académie Royale de Belgique* 14 (1841): 'Mémoire sur la part que le clergé de Belgique et spécialement les docteurs de l'université de Louvain ont prise au concile de Trent', 17-45.

[267] Cf. Cockx-Indestege (1968), 573: In 1562 the three major Leuven printers, Johannes Bogardus, Bartolomaeus Gravius and Valerius Stephanus only published four other theological works in addition to Smyth's original works (of which 1562^2 was published at two presses simultaneously, by Bogardus and Stephanus). Among the other theological works were two patristic works, as well as a scholastic work by Aquinas. The only other contemporary theological work to be published in 1562 was the first edition of a polemic tract by the local professor Jan Hessels, whose *Tractatus pro invocatione Sanctorum contra Joannem Monneminem* was printed by Bogardus.

said deputies were particularly instructed to locate men of learning in Leuven'.[268] At first the magistrates from Douai were wholly unimpressed with the standard of theological education at Leuven. None of the local theologians appear to have fulfilled their expectations of genuine 'men of excellence' required for their new faculty.[269] The English exile, on the other hand, must have given the impression of being an ideal candidate—a scrutinising theologian with excellent references and a convinced catholic whose exile added further credibility to his orthodoxy.[270]

In his report, de France made clear that the search-party did not find any theologian

> who could satisfy the said deputies, with the exception of Richard Smyth, an Englishman, who was made a refugee because of the sectarianism and heresy in his homeland where, for a long time, he had been a lecturer, principally at Exeter [sic], with great influence and a good reputation; likewise, his profound nature and his knowledge of Sacred and Holy Theology—as well as his effortless interpretation of the same—were very easy to recognise.[271]

The flurry of activity in early spring 1562 had evidently borne fruit, for it was Richard Smyth who was subsequently approached and appointed as first professor of Sacred Scripture at Douai.[272]

Three other academics were appointed to head the newly-established faculties of civil and ecclesiastical law.[273] Once ap-

---

[268] De France, Bibliothèque municipale de Douai, MS 1304, f. 76: 'Et quand à la théologie, pour le respect de laquelle ladicte Université avoit été construicte, lesdits depputez feirent pareillement debvoir de recouvrer audict Louvaign gens sçavans'.

[269] Ibid.

[270] The Douai magistrates were evidently unaware that Smyth had recanted twice before, see above 2.1.

[271] De France, Bibliothèque municipale de Douai, MS 1304, f. 76: 'quy peut donner contentement ausdits députez, sinon Richard Scemiteus, anglois, quy estoit illecq refugiez pour la secte et hérésie de son païs, où avoit esté plusieurs années professeur et principalement à Exone [sic], aveq grand bruict et réputation, comme aussy la profondité de son sçavoir et intelligence de la saincte et sacrée théologie et la facile interprétation d'icelle le donnoient facilement à cognoistre'.

[272] Archives de Douai, MS CC 19: Comptes de l'Université 1561-1562, f. 11v.

[273] Vendeville was appointed professor of civil law, while Ramus was signed up as a professor of ecclesiastical law. Boetois Epo senior was enlisted 'to provide a comprehensive interpretation of the articles of Canon Law and the Institutes' (pour faire sommaire interprétation des tiltres du droit canon et les Institutes), cf. De France, Bibliothèque Municipale de Douai, MS 1304, f. 73.

pointed, the four professors actively concerned themselves with the further organisation and establishment of the new university, especially by searching for 'other men of learning' for the Faculty of Arts as well as for the projected College.[274] The diocesan bishop of Arras, Mgr François Richardot, had been approached to share the chair of Sacred Scripture with the sixty-two year-old Smyth, thus providing the faculty of theology with two very different but nonetheless remarkable lecturers. When Richardot had died twelve years after this joint appointment, it was another English exile and Douai colleague, Thomas Stapleton, who explained in his eulogy that 'he undertook by his deeds to commend the university of Douai in fulsome words everywhere, among the leading men'.[275] Although the brunt of academic teaching was probably borne by the older Smyth, the bishop seems to have enjoyed his appointment and a town councillor enthusiastically wrote to the king that the city considered itself

> flattered by the honour His Majesty so graciously bestowed, the said town was well aware that it had placed a large part of its hope of success in [Richardot's] person, in consideration and on authority of which it was hoped that all would turn out for the best.[276]

Following the organisation of the university's flagship, the faculty of theology, new contracts were signed almost every day: Adriaan Puessius, a lawyer from Mechelen and an 'excellent administrator', was signed up to 'give a good lecture every day', while Jean Dubuisson (Rubus), a lecturer at the Leuven theology faculty, accepted the position as principal of the projected Collège du Roi.[277] The Leuven professor of classics, Jean Cospeau Montois accepted a joint appointment with Jean Petreius, 'to read Latin and Greek', while the three Leuven lecturers Johannes Ferrarius, Wilbrand

---

[274] Ibid.: 'autres gens sçavans'

[275] F. Richardot, *Richardoti Orationes*, Douai, 1608, 90: 'Quibus umquam laboribus percipit ... ut Universitatem Duacensem ... verbis amplissimis apud principes viros sedulos commendaret'.

[276] De France, Bibliothèque municipale de Douai, MS 1304, f. 98: 'Flatté de l'honneur que luy avoir porté tant Sa Majesté que ladicte ville laquelle scavoit bien avoir fiché une grande partie de son exspectation du bon succès en sa personne pour considération et auctorité de laquelle l'on espéroit le tout debvoir aller aux mieulx'.

[277] Both on 15 June 1562: 'excellent institutionnaire'; 'faire une bonne lechon par jour'.

Bornstra and Louis Cospeau were appointed to assist Montois at the faculty of *Litterae humaniores*.[278] The sudden speed with which appointments were made is nearly as astonishing as the readiness with which such a large quantity of Leuven lecturers gave up their positions to take up work at the new foundation. The faculties were soon gaining shape and, more importantly, were quickly building up a good reputation.

As a further enticement, the magistrates decided to grant the four new professors an advance on their salary, money having been 'the chief point of contention among the deputies and the teaching staff'.[279] Payment was an issue of division in any case, since professors did not all receive the same wages, but were paid staggered rates according to the seniority of their faculties. In order to avoid antagonism among their staff, the magistrates were anxious to make financial arrangements as amenable as possible. As the president of the council (*Raad van State*) Viglius van Aytta had already pointed out to de France as early as 1560, the town had to consider 'to appropriate some prebendaries from both the Collégiale Saint-Amé as well as the Collégiale Saint-Pierre for said prospective university, in order to provide salaries for the teaching staff'.[280]

The two main Douai churches were both collegiate foundations drawing substantial tithes on their prebends. The respective provosts held the right of collation to seventeen prebends, of which the rector of Saint-Amé was able to appoint five while the provost of Saint-Pierre held twelve in his gift.[281] The city council took up van Aytta's suggestion and swiftly demanded eleven or twelve prebends to pay for the salaries of their theology lecturers. Agreement between chapter and council seems to have been

---

[278] De France, Bibliothèque municipale de Douai, MS 1304, f. 73: 'pour lire en grec et en latin'.

[279] Cardon (1892), 189: 'le point capital du débat entre les députés et les professeurs'.

[280] De France, Bibliothèque municipale de Douai, MS 1304, f. 8: 'Annexer aulcunes prébendes tant de Saint-Amé comme de Saint-Pierre à ladicte Université future pour salarier les professeurs'.

[281] For the Collégiale Saint-Pierre, see above, 17, n. 23; for Saint-Amé, see M. Rouche, ed., *Histoire de Douai*, Condé-sur-l'Escaut, 1998, 61-63; for its destruction in 1734, see P. Héliot, *Revue Belge d'archéologie et d'histoire* 28 (1959), 129-173 'Quelque moments disparus de la Flandre wallonne: L'abbaye d'Anchin, les collégiales Saint-Pierre et Saint-Amé de Douai'.

found swiftly and soon the magistrates petitioned Margaret of Parma to appoint Smyth to the vacant deanery of the Collégiale Saint-Pierre. The matter was passed on to the Escorial:

> Regarding the praelector in said university: the above-mentioned deanery generates too little revenue and, in the absence of a dean of the Collégiale Saint-Amé, the deanery was coupled with the office of vice-chancellor of the university. As it is essential that the person appointed to said deanery be also sufficiently qualified and knowledgeable in the execution of the tasks pertinent to a chancellor of that university, among others the said Smyth is well equipped. And in order to encourage and attract others by his example, it would seem that Your Majesty could do, by way of revision, a good work by assigning the above-mentioned deanery to the said Smyth.[282]

By the time the letter reached Spain, Smyth had already arrived at Douai and was accommodated in the deanery of Saint-Amé 'with the greatest convenience possible'.[283] Before word returned from Philip II, admitting him to the deanery and another vice-chancellorship, the university had been formally opened and the new professor had delivered his inaugural lecture together with his episcopal colleague in the chair of theology, François Richardot, on the market square of Douai—for want of a large enough building.[284]

---

[282] Gachard (1881), 2.419: 'Pour le premier lecteur en ladicte université: estant ladicte prévosté de peu de revenu, et à icelle annexé l'office de chancellier de l'université, en l'absence du prévost de Sainct-Amé, et qu'il est nécessaire que celluy qui sera pourvenu de ladicte prévosté soit personnage qualiffié pour sçavoir convenablement exercer les actes que conviennent à ung chancellier de telle université, y joinct que ledict Smitheus est destitué de autre bien. Et pour l'encouraiger et attirer autres par cest example, il a semblé que Vostre Majesté feroit, à correction, bonne oeuvre de pourvenir de ladicte prévosté ledict Smitheus'.

[283] De France, Bibliothèque municipale de Douai, MS 1304, f. 97: 'à la plus grand commodité que lon sceut faire'.

[284] For Smyth's vice-chancellorship of Oxford university in 1553, see above, 32; for the opening of the university of Douai on 5 October 1563, see *Bref Recueil & recit de la solemnite faicte a lentree et consecration de L'Uniuersité faicte & erigée en la Ville de Douay, en Flandre. Par le tres catholicque & tres uertuex Prince Philippe, Roy Despaigne, Conte de Flandre &c. le v Doctobre, L'an M.CCCCCC.Lxij*, Douai, 1562; for Smyth's inauguration lecture, see De France, Bibliothèque municipale de Douai, MS 1304, f. 114, 116.

72   CHAPTER ONE

5.1.4. *Smyth and the English College*

The foundation of the university of Douai proved an immediate success. Within a relatively short time the professors and lecturers had gained a reputation for excellence which attracted substantial numbers of students at a time when its Brabant counterpart began to experience a quiet lull. Douai university had a vested interest in attracting large numbers of students, and proceeded with verve on the way to economic and academic achievement. A particular group of exiled English scholars, the *Louvain School of Apologetics* or *Louvainists* played a key role in accomplishing this goal. A movement of conservative exiled students and teachers who by their theological works countered English evangelical doctrine, the *Louvainists* later settled in Douai and there established the English College.[285] It can be assumed that the appointment of an Englishman as first professor of theology was made with the deliberate intention of attracting this group of students to move from Leuven to the new university.

Richard Smyth was an old man by the time he arrived at Douai. He was a prominent theologian of his age, looking back on nearly thirty years of lecturing at the various centres of catholic learning in Northern Europe when he accepted the position. Smyth had retained much of his passion, and played himself into the foreground of current academic debate to orchestrate his later appointment as *premier lecteur* at the newest and most privileged university in the Low Countries. It was from this platform that he continued his mission of questioning the doctrinal innovations in his mother country with undiminished fervour. The last two years of his life saw more polemical publications than the six years as professor in Oxford following his first exile.[286]

---

[285] For the *Louvain School of Apologetics* or *Louvainists*, see e.g. *Messager des Sciences Historiques* 1875: 'Les numbres du Collège d'Oxford refugiés à Anvers', 284; Lechat (1914), 31-33; P. Guilday, *The English Catholic Refugees on the Continent, 1558-1795*, London, 1914, 11-13; J. Bossy, *Past and Present* 47 (1970): 'The Counter-Reformation and the People of Catholic Europe', 52-54, 62-67; C. Haigh, ed., *The English Reformation Revised*, Cambridge, 1987: idem, 'The Continuation of Catholicism in the English Reformation', 176-208; for the English College at Douai, see Knox (1878-1882).

[286] The six 1563 Leuven publications were followed by two further works: R. Smyth, *Refutatio locorum communiorum theologicorum Philippi Melanchthonis Germani*,

If it had been the university's intention to draw students from its Dutch-speaking rival institution, the English exiles would have been an ideal group: uprooted and not yet settled long enough, the offer of being taught by a fellow-countryman was a substantial incentive to move to Douai. Later local historians insinuated that it was indeed due to Smyth's presence at Douai that the English College was eventually established there.[287] By 1562, a large contingent of catholic Oxonian lecturers and students had left for the continent—New College seems to have contributed disproportionally to this movement.[288] Nicholas Sander estimated that about three-hundred students altogether left Oxford and Cambridge for the Leuven faculty, an impressive number considering the overall size of the student body at the two British universities.[289] The matriculation registers of the university of Leuven bear witness to this: while 1558 did not see the classification 'anglus' at all, by the following year eighteen Englishmen had been registered, while the first eight months of 1560 alone saw the arrival of fifteen men from the British Isles.[290] Among the exiled members of the two British universities were prominent theologians and, as many of Smyth's former Oxford colleagues settled in the Low Countries, familiar names such as Francis Babington, Thomas Harding, Henry Henshaw and Morgan Philips (who stood in for Smyth at Oxford in the 1549 debate against Peter Martyr Vermigli) were added to the Leuven registers. Once they had organised themselves in their study-houses, 'Oxford' and 'Cambridge', the exiles began to react to the developments in their home-country.[291] Christopher Haigh characterises their new role succinctly:

> The Louvainists regarded themselves as a Church government in exile. They bombarded their co-religionists at home with advice and instruction, Elizabeth and her councillors with threats and promises,

---

M. Lutheri discipuli primarii, Douai, 1563[1]; *De libero hominis arbitrio adversus Joannem Calvinum, et quotquod impie ... Lutherum imitati*, Douai, 1563[2].

[287] Leuridan (1904), 28.

[288] C. Haigh, *The English Reformations*, Oxford, 1993, 253, cf. Lechat (1914), 31-35, 211.

[289] N. Sander, *The Rise and Growth of the Anglican Schism*, London, 1877, 287.

[290] K. Baron de le Henhove, *Relations politiques des Pays-Bas et de l'Angleterre sous le règne de Philippe II*, Brussel, 1882-1900, 8.73.

[291] T. F. Knox, *Cardinal Allen's Letters and Memorials, 1532-1594*, London, 1878-1882, 53, n. 4.

and English Protestants with great tomes of theological controversy.[292]

The new university seems to have taken a considerable chance in appointing one of the English exiles to head their most prestigious faculty in order to win over the *Louvainists*. Their investment was successful. The aged Smyth evidently still had the necessary charisma to take a large following with him to Douai. Once he had left Leuven to take up his position as head of the newly-founded faculty, many prominent theologians followed suit to pursue their studies there: Owen Lewis, Thomas Stapleton and John Marshal are just a few of those who chose to follow their professor to Douai.[293] The attraction of a vibrant and flourishing university community would already have provided ample incentive to leave Leuven. The fact that an experienced Oxford don was chosen from their midst to teach there made the decision to leave the new 'Oxbridge' for Douai even less difficult. When the people of Douai petitioned the regent for a new professor of theology following Smyth's death on 9 June 1563, Margaret wrote to her brother in acknowledgement of his achievements: 'Because of his reputation many other English Catholics also went there'.[294]

Neither the founders nor the professor himself would have contemplated as early as 1562 that a few decades later Douai was to become the chief centre of learning for the English exiles. The foundation of the English College lay firmly in the hands of the second generation of Douai lecturers, among them the main driving force behind the College, William Allen.[295] The future president and Cardinal protector of the English mission was still principal of St Mary's Hall at Oxford when the university of Douai began to take its first steps.[296] By 1568, however, nearly ten years into the reign of Elizabeth, even the most hopeful of recusants had realised that the Queen's government was stable enough to

---

[292] Haigh (1993), 254.
[293] Knox (1878-1882), appendix, 270; Leuridan (1914), 34.
[294] Gachard (1881), 3.114: 'Pour son respect, y estoient venues plusieurs aultres anglois catholiques'.
[295] Cf. W. Allen, *An Apology and True Declaration of the Institution and Endeavour of the Two English Colleges*, Rheims, 1581.
[296] Now part of Oriel College, cf. Haigh (1993), 254; Allen left for the Low Countries in 1561 but frequently returned to his homeland. By 1565 he had settled in Leuven for good.

withstand the attacks from the continent, and consequently sought possibilities to provide a centre of English Catholic learning abroad. It would have made sense for the fathers of the English College, William Allen and Jean de Vendeville, to establish such an institution in the shadow of a settled yet still lively university, especially since Vendeville had then been on the professorial staff of Douai for more than a decade. Furthermore, the newly-founded university possessed sufficient impetus and continuity to grant the exiled theologians the security they lacked in their homeland.

The great number of students that went through the seminary each year bear witness to the English College's success. But this institution would not have been established at Douai at all, had there not been an earlier exodus of *Louvainists* from Brabant to Artois. The story of the foundation of the English College is as much the story of two conservative catholic institutions in Douai which remained faithful to a common goal, as well as a story of two rival universities in the Low Countries. The English College at Douai benefited from the conservative spirit of its mother–university and soon proceeded to provide both English underground clergy and fierce conservative tracts. In turn the English formed a sufficiently large student body to benefit the economy and influence of Douai and contributed to weakening the predominance of the new university's counterpart in Brabant.

5.2. Evangelical Polemicists

A notorious polemic writer like Smyth had no friends among his evangelical opponents. Contemporaries like Peter Martyr Vermigli and his student John Jewel took every opportunity to provide more intriguing details of Smyth's private life.[297] These allegations found

---

[297] Cf. for instance P. M. Vermigli to M. Bucer, in: Gorham (1857), 154: 'He had a manservant who took to himself a wife: he lodged with them and, as it is generally reported, they had all things in common. Such are the advocates of the Celibacy of Clerks and Monks'; Jewel's biographer L. Humphrey added a verse: 'Smyth did not treat crafts like a craftsman, / He wrote a book on the life of chastity / While he praised modesty, while he praised monastic vows / He fornicated, staining the sacred bond of marriage' (Haud satis affabre tractatus fabrilia Smithus, / Librum de Vitâ Coelibe composuit / Dumque pudiciam, dum Vota Monastici, laudat / Stuprat; sacra notans foedera Conjugii).

their way into a number of scholarly publications, ranging from Ellen Macek's *The Loyal Opposition* to Diarmaid MacCulloch's magisterial *Cranmer: A Life*.[298] Vermigli and Jewel both routinely depicted Smyth as an inconsistent careerist with a strong propensity to contradict his writings by his deeds. A great advocate of clerical celibacy with little sympathy for married ministers, Smyth often found himself accused of sexual laxity. This, rather than his opposition to royal supremacy, was given as the reason for his second dismissal from Oxford in 1559.[299] Jewel modelled a report to Vermigli on Cicero's Catalinian oration:

> Smith has gone into Wales, where, they say, he has taken a wife, with the view of refuting all your arguments. He now gains his livelihood by a hired tavern, despised by our friends and his own; by those who know him, and those who do not, by old and young, by himself, by everyone.[300]

Throughout his Netherlandish exiles, on the other hand, he enjoyed the highest of reputations. His Leuven friends and patrons valued his orthodoxy and his didactic abilities. It has already been noted that the regent of the Low Countries commended him to her brother, king Philip, as 'a person of unblemished doctrine and good faith and highly recommended by those of the university of Leuven, where he has dwelt for some time'.[301] Among English catholics, Smyth was remembered as a 'learned catholic in exile', whose two recantations did not detract from his learning.[302] His

---

[298] Macek (1996), 29: 'After a flight from Oxford, Smyth retired to Wales where he married and kept a tavern. His excursions into lay-activities must have been brief'; MacCulloch (1996), 489.

[299] J. Jewel to P. M. Vermigli, in: H. Robinson, ed., *The Zurich letters, comprising the correspondence of several English bishops and others, with some of the Helvetian reformers, during the reign of queen Elizabeth*, Cambridge, 1842-1845, 1.45: 'Your renowned Smith, the patron of chastity, has been taken on adultery, and on that account is rendered to retire from the theology chair … the like was never done in Mary's time'.

[300] Robinson (1842-1845), 1.85.

[301] Gachard (1881), 2.419f.: 'A ung personnaige de singulière doctrine et bonne vye et fort recommandé par ceulx de l'université de Louvain où il s'est tenu quelque temps'.

[302] C. G. Bayne, *Anglo Roman Relations, 1558-1565*, Oxford, 1913, 284: 'vir catholicus et doctus citra Mare'; 'Richardus Smitheus vir omnium doctissimus sed infamis tum propter alia, tum quod saepe in Anglio palinodiem cecinet'. I am grateful to C. Armstrong for pointing out this document which suggests that

colleagues and students and Douai valued his academic talents and catholic fervour.[303] Smyth's epitaph in the Collégiale Saint-Pierre Douai, composed by a contemporary, is a lasting testimony to his impeccable reputation:

> Richard Smyth, Englishman, Doctor of Theology, had already performed the office of royal praelector of sacred scripture at Oxford in England with the greatest merit for many years. While he was repeatedly exiled from his homeland at length for the sake of the catholic faith, he was honoured by the noble and truly catholic prince Philip, king of Spain, with the deanery of the Collégiale Saint-Pierre in Douai; he was made first public praelector of sacred scripture at the university which had been set up there for the proper studies of the good citizens. When he had been in office for a year with the greatest success he left, in his public writings, clear testimonies of his integrity against those who spread heresies in his time. He died on the seventh day of the Ides of July, in the 1563th year from the child-bearing of the Blessed Virgin, at the actual age of 63. Great sorrow was shared by people of all ranks. He was honoured by a public funeral and buried in this Chapel of the Virgin-Mother. May you, good reader, pray for his soul, that God, the greatest and best, may be merciful in his clemency: pour prayers to our Lord, and go joyfully on your way.[304]

Smyth's promotion to an English bishopric or deanery during Mary's reign may have been hindered by his two recantations rather than his credentials.

[303] Cf. for instance Jean Dubois (Joannes Sylvius), *Academiae Duacensis, eiusdemque Illustrium Professorum, Encomium, Anno M.D. LXII. Tert. Non. Octobris Dvaci, Typis Iacobi Boscardi, Typographi iurati*, Douai, 1563, 2 r-2 v.

[304] Foppens (1739), 2.1069f.: 'Richardus Smythaeus, Anglus, Theologiae Doctor, Regii Sacrarum Litterarum Professoris munere Oxonii in Anglia multis jam annis summa cum laude functus, dum fides tandem catholicae causa patria iterum exulat, ab optimo vereque Catholico Principe Philippo Hispaniarum Rege Praepositura Collegii D. Petri Duacensis ornatur, publicaeque ibi institutae scholae propensissimis optimorum civium studiis primus Sacrarum Litterarum publicus Praelector creatur, Quo in munere cum annum jam paulo minus felicissime versatus esset, praeclaraque ingenii monumenta contra grassantes sui temporis haereses publicis mandata litteris reliquisset. VII Idus Julias anno a parto Virgineo M.D.LXIII. aetatis vero suae LXIII. magno omnium ordinum maeore fato concessit, publicoque elatus funere hoc virginis matris sacello sepultus est. Cuius animae, ut Deus Opt. Max., pro sua clementia misericors esse relit, prias candide lector ad communem Dominum preces fundito, felixque age'.

CHAPTER TWO

EXEGETICAL LECTURES

The university of Douai had been founded by king Philip II to be a bulwark of catholic orthodoxy on the borders with protestant France.[1] The Flemish plains were deemed to be particularly vulnerable to the message of evangelicalism. Soon after its hurried establishment, in October 1562 the university opened its gates with a dazzling demonstration of 'true religion and catholic faith'.[2] The market square and one of the town's many chapels served as locations for the two inaugural lectures included in the opening ceremonies. Following the festal procession of the blessed sacrament on 5 October, the two lecturers chose to expound two Pauline epistles. François Richardot, the diocesan bishop of Arras, devoted three hours to the first epistle to Timothy, while the exiled Oxonian, Richard Smyth, continued the lectures: 'The same day, at said chapel of Saint Catherine, Monsieur Richard Smyth, the Englishman, doctor of theology, lectured before the university from eight o'clock in the morning'.[3] Smyth had chosen to read on Romans, an epistle on which he continued to lecture for the rest of the term.[4]

---

[1] During an address given at the opening ceremony, Mgr François Richardot's praise of the new university city culminated in 'and what is most, an exemplar in Religion' (quodque summum est, Religione spectabilis), see F. Schott, ed., *Reverendissimi et Eloquentissimi Viri D. Francisci Richardoti Atrebatensium Episcopi Orationes, ad Noblissimus, & Amplissimum virum Dominum Ioannem Richardotvm, Equitem Auratum, Dominum de Barly &c.*, Douai, 1608, 50.

[2] 'La vraye Religion et Foy catholique', Archives de Douai, Layette 172: 'Lettres de Vidimus Données des Eschevins de la Ville de Doüay des Lettres Patentes du Roy D'Espagne en forme de convention des Droits & Privileges de l'Université de Doüay en 1561' (1562 n.s.); cf. M. Rouche, ed. et al., *Histoire de Douai*, Condé-sur-l'Escaut, 1998, 105.

[3] J. de France, *Discovrs de la Povrsvite et Erection De L'Vniuersité De Douay*, Bibliothèque municipale de la Ville de Douai, MS 1304, c. 1570-90, f. 114: 'Lesquelz jour suivant ... ay ladicte chapelle de St Catherine a sçavoir Monsieur Richardus Scimetheus, anglois, docteur en theologie, le universitaire cours depuis viii heures matin'.

[4] De France, Bibliothèque municipale de la Ville de Douai, MS 1304, f. 116.

1. THE EVIDENCE FROM FRANÇOIS DE BAR'S STUDIES

From late 1562 until September 1573, a Benedictine monk, François de Bar of Anchin Abbey, attended a course of exegetical lectures at Douai university.[5] Whether de Bar had begun his studies immediately after the solemn inauguration of the university remains unknown, but he was certainly attending lectures during winter 1562-1563. Until the establishment of the first monastic study-house at Douai, the Collège d'Anchin in 1568, de Bar would either have been a member of the Collège du Roi, the first college to be established, or would have travelled from nearby Anchin Abbey to attend lectures.[6] For nearly ten years he frequented a course of lectures that expounded the entire New Testament. This enormous undertaking was the work of the whole faculty staff. Until his death in July 1563, Smyth set the pace by commenting on the Gospels, Romans, and 1 and 2 Corinthians in a mere eight months. In autumn 1564, Richardot took over with a painstaking exegesis of Ephesians, which he concluded fifteen months later.[7]

In addition to the episcopal lecturer and his English colleague, three Leuven theologians, Jean Bouche, Adriaan Bessemer and Nicholas Zeghers OFM, as well as the prior of Anchin Abbey, Dom Oostrel, lectured on the remaining epistles, commencing with Bouche's interpretation of Hebrews in 1564 and concluding with Zegher's exposition of Revelation nine years later.[8] The fact that six highly qualified theologians took about ten years to complete the task indicates not only the arduous nature of the enterprise,

---

[5] For de Bar see E. A. Escallier, *L'Abbaye d'Anchin, 1079-1792*, Lille, 1852, 2.263-306; H. R. Douthilloeul, *Galerie douaisienne, ou biographie des hommes remarquables de la ville de Doaui*, Douai, 1844, 14ff; for Anchin Abbey, see J.-P. Gerzaguet, *L'Abbaye d'Anchin de sa fondation (1079) au XIVe siècle*, Lille/Arras, 1997; P. Héliot, *Revue Belge d'Archéologie et d'Histoire* 28 (1959), 129-173: 'Quelques moments disparus de la Flandre wallone: l'Abbaye d'Anchin, les Collégiales Saint-Pierre et Saint Amé de Douai'.

[6] Escalier (1852), 2.272; Rouche (1998), 107: 'The college was inaugurated on 20 October 1568, the Abbot of Anchin signed its charter of foundation on 17 July 1570' (Le collège fut inauguré le 20 octobre 1568; l'abbé d'Anchin signa l'acte de fondation le 17 juillet 1570).

[7] F. de Bar, Bibliothèque municipale de la Ville de Douai, MS 57, 1563-1573.

[8] De Bar, Bibliothèque municipale de la Ville de Douai, MS 57, unpaginated entries.

but also the considerable significance attached to biblical exegesis at the university. The magistrates of Douai had put great emphasis on scriptural studies and set out to select a resolute *premier lecteur* for that particular subject. In choosing two conservative celebrities to share the chair, they had accomplished this intention.[9]

In autumn 1562, Jean Dubois composed poetic characterisations of the newly appointed professors. Smyth's not only honours the exiled Englishman, but also provides a contemporary testimony about the importance attributed to biblical exegesis by the general public. Dubois wrote in admiration

> First enters Smyth, venerable for those very white hairs,
> His breast imbued with the Sacred Scriptures,
> Which act as guide to the easy way: he will make clear to you
> What every divine letter signifies
>   and the oracles of the gods and heavenly things.
> A crowd from every rank follows the man to honour him,
> Wearing a crown on his brow, the reward of his labours,
> Which, holy Justice, you weave with Elysian herbs.[10]

It is noteworthy that the adroitness with which Smyth steered students through the maze of biblical exegesis is given particular prominence in the sketch, a reputation the English exile had already built up at Leuven.[11] The same fervour for the interpretation of Scripture which Douai magistrates attributed to Smyth and his episcopal colleague can be detected among his successors, who continued their work in the same spirit of orthodoxy.

---

[9] J. A. Löwe, *Nederlands Archief voor Kerkgeschiedenis* 72/2 (1999), 142-169: 'Richard Smyth and the foundation of the university of Douai', 153, 161; De France, Bibliothèque municipale de Douai, MS 1304, f. 76: 'gens fort excellens'.

[10] J. Dubois (Joannes Sylvius), *Academiae Duacensis, eiusdemque Illustrium Professorum, Encomium, Anno M.D. LXII. Tert. Non. Octobris Dvaci, Typis Iacobi Boscardi, Typographi iurati*, Douai, 1563, 2 r-2 v: 'Proximus incedit, canis venerabilis ipsis / Smyttaeus, sacris imbutus pectora scriptis, / Quo facilem monstrante viam, tibi dia patebit / Litera quidquid habet, Superûmque oracla deorum. / Hunc veneranda virûm sequitur quendam ordine turba / Praemia sudorum gestans in fronte coronam, / Elysijs quam sancta Dice contextuis herbis'.

[11] L. P. Gachard, ed., *Correspondance de Marguerite d'Autriche*, Brussel, 1881, 2.419.

2. DE BAR'S LECTURE NOTES

For over nine years the Benedictine student transposed his lecture notes faithfully from a note-book into his study Bible, a version of Jerome's Vulgate text published at Leuven in two volumes early in 1563.[12] The fact that this extraordinary record survives today is chiefly due to the monk's subsequent illustrious career. Appointed grand prior of his abbey in April 1575, de Bar bequeathed his bible to the monastery library.[13] Following the dissolution of Anchin Abbey in 1792, the two densely annotated volumes escaped the fate of destruction or sale and were instead transferred to the municipal library at Douai, where the second volume comprising the epistles and Revelation remains to this day.

Sadly, the first volume of de Bar's did not survive the turmoil of the Second World War. Since no studies of the annotated volumes were conducted prior to the present analysis, Smyth's exegesis of the Gospels is lost.[14] The remaining volume, however, still offers a wealth of information regarding biblical studies at Douai in the 1560s and 1570s. De Bar proved a thorough notator and covered most epistles in great detail. He took down commentaries in the margins of the text, on blank pages bound between the printed text for that purpose, and even pasted his own pages into the book to provide additional space.[15] His annotations are tightly woven around the printed text itself, they often occupy the entire margin, study pages and, in his notes from Hebrews, are even supplemented by minute notes tracing the border of the page.

De Bar dated the beginning and end of most lecture series, and acknowledged the sources of his annotations. At the end of the second volume he wrote:

> For I remember that I have taken notes from the lectures of the Englishman Smyth, a Doctor of Divinity, and have woven this text

---

[12] *Sanctum Jesu Christi evangelium secundum Matthaeum, secundum Marcum, secundum Lucam, secundum Joannem, Acta Apostolorum*, Lovanii, excudebat Bartholomaeus Grauius suis sumptibus, & Petri Zangri Tiletani, Leuven, 1563; *Pavli Apostoli Epistolae*, Lovanii, excudebat Bartholomaeus Grauius suis sumptibus, & Petri Zangri Tiletani, Leuven, 1563.

[13] For de Bar's ensuing monastic career, see Escalier (1852), 2.306f.

[14] A description of the lost volume survives in: C. Dehaines, *Catalogue des Manuscrits de la Bibliothèque de Douai*, Paris, 1878, 38.

[15] In the case of 1 Tim, Titus, and Rev.

around the Gospels. From the same author I noted much concerning the epistles of Paul in a parchment book.[16]

The lecture-notes had first been noted in an ordinary notebook ('libello quodam chartaceo') and then transferred into the study Bible and woven around the text ('contextum'). In addition to lecture notes, some of de Bar's annotations were evidently based on his private reading of standard patristic commentaries or 'from the *Annotations* of Erasmus'.[17] The passages not covered by private study or the lectures of Smyth and Richardot were taken from 'the expositions of Dr Johannes Bouche, Dr A. Bessemer, and the prior of Anchin, the Reverend Dom Oostrel', the monk explained, confirming that the whole faculty of divinity had shared in the effort of expounding the Psalter and the New Testament.[18]

Since most sixteenth-century theology courses centred on the Pauline epistles, de Bar spent much less time on the Catholic and the pastoral epistles.[19] They merely contain brief introductory notes, except for the *comma Iohanneum* (1 Jn 5.7f), which warranted half a page.[20] Most attention, however, is devoted to a commentary on Revelation, a text Smyth had probably covered already during his second exile in Leuven.[21] Unlike Thomas de Vio

---

[16] De Bar, Bibliothèque municipale de la Ville de Douai, MS 57, unpaginated entry: 'Memini enim me imprimis ex praelectionibus D. Doctoris Smithaei, Angli, ad similem huius libri contextum in Evangelia scripsisse atque ex eodem in epistolis Pauli annotasse plurima in libello quodam chartaceo'.

[17] 'Ex annotationibus Erasmi'; for instance Isidore, *De nativitate Domini & resurrectione regno atque juditio libri duo. Item Allegoriae quaedam, ex utroque Testamento excerptae*, Hagenau, 1529; Basil the Great, *Basilii Magni Caesariensis Episcopi singularis eruditionis libellus de ueterum scriptorum, & praesertim poetarum libris, & an Christiano homini eos manibus attrectare*, Wien, 1518; Desiderus Erasmus, *In Novvm Testamentvm ab Annotationes: ingenti nuper accessione per autorem locupletatae*, Basel, 1519.

[18] De Bar, Bibliothèque municipale de la Ville de Douai, MS 57, unpaginated entry; according to the same source, Smyth also lectured on the Psalter: 'de exhibitionibus D. Joannes Bouche, D. Doctoris A. Bessemeris, Aquicinctensi quodam prioris Rev. Domini Oostrellij'.

[19] For a thorough analysis of late medieval theological education, see for instance F. W. Oedinger, *Über die Bildung der Geistlichen im späten Mittelalter*, Leiden, 1953.

[20] For the *comma Iohanneum* see particularly W. Thiele, *Zeitschrift für die neutestamentliche Wissenschaft und die Kunde des Urchristentums und der älteren Kirche* 50 (1959), 61-73: 'Beobachtungen zum Comma Iohanneum' and B. M. Metzger, *The Text of the New Testament*, Oxford ³1992, 101f.

[21] A. Wood, *Athenae Oxoniensis: An exact History of all the Writers and Bishops who have had their Education in the University of Oxford*, Oxford, 1813-1821, 1.193.

Cajetan, who shrank back from interpreting the cryptic visions of John and felt that its exegesis required divine inspiration (*exponat cui Deus concesserit*), the Leuven-educated Nicholas Zeghers spent the summer term of 1573 expounding on the text in great detail.[22] Once more, the generous space provided in the monk's study Bible was not sufficient for his extensive notes and de Bar supplemented his own pages which he then pasted into the text. In September 1573, on completion of his weekly lectures on the New Testament, more than nine years after first attending an academic exposition on the Pauline epistles, de Bar remarked that he had finally reached 'the end of ... studying the Epistles and Gospels, then the letters of Paul and the Catholic epistles and then, finally, the Revelation of John'.[23] One can almost sense the sigh of relief when he took pains to spell out the momentous date in all its fullness: 'on the fourth day of the Nones of September Anno Domini 1573'.[24]

3. Smyth's Introductory Lectures on Romans (1562-1563)

In the dedicatory letter introducing his last published work, Smyth confirmed that in winter 1562-1563 'I had undertaken to expound the epistle of St Paul written to the Romans in the recently established university of Douai'.[25] Romans lent itself well to such a course. Located at the beginning of the canon of apostolic letters, it touches on a number of controverted subjects which Smyth had already covered in depth in England. He had been lecturing on scripture since 1536. The faculty of divinity at Oxford had heeded

---

[22] T. de Vio Cajetan, *Opera omnia quotquod in Sacrae Scripturae expositionem reperiuntur, cura atque industria insignis Collegii S. Thomae Complutensis OP*, Lyon, 1639, comprising his *Evangelia cum Commentariis Reverendissimi Domini Thomae de Vio Cajetani, Cardinalis Sancti Xisti, in quatuor Evangelia et Acta Apostolorum ad Graecorum codicum veritatem castigata, ad sensum quem vocant literalem Commentarij*, Paris, 1532.

[23] De Bar, Bibliothèque municipale de la Ville de Douai, MS 57, unpaginated entry: 'finem ... studij in Epistolas et in euangelia, uel in epistolas Pauli ac Catholicas, uel denique in apocalypsim Johannis'.

[24] Ibid: 'quarto nonas septembris, anno domini millesimo, quinquacentesimo, septuagesimo tertio'.

[25] R. Smyth, *De libero hominis arbitrio adversus Joannem Calvinum, et quotquod impie Lutherum imitati*, Leuven, 1563: 'epistolam Divi Pauli ad Romanos scriptam suscepissem enarrandam in Duacensi academia recens jam instituta'.

Thomas Cromwell's injunctions to the universities right from their promulgation in 1535, and began to replace the traditional scholastic curriculum by a more Scripture-based course of lectures.[26] Smyth had commented on Romans previously, and many of the subjects called into controversy by contemporary debate (such as the dispute about justification by faith) later found their way into his published works.[27] Since François de Bar began his studies in the autumn term of 1562, he attended Smyth's series of lectures on Romans. His notes are an invaluable supplement to the extensive corpus of Smyth's published works.

Smyth began his teaching not by reiterating his well-known opposition to the evangelical teaching of justification by faith alone, but by considering a much more fundamental issue instead. In the first few lectures he set out to reject evangelical claims about *perspicuitas scripturae* (the evangelical idea that God's authorship of the bible precluded obscurity). Such a rejection not only called into question the evangelical understanding of justification by faith but, more significantly, that of *scriptura sui interpres*.[28] François de Bar left fascinating notes which he later pasted neatly into the vellum of the front cover of his epistles. They cover not only Smyth's extensive rejection of *perspicuitas scripturae*, but also include general notes on the benefit of biblical studies, the canonicity of biblical books, and the origin of the name of the Apostle Paul.[29] Sadly, de Bar's exegesis of Romans itself dates from summer

---

[26] For an analysis of the effects of Cromwell's injunctions on the English universities, see D. R. Leader, *History of Education* 13 (1984), 215-217: 'Teaching in Tudor Cambridge'.

[27] According to Peter Martyr Vermigli's statement, in P. M. Vermigli, *D. Petri Martyris Vermilii Florentini divinarum Literarum in Schola Tigurina Professoris Oxoniensis duos Libellos de Caelibatu Sacerdotum, & Votis Monasticis, Nunc Primum in lucé edita*, Basel, 1559, 643, Smyth had already read on the subject at Oxford in about 1539: 'Richard Smyth ... expounded the fifth chapter of Romans' (Richardus Smythaeus ... è quinto capite ad Romanos interpretabatur), considering in particular the *topoi* on justification; for Smyth's published works on the subject see R. Smyth, *Diatriba de hominis justificatione aedita Oxoniae anno 1550 mense februario adversum Petrum Martyrem Vermelium nunc apostatam*, Leuven, 1550 and R. Smyth, *De libero hominis arbitrio adversus Joannem Calvinum, et quotquod impie Lutherum imitati*, Leuven, 1563.

[28] For another traditional rejection of *perspicuitas scripturae* see for instance F. Titelmans OFM, *Collationes qvinqve svper Epistolam ad Romanos beati Pauli Apostoli*, Antwerpen, 1529, c viij r.

[29] Smyth probably derived his reflections on the name 'Paul' from the *glossa ordinaria*, for instance in: K. Froehlich, M. T. Gibson, edd., *Glossa ordinaria editio*

1567 and therefore does not include any notes taken at Smyth's 1562-1563 lectures. His introductory notes and the annotations covering the first and second epistle to the Corinthians remain the only record of Smyth's lectures at Douai.

De Bar's set of notes first records the debate about whether scripture could be regarded as self-revelatory. Smyth impressed his students by his progressive lecturing techniques. He had already taken on board a radical change in sixteenth-century teaching method and arranged his material in tables. Departing from the systematisation of formal logic as proposed by Aristotle and used extensively by earlier scholastic scholars, the summary of theses in logical groups reflected a move to the spatial systems of logic expressed in many contemporary *Loci Communes*. The publication in 1479 of Rudolph Agricola's *De inventione dialectica* had already marked a radical departure from traditional scholastic logic.[30] Three decades later, the evangelical Philipp Melanchthon and the catholic Melchior Cano both proceeded to refine Agricola's principles and soon topical lists arranged by subject headings had superseded the traditional commentaries on the sentences in university curricula.[31] Smyth's teaching method at Douai, however, went beyond the mere topical systematisation of facts. In his lectures, he made use of the most up-to-date presentation techniques available and classified his information in bracketed tables,

---

princeps, Turnholt, 1992. For the contemporary evangelical use of the *glossa* on the name 'Paul', see Ch. Krieger, M. Leinhard, edd., *Martin Bucer and Sixteenth Century Europe: Actes du colloque de Strasbourg (28-31 août 1991)*, Leiden, 1993, 1.55-69: I. Backus, 'Martin Bucer and the Patristic Tradition', 62-63; for the *glossa* as a tool for late medieval exegetes, see M. D. Jordan, K. Emery, edd. et al., *Ad Literam: Authoritative Texts and their medieval Readers*, Notre Dame IN, 1992, 5-27: M. T. Gibson, 'The place of the *Glossa ordinaria* in medieval Exegesis'.

[30] The sentiments expressed by John Fisher who, on reading Agricola, exclaimed 'would that as a young man I could have obtained that man as a teacher!' (utinam iuvenis praeceptorem illum fuissem nactus!), could be applied to a whole generation of scholastically educated divines, in: P. S. Allen, ed., *Opus Epistolarum Desideri Erasmi Roterodami*, Oxford, 1906-58, 2.90: epistola 336 from Fisher, c. May 1515; cf. R. Rex, *The Theology of John Fisher*, Cambridge, 1991, 17; for Agricola's rhetoric priciples, see P. Mack, *Renaissance argument: Valla and Agricola in the traditions of rhetoric and dialectic*, Brill Studies in Intellectual History 43, Leiden, 1993.

[31] For the shift in curricula from the *trivium* of grammar, logic and rhetoric, see for instance W. J. Ong SJ, *Ramus: Method and the Decay of the Dialogue*, Cambridge MA, 1958, especially 314-318: 'The Spatial Model as Key to the Mental World'; for an English application, see Rex (1991), 14-22.

each consisting of sets of logically assembled *topoi*.[32] He presumably used wall-charts or a black-board,[33] the ingeniously simple equivalent of modern wall projections, to communicate his thoughts on the problem of the obscurity of the epistle to the Romans.[34]

3.1. *Obscurity in Romans*

As early as the second century and the composition of the second epistle of Peter, biblical writers and their exegetes had acknowledged the difficulties posed by some of the Pauline writings. The earliest testimony to Pauline 'obscurity' is contained in 2 Pet 3.16: 'In all [Pauline] letters there are of course some passages which are hard to understand, and these are the ones that uneducated and unbalanced people distort ... to their own destruction'. This biblical proof text was employed routinely to justify attacks on evangelical claims that scripture, as the Word of God, was devoid of obscurity.[35] Since the theology of justification by faith alone chiefly hinged on Romans, conservative theologians plausibly argued that if the whole letter was found obscure it could never be

---

[32] For the introduction of spatial systems of logic into the Eton timetable in 1530, see P. Mack, ed., *Renaissance Rhetoric*, Basingstoke, 1994, 81-102: B. Vickers, 'Some reflections on the Rhetoric Textbook', 87.

[33] This system had been popularised by P. Mosellanus, *Tabvlae de Schematibvs Petri Mosellani, à pluribus mendis quam diligentissime repurgatae*, Köln, 1541. In his *De tradendis Disciplinis*, Vives remarked, F. Watson, tr., *Vives: On Education*, Cambridge, 1913, 134: 'Peter Mosellanus has also prepared for use a table of figures of speech, which can be hung up on the wall so that it will catch the attention of the pupil as he walks about it, and force itself upon his eyes'.

[34] Smyth presumably chose to arrange his material in tables for the same reasons as Mosellanus, who explained in his preface, Mosellanus (1541), A i v: 'For which reason, as so many diagrams, so many insertions are no less necessary for understanding than they are difficult to remember ... I have gathered them together in this short table' (Quamobrem cum tot figuram, tot Troporum non minus sic necessaria cognitio, quam memoria difficilis ... in brevem hanc Tabellam congressero). The method is also shared by many Reformed scholastics, so for instance by Theodore de Bèze in his *Tabula praedestinationis*, cf. *Apologia pro iustificatione per vnius Christi viua fide apprehensi iustitiam gratis imputatam, aduersus anonymi scriptoris tractatum*, Genève, 1592.

[35] As in H. Zwingli, *Von Clarheit vnnt gewüsse oder vnbetrogliche des wort gottes*, Zürich, 1524, of which a contemporary English translation was consulted: *A short pathwaye to the ryghte and true vnderstanding of the holye and sacred Scriptures set fourth by that moste famous Clerke, Huldrich Zwinglius*, Worcester, 1550; H. Bullinger, *In omnes Apostolicas Epistolas, divi vidilicet Pauli XIIII et VII Canonicas, Commentarii Heinrychi Bullingeri*, Zürich, 1558.

claimed without reasonable doubt that Paul taught a clear doctrine of justification.

In his lectures Smyth also resorted to the Apostle Peter's judgement and elaborated on 'those opinions from the second letter of Peter which are hinted at in chapter three', before setting out to prove that among the Pauline epistles Romans was certainly the most obscure.[36] Evangelical theologians were hard pressed to reject such arguments, particularly as they derived from scripture themselves. The propagators of *sola fide* recognised that they could not permit large chunks of explicit scriptural evidence to be discredited by the argument of obscurity, and instead set out to prove that *scriptura sit perspicua*. Consequently, in his commentary on Romans, the reformed theologian Heinrich Bullinger argued that if God was the author of scripture, his very nature ruled out any obscurity. He explained that catholics

> reject simplicity in holy matters and, having got hold of some perverse opinion, they believe that no-one truly practises theology unless he harms what has been said simply with many and diverse meanings and binds it up in some wonderful way: they deliberate in such a perplexing and intricate way about religion that they do not understand it themselves and scatter wherever they like whatever they like.[37]

Perspicuitas or *claritas scripturae* excluded any misunderstanding. Misinterpretations of Scripture, and in particular in the letter to the Romans, were based on human ineptitude (*ineptia*). True believers, however, possess 'the light and spirit of simplicity', Bullinger made clear.[38] Anyone who argued that Romans was obscure, he insinuated, was therefore excluded from the circle of rightful believers.

In his introductory lectures on Romans, Smyth tackled these and similar evangelical claims by amassing evidence from Scripture and the Fathers. Unlike one of his more notorious Leuven prede-

---

[36] De Bar, Bibliothèque municipale de la Ville de Douai, MS 57, unpaginated inlay, recto: 'quae a Petro 2 opiniones cap. 3 insinuatur'.

[37] Bullinger (1558), a i r: 'Simplicitatem in sacris respuunt, & peruersa quandam opinione concepta neminem uere theologicari credunt, nisi qui simpliciter dicta multis & uarijs sensibus laceret atque miro quodam modo implicet: de religione item tam spinose & intricate disserat, ut ne ipse quidem sese intelligat, adde & quidlibet quolibet in loco spargat'.

[38] Ibid: 'illis est illuminatus & simplicitatis spiritus'.

cessors, the Carmelite Frans Titelmans, who in his own commentary on the Pauline epistles simply restricted himself to stating that 'we will try to embrace the letter, which is full of obscurity, like an Epitome running through individual chapters', Smyth set out to provide his students with more substantial evidence.[39] In particular he fervently denied the segregation of believers into two classes. There could be no distinction between those who read Romans in its 'clarity' and those who found it obscure. The dictum 'to you is granted to understand the mysteries of the kingdom of Heaven' applied to all, Smyth stated.[40] He assured his students that 'you shall be able to understand the mysteries' and proceeded to provide them with patristic evidence:[41] Augustine maintained that 'in Christian life, men demand true understanding from God concerning the prayers they offer'.[42] Chrysostom and Theophilus echoed the Apostle Peter's opinion that the epistle was obscure. Smyth emphasised that opinions such as those uttered by Bullinger (or by his evangelical successor at Oxford Peter Martyr Vermigli) were to be rejected.[43] He employed arguments from the Fathers and tradition to demonstrate that the obscurity in Romans could not be resolved with the same ease his evangelical successor suggested. How could a letter full of diametrically opposed *topoi* ever be considered unambiguous? Smyth asked and, by way of

---

[39] F. Titelmans OFM, *In Omnes Epistolas Apostolicas Elucidatio*, Antwerpen, 1540, A iv r: 'tamen clarior fiat: epistola, quae tota obscuritas est plena, per singula capita discurrentes, uelut Epitomate eam complecti tentabimus'.

[40] Mt 13.11.

[41] De Bar, Bibliothèque municipale de la Ville de Douai, MS 57, unpaginated inlay, recto: 'a mysteriorum intelligentia vobis est posse'.

[42] De Bar, Bibliothèque municipale de la Ville de Douai, MS 57, unpaginated inlay, recto: 'homines Christiana vita de orationibus supplicentibus a deo postulant veram intelligentiam'.

[43] P. M. Vermigli, *In Epistolam S. Pavli Apostoli ad Romanos D. Petri Martyris Vermilii Florentini Professoris diuinarum literarum in schola Tigurina, commentarij doctissimi, cum tractatione perutili rerum & locorum, qui ad eam epistolam pertinet*, Basel, 1560, γ 4 r: 'The Apostle Peter acknowledges in his later letter that Paul has many things in his epistles which are difficult to understand, which men who are not learned or reliable enough distort to their own ruin. That which Augustine and Chrysostom handed down appear to be opposed to these thoughts: but they are easily solved' (Petrus Apostolus in posteriori sua epistola fatetur, Paulum habere in suis epistolis multa difficilia intellectu, quae parum eruditi & firmi homines ad suum exitium peruertant. Ista videntur his opponi quae Augustinus & Chrysostomus tradiderunt: sed facile soluuntur).

conclusion, painstakingly noted the opposing themes that contributed to the letter's obscurity:[44]

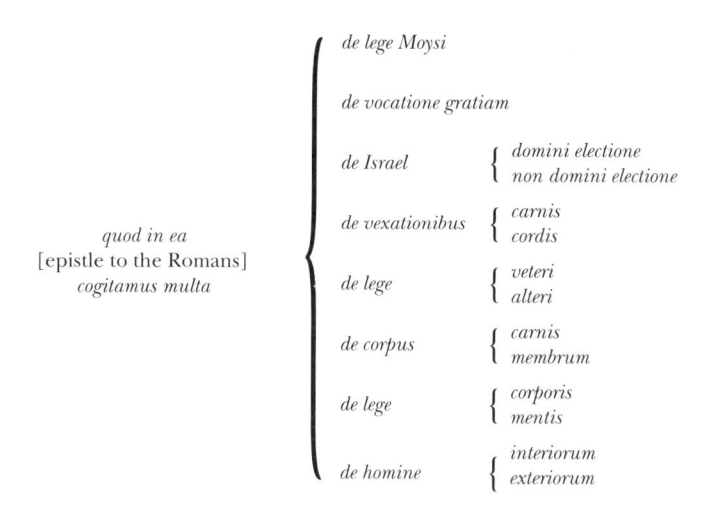

$$
\begin{array}{l}
\text{quod in ea} \\
\text{[epistle to the Romans]} \\
\text{cogitamus multa}
\end{array}
\left\{
\begin{array}{ll}
\textit{de lege Moysi} & \\
\textit{de vocatione gratiam} & \\
\textit{de Israel} & \left\{ \begin{array}{l} \textit{domini electione} \\ \textit{non domini electione} \end{array} \right. \\
\textit{de vexationibus} & \left\{ \begin{array}{l} \textit{carnis} \\ \textit{cordis} \end{array} \right. \\
\textit{de lege} & \left\{ \begin{array}{l} \textit{veteri} \\ \textit{alteri} \end{array} \right. \\
\textit{de corpus} & \left\{ \begin{array}{l} \textit{carnis} \\ \textit{membrum} \end{array} \right. \\
\textit{de lege} & \left\{ \begin{array}{l} \textit{corporis} \\ \textit{mentis} \end{array} \right. \\
\textit{de homine} & \left\{ \begin{array}{l} \textit{interiorum} \\ \textit{exteriorum} \end{array} \right.
\end{array}
\right.
$$

Figure 3: 'Obscurity in Romans': F. de Bar, *Bibliothèque de la Ville de Douai, MS 57*, unpaginated inlay, recto.

In pairs, Smyth listed some of the paradoxes found in the letter, such as for instance the 'election of Israel' and her 'non-election' (cf. Rom 11), or the juxtaposition of the 'old Law' and the 'new'.

3.2. *The Fruits of Scripture*

An intriguing table of five 'prerequisites' for the study of Scripture followed the detailed rejection of the *perspicuitas scripturae*. Smyth suggested that if his students took these to heart, 'abundant fruit would follow'.[45] With the zeal of a disciplined undergraduate, the novice theologian de Bar noted down his teacher's every aside, even the exhortation to take especial care when analysing 'the grammatical meaning of the Pauline epistles'.[46] Smyth counselled his students to devote ample time to the study of patristic commentaries and particularly suggested that they learned the passages they studied by heart. Thorough knowledge of the biblical

---

[44] De Bar, Bibliothèque municipale de la Ville de Douai, MS 57, unpaginated inlay, recto.
[45] Ibid: 'copiosum ... consequit fructum'.
[46] Ibid: 'grammaticam epistolarum Pauli sententiam'.

text was not sufficient. Learning had to go hand in hand with understanding; knowledge with the practical application of the scriptural precepts in the daily life of a theologian. The student was to embrace all that 'makes morals, either to root out vices or to gather virtues', Smyth emphasised.[47] Consonant with his remaining exegetical work, pastoral formation and the academic study of divinity also went together.[48] His students were not only to become good exegetes but good catholic priests. The *studium theologicum* was principally concerned with the exploration and exegesis of Scripture. From their study, from comparing the obscure with the evident and the unknown with the familiar, the new theologians were to gain deeper insights into their faith.[49] He pointed out that, 'if afterwards, if he ... shall commit to memory what is to be built up and clearly endeavour to understand, he will demand a summary of learning from time to time, as if his learning were to be examined'.[50]

3.3. *The Biblical Canon*

Thus equipped for his studies, the Benedictine de Bar took down two further tables of introductory comments which, all entered on the same page, probably formed part of the same lectures.[51] In them Smyth outlined the criteria employed for the composition of the biblical canon. This was a consideration very much in keeping with his other hermeneutic concerns. Before any biblical text could be interpreted, a binding decision had to be taken as to which books bore authentic testimony to the Word of God, and which could only be affirmed as building up the Christian faith by their moral or ethical example. The question about whether or

---

[47] Ibid: 'ad mores facit, vel vitia extirpanda, & virtutes comparandas'.

[48] See de Bar, Bibliothèque municipale de la Ville de Douai, MS 57, 29 v: annotations on 1 Cor 11.

[49] Here Smyth's own perception echoes those of late medieval predecessors; see Gabriel Biel's exposition on the subject, in: G. Biel, *Epitome et collectionem ex Occamo circa quattuor sententiarum libros*, Tübingen, 1501, 3 sent., dist. 24, q. un., a. 2, concl. 6.

[50] De Bar, Bibliothèque municipale de la Ville de Douai, MS 57, unpaginated inlay, recto: 'Si posteaquam ... memoriae mandare profecit aedificanda, & plane profecit intelligenda aliquotius quasi sit examinanda exigat profectum eruditionis'.

[51] De Bar, Bibliothèque municipale de la Ville de Douai, MS 57, unpaginated inlay, recto.

not a book could be accepted into the biblical canon preoccupied the bishops at Trent in the middle of the sixteenth century as much as it had concerned exegetes such as Erasmus and Cajetan nearly three decades earlier.[52] Smyth thought the subject important enough to devote considerable time to elaborating on the four *modi canonici* received by the church.

Smyth followed a traditional patristic definition of canonicity, very similar to Jerome's. Jerome held that while some deuterocanonical books, such as Wisdom, Ecclesiasticus, Judith and Tobit should be read for edification, they did not enjoy canonical authority.[53] Contemporary biblical scholars on the whole agreed that the church was particularly indebted to Jerome 'for distinguishing canonical from non-canonical books'.[54] Smyth shared this opinion and adopted Jerome's *modi* for his own teaching. Each distinctive *modus* had shaped the biblical canon. Among those, apostolic tradition ranked highest. In the very beginning, the Apostles themselves had identified scriptures now considered canonical (*per traditionem apostolicam*).[55] They had either written, cited or approved them by inspiration of supernatural charisma. It had been confirmed by the testimony of martyrs; later, patristic writers had shaped its adoption in their rejection of heresy (*diffudius elicuerunt*).[56] Their judgement had subsequently been confirmed (*per oecumenica concilia*), although Smyth urged caution in accepting their judgement too readily.[57] He elaborated that

---

[52] Cf. Cajetan (1639), 5.130ff.

[53] Jerome listed Esther among the deuterocanonical books, a book later added to the canon, cf. his preface to Proverbs, cited in H. F. D. Sparks, ed., *Novum Testamentum secundum editionem s. Hieronymi I-III*, Oxford, 1959; for an introduction to the life and work of Jerome, see J. N. D. Kelly, *Jerome: His Life, Writings and Controversies*, London, 1975.

[54] De Bar, Bibliothèque municipale de la Ville de Douai, MS 57, unpaginated inlay, verso: 'propter discretos ab eodem libros canonicos a non canonicis'. This view resembles Cajetan's commentary on Heb closely; cf. Cajetan (1639), 5.329: 'Since we follow the rule of Jerome, we shall not err in our determining canonical books, since we consider those books which he separated from the Canon to be extracanonical' (Quoniam Hieronymum sortiri sumus regulam ne erramus in discretione librorum canonicorum, nam quos ille a canonicis discrevit, extra canonem habemus).

[55] De Bar, Bibliothèque municipale de la Ville de Douai, MS 57, unpaginated inlay, verso.

[56] Ibid.

[57] Ibid.

while councils had met 'with the authority of Scripture', the primacy of Peter authorised the infallible magisterium of the Latin Church to exercise the same rights as bishops assembled at ecumenical councils: a view shared by the Fathers at Trent.[58] Smyth put magisterial authority on a par with patristic evidence: the authority of the pope to settle disputes on the validity of Scripture was equal to patristic tradition and conciliar decisions, he stated in accordance with earlier exegetes such as Cajetan.[59]

In conclusion, Smyth proceeded to explain on what ground apocryphal texts could be excluded from the corpus of Scripture. He made clear that, despite the fact that some texts had fulfilled one or more of the criteria which justified inclusion in the canon noted above, some texts had not been given a place in the canon after all. He referred in particular to the *prophetia Enoch* (*quod apocrypha est*) which, while quoted by the Apostle Jude in Jude 1.14, had not been accepted among canonical writings. Again, Smyth enjoined his students to caution: 'Quotations in Holy Scripture are not adequate to prove that it is authentic Scripture'.[60]

4.1. Smyth's Hermeneutical Method

The sixteenth century saw a remarkable expansion in biblical scholarship, not only in the refinement of exegetical skills, but also in the endeavour to produce as close a Latin translation of the original Greek and Hebrew texts of the New Testament and Old Testament as possible. From the publication of the Gutenberg Bible (c. 1452) until the resolution of the council of Trent nearly a century later to produce a single, unified, improved Latin text of

---

[58] Ibid: 'in auctoritate scripturae'; cf. Görres-Gesellschaft, ed., *Concilium Tridentinum*, Freiburg im Breisgau, 1901—, (cited as: CT), Sessions 3 and 4 [=CT 1.36-40].

[59] Cajetan (1532), letter dedicatory: the Holy Father had the right of 'censure of the teachers whose publications are legally submitted. For nothing is trustworthy in the Church of Christ which does not square with the doctrine of the Apostolic See' (censurae doctorum quorumque documenta iure subduntur. ... Nihil enim in Christi Ecclesia tutum est quod apostolicae sedis doctrinae non quadrat).

[60] De Bar, Bibliothèque municipale de la Ville de Douai, MS 57, unpaginated inlay, verso: 'Citationes in S. Scripturam non sunt efficaces ad probandum Scripturam esse authenticam'.

the Bible, numerous scholars devoted their philological and theological skills to this end.[61] Following Lorenzo Valla's groundbreaking critique of traditional translations which led to the preparation of a new Latin text,[62] more and more catholic scholars took it upon themselves to improve the fifth-century translation of the Vulgate by critical textual study.[63] Most notable among them was Desiderius Erasmus.[64] His revision of the Vulgate, first published in 1516 and revised in 1522, set out to correct 'clearly erroneous passages' (*loci manifeste depravati*) in Jerome's text. Despite substantial criticism from Sorbonne theologians in 1526, it became a text widely acknowledged not only for its textual subtlety (*textus elegantissimus*), but also for its scholarly corrections.[65] Both exegetes and compilers of later translations into Latin made extensive use of Erasmus' text and *Annotationes*.[66] It is noteworthy, therefore, that his translation was not used as a basis for biblical lectures at Douai where, in accordance with the judgement of prominent conservative Leuven lecturers and, more significantly, recent council rulings, Jerome's text was given preference.[67]

---

[61] On 17 March 1546, CT 1.36: 'The first offence is to possess differing editions of Holy Scripture and to seek to use them as genuine for public readings, debates, expositions and preaching' (Primus abusus est habere varias editiones Sacrae Scripturae et illis velle uti pro authenticis in publicis lectionibus, disputationibus, expositionibus et praedicationibus).

[62] For a scholarly edition of Valla's text see A. Perosa, ed., *Collatio Novi Testamenti*, Firenze, 1970.

[63] The Dominican Albert de Castello, for instance, produced a new edition of the Vulgate text in 1511 while Jacques Lefèvre d'Etaples provided two new Latin translations, one of the Psalter (1509) and another on the Pauline Epistles (1512); see also B. Metzger, *The Text of the New Testament: Its Transmission, Corruption and Restoration*, Oxford, 1968, 98-106; I. Backus, *Renaissance Quarterly* 51 (1998), 1169-1198: 'Renaissance Attitudes to New Testament Apocryphal Writings: Jacques Lefèvre d'Etaples and his Epigones'; and G. Bédouelle, *Lefèvre d'Etaples et l'Intelligence des Ecritures*, Genève, 1976.

[64] For Erasmus' Vulgate translation see in particular E. Rummel, *Erasmus' 'Annotations' on the New Testament: From Philologist to Theologian*, Toronto, 1986, 3-35 and 89-122, and H. J. de Jonge, *Journal of Theological Studies* 35 (1984), 394-400: 'Novum Testamentum a nobis versum: The Essence of Erasmus' edition of the New Testament'.

[65] Cf. Vosté (1934), 459.

[66] Vosté (1934), 466-472.

[67] For the Leuven preference of the Vulgate over and above new translations of the Bible, cf. Titelmans (1529), a v r: 'Jacques Lefèvre d'Etaples and Erasmus of Rotterdam endeavoured to create a new version [of the New Testament] from the Greek source. ... It is certain enough that because of this hate and contempt against the interpretation of the Church was incited among the unskilled and the

94   CHAPTER TWO

But catholic scholars were not only concerned with the philological precision that led to an accurate Latin translation of scripture. They also set new standards in biblical exegesis. While scholastic method still knew the traditional four *sensus* of biblical exegesis, in the course of the sixteenth century the literal interpretation of the text slowly superseded the three other *sensus*.[68] In his Douai lectures, Smyth essentially adopted a similar system to that favoured by Cajetan who, in his commentary on the Gospels, had strongly advocated the new hermeneutic programme: 'consider, careful reader, the text of the Gospel: and consider yourself according to the Gospel, not the Gospel according to your own opinion'.[69] Likewise, Smyth emphasised that it was the text which 'brings the faithful to the meaning' rather than the students' abilities which led to understanding.[70] The use of exegetical methods akin to those of Cajetan (a scholar who, despite his orthodoxy, was often accused of excessive humanism), rather than those of his conservative scholastic Leuven colleagues, once more underlines Smyth's modern approach to biblical studies.

However, while Cajetan and, to a certain degree Erasmus, chiefly propagated the *sensus litteralis* in their exegetical work, traces of the late medieval hermeneutic system still lingered in Smyth's exposition. In his introductory lectures he still identified

---

common man unaware of the opinion of scholars. While this version was criticised—which is proved by the reaction of so many—they seemed to change it at a whim; they judged it worthy of no consideration, but rather considered it condemnable and, beyond that, negligible' (Iacobus Stapulensis atque Erasmus Roterodamus nouam insuper tentauerunt de graeco fonte uersionem [Novi Testamenti] facere. ... Hinc uero, illud apud imperitos & expers iudicij literatorum uulgus erga Ecclesiasticam interpretationem odium & plane contemptum extorta fuisse, satis est euidens: dum eam quam a tantis uiris coargui, reprehendi, taxari atque pro libitio immutari uidebant, nulla dignam existimatione iudicarent, sed contemnendam potius censerent, & prorsus negligendam); for the rulings of Trent, see CT 1.48-49.

[68] For the fourfold *sensus* (i.e. the literal sense, the allegorical sense, the anagogical sense, the moral or tropological sense), see for instance B. Smalley, *Speculum* 6 (1931), 60-76: 'Stephen Langton and the Four Senses of Scripture'; H. Caplan, *Speculum* 4 (1929), 282-90: 'The Four Senses of Scriptural Interpretation'; E. v. Dobschütz, *Zum vierfachen Schriftsinn. Die Geschichte einer Theorie*, Berlin, 1921, 1-13.

[69] Cajetan (1532), XVIII r: 'considera prudens lector evangelii textum: et teipsum evangelio non evangelium tuo accommodata sensui'.

[70] De Bar, Bibliothèque municipale de la Ville de Douai, MS 57, unpaginated inlay, verso: 'doceret fideles ... ad sensu'.

the four ancient *sensus* (1) as the manner by which 'you are able to understand the mysteries of heaven'; (2) as the inspiration received 'when, in their Christian life, men demand true understanding from God by prayers offered'; (3) the future hope that the sense 'will be revealed by the exactness of human understanding'; (4) the moral guidance by which 'human pride' is reined.[71] The application of Scripture for the development of Christian doctrine is still standard practice, even though direct allegorical exposition has long been since eschewed. Smyth, however, often went beyond the mere adoption of scriptural precepts into the doctrinal framework and propagated forcefully the adoption of allegorical or tropological interpretations of the text. The moral and doctrinal precepts which could be drawn from Scripture were as important for Smyth as the clarification and understanding of its literal meaning. This is consonant with much of Smyth's earlier doctrinal and catechetical teaching, and is reflected particularly in his two vernacular works on the eucharist and the *Bouclier of the Catholike Fayth*.[72]

Not only Smyth's lectures bear testimony to his lingering predilection for scholastic hermeneutics. His evangelical opponents also frequently accused him of overly allegorical interpretations in his published works. What his evangelical opposition regarded as one of his greatest weaknesses, however, was regarded as an invaluable asset by both his catholic superiors and his later biographers. In a letter to her brother Philip II of Spain, the regent of the Low Countries, Margaret of Parma, described the efforts of the *premier lecteur* as contributing considerably to the building-up of the catholic faith at Douai.[73] A later catholic biographer regretted in particular the fact that Smyth's exegetical lectures were cut short by his untimely death. By his orthodox teaching, 'when he had spent a year in this office with the greatest success he left, in his

---

[71] Ibid: 'a mysteriorum intelligentia ... vobis est posse'; 'ut homines Christiana vita de orationibus supplicentibus a deo postulant veram intelligentiam'; 'humanis intellectis euoluetur a fastidio'; 'superbia humana'.

[72] R. Smyth, *A Bouclier of the Catholike Fayth of Christes Church, conteynyng diuers matters now of late called into controversy, by the newe gospellers. Made by R. Smith*, London, 1554.

[73] Gachard (1881), 2.419.

public writings, clear testimonies of his integrity against those who spread heresies in his time'.[74]

4.2. Smyth's Exegesis of 1 Corinthians 10 and 11

Among the most prominent testimonies composed to refute contemporary evangelical doctrine were Smyth's eucharistic writings. The conviction that Christ continually offered Himself fully in bread and wine for humankind captivated Smyth throughout his life and led to numerous publications in defence of the sacrament. Just as he employed his extensive theological expertise and exegetical skill to defend 'the chiefest and the most weighty matters of our religion and fayth ... [now] called into question, babled, talked and tangled upon' in his books; in his lectures on the same subject the rejection of evangelical doctrine and the preparation of his ordained students for their priestly life also went hand in hand.[75]

The interpretations of 1 Cor 10.16f and 1 Cor 11.24f are among the few extensive stretches of text the Benedictine monk gleaned exclusively from Smyth's lectures. As Smyth had lectured chiefly on the Gospels and only dealt with three Pauline epistles during the course of 1562-1563, most entries in the second volume of de Bar's annotated study Bible must be attributed to later lecturers. De Bar's own testimony suggests that only the exegetical treatment of 1 and 2 Cor derived from Smyth's lectures.[76] The interpretation of 1 Cor is restricted to the eucharistic pericopae in chapters 10 and 11, as well as 1 Cor 3.12, and an isolated commentary on 1 Cor 7.16. The two eucharistic pericopae provide the only extended commentary on the epistle. Smyth's fervent concern for the eucharist radiates through de Bar's notes, who provides a vivid record of his lecturer's views.

Smyth's exposition of the eucharistic pericopae at Douai lends itself well to direct comparison with earlier catholic exegetes. In

---

[74] Foppens (1739), 2.1069-1070: 'in munere cum annum jam paulo minus felicissime versatus esset, praeclaraque ingenii monumenta contra grassantes sui temporis haereses publicis mandata litteris reliquisset'.

[75] Smyth (1546¹), 2 v.

[76] For instance de Bar, Bibliothèque municipale de la Ville de Douai, MS 57, notes on 30 v.

this study, the commentaries of Aquinas, Erasmus, Cajetan and Titelmans were chosen as benchmarks, to offer a comprehensive range of catholic theological opinion for comparison.[77] The monumental commentary on the Pauline epistles composed by Aquinas in the late 1260s was still a favourite among sixteenth-century biblical scholars. The fine copy preserved in Cambridge University Library, for instance, is littered with comments by its evidently catholic sixteenth-century owner. The later proprietor of the book, a seventeenth-century Anglican bishop of Lichfield, also added his own extensive marginalia.[78] Erasmus' *Annotationes*, on the other hand, were not held in quite the same universal esteem. Titelmans' slighting dismissal of Erasmus' *Annotationes* as superfluous insights is countered by the general respect paid by evangelical scholars.[79] Similarly, Cajetan's 1529 commentary was not uncontroversial, either. Censure of his biblical exposition came from various sources, among which Ambrosius Catharinus' condemnation was the most prominent.[80] The doctors of the Sorbonne could only be deterred from severe censure of Cajetan's work by the personal intervention of pope Clement VII in 1533. While he was regarded as a faithful exponent of Aquinas, his biblical interpretation was not beyond suspicion. Undoubtedly one of the foremost scholastic theologians of his day, his critics regarded his exegetical work as too humanist and too similar to contemporary heretics, in particular those whom Cajetan sought to refute.[81] The last com-

---

[77] The comparative interpretations derive from Thomas Aquinas, *Diui Thomae Aquinatis in omnes beati Pauli Apostoli epistolas commentaria*, Paris, 1541; Erasmus (1519), in: J. Leclerc, ed., *Desiderii Erasmi Roterodami opera omnia*, Leiden, 1703-1706, 9-10; Cajetan (1639), 5 and Titelmans (1540).

[78] W. Pye, and J. Hackett, bishop of Lichfield (1661-1671); Cambridge University Library, P * 7.35 (B).

[79] See Titelmans (1529), a v v. The fact that Titelmans based his entire work on an imagined disputation between Lefèvre, Erasmus and himself demonstrates his bias amply. Erasmus was not sparing in his criticism of the Leuven *praelector*, either, when he wrote to a friend: 'There is at Louvain a certain Titelmans ... prodigious in his boasting and more impudent loquaciousness', quoted in: Allen (1906-1958), 8.406.

[80] For the controversy with Catharinus, see L. Scheffczyk, ed., *Wahrheit und Verkündigung*, München, 1967, 551-577: U. Horst OP, 'Der Streit um die Heilige Schrift zwischen Kardinal Cajetan und Ambrosius Catharinus'.

[81] For a concise English summary of the Sorbonne criticism, see for instance J. Wicks SJ, ed., *Cajetan responds. A reader in Reformation Controversy*, Washington DC, 1978, 34: 'The Sorbonne masters charged Cajetan with imprudently taking these notions [i.e. his interpretations] from Erasmus or even Luther'.

mentary to feature as a yardstick of theological opinion was not controversial at all, but a fine example of conventional orthodoxy. Frans Titelmans' exegetical writings not only made a strong case against the use of primary texts other than the Vulgate in biblical exegesis, but also countered the literal interpretation of Scripture by his traditional tropological exegesis.[82] While his commentary on the Pauline epistles shared the same catholic orthodoxy generally associated with Aquinas' work, it did not share its lofty graciousness. A modern commentator points out: 'Titelmans shows us that not every teacher at the trilingual college at Louvain was an enlightened scholar'.[83] Seen at best as conservative fervour, at worst as narrow-minded piety, the work has been chosen to represent the Leuven school, of which both Titelmans and Smyth were distinguished exponents.

Smyth began his exposition of 1 Cor 10.16f by a close analysis of the idea of Christ as the spiritual rock.[84] Unlike Titelmans who began his exposition of the eucharistic pericopae by a pious narrative of the arrest in the garden Gethsemane, Smyth chose to draw logical parallels between the Covenent of God with the people of Israel, and that instituted by Christ at the last supper which superseded it; a common theme in his earlier eucharistic writings.[85] Smyth not only strongly emphasised the common nature of the two Covenents, he also made use of his exegesis for a strong affirmation of the Petrine primacy, when he elaborated: 'our Fathers used to drink ... not from the material in that rock, from which dripped water, but from the spiritual in it, which came from God: this rock was the Spirit of God; or Christ!'[86] The rock in question both provided continuity between the earliest rock of salvation, the foundation stone on which the children of Israel were to erect a godly commonwealth, and the rock on which the

---

[82] For instance Titelmans (1529), b vij r.
[83] T. H. L. Parker, *Commentaries on the Epistle to the Romans, 1532-1542*, Edinburgh, 1986, 13.
[84] 1 Cor 10.3: 'All ate the same spiritual food, and all drank the same spiritual drink, since they drank from the spiritual rock which followed them, and that rock was Christ'.
[85] Titelmans (1540), K i r.
[86] De Bar, Bibliothèque municipale de la Ville de Douai, MS 57, notes on 29 r: 'Bibebant patres ... non de materiali illa petra, ex qua manauerant aquae, sed de spirituali illa quae deo consequabantur, quae dei spiritus petra erat, vel Christus!'

church was founded (cf. Deut 32.15). It also represented the basis of all sacred ecclesiastical authority, the rock of Peter (cf. Mt 16.18): 'This is Paul's meaning: he calls Christ a rock not in terms of an allegory but speaks of the spiritual rock which ... was granted to them'.[87]

Smyth next considered at some length the meaning of the 'spiritual drink' in 1 Cor 10.4 and proceeded to link it to Paul's rhetorical interjection 'the blessing-cup, which we bless, is it not a sharing in the blood of Christ?' (1 Cor 10.16). He instructed his students that the passage did not refer to a mere spiritual communication with a distant Christ, seated locally at the right hand of the Father, but rather a direct participation in the person of the divine Son and His merits. He pointed out in particular that the 'communion of blood surely is communion. It is Christ Himself!'[88] By receiving the gifts of the altar, the communicant partook directly and bodily in Christ Himself and shared in the life of the hypostatic union, a conviction Smyth had derived from Fisher's *De Veritate Corporis et Sanguinis Christi in Eucharistia* and propagated passionately in his *Assertion and Defence of the Sacrament of the Aulter*.[89] This mediation of divine grace could not be said to depend on the feeble faith of the believer, but rested on Christ alone. Likewise, the nature of the officiating priest alone did not bring about this communication of divine grace, but solely the fact that he stood in Christ's stead and performed the consecration *in persona Christi*.[90] Once more, Smyth took every opportunity to instil the Douai seminarians with his catholic understanding of the sacerdotal office: 'we priests bless this cup, although its consecration only occurs by divine grace'.[91] No priest was able to accomplish this by human achievement; the act of consecration was entirely dependent on his office as a *minister Christi*. The priest had been called to

---

[87] Ibid: 'Hic est Pauli sensus, quum appellat Christus petra, non in figuram ... sed petram istam spiritualis quae ... eis sequebantur'.

[88] De Bar, Bibliothèque municipale de la Ville de Douai, MS 57, notes on 29 v: 'Communicatio sanguinis nonne est communicatio. Christus est!'

[89] J. Fisher, *De Veritate Corporis et Sanguinis Christi in Eucharistia*, Köln, 1527, xxx v; R. Smyth, *Assertion and Defence of the Sacrament of the Aulter*, London, 1546, 53 v, 70 r.

[90] Ibid.

[91] Ibid: 'eum [calicem] benedicimus, nos sacerdotes, quamquam eius consecratio ista fiat sola diuina virtute'.

this office by Christ and exercised it on His behalf. It was Christ who effected the consecration through His sacerdotal ministers: 'If priests are able to carry out that consecration, it is not in their own stead, but in the person of Christ, as they are His ministers'.[92] Just as he had argued in his *Assertion and Defence* sixteen years earlier that 'the priest is but a minister, and God is the worker and bringer of the thinge to passe', so here he held that, despite their human frailty, priests were central to bringing about the participation in the person of Christ Himself.[93] Smyth followed broadly the opinion of Aquinas who, in his own commentary on 1 Cor 10-11, emphasised repeatedly that 'while the priest consecrates, he does not bring forth those words as if he was himself, but as if he consecrated in Christ's stead'.[94] The strong emphasis on the effects of grace which resulted from the sacerdotal offering also finds its roots in Aquinas' teaching.[95] In words echoing closely his earlier convictions, Smyth told a student body that consisted chiefly of religious and candidates for the priesthood that there could be no question of a memorial meal, in which a congregation commemorated the last supper.[96] 'We priests' offer the sacrament for the sake of human salvation: 'this is our gratitude for God's graciousness'.[97]

Smyth next considered the tradition Paul had received concerning the eucharist (1 Cor 11.23ff). He did not make use of his reflection for a further excursus on the subject of apostolic tradition, but provided a straightforward interpretation of the passage. His exegesis lacked the pious overtones of Titelmans' commentary. Rather than offer a spiritual (or mystical) interpretation of the text which, like that of his Leuven colleague, emphasised the merit of

---

[92] Ibid: 'Si sacerdotes proficiant consecratio ista nonne persona propria, sed in persona Christi, quum sunt eius ministri'.
[93] Smyth (1546), 204 r.
[94] Aquinas (1541), 97 r: 'quia sacerdos dum consecrat, non profert ista verba quasi persona sua, sed quasi ex persona Christi consecrat'.
[95] Aquinas (1541), 96 v: 'firstly ... His strength and merit operate through the sacraments; secondly, because the sacrament is sanctified through His name' (primo ... virtus & meritum eius operetur in sacramentis' and 'secundum quod in nomine eius sanctificetur sacramentum).
[96] For instance Smyth (1546), 57 r.
[97] Ibid: 'hoc est gratiarum actio quam offeremus pro gratiarum actione dei'; see his earlier teaching, in: Smyth (1546^2), lxvi r-lxvi v: 'the death and passion of Christ is remembered ... by offeringe of his verye bodye and bloude in sacrifice, whiche is done of the preist at his masse'.

'this sacrament of the passion and death of the Lord', he restricted himself to an exposition of the sacramental theology illuminated by the passage.[98] He set out by comparing the dominical words in 1 Cor with their Gospel counterpart, Mt 26.26. All was just 'as in Matthew', Smyth made clear and in an isolated aside added that the purpose of the sacramental self-giving of Christ was the 'restoration of mankind'; this mirrored Aquinas who held that 'Christ re-creates to bring about salvation ... according to His own substance'.[99]

The verse-by-verse exegesis that follows is the only such example in de Bar's notes deriving entirely from Smyth's lectures.[100] The three isolated exegetical passages from the first epistle to the Corinthians only ever dealt with individual verses (1 Cor 3.12; 1 Cor 8.4; 1 Cor 10.2). In his exegesis of 1 Cor 11, however, Smyth elaborated carefully on the meaning of the four successive verses that make up one of the earliest testimonies to the eucharist (1 Cor 11.23-27).[101] Like Aquinas or Cajetan, he took a single verse, or a fragment of a verse, and then proceeded to offer his interpretation. In his study Bible, the student distinguished the Pauline passages from Smyth's exegesis by switching to an italic hand.[102]

Making use of Erasmus' annotations of 1 Cor 11.24 rather than the *glossa ordinaria* for his revision of Jerome's text, Smyth began his exposition by reiterating how Christ broke (*fregit*, rather than *tradit*) the bread before consecrating it 'and He gave it: because

---

[98] Titelmans (1540), K i r: 'sacramentum hoc passionis ac mortis domini'.
[99] De Bar, Bibliothèque municipale de la ville de Douai, MS 57, notes on 30 v; Aquinas (1541), 96 v: 'Christus regenerat ad salutem ... secundum suam substantiam'.
[100] De Bar identified the author of the exegetical notes by the recurring prefix 'Smtt:'. As shown above, 3, at Douai Smyth's name was often spelled 'Smytthaeus' when latinised.
[101] 1 Cor 11.23-27: 'For I received from the Lord what I also handed on to you, that the Lord Jesus on the night when He was betrayed took a loaf of bread, and when He had given thanks, He broke it and said, "This is my body that is for you. Do this in remembrance of me". In the same way He took the cup also, after supper, saying, "This cup is the new covenant in my blood. Do this, as often as you drink it, in remembrance of me". For as often as you eat this bread and drink the cup, you proclaim the Lord's death until He comes. Whoever, therefore, eats the bread or drinks the cup of the Lord in an unworthy manner will be answerable for the body and blood of the Lord'.
[102] De Bar's own italics have been maintained in quotation.

He consecrated this form which He gave to us, for *this is my body*.[103] Smyth's interpretation principally followed those of his catholic predecessors, such as for instance Cajetan and, closer to his own convictions, Aquinas. His exegesis commenced with a confession of his faith in the corporeal presence of Christ in the elements of the sacrament. Unlike Titelmans, Smyth not only stated his beliefs but supported his credo by his ensuing exegesis in which he recalled his earlier teaching:[104] 'Paul did not say "here", that is, "in this place", but "this", that means "this substance", showing that He was going to give them what He had in His hands'.[105] In emphasising that Jesus had provided a clear point of reference by holding the eucharistic bread in His hands, Smyth echoed Cajetan very closely, who had stated: 'it is therefore the most accurate and truest sense "this", that is, "this substance", by demonstrating what He was holding in His hands'.[106] Elaborating further, Smyth argued that the bread offered at the last supper was not merely a metaphor for the body of Christ, but 'an absolute substance by its nature', the very essence of Christ's being.[107] Christ did not say 'this

---

[103] De Bar, Bibliothèque municipale de la ville de Douai, MS 57, notes on 30 v; cf. Leclerc (1703-1706), 10.1566b: 'et dedit: quia consecravit hac forma, quid nobis dedit, *hoc enim est corpus meum*'.

[104] De Bar, Bibliothèque municipale de la ville de Douai, MS 57, notes on 30 v: 'I am unaware of the metaphor here, I adore the truth' (hic metaphoram agnosco, solam veritatem adoro); cf. for instance Titelmans (1540), K i r.

[105] De Bar, Bibliothèque municipale de la ville de Douai, MS 57, notes on 30 v: 'Non dixit Paulus "hic", id est, "in hoc loco", sed "hoc", id est, "hic substantia", demonstrans quod in manibus habet se illis daturum'; cf. Smyth (1546¹), 15 r: '[Here, Christ was] not poyntynge, as some folishe fantasticall fooles do fantasyse, to his visible body, then sittynge at the table, which had ben a fond trifling, & iugglyng, but poynting, and meaning of that his body, which then was really conteined vnder the forme of bread, then gyven there to his apostles'.

[106] Cajetan (1639), 4.118: 'est itaque propiissimus et verissimus sensus, *hoc*, id est, haec substantia demonstrando quod habebat in manibus'; Aquinas (1540), 97 r has: 'The change of the bread into the Body of Christ occurs at the end of the duration of these words ... for they bring about the form, by signifying the sacraments, and therefore what occurs next is that, at the beginning of the saying it is pointed out that the body of Christ is not present, but only the substance of bread—which is initiated by the pronoun "hoc", when it is a demonstrative of the substance' (Conuersio enim panis in corpus Christi fit in termino prolationis horum verborum. ... Formae enim sacramentorum significando efficiunt, & ideo sequitur quod in principo locutionis quando dicitur quod non sit ibi corpus Christi sed sola substantia panis quae demonstratur per hoc pronomen 'hoc', quando est demonstratium substantiae).

[107] De Bar, Bibliothèque municipale de la ville de Douai, MS 57, notes on 30 v: 'substantiam absolutam ex suo qualitate'.

was, but *this is*, for this *is body*, not *bread*. But *my body*.'[108] Here, de Bar's notes convey some of the vigour of the lectures in which the central premise was reiterated again and again: 'not bread, but my body'.[109] This concern is in full accordance with Smyth's previous teaching on the eucharist, in which he devoted page after page to affirm the corporeal presence of Christ in the sacrament of the altar. In 1546 he wrote:

> Now if the very true bodye & bloud of christ were giuen & shed really, & in dede (as euery true christen man doth perfectlye beleue they were, & so confesse without any scruple or doubt) then doth it folow, that the body and blud which christ at his last supper gaue to his apostles vnder the forme of bread & wine (& so in the sacrament, to be received & taken) they were trulye, & in dede, without any doubt, the very body & bloud of our sayd sauyour Jesus christ.[110]

The debate over the corporeal presence was pivotal in catholic interpretations of the eucharistic pericopae. The general agreement between Smyth and Cajetan suggests that Smyth relied on the cardinal's writings in addition to his own dogmatic works. This is confirmed by his direct reference to Cajetan, the sole quotation from a contemporary author in an analysis based almost entirely on biblical or patristic citations.[111] In his commentary on the Pauline epistles Cajetan had explained the correlation between signified and signifier in a manner closely akin to Smyth's teaching at Douai:

> *It is*, not *it appears*, not *it signifies*, but *it is my body*, not the *body of bread*. Know that saying of the Lord is *not only a pronouncement of truth* (for it is most true that this substance is the body of Christ), *but it is also a deed of signified truth*. And because of this, the pronoun *hoc* does not indicate the bread nor the body of Christ, but this substance.[112]

---

[108] De Bar, Bibliothèque municipale de la ville de Douai, MS 57, notes on 30 v: 'hic *erat*, sed *est*, hic enim *est corpus*, non *panis*. Sed *meum corpus*'.
[109] De Bar, Bibliothèque municipale de la ville de Douai, MS 57, notes on 30 v: 'non panis, sed meum corpus'
[110] Smyth (1546¹), 15 r.
[111] De Bar, Bibliothèque municipale de la ville de Douai, MS 57, notes on 30 v: 'At this point Cajetan refers to the early Church' (Caietanus in hunc locum refert in primitiva ecclesia), cf. Cajetan (1639), 4.119.
[112] Cajetan (1639), 4.118, the italics are his own: '*Est*, non *apparet*, non *significat*, sed *est Corpus meum*, non *corpus panis*. Ubi scito quod sermo iste dominicus est *non*

However, while Cajetan and, at some considerable length, Aquinas elaborated on the corporeal presence of Christ under the elements of bread and wine, Smyth did not use his lectures to discuss the doctrine of transubstantiation as much as to point to the role of the priest in effecting this change.[113] He proceeded to tell his students that in Christ's commandment to His Apostles, 'do this as a memorial to me' He also 'charged the priests'.[114] The statement that Christ had commanded the eucharist to be celebrated in His memory was of greatest importance to the Benedictine notator. It is revealing that priests is the one word underlined in the entire exegetical section. Christ had not only commanded His Apostles to 'do this' but His mandate clearly applied to their successors also, Smyth had told his students. Christ had instructed them

> to do what He did, because as He used expressly to do, so He gave them the commandment to do, which is this: He taught His priests with direct words. He did not say 'say this', but 'do what is done'.[115]

Once again, Smyth's emphasis is on the sacerdotal action rather than the words of institution themselves (although only the words of Christ effect the consecration proper), a concern first expressed in his *Assertion and Defence*. Christ's actions at the last supper, that is, 'He took bread, gave thanks, broke and consecrated, and gave what was consecrated to His companions', were unalterable instructions left to the church which had charged her priests to repeat them.[116] Smyth regarded the last supper not only as the institution of the eucharist itself, but more so as the dominical ordination, and first instruction, of a new apostolic priesthood. His students were called to share this priesthood, which he had embraced himself.

---

solum enuntiativus veritatis (verissimum enim est quod haec substantia est corpus Christi), *sed est etiam factivus veritatis significatae*. Et propterea pronomen *hoc* non demonstrat panem neque corpus Christi—sed hanc substantiam'.

[113] For Aquinas' definition of the doctrine of transubstantiation, see Aquinas (1540), 97 r; for Cajetan's, see Cajetan (1639), 4.118.

[114] De Bar, Bibliothèque municipale de la ville de Douai, MS 57, notes on 30 v: 'praescripsit sacerdotibus'.

[115] De Bar, Bibliothèque municipale de la ville de Douai, MS 57, notes on 30 v: 'facere quam fecit, quod expressius ut facebat, dedit illis exhortationem facendi, hoc est; sacerdotes expressis verbis educavit. Non dixit "hoc dicite", sed "facite quod fieri" '.

[116] Ibid: 'accepit panem, gratias agit, fregit, et consecravit, consecratum famulos dedit', cf. 1 Cor 11.24.

In his exegesis of 1 Cor 11.23-27 Smyth clearly built on the work of his catholic predecessors. The links with the hermeneutic work of Cajetan and Aquinas have been documented. The fact that Smyth did not make much use of Erasmus' work is not surprising, considering the council rulings on the use of new translations and the general catholic misgivings about Erasmus' work.[117] The considerable difference between Frans Titelmans' work and Smyth's lectures is more surprising. Both share a similar scholastic education and the same conservative convictions; yet in his lectures Smyth resorted neither to overt late scholastic expressions of piety nor to the explicit usage of the same fourfold *sensus* on which he had elaborated in his introductory lectures on the epistle to the Romans. Smyth did not merely reproduce, or protect old methodologies. While he showed a close affinity with scholastic doctrine, he incorporated his views subtly into the context of his exegetical work, again following the example first propagated by Cajetan.

5. 'LA VRAYE RELIGION ET FOY CATHOLIQUE'

De Bar's notes from the first Douai lecture series on the New Testament reinforce the view that Smyth was an experienced teacher and pedagogue. Making use of advanced contemporary teaching methods such as wall-charts and tables, his most outstanding quality was the fact that he regarded the needs of the student body as the guiding principle for his hermeneutic work. In 1563, Smyth had been lecturing for nearly thirty years. His last (and only documented) lecture series demonstrates that the ideas he passed on to his students were shaped as much by their concerns as by his own convictions. The fact that in his exegetical lectures Smyth revealed conservative doctrinal views and their scholastic roots, does not startle. It is not surprising, either, that his lectures often took up arguments from his written works.[118] The secret of Smyth's successful lecturing was the same as in his earlier

---

[117] Cf. CT 1.36-49.

[118] In 1547 he had been forced to recant that Christ's priesthood was derived from Aaron; he later composed a succinct work devoted to the priesthood of Christ, R. Smyth, *Defensio comprehendaria, et orthodoxa, sacri externi, et visibili Iesu Christi sacerdotii. Cui addita est sacratorum Catholicae Ecclesiae altarium*, Leuven, 1562.

writings: he tailored his views to the needs of the audience he addressed. In his lectures, this is shown clearly in the continual emphasis on the sacerdotal office and the tasks to which priests, indeed 'we priests', were called.[119] Smyth's lectures evidently inspired his students, as François de Bar's thorough and dynamic notes reflect 450 years after they had first been taken. Both the lecturer's deep convictions and his apparent enthusiasm are captured in de Bar's notes. It seems that Smyth's exposition enabled his students to become a living part of the pericope that was being explained, emulating the first disciples gathered around the eucharistic table to celebrate the mysteries Christ had commanded His Apostles to perpetuate.

Smyth not only extracted theological doctrine by scriptural exegesis, but developed a eucharistic theology that centred on his students' role in the eucharistic mysteries rather than the Apostles assembled round their master (Mt 26.18ff). Seen through the eyes of his student it was the circle of disciples assembled at Douai that was at the heart of Smyth's hermeneutic method. His message to them was distinct, and of lasting appeal. Just as Christ had charged the Apostles, so they also were commanded 'do what is done' (*facite, quod fieri*).[120] In his lectures on 1 Cor 11 this message is reiterated in manifold forms. His students were called to stand in Christ's stead to offer the sacrifice of salvation, their lecturer emphasised again and again. It must have been Smyth's teaching fervour rather than his theological method, that led the fathers of the university of Douai to appoint the elderly English exile to be their first *premier lecteur* of holy scripture.

François de Bar's notes on the New Testament are a treasure. They grant insights into the teaching at a catholic university at the outset of the catholic reformation which could not simply be gained from lecture schedules, published commentaries, or doctrinal works dating from the same period.[121] By transferring his exact commentary from his note-book to his study Bible, the Benedictine monk not only recorded the exegesis of his lecturer,

---

[119] De Bar, Bibliothèque municipale de la ville de Douai, MS 57, notes on 29 v.
[120] De Bar, Bibliothèque municipale de la ville de Douai, MS 57, notes on 30 v.
[121] Such a lecture schedule survives in Archives de Douai, Layette 172. Indicating a number of exegetical lectures for the year 1562 from the *Collegium linguarum* at Tournai, no notes of the actual lectures survive.

but also provided a lively impression of Smyth's fundamental theological concerns. Smyth had been appointed to the newly created chair in scripture for two reasons: his faultless catholic credentials and his popularity among his colleagues and students at Leuven.[122] Both are reflected in the lecture notes taken at his exegetical discussions. By his exegesis he set out as much to prepare his students for ordination as to defend orthodox catholic doctrines. For the English exile these two concerns always went hand in hand.[123] Based on contemporary hermeneutic principles such as those propagated by Cajetan in the 1520s, and the pedagogic theories developed by Agricola and Mosellanus, Smyth's biblical exegesis at Douai not only served the purpose of gaining a deeper understanding of scripture, but was in itself a tool to defend traditional doctrine.[124] In his interpretation of scripture Smyth was not breaking new ground. His theological views did not differ greatly from those of earlier orthodox scholars. Yet his teaching methods and his fervour in bringing traditional catholic teaching alive by his interpretation of the bible were remarkable.

For the catholic scholars at Douai the study of divinity was primarily a preparation for the priesthood or religious life.[125] The appointment in 1562 of a weathered yet still enthusiastic teacher to the chair of scriptural interpretation underlines the belief that the study of the biblical text, and not the analysis of patristic or scholastic sources, was at the very heart of the *studium theologicum* in the newly-founded catholic university. Douai was to be a fortress against the threat of theological innovations from evangelicals in France.[126] François de Bar's exegetical annotations demonstrate Smyth's conviction that this faith was to be found in the contemplation of scripture and its application in the sacerdotal office.

---

[122] Cf. Gachard (1881), 2.419f.
[123] Cf. above, 2.2.
[124] Cf. Cajetan (1532), XVIII r.
[125] Cf. C. Haigh, ed., *The English Reformation Revised*, Cambridge, 1987, 176-208: idem, 'The continuity of catholicism in the English reformation', 195-196.
[126] Archives de Douai, Layette 172.

CHAPTER THREE

JUSTIFICATION

The question of how sinners were made righteous was a life-long concern for Richard Smyth. At the outset of his academic career, he made the doctrine the subject of a number of prominent sermons at Oxford (1536).[1] In 1539 he gave a university lecture series on justification and two years later attacked Alexander Seton's evangelical doctrine of justification publicly at St Anthony's Budge Row.[2] At his recantation in 1547, Smyth tried to tone down his thoroughly catholic understanding of justification by an equivocation:

> I vnderstande that some were offended with me for certain pointes on my doctrine ... reportinnge that I shulde say that these iii thinges were required to justification: the promis of god, the merites of christ: the worthiness of the person: and the worthiness of the worke. The truth is they dyd mistake me, applieng those wordes to our justification whiche I spake of the workes of a man that is alreadie justified.[3]

In autumn 1550 he consolidated his catholic understanding of justification in print. His first publication on the doctrine is a treatise which approached the topic through the eyes of a systematic theologian rather than the polemicist. The work belies its belligerent title *Diatriba de hominis ivstificatione aduersus Petrum Martyrem Vermelium.*[4] Rather than a vilification of Peter Martyr, it is

---

[1] Oxford University Archives, Registrum Cancellarii Ꮒ, Registrum Curiae Cancellarii, Ab An. 1527 ad An. 1543, f. 366 r; *Letters and Papers Foreign and Domestic Henry VIII*, 10.396.

[2] J. Foxe, *Actes and Monumentes of these latter and perillous dayes ... newly recognised and inlarged by the Authour*, London, 1583, 2.1205-1206 [=J. Foxe, *The Acts and monuments of John Foxe. New and complete edition, with a preliminary dissertation by G. Townsend. Edited by S. R. Cattley*, London, 1837-1841, 5.448-450].

[3] R. Smyth, *A godly and faythfull Retraction made by R. Smyth. Reuokyng certeyn errors in some of hys books*, London, 1547, E iii r-v.

[4] R. Smyth, *Diatriba de hominis ivstificatione aedita Oxoniae in Anglia, anno à natiuitate Domini nostri Iesu Christi. 1550. Mense Februario aduersus Petrum Martyrem Vermelium, olim Carthusianum Lucensem in Italia, nunc apostata in Anglia Oxoniae, acerrimum improborum dogmatum assertorem, sed imperitum, & impudentem cum primis*, Leuven, 1550.

a well-crafted piece of theological reasoning. An excursus delivered during an earlier Oxford lecture-series on Romans (derided in a later account by his evangelical successor for its alleged theological inconsistencies) formed the basis for the publication.[5] Unlike his polemic works this reflection on justification lacks the incessant salvos on Vermigli. Instead, the reader is offered a systematic introduction to the doctrine of salvation extracted, like most of Smyth's work, from Scripture and the Fathers. At times the work's theological rigour is complemented by exquisite prose that verges on the poetic. As a theological deliberation and linguistically, the *Diatriba* must be ranked among Smyth's finest achievements and was regarded as such by his catholic contemporaries.[6]

Smyth did not approach the subject again until his return to England. Once safely re-established at Oxford he devoted a small part of his *A Bouclier of the catholike fayth of Christes church* to the causes of justification and supererogatory works.[7] The *Bouclier* set out to repeal the doctrines of 'Peter Martyr & the other new brethren', in particular their insistence 'that no worke pleseth god, except it be commanded of hym to bee doone'.[8] In this popular exposition, written to confute the 'new preachers euil sermons and wicked books', Smyth attacked the evangelical rejection of human co-operation in justification propagated in the Edwardian Catechism.[9] He emphasised that it was not only 'lawfull and good' to put one's trust in good works, but that works of supererogation would merit a sure and certain reward.[10]

His third and last contribution to this controversy is contained in an extensive refutation of Melanchthon's *Loci Communes*,

---

[5] P. M. Vermigli, *D. Petri Martyris Vermilii Florentini divinarum Literarum in Schola Tigurina Professoris Oxoniensis duos Libellos de Caelibatu Sacerdotum, & Votis Monasticis, Nunc Primum in lucé edita*, Basel, 1559, 643.

[6] Quoted for instance by Ruard Tapper in his *Articuli*; cf. R. Tapper, *Rvardi Tapperi ab Enchvsia, Ecclesiae Collegiatae S. Petri Lovanienis Decani, et eivsdem florentissimae academiae cancellarii, omnia, qvae heberi potvervnt Opera*, Köln, 1582, 2.78 a.

[7] R. Smyth, *A bouclier of the catholike fayth of Christes church, conteynyng diuers matters now of late called into controuersy, by the newe gospellers. Made by Richard Smith, doctour of diuinitee, & the Quenes hyghnes Reader of the same in her graces vniuersite of Oxford*, London, 1554.

[8] Smyth (1555), B ii r.

[9] Smyth (1555), ∀, vi v; cf. D. G. Selwyn, ed., *A Catechism set forth by Thomas Cranmer from the Nuremberg Catechism translated into Latin by Justus Jonas*, Appleford, 1978.

[10] Smyth (1555), E vi r.

composed at Douai during the last year of his life.[11] In choosing as his target 'the leader of Martin Luther's cause' Smyth addressed himself once more to the Lutheran position of justification by faith as defined in the *Confessio Augustana* (1535) and Melanchthon's *Loci Communes* (1543).[12] He attacked the evangelical view that 'we cannot gain remission of sins and justification in the presence of God ... but that we shall be pardoned and justified before God freely', and urged instead the benefits of freely-willed good works and traditional catholic sacramental theology.[13] He reiterated his belief of a lifetime that man could only ever be justified if he consented to four preconditions: membership of the catholic church, a certain belief in Christ, participation in the sacrament of reconciliation, and the strict observance of God's commandments.[14]

1.1. The Medieval Understanding of Justification

The church held that while man bears the sin of Adam as well as his own, he was enabled to share in Christ's resurrection to eternal life by confessing his belief in Christ's merits. In order to acquire this salvation, he first had to show regret for past sins and make satisfaction for his offences. Man did not only need to make up for

---

[11] R. Smyth, *Refvtatio Locorum communiorum Theologicorvm, Philippi Melanchthonis, Germani, M. Lutheri discipuli primarij dedicata Principum Philippo, Regi Hispaniarum &c.*, Douai, 1563; cf. Ph. Melanchthon, *The Common Places 1543*, St Louis MO, 1992.

[12] Smyth (1563), B 3 r-v: 'Martini Lutheri coryphaeus'; cf. *Confessio Augustana* (cited as: CA), in: E. Kinder and K. Haendler, edd., *Lutherisches Bekenntnis. Eine Auswahl aus den Bekenntnisschriften der evangelisch-lutherischen Kirche*, Berlin and Hamburg, 1962. An English rendition can be found in: *Concordia Triglotta: Libri symbolici Ecclesiae Lutheranae Germanice, Latine, Anglice*, St Louis MO, 1921.

[13] CA 56.2-7: 'Daß wir Vergebung der Sunde und Gerechigkeit vor Gott nicht erlangen mogen, ... sondern daß wir Vergebung der Sunde bekommen und vor Gott gerecht werden' (homines non possint iustificari coram Deo ... sed gratia iustificantur); CA 94.9ff: 'That we gain grace before God by faith and not by works' (Daß wir vor Gott Gnade erlangen durch Glauben und nicht durch Werk; nos coram Deo iustificari per fidem in Christum).

[14] Smyth (1563), 41 r: 'To members of the catholic church, to true believers in Christ, to penitents by rite and to those who observe the rest which scripture teaches is to be observed by them' (Esse in ecclesia catholica, verè credentibus in Christum, ritè poenitentibus, et caetera obseruationibus quae scriptura docet illis obseruanda).

his individual sins but was also required to pay the price for the sin of Adam, which he had inherited at birth.[15] Both his own sinfulness and the burden of original sin passed on from his first forebear compelled the Christian to strive continually towards a state of grace that would enable him to become justified and ultimately merit eternal life.[16]

The question of whether and how believers were able to co-operate in the work of their salvation was not restricted to the reformation era. Ever since Augustine's rejection of Pelagianism, the interaction of grace, faith and works had been laid down in a complex form that was expanded and developed throughout the writings of the later Fathers.[17] What had been a delicate order uniting the human will with the sacraments of the church and the workings of the Holy Spirit had, by the time of the publication of Smyth's first work on the subject (1550), often been reduced to a crude juxtaposition of faith versus works. Either faith in Christ's redemptive work alone, or the interaction of faith and human works were seen as contributing factors to human justification.[18] This reformation polarisation reduced the medieval trinity of co-

---

[15] Tertullian held that at the moment of baptism the stain of original sin was washed away. Baptism was no antidote to sin, it required human co-operation by works of charity; cf. Tertullian, *De baptismo*, 15.3 [=A. Reifferscheid, G. Wissowa, edd., *Corpus Scriptorum Ecclesiaticorum Latinorum*, Wien, 1890, (cited as: CSEL), 20.215]: 'semel delicata abluuntur'. For Aquinas, the first infusion of the habit of grace occurred at baptism. The newly-baptised were granted the *habitus virtutum* that rendered them capable of performing works of charity towards their own salvation. This habit had to be maintained by satisfaction for venial sins committed. It was obliterated by mortal sin; cf. G. Philips, *L'Union personelle avec le Dieu vivant. Essai sur l'origine et le sens de la grâce créée*, Bibliotheca Ephemeridum Theologicarum Lovaniensium 36, Leuven, 1989, 42-46.

[16] For a summary of medieval doctrines of satisfaction and justification, see A. E. McGrath, *Iustitia Dei, A history of the Christian Doctrine of Justification: The Beginnings to the Reformation*, Cambridge, 1993, 1.43-1.50.

[17] First taken up in the decrees of the council of Carthage (418), canons 3-5; cf. H. Denzinger and A. Schönmetzer, edd., *Enchiridion symbolorum et definitionum de rebus fidei et morum: Kompendium der Glaubensbekenntnisse und kirchlichen Lehrentscheidungen*, Freiburg im Breisgau and Rome, [38]1999 (cited as: DS), 103-105 and DS 176f, 180.

[18] Both positions can be derived from scripture; cf. especially Rom 4.3, 5.1 etc. and Jas 2.14-17. Many Fathers, in particular Augustine, saw faith (the human *fides quae creditur* or *assensus*) as a human-willed contribution towards salvation. Faith can therefore also be an 'act' or a 'work', cf. in particular Augustine, *Enchiridion de fide, spe et charitate*, 20.7, in: J. P. Migne, *Patrologia cursus completus, series Latina*, Paris, 1844-1855 (cited as: PL), 40.242.

operating faith, the sacraments and works of grace to a contentious and futile debate.[19]

The scholastic economy of salvation laid down that in order to acquire justification man needed to co-operate actively in the process of justification. No-one was able to please God solely by faith in Christ's saving work.[20] Faith that assented to the act of salvation (*fides formata*) needed to be inspired by charity, the principal agent of salvation according to Aquinas.[21] Only faith combined with charity was worthy of the increase of grace that ultimately led to the building up of merit towards eternal life.[22] For Aquinas, the act of justification was initiated by God, who sought to work salvation through imparting grace to believers. God's infusion of grace moved believers to a response of faith that allowed them to perform the works of charity which merited salvation.[23]

For medieval theologians justification was an internal process that prepared the soul to build up merit towards salvation, rather than the external deliverance from sin in the sight of God propagated by the Lutheran reformation.[24] Aquinas described it as 'a

---

[19] Cf. for instance Hugh of Saint-Victor, *De Sacramentibus legis naturalis et scriptae*, PL 176.35: 'What are those things without which salvation cannot be gained from the beginning? They are three: that is, faith, and the sacraments of faith, and good works' (Quae sunt illa sine quibus salus ab initio haberi non potuit? Tria sunt, id est fides, et sacramenta fidei, et opera bona).

[20] Hugh of Saint-Victor, ibid., stated that 'no-one can please God by faith alone unless charity is allied to him' (sola fide nemo potest placere Deo nisi charitas illi sociata fuerit).

[21] Th. Aquinas, *Summa Theologica*, London, 1963-1966 (cited as: ST), 3a, q. 49, a. 1: 'But through charity we acquire the forgiveness of sinners' (Per charitatem autem consequimur veniam peccatorum).

[22] ST 1a.2ae, q. 114, a. 4: 'And for this reason, the reward of eternal life depends firstly on charity' (Et ideo meritum vitae aeternae primo pertinet ad caritatem).

[23] Philips (1989), 161: 'Simply because of their profound and free nature, life and charity bring about a lasting disposition on which man can call freely. ... God's beloved is not merely put in action ... he himself also acts (non tantum agitur sed agit)' (La vie et l'amour, précisément à cause de leur profondeur et de leur liberté, exigent une disposition permanente à laquelle l'homme puisse faire appel à volonté. ... L'amant de Dieu n'est pas seulement mis en action ... il agit lui-même—*non tantum agitur sed agit*).

[24] Bonaventure, *Sententiae* 4, dist. 17, p. 1, d. 4, in: Bonaventure, *Sancti Bonaventurae Opera Omnia*, Quaracchi, 1882-1902: 'preparatio animae'; contrasted by CA 94.9: 'We are justified in the sight of God through faith in Christ' (Nos coram Deo iustificari per fidem in Christum).

change from the condition of injustice to the condition of justice' or a complete remission of sin which prepared man to merit his own salvation through the increase of works of grace.[25] Once in a state of grace (and therefore able to perform works that counted towards their justification), believers were able to cherish a reasonable hope that God would be a gracious judge.[26]

Christians were not able to perform meritorious works entirely on their own. Every work of charity was initiated by grace, and could never be claimed as something the person 'owned' or 'willed' himself. A modern Roman Catholic expositor, Gérard Philips, points out:

> It is not the accomplishment which bestows dignity, ... but rather the state of being which determines and sublimates both action and person. The object does not convey merit, rather the subject.[27]

According to scholastic concepts of justification, the believer was only entitled to receive the merit earned for his act of charity because he was himself co-operating in the work of salvation through the agency of the Holy Spirit.[28] Works that involved human co-operation with the infused habit of grace presupposed a state of grace and were therefore deemed to be of higher intrinsic value than those bestowed on the believer without the gift of grace.[29] Indeed, most classic scholastics—Aquinas, Bonaventure

---

[25] ST 1a.2ae, q. 113, a. 1: 'Transmutatio quaedam de statu iniustitiae ad statum iustitiae'.

[26] Cf. ST 1a.2ae, q. 114, a. 8 ad 3: 'By whatever meritorious act a man deserves an increase of grace' (Quolibet actu meritorio meretur homo augmentum gratiae).

[27] Philips (1989), 161: 'C'est ne pas "l'avoir" qui l'emporte en dignité ... c'est "l'être", qui qualifie et qui dignifie notre action et notre personne. L'objet n'est pas méritoire, mais le sujet'.

[28] Cf. ST 3a, q. 19, a. 3.

[29] Ibid.: 'What is achieved by merit is considered more noble in itself than what is achieved without merit' (Nude nobilius habetur id quod habetur per meritum quam id quod habetur sine merito); Philips (1989), 161: 'Merit does not consist of the cost of the work performed, but of the worth of its agent. ... It is the raising up of the person, not the payment of petty cash for some merchandise' (Le mérite ne consiste pas dans le prix de l'oeuvre produite, mais dans la valeur de celui qui est l'auteur. ... Il est une dignification de la personne, non le payement de gros sous pour une marchandise). V. Pnür, *Einig in der Rechtfertigungslehre? Die Rechtfertigungslehre der Confessio Augustana (1530) und die Stellungnahme der katholischen Kontroverstheologen zwischen 1530 und 1535*, Wiesbaden, 1970, 37, cited this Lutheran derision: 'Whoever merits *de condigno* no longer depends on the mediation of Christ, since his works already were the price which merited life

and Richard of Middleton—held that works performed without the assistance of grace neither contributed to justification nor the remission of sins, since they lacked the assistance of the Holy Spirit.[30] The Austrian Roman Catholic Johann Heinz elaborates:

> By the moving of the Holy Spirit on free will, a qualitatively corresponding relationship between free will and the reward arises in the meritorious act. The Holy Spirit as *causa prima* [first cause] bestows on the work a supernatural worth which God must reward in a supernatural way, if He is just to Himself. As *causa secunda* [second cause], the believer has a share in it. As he co-operates with the Holy Spirit, he ... becomes worthy (*condigno*) of the reward. As to whom the merit really belongs—the Holy Spirit or the person—it is important to grasp that the works would be impossible without the Spirit, but it is the person ... who earns it.[31]

1.2. Objections to the Late Medieval Understanding of Satisfaction and Merit

At the centre of the reformation debate about justification was a quarrel about human co-operation in the process of salvation. For their late medieval predecessors, justification involved as much making satisfaction (*satisfactio*, i.e. the *operatio ad placandam divinam offensam*) as it depended on living up to the potential God had granted the believer (*facientibus quod in se est*).[32] This is reflected particularly well in Gabriel Biel's commentary on the *Sentences*, which adopted a clear Scotist definition of justification and satisfaction:

---

eternal' (Wer *de condigno* verdiene, der habe Christus als Mittler nicht mehr nötig, da seine Werke selber der Preis seien, für den ewiges Leben geschuldet wird).

[30] Scotus held that works performed in the state of mortal sin, or *extra charitatem*, merited neither the habit of grace nor salvation, but nonetheless cancelled the sin committed; J. Duns Scotus, in: L. Wadding OFM, ed. et al., *Quaestiones quodlibetales*, Lyon, 1639, 6.15, 1.

[31] J. Heinz, *Justification and Merit: Luther versus Catholicism*, Andrews University Seminary Doctoral Dissertation Series 8, Berrien Springs MI, 1984, 148f; i.e. not *valor operis* but *valor personae operantis*, see especially, ST 1a.2ae, q. 114, a. 3.

[32] For a history of the development of the doctrine 'facientibus quod in se est Deus non denegat gratiam', see McGrath (1993), 1.83-90; for a more critical reflection on the doctrine, see H. A. Oberman, *Harvard Theological Review* 55 (1962), 317-342: 'Facientibus quod in se est Deus non denegat gratiam'.

> In the following satisfaction is defined rigorously in order to distinguish it from the other aspects of penitence. Scotus describes it in this way: satisfaction is the laborious external working, or a freely accepted penalty to punish one's own sins, to placate divine wrath. It is suffering or freely chosen punishment both in a sinful state, or a state of forgiveness.[33]

For late medieval theologians satisfaction, the precondition of grace, was 'an exerting external action through which laborious internal action is excluded ... as is the ensuing contrition and sadness'.[34] All works held to contribute towards justification stemmed from this external operation. Among them, Biel emphasised in particular fasting, prayer and almsgiving; a triad that echoed apostolic principles and was later endorsed by most sixteenth-century catholic theologians and the council of Trent.[35] Man was not only obliged to undertake these works in order to live up to his promises but, by that operation and the assistance of the infused habit of grace, was also enabled to contribute towards his own salvation.[36]

Luther was still able to embrace the late medieval formula '*facientibus quod in se est*' when he commenced his lectures on the Psalter (1513-1515), yet he already had put himself at odds with certain scholastics by his strong rejection of the doctrine of merit

---

[33] G. Biel, *Epitome et Collectorium ex Occamo circa quattuor sententiarum libros*, Basel, 1508, reprint Frankfurt am Main, 1965, 1. IV d. 16 q. 2 a 1 not. 1 lit. C.: 'Secundo modo accipitur satisfactio stricte ut distinguitur contra alias partes penitencie: et sic eam describit Scotus. Satisfactio est operatio exterior laboriosa seu penalis voluntarie assumpta ad puniendum peccatum commissum a se: et ad placandam divinam offensam: vel est passio aut pena voluntarie tolerata in ordine ad peccatum vel peccati remissionem'.

[34] Biel (1965), ibid.: 'Operatio exterior laboriosa per quod excluditur actio laboriosa interior ... ut est contritio et tristia eam consequens'.

[35] Ac 10.2-4; cf. Pfnür (1970), 41: fasting included 'everything that ... promotes self-discipline' (all das ... was der Selbstzucht dient), i.e. vigils, pilgrimages, flagellation, etc. Prayer was interpreted to imply meditations, reading of scripture, sermons, study of divinity, disputations and the refutation of heretics. Almsgiving was striving for justice, and the giving up of temporary goods for 'the least of these who are members of my family' (Mt 25.49).

[36] See especially Pfnür (1970), § 2 aa.

ex condigno.[37] In a subsequent lecture series on the epistle to the Romans (1515-1516), he began to develop his own concept of justification.[38] Justification was seen as an external process imposed on the believer (*iustificatio extranea*), rather than the internal and spiritual process upheld by earlier scholastic exponents. Believers were able to contribute nothing at all to their own salvation and needed to rely entirely on God to bestow both the will and His grace to accomplish good works.[39] In Luther's theo-logy there was no room for works *de congruo* performed without the aid of the Holy Spirit.[40] For Luther, Aquinas's 'agent of salvation', *fides formata* (faith perfected by the infusion of charity), had become an 'accursed word'.[41]

In a second step, Luther turned to the scholastic doctrine of human co-operation. The habit of grace infused into the human soul to bring forth works worthy of merit, at the heart of medieval systems of justification, came under attack. While Luther had originally acknowledged a human component in salvation, he soon dismissed the concept of a habit of grace as artificial pedantry. Faith was no longer seen as an essential factor that was preparatory to all works of grace, but as the essential trust (*credulitas, fiducia*) in the salvific act of Christ. By the time of his 1515-1516 lectures on Romans the reformer had become indignant at the late medieval notion that believers were able to love God by their own power (*ex puris naturalibus*) and thereby were able to procure grace towards their own salvation. On the contrary, man was entirely passive in the process of salvation and not able to contribute anything of

---

[37] Cf. M. Luther, *Werke. Kritische Gesamtausgabe*, Weimar, 1883— (cited as: WA), 4.262.3-7: 'For everyone who asks, receives etc. From this, teachers correctly deduce that, without fail, God gives grace to the man who does what is in himself. While man is not able to prepare himself for grace through his own self-worth, because it is unobtainable he may prepare himself well *de congruo* according to the promise of God and His covenant of mercy' (Omnis enim qui petit, accipit etc. Hinc recte dicunt doctores, quod homini facienti quod in se est, deus infallibiliter dat gratiam, et licet non de condigno sese possit ad gratiam praeparare, quia est incomparabilis, tamen bene de congruo propter promissionem istam dei et pactum misericordiae), see also WA 4.312, 38-41.

[38] For a succinct analysis of Luther's theology of justification, see A. E. McGrath, *Luther's Theology of the Cross. Martin Luther's theological breakthrough*, Oxford, 1993, 93-128; 153-161.

[39] E.g. WA 56.398, 11-14.

[40] Cf. WA 56.172, 10-11.

[41] WA 56.287, 17-24: 'maledictum vocabulum'.

worth to justification.[42] In his lectures, he rejected the mainstream late medieval understanding of human co-operation in the process of salvation as Pelagianism:[43]

> Those merits of which they speak are mere figments of the imagination: that, by his own strength, a man can love God more than anything and perform the works of the actions that are commanded by his own nature. However, those are never performed according to the will of the One who commanded them, since they are not performed in grace. O fools, o rotten theologians.[44]

By 1519 and his published commentary on Galatians, Luther had reached the logical terminus of his departure from the late medieval understanding of justification, and openly began to equate the merits of works of grace (*meritum gratiae*) with the faith of the individual.[45] Only a few months later, in his *De libertate Christiana* (1520), he had publicly expounded the position with which he is generally associated—justification by faith alone:[46] Believers were not able to merit anything by their own powers, neither *de congruo* nor *de condigno*, such distinctions were nothing but the 'tricks of Satan'.[47] Everything needful for salvation stemmed from Christ Himself. Whoever held that to be true would naturally perform

---

[42] In the 'autobiographical fragment' prefacing his *Opera Latina*, Wittenberg, 1545 [=WA 54.185ff], Luther declared: 'How does the just man live by the gift of God? Surely by faith ... in the justice of God, which is obviously a passive justice by which a merciful God justifies us by faith' (Qua iustus dono Dei vivit, nempe ex fide ... iustitiam Dei, scilicet passivam, qua nos Deus misericors iustificat per fidem).

[43] For the strict Thomist and neo-Augustinian doctrines of justification left untouched by Luther's 1516-1517 lectures, see C. Mayer, W. Eckermann, edd. et al., *Scientia Augustiana. Festschrift Zumkeller*, Würzburg, 1975, 349-394: H. A. Oberman, '"Tuus sum, salvum me fac". Augustinréveil zwischen Renaissance und Reformation'; for the *schola Augustina nova*, see idem, *Masters of the Reformation: The Emergence of a New Intellectual Climate in Europe*, Cambridge, 1981, 64-110.

[44] WA 56.502, 14-20: 'Quodcirca merita deliria sunt, que dicuntur, quod homo ex viribus suis possit deum diligere super omnia et facere opera precepti secundum substantiam facti, sed non ad intentionem precipientis, quia non in gratia. O stulti, o Sawtheologen'.

[45] WA 2.46, 6: 'faith is all merit' (fides est meritum totum), cf. especially WA 2.511, 27-8 and WA 2.537, 2-3.

[46] M. Luther, *De libertate Christiana dissertatio*, Nürnberg, 1524 [=WA 7.49-73].

[47] WA 40/1.223, 14-20; cf. WA 40/1.224, 25-28: 'ludibriae satanae'.

good works, for 'a good and pious man performs good and pious works'.[48]

Rejecting a system based on meriting salvation, Luther instead upheld the doctrine of external salvation imparted to the believer by God. God justified mankind by the gift of His grace. By this gift sinners received forgiveness and the need for human satisfaction was nullified. Similarly, 'sanctification' meant that God healed human sinfulness by accepting sinners in an act they could never have achieved themselves. This underlies Luther's principle *simul iustus et peccator*: no Christian could ever be proclaimed entirely righteous since he continually needed to grow in faith in order to attain a state of righteousness. Analogously, he could only ever be deemed sinner in part because he had 'taken up the battle with sin, and is continually challenged to overcome sin within and outside himself'.[49] A modern German Lutheran commentator summarised the reformer's position succinctly:

> It is God's prerogative that justification can only ever be attained through Christ (*sola Christo*), by grace (*sola gratia*) and faith (*sola fide*) alone. It is the human prerogative vis-à-vis God that man is only ever able to attain a justification beyond his own capacities (*extra nos*) by faith (*sola fide*). His own good works are merely the fruit of this process (*fructus*). Sin, therefore, is to be seen as the exact mirror-image of the believer's relationship with God and his own self (*peccatum, radicale, personale*). It is thus that we perceive the centre and basis of justification as nothing but the Gospel of Jesus Christ.[50]

---

[48] WA 7.30, 31-32: 'Eyn gutt frum man macht gutte frum werck'; a typical catholic position would be Fisher's 'a just man, by acting justly, gains further justification' (homo iustus iuste operando iustificatior evadit), J. Fisher, *Assertionis Lutheranae Confutatio*, Antwerpen, 1523, 1.26 r.
[49] Heinz (1984), 193.
[50] D. Lange et al., *Überholte Verurteilungen? Die Gegensätze von Rechtfertigung, Abendmahl und Amt zwischen dem Konzil von Trient und der Reformation—damals und heute*, Göttingen, 1991, 28: 'Dem Gottsein Gottes entspricht es, daß die Rechtfertigung allein durch Christus (*sola Christo*), allein aus Gnade (*sola gratia*) und allein im Glauben (*sola fide*) geschieht. Dem Menschsein des Menschen vor Gott entspricht es, daß er in der Rechtfertigung sein Heil außerhalb seiner (*extra nos*) im Glauben (*sola fide*) hat und seine eigenen Werke daraus nur folgen können (*fructus*) während umgekehrt die Sünde als wurzelhafte Verkehrung seines Abhängigkeitsverhältnisses zu Gott und damit auch seines Verhältnisses zu sich selbst zu bestimmen ist (*peccatum, radicale, personale*). In diesem Sinne muß verstanden sein, daß nichts anderes als das Evangelium von Jesus Christus Sache und Inhalt der Rechtfertigung ist'.

For Luther and his later followers justification at its most basic could be defined as the divine act of forgiveness for the sake of Jesus Christ.[51] External justification, initiated by God, reflected 'the Gospel of Jesus Christ' while any doctrine of human contribution in salvation, or even the notion of fulfilling divine ordinances, was seen as 'lex' (e.g. Rom 3.20), and therefore Pelagianism (*Selbstrechtfertigung*).[52] Believers were not able to contribute anything to their own salvation, still less to fulfil the law of God in order to placate or please Him. Only the 'Gospel', the message of Christ's redemptive death and claim for His saving justice, could confer righteousness.[53] Justifying righteousness was imputed to the sinner on account of his belief in the Gspel of salvation. This was an external process, *extra nos* and therefore *iustitia aliena*, extraneous righteousness.[54]

By the publication of the *Confessio Augustana* (1530) Luther, and with him Melanchthon (the target of Smyth's third publication on the subject), held a doctrine of justification diametrically opposed to that of the late medieval schoolmen. Salvation could be attained only through absolute faith (*fiducia*) in the promises of Christ, which in turn freed the believer from a false dependence on his own powers and inspired him to turn instead to God for his salvation. Lange added:

> Such faith can only ever be thought of as genuine confidence, if it is wholly based on Christ's Word. ... Christ acts on the life of the sinner by His spoken and sacramental Word, which man encounters externally.[55]

---

[51] Documented well in H. A. Oberman, *Harvard Theological Review* 59 (1966), 1-26: '"Iustitia Christi" and "Iustitia Dei". Luther and the Scholastic Doctrines of Justification'.

[52] Rom 3.20: 'No human being will be justified in His sight by deeds prescribed by the law'; for a modern perspective see Lange (1991), 27-29.

[53] E.g. CA 104.28ff: 'Wir glauben durch die Gnad unseres Herrn Jesu Christi selig zu werden' (*per gratiam Domini nostri Jesu Christi credimus salvari*); cf. M. Brecht, *Zeitschrift für Kirchengeschichte* 89 (1978), 45-77: 'Der rechtfertigende Glaube an das Evangelium von Jesus Christus als Mitte von Luthers Theologie'.

[54] E.g. CA 71.11-14: 'Das Evangelium lehrt nicht ein äußerlich, zeitlich, sondern innerlich, ewig Wesen der Gerechtigkeit' (*Evangelium tradit iustitiam aeternam cordis*).

[55] Lange (1991), 29: 'Solches Vertrauen bleibt reines Vertrauen nur dann, wenn es seinen Halt einzig und allein in Christi Wort findet. ... Christus handelt am Sünder durch das—mündliche und sakramentale—Wort, das dem Menschen von außen begegnet'.

It is the external word which renders the sinner at once justified in relationship to God and a sinner according to his deeds and life.[56] The believer can contribute nothing at all to his salvation. 'This passive reception should not be regarded in a merely mechanical way, or as a divine causal operation in humankind', Lange elaborated, 'rather, by this action a new identity is bestowed upon the recipient, his new and lasting reality in the eye of God'.[57] In Luther's theology of justification the correlation between faith and grace was set up as a check to ensure that no human work should ever be regarded as an additional means towards salvation.[58] As formalised in the *Confessio Augustana*, the Lutheran doctrine of justification was as far removed as possible from late medieval doctrine, and as such formed a favourite target of contemporary catholic theologians.[59]

2.1. Smyth's 'Diatriba de Hominis Iustificatione' (1550)

Smyth's 1550 publication primarily sought to address the doctrinal innovations in his home-country, rather than counter German teaching. The exile lamented that England had been corrupted 'wretchedly by the infection of many heresies' among which justification by faith featured prominently.[60] Out of this conviction he had put pen to paper previously and would do so again in refutation of the doctrines of the Edwardian religious

---

[56] Ibid.

[57] Lange (1991), 41: 'Diese Passivität darf aber nicht mechanistisch verstanden werden, im Sinne kausaler Einwirkung Gottes auf den Menschen. In diesem Geschehen [erhält] der Empfänger sich selbst neu und darin bleibend seine Wirklichkeit vor Gott'.

[58] For instance the identification of faith with charity or the three cardinal virtues. Any idea of 'responding love' (*fides caritate formata*), e.g. in DS 1531, was rejected; cf. *Apologia Confessionis Augustanae* (cited as: *Apologia*), 109-119, in: H. G. Pöhlmann, ed., *Die Bekenntnisschriften der evangelisch-lutherischen Kirche*, Gütersloh, 1987, 160-172.

[59] So for instance Cajetan, Cochlaeus, Dietenberger, Mensing, Rauch, Vehe, and Tapper; for an exhaustive survey of contemporary German catholic refutations see Pfnür (1970), §§ 14-19. For a succinct introduction, see H. Jedin, *Catholica* 21 (1967), 85-100: 'Wo sah die vortridentinische Kirche die Lehrdifferenzen mit Luther?'

[60] Smyth (1550), A iii v: 'multarum haereseon contagionibus miserrime'.

establishment.[61] From 1547 until 1553 and the publication of the distinctively reformed *Forty-Two Articles*, the English position was still influenced strongly by Luther and Melanchthon.[62] What Smyth had detected in the 'new' English teaching was the notion of justification by faith which he identified as the position of the Lutherans.[63] Finally, as so often in Smyth's case, the work was not only intended to be an exposition of sound catholic teaching, but also a sign of gratitude to a newly-gained patron. Smyth's latest 'best friend and friendliest of the best' was Ruard Tapper, inquisitor–general of the Habsburg Low Countries and chancellor of Leuven university.[64] The influential recipient of the book not only gave Smyth a platform from which to launch his polemics safely, but himself made good use of the work in a later defence of justification against evangelical opponents.[65]

In order to refute the view that man could be justified solely by faith, in his *Diatriba* Smyth provided the reader with a systematic analysis of the process of justification. The work gives a distinctive insight into the doctrinal views of English catholic theologians during the Edwardian reformation. Smyth set out to analyse the classic *topoi* of justification: he contrasted unformed faith with theological faith, defined the hope of grace, made a case for the merit of good works, and upheld the concepts of supererogatory

---

[61] Smyth (1550), A iii v: 'I wrote ... three books which strongly criticised the promoters of new and irreligious doctrines, and the advocates of heresy' (Scripsi ... tres libellos qui nouorum ac impiorum dogmatum promachis, accorypheis assertoribus vehementer displicuerunt), i.e. R. Smyth, *The assertion and defence of the sacramente of the aulter*, London, 1546; ibid., *A defence of the blessed Masse and the sacrifice thereof, prouynge that it is aualable bothe for the quycke and the dead*, London, 1546; ibid., *A brief treatyse settynge forth diuers truthes left to the Church by the apostles tradition*, London, 1547.

[62] Cf. E. C. S. Gibson, *The Thirty-Nine Articles of the Church of England*, London, 1896, 1.70-89, see particularly 12-29.

[63] E.g. Smyth (1550), 1 r, 2 v, 6 r, 38 r, 40 r, 60 r, etc. Smyth used the term 'Lutheran' to refer to evangelical doctrines in general.

[64] Smyth (1550), A iii r: 'amicorum optime & optimorum amicissime'.

[65] Tapper, (1582), 2.78 a; for Tapper's doctrine of justification, see esp. V. J. Peter, *The doctrine of Ruard Tapper (1487-1559) regarding original sin and justification*, Ph.D. dissertation, Pontificia Studiorum Universitas a S. Thoma Aquino in urbe, Rome, 1965; and J. Etienne, *Ruard Tapper, interprete catholique de la pensée protestante sur le Sacrement de penitence*, Leuven, 1954.

works, merit *de congruo*, and the sacrament of penance.[66] The *Diatriba* is a 'period piece'; largely though not entirely a didactic work, yet to a lesser extent also a work of polemic. It has its roots in late medieval scholasticism and seeks to defend the theology of the divine *pactum* (the soteriological framework within which man was enabled to contribute *quod in se est* to salvation) against contemporary evangelical innovations by constant reference to biblical and patristic sources.[67]

2.1.1. *Fiducia*

Smyth's chief criticism of the Lutheran position that a firm trust in the salvific work of Christ sufficed for justification was that it equated initial or unformed faith with *fiducia*—the Pauline 'faith working through love', a gift from God that caused man to be confident in faith and grow in charity.[68] Evangelical theologians frequently defined *fiducia* as the infallible, certain belief that God, for the sake of Christ, would no longer hold sins against the believer and thereby grant him eternal salvation. Smyth was convinced that it was impossible to be certain of salvation merely on the basis of a firm belief in the words and promises of God. In his view certainty of salvation could only be reached by the grace of direct divine revelation.[69] Faith in the promises of Christ was common to all believers: 'For which Christian does not believe that

---

[66] Smyth (1550), *causae iustificationis*: A iv v-1 r; *fides theologica*: 1 r-12 v; *fides informis*: 13 r-17 r; *opera*: 17 v-26 r; *meritum de congruo*: 26 v-39 v; *poenitentia*: 30 v-49 v; *opera poenitentiae*: 49 v-64 r; *conditiones iustificationis*: 64 v-71 v; *de timore*: 71 v-76 r; *de eleemosynae*: 76 v-'81 r' [=80 r]; *de oratione differens*: 80 r-'83 r' [=84 r]; *de confessione*: 84 v-91 r; *de ieiunio*: 91 v-92 r; *de spe veniae*: 92 v-93 r; *de remittendis proximis*: 93 v-101 r; *de baptismo*: 101 r-103 r; *de charitate*: 103 v-113 v; *opera supererogatoria*: 117 v-125 r; followed, as with most other works, by a lengthy set of practical test-cases or 'objections and responses'.

[67] For a succinct summary of the *pactum*, see Philips (1989), 186-188; Smyth maintained that the doctrine derived from Rom 10.14.

[68] Gal 5.6; Smyth (1550), 2 v.

[69] Smyth (1550), 2 v: 'To know with certainty that one pleases God, and that He forgives one's sins, is false' (Certo scire se Deo placere, illumque sibi noxas ignoscere, quam sit falsum); 'It is impossible to know for sure that one stands in the favour of God' (Ne posse certo scire se Deum habere propitium). This view is also shared by Fisher (1523), 1.33 r; cf. R. A. W. Rex, *The Theology of John Fisher*, Cambridge, 1991, 120f.

the promises of God and all His sayings are true?'[70] The key to human salvation could not depend on anything so brittle as the faith of the individual. Like Aquinas, Smyth was a firm believer that the process of salvation was initiated by God, the 'main initiator and effective cause' of justification, who moved man to share in the work of salvation through works of charity.[71] In a second step God would render them just, by the mediation of the merits of Christ to those who had previously been awarded the habit of grace and were able to demonstrate this by the fruit of their good works.[72] These received preconditions for salvation precluded any notion of justification by faith alone.[73]

Smyth held that Melanchthon in particular conflated the two stages of justification by equating unformed faith (*fides informata*) with confidence (*fiducia*).[74] In his seminal analysis of the catholic response to Melanchthon's *Apologia Confessionis Augustanae* the German Roman Catholic scholar Vinzenz Pfnür identifies this position as a common repartee.[75] In an unsuccessful attempt to reconcile the scholastic understanding with Melanchthon's doctrine, he dismisses these accusations as too simplistic:

> The Reformation statement *justification by faith alone* followed the same intentions as the scholastic notion of *justification by gratia creata*. Both underline that we are justified by the grace and mercy of God which we receive in fullness.[76]

---

[70] Smyth (1550), ibid.: 'Quis enim est inter Christianos, qui non credit Dei promissis ac vera esse quae is vnquam dixerit?; cf. Fisher (1523), 1.22 v-1.23 r.

[71] Smyth (1550), A iv v: 'Autor princeps & efficiens causa'; cf. Isa 43.25 and 50.8.

[72] Smyth (1550), ibid: 'God justifies alone by merit' (Deus iustificat ... solus meritorie [sic]); cf. Rom 3.24, 1 Tim 2.5.

[73] Smyth (1550), ibid: 'It is a great claim, indeed impertinent ... to state that it is faith alone that makes man just or unjust' (Magna constantia immo pertinacia ... solam fidem id esse, quo quis per se sit iustus et iniustus).

[74] Smyth (1550), 3 r, quotes Melanchthon: 'Justifying faith is confidence (fiducia), which is knowledge of Christ and of the will by which it desires and receives the promise from Christ, whether effected by character or deed, and it accepts both' (Fides iustificans est fiducia, quae noticiam de Christo, atque voluntatis seu habitum, seu actionem complectitur, qua vult, & accepit promissionem de Christo, & in illos acquiescit).

[75] Pfnür (1970), 153; cf. op. cit., 209, 213.

[76] Pfnür (1970), 152: 'Die reformatorische Ausdrucksweise: *Rechtfertigung durch den Glauben* verfolgt so dieselbe Intention wie die scholastische Formulierung: *Rechtfertigung durch die gratia creata*. In beiden Fällen geht es darum, zum Ausdruck zu bringen, daß wir durch die Güte und Barmherzigkeit Gottes, die uns ganz zuteil

Smyth held that justifying faith led to the building up of confidence (*fiducia*) which in turn brought about certainty of grace (*certitudo*). His position is both logically tenable and reflects orthodox teaching, especially when considering his strong conviction that it was impossible for justifying faith to generate itself: 'now if faith is confidence, then faith itself generates faith'.[77] Justifying faith could only be gained through the co-operation of unformed faith with good works, the love for God, and the keeping of his commandments.[78] Smyth concluded, 'I press on, unless I were to teach that faith is not confidence and no-one is permitted to be justified without that'.[79] *Fiducia* could not simply be held; the believer constantly needed to labour to reach and remain in this state.[80] If *fiducia* was based on previous good works anyone who, like Melanchthon, claimed that justifying faith was merely a habit requiring no human co-operation other than the acceptance of God's grace and promises, denied the distinctive function of the human will in salvation.[81] It was the human will that led the be-

---

wird, gerechtfertigt werden'; cf. the proposed compromise between evangelicals and conservatives at the diet of Augsburg, in: K. E. Förstermann, ed., *Urkundenbuch zu der Geschichte des Reichstages zu Augsburg im Jahre 1530*, Halle, 1833-1835, 2.227: 'Sins are forgiven *per gratiam gratum facientem, per fidem formaliter* and *per verbum et sacramenta instrumentaliter*' (Daß die Vergebung der Sünden sei per gratiam gratum facientem et fidem formaliter et per verbum et sacramenta instrumentaliter). Pfnür's view overlooked that the reformation statement intended to eliminate all human co-operation in salvation, while the scholastic doctrine did not.

[77] Smyth (1550), 3 v: 'Iam si fides fiducia esset, fides seipsam pareret'.

[78] Smyth (1550), ibid: 'Confidence stems from the good works of the pious' (Fiduciam gigni ex benefactis piorum); 4 r: 'He declares that confidence stems from the love of God and the keeping of His commandments' (Declarat fiduciam prognasci ex … dilectione Dei, atque obseruatione illius mandatorum).

[79] Smyth (1550), 4 v: 'Inculco, nisi vt persuadeam fidem non esse fiduciam, licet sine illa iustificari neminem posse', cf. Heb 4.16.

[80] Smyth (1550), 12 r: 'Confidence is not contained in present matters, but either in the present act and certainly the future' (Fiducia non est rei praesentiae, sed aut praesentis aut certe futurae).

[81] Smyth (1550), 5 v, referring to Melanchthon, *Apologia*, 172, 52ff; 172, 21ff, cf. 162, 42. In his *Assertion and Defence of the sacramente of the aulter. Compiled and made by mayster Richarde Smythe doctour of diuinitie, and reader of the kynges maiesties lesson in his graces vniuersitie of Oxforde, dedicate vnto his hyghnes, beynge the excellent and moost worthy defendour of Christes faythe*, London, 1546, he held: 'for there are only ii principall wayes to auoyde synne, the one by vertue, for the loue whereof, good men abstayne from synne, & ye other by ponishment, for feare whereof, vnthryftes & noughty packes, are kept vnder'. Pfnür (1970), 159, commented: 'In the *Apologia* Duns Scotus's doctrine of attrition [i.e. an imperfect natural form of repentance for sin out of fear of divine punishment] and Biel's strong emphasis

liever 'beyond true repentance and a pious state of mind, or rather love for God, and so the author [Melanchthon] cuts his throat with his own sword'.[82] Without the will to undertake good works for the sake of loving God faith was empty.[83]

In outlining the twofold process of justification Smyth reiterated his conviction that God was the origin of salvation. By granting faith to the believer, God allowed the individual to cherish a reasonable hope in salvation that, through the aid of his prayers and good works, he would eventually attain *fiducia*:

> This unformed faith is then given when God gives power to those who believe in His name to become children of God, so that they may obtain the help of God and the grace for which they beg.[84]

Under the terms of God's promises of salvation revealed to humankind (*diuinarum promissionum*), He would not refuse to impart Christ's merits to the believer once He had received the gift of *fiducia*. Smyth did not make much use of the late medieval language of the *pactum* but, unlike Fisher, clearly shared its concerns.[85] For Smyth, the basis of salvation was initial faith which

---

on human contrition [i.e. a perfect form of repentance for sin arising out of *amor amicitia*, the love of God, and the infusion of grace], as seen through the eyes of Biel, are contrasted by justification through ... faith alone' (Dem durch die Brille Biels gesehenen Attritionimus von Duns Skotus und dem Kontritionismus von Biel setzt die *Apologia* die Rechtfertigung ... durch den Glauben entgegen). For a summary of the respective positions, see J. Périnelle, OP, *L'Attrition d'après le Concile de Trente et d'après Saint Thomas d'Aquin*, Bibliothèque Thomiste 10, Paris, 1927.

[82] Smyth (1550), 5 v.: 'Citra poenitentiam veram, piumque affectum mentis, seu dilectionem erga Deum, vt autor ipse suo iuguletur gladio'. Fisher, *Public Record Office, State Papers 2/R*, 32 r, held that while *fiducia* was a gift from God it needed to be nourished 'show me ... works' (nobis tamen assentientibus et cooperantibus), cf. Rex (1991), 121.

[83] Smyth (1550), 15 r: 'ostende ... operibus', cf. Jas 2.14.

[84] Smyth (1550), 17 r: 'Haec fides informis tum data est, quando potestatem dedit Deus his, qui credunt in nomine eius, vt filij Dei fierent, vt qua auxilium Dei, & gratiam, implorantes impetrent'.

[85] Fisher (1523), 215 r: 'There are several among the debaters whose opinions I do not share, who think that the man who is in a state of mortal sin can act well and morally without the help of special grace and thereby can prepare himself, not by his own merit but hoping that God should give him grace *ex congruo*' (Ex disputatoribus nonnulli, quorum iudiciis ipse non subscribo, sentiant eum, qui mortali peccato gravatus sit, absque speciali auxilio gratiae, posse bene moraliter agere, ac proinde se praeparare posse, non quidem ut ex merito, sed ut ex congruo, deus ei sit daturus gratiam), cf. Rex (1991), 115: '[Fisher] explicitly

'is given first, so that the rest may be acquired subsequently'.[86] This was not only held by Augustine but implicit in Rom 10.14, on which he based most of his argument.[87] At the beginning of the journey of justification stood the gift of initial faith, granted by God to all the baptised. This gift constantly needed to be nourished and built up by prayer, or acts of charity, to be worthy of the second gift that God imparted—*fiducia*. Smyth concluded with a pointed reference to his Pauline sources, 'without charity, faith may exist, but it is of no benefit'.[88] He rounded off his argument by directing the reader once more to Augustine: even with the initial gift of unformed faith, the believer stood in constant need of charity, 'but without charity [the gifts given by the Holy Spirit] profit nothing'.[89]

The key to attaining the 'second justification' was the believer's active response to God's gift of faith.[90] This would normally take the form of contrition, followed by seeking remission of sins and the obligation to undertake works of charity.[91] Smyth took great pains to reflect on their precise nature and the scriptural traditions that supported their practice.[92] Works of charity were not necessary hurdles to be taken on the way to salvation, but rather a

---

repudiated the theory of "meritum de congruo" favoured by the Scotists, some Thomists and almost the entire *via moderna*'.

[86] Smyth (1550), ibid.: 'primo datur, vt caetera impetrentur', quoting Augustine, *De Praedestinatione*, 7 [=PL 44.969].

[87] Smyth (1550), 24 v: 'They fist derived ... the concept of this pact from Saint Paul' (Primum hoc pacto ... colligunt ex D. Pauli); cf. Rom 10.14: 'But how are they to call on one in whom they have not believed? And how are they to believe in one of whom they have never heard?'

[88] Smyth (1550), 16 r: 'Sine charitate quippe fides potest esse, sed non & prodesse'.

[89] Smyth (1550), ibid.: 'Sed sine charitate [munera per spiritum sanctum dantur] nihil prosunt', cf. Augustine, *De Trinitate*, 15, 18 [=PL 42.1082].

[90] Smyth (1550), 20 r: 'To be works which anticipate justifying faith, by which man's soul should be made capable of receiving forgiveness of sins and the infusion of divine grace' (Esse opera, fidem iustificantem anteuertentia quibus hominis anima reddi debet capax remissionis peccatorum, & diuinae gratiae infundendae).

[91] Smyth (1550), 20 v, echoed Ambrose's view, *Expositio Evangelii secundum Lucam*, 7 [=PL 15.1673B]: 'Good tears, which are able to wash away our crime. Good tears, in which is not only the redemption of sinners, but even the recreation of the just' (Bonae lachrymae, quae nostrum possunt lauare delictum. Bonae lachrymae, in quibus non solum redemptio peccatorum, sed etiam refectio est iustorum).

[92] Cf. above, n. 66.

spiritual journey of preparation resulting in the infusion of divine grace into the heart of man. They were 'a way of preparation to receive divine grace'.[93] In order to match the emphasis on Scripture by his evangelical opposition, Smyth made use of arguments from Old Testament prophecies and the Gospels, as cited by Fisher and Eck.[94] The pleading of the Ninevites in Jon 3.10 found its culmination in the prophecies of hope in Ezek 18.31, Isa 45.22 or Jer 15.19.[95] In a commentary that verges on the poetic and brings to life the prophet's rich language of colour, Smyth reflected on Isa 1.18:

> See how φοινικοῦν ['they are scarlet'], that is 'scarlet' and 'red', are emphasised. Both colours describe the blemish and the charges of blood. However, by good works of mercy, true judgement, by helping widows and defending orphans, they are turned to the spotless of wool, are transformed into the whiteness of snow.[96]

The Old Testament prophecies are joined by the petition for forgiveness in the Lord's prayer in Mt 6.12, and the parable of the Prodigal Son in Lk 15.18ff.[97] The final plea for mercy of the criminal crucified alongside Jesus in Lk 23.42 also formed a central part of Smyth's argument that God was able to effect a conversion of heart in believers and non-believers alike.[98] All

---

[93] Smyth (1550), 22 r: 'Preparamenta quaedam ad suscipiendam diuinam gratiam'.

[94] Cf. Fisher (1523), §§ 5 and 21; and J. Eck, *De Satisficatione et aliis penitentie annexis*, Rome, 1523, D ii r-v, and idem, P. Fraenkel, ed., *Enchiridion locorum communiorum adversus Lutherum et alios hostes ecclesiae (1525-1543)*, CC 34, Münster, 1979, 126-128.

[95] Jon 3.10: 'When God saw, what they [the inhabitants of Nineveh] did, how they turned from their evil ways, God changed His mind'; Ezek 18.31: 'Cast away from you all the transgressions that you have committed against me, and get yourselves a new heart and a new spirit!'; Isa 45.22: 'Turn to me and be saved, all the ends of the earth! For I am God, and there is no other'; Jer 15.19: 'If you turn back, I will take you back, and you shall stand before me'.

[96] Smyth (1550), 48 r-48 v: 'Ecce quomodo φοινικοῦν, hoc est rubrum, & coccinum, in quo vtroque macula est, & crimina sanguinis indicantur, per misericordias bona opera, & recta iudicia, & per auxilium viduarum, & defensionem orphanorum, ad purgationem lanae vertitur, & ad candorem niuis mutatur'.

[97] Mt 6.12: 'And forgive us our debts, as we also have forgiven our debtors'; Smyth (1550), '83 r' [=L viii r] also cited Mt 18.32: 'I forgave you all that debt because you pleaded with me'.

[98] Smyth (1550), 88 r: 'Latro confessione fit iustus, non tantum fide'; Lk 23.42: 'Jesus, remember me when you come into your kingdom'.

communicated the same divine appeal believers were to emulate: 'repent and do penance'.[99]

The believer was not able of himself to will this process of turning to God. God's grace effected contrition, and led man to make an act of penance.[100] Following the sacerdotal pronouncement of remission of sins, man was called upon to perform a work of charity worthy of merit towards the justification to eternal life.[101] Smyth was well aware that it was not the work in itself which gained the infusion of justifying grace.[102] Man had to rely fully on the infusion of the habit of grace in order to perform works worthy of salvation, otherwise such works were vanity and even sinful.[103] Believers were 'drawn' to the Father through the teaching and the merits of the Son, while the Holy Spirit imparted the necessary graces to accomplish works prerequisite towards salvation:[104]

---

[99] Smyth (1550), 22 v: 'convertemini & agite poenitentiam'; Mk. 1.15.

[100] Smyth (1550), 23 r: 'So that I shall argue that it is a man's duty—enlightened by a form of divine prevenient grace—to obey God's commandment, by His help, and so to prepare himself as much as possible for God to bestow His grace on him' (Vt persuadeam hominis esse, praeuenienti quadam gratia Dei illustrati, obedire suasioni Dei per ipsius adiutorium, atque quantum liceat illi impartiendae gratiae se idoneum reddere).

[101] Smyth (1550), 22 v: 'I do not say this because I am unaware that no-one can—by his own strength—truly and fully turn to God. ... Change me and I shall be changed, because after you changed me, I did penance' (Non haec dico, quod sim ignarus neminem posse ad Deum vere & plene sese conuertere. ... Conuerte me & conuertar quia postquam conuertisti me, egi poenitentiam).

[102] Smyth (1550), 23 v.

[103] Ibid; unlike Scotus (1639), 4.15, 1, Smyth emphasised that not every work was worthy to merit eternal life, see in particular Smyth (1550), 25 v: 'That which is not done by faith is certainly sinful, and those men miss the point who turn many other things against their faith or conscience to faith (which is a theological virtue), so that they argue that every deed which precedes grace and justifying faith is truly sinful and that the faithful sin greatly through faith—that is from the knowledge of good and proper action' (Quod non est ex fide, peccatum est, isti, vt pleraque alia, contra suam ipsorum fidem seu conscientiam, ad fidem, quae virtus est Theologica, detorqueant, vt persuadeant omne opus, quod gratiam et fidem iustificantem anteuertat, esse vere peccatum, fideles peccatores multa ex fide, hoc est, ex conscientia honesti atque recti facere).

[104] The argument derived from Jn 6.44: 'No one can come to me unless drawn by the Father who sent me; and I will raise him up on the last day'; cf. Philips (1989), 45: 'By His example Christ ... draws His disciples to follow Him to the Father but, in order to enable them to do so, on a much deeper level He infuses grace into [their hearts] which, although initially hidden, is itself gradually manifested' (Le Christ ... attire par son exemple ses disciples à le suivre vers le Père, mais à un niveau plus profond il leur infuse pour ce faire un grâce qui d'occulte qu'elle était, se rend de plus en plus manifeste).

Both by acknowledgement [of their deeds] and faith the Father leads to the Son those whom He has judged worthy of this grace. ... Surely the preparation of the minds of those to whom grace shall be imparted, by which process they are made fitting and in some way worthy, is their very worthiness?[105]

2.1.2. Merit

Merit (*meritum*) is generally understood to be the property of a good work which entitles the doer to receive a reward (*praemium, merces*) from the person for whom the work is done. In its theological sense, supernatural merit is the quality of a salutary act (*actus salutaris*), to which God in consequence of His infallible promise awards a supernatural reward, consisting ultimately in eternal life.[106] In order to procure merit towards eternal life, believers depend on their initial merit, 'that merit consists in the preparation of our own mind which, by the grace of God, moves us from unformed faith to penitence'.[107] Under the terms of His promises revealed to mankind, God would not withhold the infusion of His justifying faith from anyone who had prepared himself to receive merit.[108] Again, Smyth took great pains to spell out that this could not be achieved by the vain striving (*inania*) of a believer but only by the aid of God's grace in conjunction with the believer's works of penitence.[109] Once he had received justifying faith, according to God's promises he would begin to build up merit towards eternal life.[110] For Smyth this God-given framework not only excluded any semi-Pelagian attempts to procure salvation through works, but also emphasised the need to rely entirely on

---

[105] Smyth (1550), 23 v: 'Pater quidem per cognitionem et fidem eos adducit ad filium, quos hac gratia dignos iudicauerit. ... Nonne haec dignitas istorum, recte dicatur mentium illorum dispositio quedam & praeparatio, qua idonei & quodammodo digni redduntur, quibus detur gratia?'

[106] Cf. *The Catholic Encyclopedia*, New York, 1911, 10.202-208.

[107] Smyth (1550), 24 v: 'Illud [meritum] consistere in hac preparatione mentis nostrae ex gratia Dei trahentis ad poenitentiam, & ex fide informi profecta'.

[108] For an introduction to the theology of merit, see W. Dettloff, *Die Entwicklung der Akzeptations- und Verdienstlehre von Duns Scotus bis Luther*, Münster, 1963; for a critical Roman Catholic reflection see L. Scheffczyk, W. Dettloff, R. Heinzmann, edd. et al., *Wahrheit und Verkündigung*, München, 1967, 2.1989ff: O. H. Pesch, 'Die Lehre vom "Verdienst" als Problem für Theologie und Verkündigung'.

[109] For an introduction to scholastic views on the 'rightful disposition' for salvation, see McGrath (1993), 78-83.

[110] Smyth (1550), 197 r.

God's initiative in the process of salvation.[111] Stimulated by the grace of God, man opened a window by which grace could enter the heart.[112] Smyth concluded: 'God is all-pervasive to us, as the all–powerful who does not know a lie, who keeps His Covenents ... because He intervenes in order to affirm His promises, He keeps them and will rule in faith over all that is good'.[113]

In the ensuing excursus, Smyth rushed to the defence of the late scholastic framework on which he had based his doctrine of justification.[114] He particularly relied on the argument from tradition, one of his trademarks. Unlike the recent 'innovations' of his evangelical opposition, the doctrines in question could not be doubted as they had been believed for more than thirteen hundred years. He had already argued that the theology of the *pactum* derived from Rom 10.14 and was only later developed by the Fathers and scholastics.[115] He now turned to the concepts of merit which had come under spirited attack in Melanchthon's *Apolo-*

---

[111] For Smyth the clearly defined interaction between God's promise of salvation and man's dutiful response to this promise (*pactum*) was an indispensable framework which gave the believer a relative certainty of salvation, cf. Smyth (1550), 17 r, 188 r-189 r. Philips (1989), 187, cautioned that the strong Ockhamist rejection of semi-Pelagianism could lead to a distorted image of a God completely unconstrained by any obligations under the terms of the *pactum*: 'An obsessive anti-Pelagian stance turned Ockhamism into the absurd concept of a God who could sanctify sinners and condemn those who love Him and respond to His love! In order to preserve the free will of God, His goodness and mercy, therefore, Ockham created an irresponsible despot' (Le souci antipélagien a projeté l'occamisme dans l'absurdité d'un Dieu qui peut béatifer les pécheurs et condamner ceux qui'il aime et qui répondent à son amour! Pour sauvegarder un Dieu libre, bienveillant et miséricordieux, Ockham en fait un despot irresponsable); cf. Ockham, I *Sententiae*, dist. 17, q. 1, in: G. Gál OFM, ed. et al., *Opera Philosophica et Theologica*, St Bonaventure NY, 1967—; and E. Iserloh, *Gnade und Eucharistie in der philosophischen Theologie des Wilhelm von Ockham. Ihre Bedeutung für die Ursachen der Reformation*, Wiesbaden, 1956, 100-101.

[112] Smyth (1550), 30 r: 'To us preparatory works [are those] by which we are made ready for the infusion of the grace of God into us. We open ourselves to Him like a window, that He may enter into us' (Nobis opera praeparatoria, quibus viam praestruamus gratiae Dei in nos transfundae, & illi velut fenestram aperiamus, vt in nos ingrediatur); cf. Rev 3.20: 'Listen! I am standing at the door, knocking; if you hear my voice and open the door, I will come in to you'.

[113] Smyth (1550), 189 r: 'Peruasissum est nobis Deum vt omnipotentem, mentiri nescium, pactorum tenacem ... quod interponere illi visum est firmandis promissis, seruantem, omnia optima fide praestaturum'.

[114] Cf. Smyth (1550), 28 r-39 r.

[115] Cf. above, n. 87.

gia.[116] Melanchthon's chief criticism of the scholastic position was that the doctrine of merit was a human invention rather than passed down by divine revelation and apostolic tradition, 'because reason, which does not regard the impurity of the heart, feels that it pleases God in this manner; and for this reason works, or other practices thought up by men in great difficulties, are merely human fears, and opposed to knowledge'.[117] By an impressive collection of patristic evidence Smyth countered that the concept was not a recent innovation,[118] but had been laid down 'more or less 1370 years before our times' in the days of the ante-Nicene Fathers.[119] He concluded by amassing further evidence from the work of Augustine, as his opposition had also relied heavily on his writings.[120] For Smyth, Augustine had left no doubt that while human works contributed nothing to justification *ex sua natura*, they were nonetheless reckoned worthy to receive merit by God:

> This passage (and other similar passages) from the riches of the works of Saint Augustine teach nothing but that works do not merit grace *de condigno*, or by virtue of their own nature, but rather *de congruo* and the graciousness of God, and the generous promise of His grace and justification.[121]

---

[116] *Apologia*, 165, 316-166, 321; cf. 177, 372-373.

[117] *Apologia*, 165, 2ff: 'Quia ratio non videns immunditiem cordis sentit se ita placere Deo, et propterea subinde alia opera, alii cultus ab hominibus in magnis periculis excogitati sunt adversus terrores conscientiae'; cf. Pfnür (1970), 206-207.

[118] Smyth (1550), 32 v: 'Those who deride this concept of merit *de congruo* should investigate more carefully, it is not as if it had recently been invented by the scholastics, and was opposed to holy scripture' (Introspicere diligentius, qui tantopere abhorrent a vocabulo meriti de congruo, perinde ac si illud esset nuper inuentum a scholasticis & scripturis sacris aduersaretur).

[119] Smyth (1550), 33 v: 'Ante haec aetatem nostram plus minus 1370 annos'; ibid.: 'It is neither new, nor derived from scholastic studies' (Nec recens esse, nec a scholasticorum profectum officina); cf. Cyprian, *Epistolae*, 3.18-19 [=CSEL 3.2]; Tertullian, *De Monogamia* [=F. Oehler, ed., *Tertulliani opera omnia, ed. maior I*, Leipzig, 1853, 761-787]; idem, *Adversus Marcionem*, 4 [=CSEL 47.533-562]; Origen, *Commentarium in Romanos*, 4 [=J. P. Migne, *Patrologia cursus completus, series Graeca*, Paris, 1857-1866 (cited as: PG), 14].

[120] Smyth (1550), 33 r-35 v; so for instance Augustine, *De diversis quaestionibus ad Simplicianum libri* 2/1, q. 2 [=PL 40.138-142]; idem, *De fide et operibus liber* 1.14 [=PL 40.211]; idem, *De spiritu et littera ad Marcellinum liber* 1.10; 1.26 [=PL 44.210; 44.226].

[121] Smyth (1550), 35 r-35 v: 'Haec & eiusmodi alia loca, quae ex diuite operum D. Augustini penu proficiscuntur, non aliud docent quam quod opera non mereantur gratiam de condigno, & ex sua natura, [sed] de congruo, & ex Dei benignitate, liberalique promissione tamen merita gratiae, et iustificationis', cf. in

Smyth acknowledged that works performed by the human will, without the assistance and grace of God, 'without doubt do not contribute at all to procure justification'.[122] It was by the grace of God that they were transformed to be worthy of receiving merit *de congruo*.

2.1.3. *Preparatory Works*

Before addressing himself to the exact nature of works of charity—a collection not unlike Biel's *operatio exterior laboriosa*—Smyth issued one of the few blows against Vermigli that are suggested by the belligerent title.[123] In a debate he would take up at greater length in his *Bouclier* and *Refutatio*, he devoted himself to the subject of preparatory and supererogatory works. Vermigli had apparently maintained in a 1549 Oxford lecture series that all 'works which are undertaken prior to justification are sinful and wicked'.[124] Unlike Scotus, Smyth had a clear understanding that any works preparing the infusion of *fiducia*, or 'first justification', only counted towards salvation when inspired by the infusion of the gift of charity.[125] While this did exclude a large number of human works from the 'first justification' of a believer, works which were performed in a rightful disposition towards God (described by Old Testament prophets and Psalmists as *timor Domini*) could not be discounted.[126] If the 'fear of the Lord'

---

particular Augustine, *Opus imperfectum contra Iulianum*, 1.138 [=PL 45.1137]; see also Philips (1989), 36.

[122] Smyth (1550), 35 v: 'Indubie nihil conducunt ad iustificationem obtinendam'.

[123] See above, n. 35.

[124] Smyth (1550), 35 v: 'Opera, quae iustificationem hominis anteuertant, esse omnia vitia & crimina'.

[125] This echoed Fisher's concerns; cf. Fisher (1523), 204 v: 'I said this because of the Fathers, whose opinion I follow, rather than the scholastics, as they disagree with each other on this point. For the Fathers assert that without God's special grace no-one can will anything that is good, nor is a general infusion [of this grace] sufficient. Some of the scholars argue the opposite, that it is indeed sufficient, so that anyone without that grace may act well—in human terms—and is able to do good' (Hoc dixi propter patres, quorum sententiam sequi, quam scholasticorum, quum in hac re mutuo sibi pugnent. Patres enim asserunt, neminem posse quicquam boni velle sine speciali dei auxilio, nec sufficere generalem illium influxum. Nonnulli contra scholastici si contendunt hunc sufficere, ut quis absque illo auxilio bene mortaliter agere, et bonum facere posset).

[126] Smyth (1550), 37 r-38 v; cf. Eccl 2.11,13; Ps 110.10; Prov 1.7, 9.10, etc.

brought believers to acknowledge their guilt and repent—a work itself—this could not possibly be dismissed.[127]

Referring back to the Pauline corpus, Smyth argued that the only works ever excluded from building up merit in the New Testament were those of the ritual law of Moses, a commonplace catholic repartee.[128] The commandments of Christ served as continual reminders of the shortcomings of a believer. Those who sought to keep them were constantly confronted with their own sinfulness which in itself was an agent of salvation as it effected a change of heart in the believer.[129] In a passage that can hardly conceal its acerbic undertones, he queried further whether it was not through the work of penitence that men and women were made just in the first place.[130] If so, God's mercy reached the believer through his attrition, rather than his insufficient faith, 'as the Lutherans boldly lie'.[131] Smyth therefore felt confident to counsel his readers that they would only ever attain the state of 'first justification' through their preparatory works:

> Now let us hurry to consider the rest: penitence and the ways in which it is demonstrated, confession, prayer, acts of mercy, fasting, fear, hope and those other free gifts of God. These are necessary for justification, so that by them men both can (and should) be justified, and not merely by faith, which some recently held.[132]

2.1.4. *Charity*

The church believes charity (*charitas*) to be a habit which disposes man to love God above all others, and to love himself and his neighbours for the sake of God. If the Holy Spirit kindles this habit

---

[127] Smyth (1550), 38 r.
[128] Smyth (1550), 36 r; cf. for instance Phil 3.3-9.
[129] Smyth (1550), 37 r.
[130] Smyth (1550), 37 v-38 r.
[131] Smyth (1550), 38 r: 'vt splendide mentiuntur Lutheristae'.
[132] Smyth (1550), 38 v-39 r: 'Iam ad reliqua properabimus ostensuri, poenitentiam, atque quibus ea paretur, confessionem, orationem, eleemosynam, ieiunium, timorem, spem & id genus alia Dei gratuita dona, esse necessaria ad hominis iustificationem, vt per quae, nedum per fidem praesertim quam nuper desuo commenti sunt quidam homo & potest & debet iustificari'; cf. 46 v-47 v, which argues that Peter's speech in Ac 8.22 refuted three common evangelical misconceptions about justification, i.e. that works prior to justification are of themselves sinful, that they add nothing to justification, and that man is justified by faith alone; see for instance Fisher (1523), 220 v.

in the human soul by an infusion of grace (*gratia gratis data*), the gift is supernatural; if it is acquired through human works, it is called natural. Unless man is already in possession of the supernatural virtue of charity, none of the preparatory works for justification is of any value. The instigation of auxiliary grace first inspired man to return to God in penance: 'God's mercy goes before us, so that we shall be justified and obtain pardon for what we have committed'.[133] The virtue of charity flowing from God's *prima misericordia* justified the sinner, caused him to turn back to God and to begin to perform works worthy of the gift that dwelt within him.[134] Once he had received his 'first justification' through the mercy of God, man was able to contribute to his salvation not by faith only, but by the works he performed with the assistance of the gift of charity.[135]

Arguing once again from Scripture, Smyth explained that the believer had to return to God through an act of penance before he could begin to merit life eternal.[136] This change of heart was caused entirely through the indwelling habit of charity, God's *gratia gratis data*, rather than any human agency.[137] Indeed, God Himself willed to make a dwelling in the believer's heart if he only chose to receive God's free gift.[138] The doctrine of indwelling

---

[133] Smyth (1550), 69 v: 'Dei misericordiam nos anteire, vt iustificemur & admissorum nostrorum veniam assequamur'.

[134] Smyth (1550), 64 r: 'Penitence is shown to us through the grace of God, and revealed, calling us back to grace by the Lord' (Poenitentia per Dei gratiam nobis ostensa, & indicta, in gratiam nos Domino reuocat); pre-scholastic theologians first identified the indwelling Holy Spirit with the gift of charity, cf. Lombard, *In Ephesianos* 5.18 [=PL 192.174-192.175]; see also McGrath (1993), 100-101.

[135] Smyth (1550), 70 r: 'This mercy is obtained by baptism, fear, hope, penitence, prayer and confession of sins, not merely by faith' (Hanc misericordiam apprehendi baptismo, timore, spe, poenitentia, oratione, atque concessione flagitiorum, non tantum fide).

[136] Cf. Jer 15.19: 'If you turn back, I will take you back, and you shall stand before me'.

[137] Smyth (1550), 42 r: 'What else could God mean by these words [Jer 15.19] other than that a sinner should repent like an enlightened man, once grace has been freely given, he has been aided by God, and turned to God who had previously turned from God through his sin?' (Quid his verbis aliud vult Deus, quam vt peccator iam Dei quadam gratia gratis data veluti illustratus & ab eo adiutus poeniteat, ac se ad Deum conuertat, qui erat antea auersus per peccatum?)

[138] Smyth (1550), 42 r: 'To receive grace, he reveals the door of the heart, i.e. he makes himself a fitting and proper vessel to assist God in the infusion of grace'

(μένειν; *mansio*) had its roots in Jn 14.23, on which Smyth reflected at some length.[139] The evangelist's clear insistence on moral obedience and love of God as a prerequisite of God's indwelling made this passage an outstanding argument for Smyth's insistence on the necessity of a habit of charity and preparatory works towards personal salvation. The Fathers, most notably Augustine, had developed the Johannine understanding of the indwelling of Father and Son in the believer 'who loved Christ and kept His word' to include the third person of the Trinity.[140] Proceeding from the union of Father and Son, the Holy Spirit was said to effect a similar union between the three persons of the Trinity and the believer.[141]

The believer's task was to respond by his love to God's merciful offer of 'first justification': 'it is firstly necessary to love Christ, since God justifies those He loves and vice versa'.[142] This love, *amor amicitiae*, was reflected in the life of the sinner who anointed Christ's feet with oil, kissed and washed them with her hair (Lk 7.37-50). To reinforce his argument that man received his primary justification through the gift of charity and not out of his own faith, Smyth recalled Christ's words to Peter: 'I tell you, her sins, which were many, have been forgiven, because she has shown great love. For the one to whom little is forgiven, loved little'.[143] He explained that 'the penitence of the sinful woman deserved pardon before the creator' only because of her love, not her

---

(Ad gratiam suscipiendam, & ianuam cordis apparuit, id est se aptum atque idoneum vas Deo adiuuare effecit gratiae infundendae).

[139] Smyth (1550), 105 r; Jn 14.23: 'Those who love me will keep my Word, and my Father will love them, and we will come to them and make our home with them'; for the origins of the Johannine understanding of μένειν, see C. K. Barrett, *The Gospel according to St John. An introduction with Commentary and Notes on the Greek Text*, London, ²1996, 456-457.

[140] For instance Augustine, *Sermo* 71, 20.33 [=PL 38.463].

[141] Cf. Philips (1989), 37: 'To unite is the prerogative of the Third Person. What happens in the Godhead between Father and Son, occurs also between the justified and the divine Three within the context of the Church' (Unir est le propre de la troisième personne. Ce qu'elle fait en Dieu entre le Père et le Fils, elle le fera entre les hommes justifiés et les divins trois au sein de l'Eglise).

[142] Smyth (1550), 105 r: 'Opus est vt primus diligamus Christum, quando Deus quos diligit, iustificat & contra'.

[143] Lk 7.47f.

action.[144] Because 'she has shown great love' that moved her to repent, her many sins had been forgiven. Her sins washed away, she was enabled to contribute to her salvation by her work of charity—the anointing and washing of Christ's feet.[145] Her repentance had not been willed, but was the result of God's gift of charity which brought her to acknowledge her sins and repent. He concluded: 'This woman was justified by penitence, which is never genuine unless it is inspired by her love for God and her hatred of sin. She therefore was justified by charity, and not merely by faith'.[146]

Referring back to 1 Cor 8.3, Smyth elaborated that in order to receive the gift of God's acceptance (*approbatio*), man first needed to respond to the love God freely granted to His creature.[147] It was man's *amor amicitiae* for God—'firstly a medicine for the ailing soul ... by which it is able to love not only friends but even enemies'— that admitted the Trinity to his heart.[148] Smyth dismissed traditional Lutheran objections to the need for the imparting of charity as a prerequisite for justification by developing Augustine's metaphor of charity as the 'chief medicine of the soul':[149] 'Does it not offer a medicine to cure the sick?'[150] Just as medicine was administered at the beginning of the healing process, so the gift of divine love, and not faith or any other human work, stood at the beginning of the process of justification. Only once man had received the gift of the indwelling Holy Spirit was he able to begin accumulating merit.

> The Trinity itself comes to man through love and dwells in him. Love, therefore, is the reason for the arrival of the Trinity in man, and its dwelling in him. This would not happen if love was not a

---

[144] Smyth (1550), 104 v: 'Poenitentia mulieris peccatricis secundum creatorem meruerat veniam'.

[145] Cf. Tertullian, *Adversus Marcionem*, 4 [=PL 2.403B-2.403C].

[146] Smyth (1550), 104 v: 'Hanc foeminam fuisse iustificatam per poenitentiam, quae nunquam est vera nisi ex amore Dei, & odio peccati prodeat. Fuit itaque haec iustificata ex dilectione, non tantum ex fide'.

[147] 1 Cor 8.3: 'Anyone who loves God is known by Him'.

[148] Smyth (1550), 120 v: 'Primum medicamentum animae aegrotanti ... per quam possit non solum amicos, sed etiam inimicos diligere'; cf. Augustine, *Sermones de Scripturis* 5.6 [=PL 38.701].

[149] So for instance in *Apologia*, 109-112.

[150] Smyth (1550), 120 v: 'Confert nihil medicamentum ad sanandam aegrotum?'.

cause of justification at all ... because the Trinity comes to man through justification, and because of his justification makes its dwelling in him.[151]

Smyth had taken great care to point out that no work contributed anything to salvation unless it was based on God's gift of charity. In her rather abrupt examination of Smyth's doctrine of justification Ellen Macek felt that he 'occasionally slips into the terminology of ... the *via moderna*. This school ... seems to have reflected semi-Pelagian connotations [sic]'.[152] She therefore gives the impression that Smyth propagated semi-Pelagian views. This was clearly not the case. While he broadly followed the terms of the late medieval *pactum* and its fundamental premise that 'God will not deny His grace to those who do what lies in them' (*facienti quod in se est Deus non denegat gratiam*), he repeatedly emphasised that in themselves 'all our works and afflictions ... neither prepare us to receive grace, nor constitute merit *de congruo*'.[153] God alone was the source of human salvation, human works *ex puris naturalibus* did not contribute at all to human justification.[154] To claim anything else, Smyth added, was nothing but hypocrisy, and concluded:[155] 'For whoever does not love justice, which is caused by contrition

---

[151] Smyth (1550), 105 v: 'Ipsam Trinitatem per dilectionem ad hominem venire & mansionem apud eum facere, ergo dilectio est causa aduentus Trinitatis ad hominem & istius mansionis, quod non poterit fieri, si dilectio nullo pacto esset causa iustificationis ... quia per iustificationem Trinitas venit ad hominem, & mansionem facit in eo'.

[152] E. A. Mack, *The Loyal Opposition: Tudor Traditionalist Polemics, 1535-1558*, Peter Lang Studies in Church History 7, New York, 1996, 55; for a defence of the school against claims of semi-Pelagianism, see H. A. Oberman, ed. et al., *Luther and the Dawn of the Modern Era*, Brill Studies in the History of Christian Thought, Leiden, 1974: 'Headwaters of the Reformation: Initia Lutheri—Initia Reformationis', 67f; 82-84 and especially 86-88; H. A. Oberman, ed. et al., *Via Augustini: Augustine in the later Middle Ages, Renaissance, and Reformation: Essays in honour of Damasus Trapp*, Brill Studies in Medieval and Reformation Thought, Leiden, 1991, 130-141f: A. Zumkeller OSA, 'Konrad Treger's Disputation Theses of 1521', 137; for a reflection on Biel, see L. Scheffczyk (ed. et al.), *Wahrheit und Verkündigung*, München, 1967, 2.1109-2.1120: H. J. McSorley, 'Was Gabriel Biel a semi-Pelagian?'

[153] Smyth (1550), 160 r: 'Opera nostra, atque afflictiones, ... non sunt praeparatoria ad gratiam suscipiendam, nec de congruo meritoria'.

[154] Smyth (1550), 160 r: 'Any works without faith, or the prompting of God are useless' (Omnia opera quae sine fide & Dei agitatione fiunt, inutila sunt).

[155] Ibid.

together with the gift of charity, is not capable of the grace and the remission of sins'.[156]

2.2. Smyth's 'Bouclier' (1555) and 'Refvtatio' (1563): Works of Supererogation

In the *Diatriba* Smyth touched only briefly on question of works of supererogation (*opera meliora*)—works not prescribed as strict obligations or prohibitions.[157] The term 'supererogatory' derived from Luke's Gospel, Smyth explained in his *Refvtatio*.[158] Just as the good Samaritan in Lk 10.35 not only fulfilled God's commandments by rescuing his neighbour from the hands of evil men, but also promised the innkeeper on the road to Jericho to repay him for all 'whatever you spend more' (*quodcunque supererogaveris*, i.e. his supererogatory work), so man was called to go and do likewise.[159] Man was not only enjoined to avoid sinful works and to fulfil Christ's commandments, but to strive to add better works, works that ultimately counted towards his salvation.

In his two later polemics on justification Smyth defended this doctrine on two different fronts, against the evangelical English doctrine reflected in the *Forty-Two Articles* (1553) and against Melanchthon's *Loci Communes* (1543). The vernacular defence in his *Bouclier* was more immediate and lacked some of the theological sophistication of the later work since it was addressed to a less academic audience.[160] Concerned with the evangelical teaching that 'works of supererogation cannot be taught without arrogancy and impiety', Smyth attributed the new doctrine to the influence of his evangelical successor at Oxford, Peter Martyr Vermigli.[161] Martyr did not have the same direct influence on the subject of justification that he had on the drafting of a reformed eucharistic

---

[156] Smyth (1550), 165 r: 'Nam quisquis non ... diligit iustitiam, quod fit per contritionem, & donum charitatis, non est capax gratiae & remissionis peccatorum'; cf. 107 v-108 r.
[157] For instance in Smyth (1550), 118 v-121 v.
[158] Smyth (1563), 34 r.
[159] Smyth (1563), 35 r; cf. Lk 10.37: 'Jesus said to him, "Go and do likewise"'.
[160] Smyth (1555), B ii r.
[161] The doctrine was later formulated in the 39 Articles of Religion, *The Book of Common Prayer*, Cambridge, 1993: Article 14.

doctrine for the Edwardian church.[162] Partly because of genuine concern for the newly-restored catholic church in England and partly because of personal enmity, the *Bouclier* fiercely defended the validity of *opera meliora*—'that thyng which is not required of vs by compulsion and yet is geuen'—in justification:[163]

> For those thinges which are doone aboue Gods commaundement, man getteth a greate rewarde, but not so muche for the doynge of thinges conteyned vnder Gods commaundement.[164]

Smyth did not cite as much patristic evidence as in his two Latin publications, instead he relied strongly on scripture in his exposition of the validity of supererogatory works, pointing his readers to the abstinence of the Rechabites in Jer 35.4-10 or the fasting of John the Baptist in Mt 3.4f. as prime examples of what it meant to do more than fulfil God's commandments. Any work beyond avoiding evil or doing good (works described as *operatio exterior laboriosa*) was worthy of greater merit than those that merely fulfilled the Gospel teaching. Among those works Smyth in particular counted the vows of chastity, poverty and obedience taken by religious in observance of the Pauline teaching on virginity in 1 Cor 7.[165]

The patristic background to the doctrine can be found in the 1563 *Refvtatio*, where Smyth documented its genesis at length. In a reflection that owed a considerable part of its argument to the third volume of Johannes Cochlaeus's *Philippicae* (a polemic that also set out to confute Melanchthon's doctrines) Smyth thun-

---

[162] For the adoption of Martyr's reformed understanding of the eucharist in England, see for instance A. Schindler, ed. et al., *Die Zürcher Reformation: Ausstrahlungen und Rückwirkungen*, Bern, 2000, 317-326: J. A. Löwe, 'The bodie and bloud of Christ is not carnallie and corporallie in the bread and wine: The Oxford Disputation revisited—Zwinglian traits in the Eucharistic Theology of Pietro Martire Vermigli'.

[163] Smyth (1555), C i v.

[164] Smyth (1555), B iv v.

[165] Cf. Smyth (1563), 36 v; 36 v-39 r; Smyth (1555), C iii r reflects the influence of his earlier defence of monastic vows and celibacy, idem, *De coelibatum liber unus. De votis monasticis liber alter (confutatio quorundam articulorum de votis monasticis P. Martyris)*, Leuven, 1550; idem, *Defensio sacri episcoporum et sacerdotum Coelibatus, contra impias et indoctas Petri Martyris Vermelii nugas nunc vero Lutetiae Parisiorum Theologiam profitentem*, Paris, 1551; for Smyth's theology of vows, see below, chapter IV.

dered:[166] 'Philipp Melanchthon was therefore himself affected by insanity when he wrote that it was insane and an opinion promoted by the devil to teach that there are good works that can be added to those of the Ten Commandments or any other commandments of God'.[167] Melanchthon had no regard at all for the dominical precepts in Mt 19.20f, where believers were not only called to obedience of God's law but to perfection, Smyth argued.[168]

In a comprehensive collection of post-Nicene sources, Smyth proceeded to support his argument that it was not only possible but also highly desirable to accomplish supererogatory works.[169] As Augustine had stated 'there are many works that can be accomplished, not because they have been commanded by the law, but in free charity. They are the most pleasing of our duties: even if we were allowed not to accomplish these works, we would want to do them for the sake of love', so Smyth pointed out that it was possible for the human will to co-operate with divine grace in pursuit of perfection.[170] Echoing a similar passage in the *Bouclier*, he ranked a number of works that had traditionally been held to fulfil that human striving, so for instance 'people can choose to retain their

---

[166] Smyth (1563), 28 v; cf. J. Cochlaeus, *Philippicae I-VII: Edited with Introduction and Commentary by Ralph Keen*, Bibliotheca Humanistica & Reformatorica 54, Nieuwkoop, 1995 and 1996; for Cochlaeus see particularly M. Samuel-Scheyder, *Johannes Cochlaeus: Humaniste et Adversaire de Luther*, Nancy, 1993, and her *Études Germaniques* 50 (1995), 467-490: 'Johannes Cochlaeus et Martin Bucer: itinéraires croisés et controverse religieuse'; a German Roman-Catholic evaluation can be found in R. Bäumer, ed., *Reformatio Ecclesiae: Beiträge zu kirchlichen Reformbemühungen von der alten Kirche bis zur Neuzeit*, Paderborn, 1980, 333-354: idem, 'Johannes Cochlaeus und die Reform der Kirche'.

[167] Smyth (1563), 23 r: 'Insania igitur affectus erat Phil. Melanchthon quando scripserat insaniam esse & vocem a diabolo sparsam docere aliquid opus bonum addi posse decalogo seu praeceptis dei'.

[168] Cf. Mt 19.20-21: 'The young man said to Jesus: "I have kept all these commandments; what do I still lack?" Jesus said to him, "If you wish to be perfect, go, sell your possessions, and give the money to the poor, and you will have treasure in heaven; then come, follow me".'

[169] Smyth (1563), 22 r-23 r; cf. Jerome, *Epistolae*, 14, 22, 52 [=PL 22.347; 22.394; 22.527], Augustine, *Epistola* 89 [=PL 33.309]; Ambrose, *Expositio Evangelii secundam Lucam*, 24 [=PL 15.1841A-1841C]; 35 r: 'it is in our power to will to be perfected' (in potestate nostra est, vtrum velimus esse perfecti).

[170] Smyth (1563), 24 r: 'Multa autem sunt facienda, non iubente lege, sed libera charitate, & ea sunt in nostris officijs gratiora: quae cum liceret nobis etiam non impendere, tamen caussa [sic] dilectionis impendimus', cf. Augustine, *De coniugiis adulteriis libri* 2/1.13 [=PL 40.479].

chastity, to abstain from wine and meat, or to sell all they own and give it up for the poor'.[171]

The scriptural basis for Smyth's teaching on supererogatory works has been touched upon already. It is revealing to trace the application of that doctrine in his own thinking. His primary motivation for writing against the recent doctrinal innovations was not his hostility to Vermigli, or his strong catholic convictions. Rather it derived from the 'commandment, not merely the advice, of the Gospel' contained in Mt 3.10: 'Even now the axe is lying at the root of the trees; every tree therefore that does not bear good fruit is cut down and thrown into the fire.'[172] In the introduction to the *Bouclier*, he wrote:

> Euery man must make a straite accompt & reckonyng to Christ at domes daye for his talentes, and giftes receiued of god. When he that hath encreased those giftes by godly usyng of them shall receiue a reward of god accordyng to his doynges, and he whiche hath not so done, shall be punished therefore. ... [This] moued me to write, and set foorth this traicte for the defence of the truth.[173]

In his own life, Smyth had evidently experienced that 'divine mercy touches a man by fear, and not only by faith'.[174] He was convinced of the truth that only the believer whose driving force to attain perfection was the fear of the Lord would receive the 'wages of justice'—God's gift of eternal life.[175] Man would only receive eternal life if he was willing to strive for perfection, something the young man who sought to follow Christ was not able to do.[176] He strongly believed that everybody had been charged to live up to his

---

[171] Smyth (1563), 24 v: 'Virginitas conseruetur, vt a vino, & carnibus abstineatur, vt vendantur omnia & erogantur pauperibus', cf. idem (1555), C i v-C iii r.

[172] Cf. Smyth (1563), 35 r: 'praeceptum, nec consilium euangelij'.

[173] Smyth (1555), ¶ vi v- ¶ vi r. He argued on similar terms in the introductions to his *Assertion and Defence*, Smyth (1546), 4 r: 'I Richard Smyth ... dreading also the great daunger & feareful punishment, which the idel & slouthful seruant incurreth hiding in the ground his talent, & not vsing the gift of god to his power [Mt 25.26-28] to thintent ye good christen religion may be advanced ... haue made this small treatise'. This sentiment also pervaded his last publication, cf. Smyth (1563), A 3 r.

[174] Smyth (1550), 38 r: 'Diuinam misericordiam homini contingere per timorem, nedum per fidem'.

[175] Smyth (1563), 65 r: 'Eternal life is a gift, or a grace, of God as well as a reward for good works (Liquet vitam aeternam esse donum, seu gratiam dei, & mercedem quoque bonorum operum); cf. 65 v.

[176] Mt 19.22: 'When the young man heard this word, he went away grieving'.

142   CHAPTER THREE

abilities. Only those who used God's gifts in them and 'encreased those giftes by godly usyng of them' could hope that God would reward them in heaven. There was no need for an answer to his concluding question: 'Why then maye I not leafullie [lawfully] lyue well, vpon hope of that euerlastinge lyfe whiche he promiseth to vs that doe well, and continue in doinge well vnto our liues end?'[177]

2.3. 'Stipendium Iustitiae Vita Aeterna'

Smyth's theology of justification is firmly rooted in the tradition of late medieval scholasticism as reflected in the works of his earlier catholic contemporaries. While most of his work does not show the influence of any one particular conservative writer, his 1550 *Diatriba* echoes some of Fisher's *Assertionis Lutheranae Confutatio* while the 1563 *Refvtatio* owes a small debt to Cochlaeus's *Philippicae*.[178] Smyth acknowledged their influences:

> This ... will be seen openly by the reader of their books, or by the writings of Dr Cochlaeus, or by those of our own [bishop of] Rochester [John Fisher], the most holy martyr and a most learned man, or the writings of any other orthodox men who have addressed the same matter in our times.[179]

For Smyth justification was a spiritual journey in which the believer recognised the gifts of God given to him and made use of them. Man was not only called to trust in the revelation of God's saving justice through Christ, but also to live up to the expectations God had of him.[180] His strong concern for the necessity of grace in

---

[177] Smyth (1555), E vii v-E viii r.

[178] For parallels with Fisher (1523), see above, n. 67-68; n. 80, n. 199 and n. 126. Some parallels with Cochlaeus (1996) can be detected in Smyth's 1563 defence of contrition and charity as preparatory works for justification: for instance Cochlaeus (1996), 83.30-34; 90.17-19 finds a parallel in Smyth (1563), 39 r; Cochlaeus (1996), 114.15-19 in Smyth (1563), 68 v; and Cochlaeus (1996), 117.21-23 in Smyth (1563), 56 r.

[179] Smyth (1563), 28 v: 'Id ... videbitur qui eorum libros leget, seu ea, quae doctor ... Cocleus, Roffensis nostra, martyr sanctissimus, nedum eruditissimus ... & alij orthodoxi viri, nostrae aetatis ea de re scripserunt'.

[180] Smyth (1563), 44 v: 'Paul teaches that the just man who assents strongly, adheres to the divine promises, who leads a reverent and holy life on earth and believes by faith in the death of Christ etc., will—in the end—gain eternal life' (Paulus docet iustum, quia firmiter assentitur, & adhaeret diuinis promissionibus

human works has been shown above, as has his personal conviction that only those believers who proved to be good stewards of *quod in se est* by their works of preparation received this grace and the subsequent forgiveness of their sins.[181] Only believers who had attained this state of grace were able to fulfil the law of God and perform works that contributed to their own salvation:

> For these [orthodox writers] assert that we are first received by God and justified, and only later, by His grace, we can satisfy the law; ... for they teach faith, confidence, hope and wholehearted love of God etc., prayer, fear of God, invocation and other other most noble works of this sort.[182]

At the end of his spiritual journey the believer who fulfilled all these preconditions could cherish the hope that good works would be rewarded and that he would receive God's gracious gift of eternal life.[183] For Smyth, the Pauline statement that 'the wages of sin is death' (Rom 6.23) not only described the progress of a sinner to eternal damnation, but also contained the key to eternal life: 'For when he said "The wages of sin is death", who would not consider it most appropriate and suitable to add that the wages of justice is eternal life?'[184] God's saving justice was within the reach of the believer who trusted in His terms of justification, and strove to

---

hic viuere piè & sanctè ... atque tandem consecuturum vitam aeternam, fide qui credidit in Christum mortuum etc.).

[181] Cf. for instance Smyth (1563), 49 r: 'He hopes that he will obtain God's grace and, by this grace, the free forgiveness of his sins' (Sperare se esse adeptum gratiam dei, & per eam remissionem suorum peccatorum gratis).

[182] Smyth (1563), 52 r: 'Asseruant enim illi [orthodoxi] prius nos à deo recipi, atque iustificari, ac postea per gratiam illius legi satisfacere ... Docent enim illi fidem, fiduciam, spem, dilectionem dei ex toto corde, &c. orationem, timorem dei, inuocationem, ac illiusmodi alia praeclara opera'.

[183] Smyth (1550), 174 r: 'We harbour no doubt at all concerning the immense and inexhaustible mercy of God, or the fulfilment of the divine promises. In us humans, you will always find reason for fear and doubt, just as in God there is trustworthiness and certain hope. Christians should take up the hope of sure salvation, and not the certitude of evidence' (De Dei misericordia illa immensa, & inexhausta, aut diuinorum promissorum impletione, haesitare non est fas. In nobis caussam formidinis, & haesitantiae comperies facile, vt in Deo fiduciae speique certissimae. Firmae salutis spem concipere debent Christiani non euidentiae certitudinem); Smyth (1563), 65 r, cf. also Smyth (1550), XIX, 'De certitudo gratiae'.

[184] Smyth (1563), 65 v: 'Cum enim dixisset, stipendium peccati mors, quis non conuenientissime & congruenter addere iudicaret, stipendium iustitiae vita aeterna?'

attain His grace by his works. Those who rejected the gift of grace and neglected to contribute to their own salvation would receive their just reward in condemnation, those who sought after a life with God through their own efforts and the gift of His grace would be rewarded by justification. Indeed, 'because as through the merit of sin, the result—like a wage—is death, so through the merit of justice, the result—like a wage—is eternal life'.[185]

---

[185] Smyth (1563), 65 v: 'Quia sicut merito peccati, tanquam stipendium, redditur mors, ita merito iustitiae, tanquam stipendium, redditur vitae aeternae'.

CHAPTER FOUR

MONASTIC VOWS

Following the dissolution of English monasteries in the 1530s, a debate about the intrinsic nature of monastic vows inevitably seems contrived. To a modern observer any such controversy, in a country that no longer knew practising nuns or monks, certainly appears futile. Yet what has been reduced to a marginal point of contention today, for more than forty years—from 1520-1560—moved a large number of scholars to consider closely the notion of celibate clergy and cloistered religious. For the evangelical advocates of married clergy, monasticism was at best an outdated expression of piety, at worst the superstitious segregation of the people of God.[1] Catholic defenders on the other hand regarded the monastic life as the purest expression of human sanctification.[2]

Richard Smyth's defence of the monastic life has to be considered in the wider context of the catholic doctrine of justification that was so central to his thought. It has been pointed out above that he understood the threefold monastic vow primarily in terms of supererogatory works, a view many of his catholic contemporaries would have shared.[3] He explained in his *Bouclier*:

> It is a thynge of greate rewarde, to offer vnto God, a thyng, which thou owest not, than to render to hym that, whyche thou art requyred to dooe of duetye by the lawe of God. ... Of this highe perfection are, or should be al religious men and women, whiche

---

[1] See for instance P. M. Vermigli, *Defensio D. Petri Martyris Vermilii Florentini diuinarum literarum in schola Tigurina professoris, ad Riccardi Smythaei Angli, olim theologiae professoris Oxoniensis duos libellos de caelibatu sacerdotum, & votis monasticis, nunc primùm in luce edita*, Basel, 1559, 58.

[2] For instance reflected in the teaching of Augustine, *De conjugiis adulteriis libri* [=A. Reifferscheid, G. Wissowa, edd., *Corpus Scriptorum Ecclesiaticorum Latinorum*, Wien, 1890 (cited as: CSEL), 41.409], who held that those who choose the monastic life can cherish 'the hope of receiving a more glorious place in Christ's inheritance'; this sentiment is echoed by the Council of Trent's ruling on matrimony 1563, H. Denzinger and A. Schönmetzer, edd., *Enchiridion symbolorum et definitionum de rebus fidei et morum: Kompendium der Glaubensbekenntnisse und kirchlichen Lehrentscheidungen*, Freiburg im Breisgau and Rome, [38]1999 (cited as: DS), 1810.

[3] Above, chapter III, 2.2.

haue vowed and professed voluntarie povrete, to haue and possesse no worldly good. ... Whiche are now thruste out of theyr monasteries.[4]

For English catholics, the abolition of monastic orders was a severe disruption of a soteriological cycle which had hitherto characterised Christianity. They believed firmly that human salvation was at risk once man no longer performed works beyond the keeping of God's commandments. In the past, people had sought to attain justification by joining religious orders and submitting themselves entirely to the will of God. Once these orders had been abolished, the ordinary 'honour and seruice of God'—penitential acts, prayers for souls in purgatory, or indulgences—would also be subjected to similar erosion, Smyth feared.[5]

In the light of this bleak prospect, in spring 1550 Smyth launched a vicious attack on his evangelical successor in Oxford, Peter Martyr. He rightly assumed that his condemnation of Vermigli's apostasy and his censure of the monk's subsequent marriage would not remain unanswered. Their vituperative exchange was part of the ongoing debate on monastic vows and celibacy that had captivated sixteenth-century theologians. In his attack on Martyr, Smyth referred to earlier exchanges between Bucer and Eberhard Billick,[6] while in his correspondence, Vermigli recalled the debates of his Cambridge counterpart with Bartholomaeus Latomus and Stephen Gardiner on the matter.[7] There are numer-

---

[4] R. Smyth, *A bouclier of the catholic fayth of Christes church, conteynyng diuers matters now of late called into controuersy, by the newe gospellers. Made by Richard Smith, doctour of diuinitee, & the Quenes hyghnes Reader of the same in her graces vniuersite of Oxford*, London, 1554, C ii v-C iii r.

[5] Smyth (1554), C iii r: 'The suppression of abbeys, or collages, and the abusing of them, and of other the churche landes, whiche men haue by impropriations (against gods lawe) haue been & are continually a gret dammage & decay vnto the honour and seruice of God, the godly bryngyng vp of scholers in vertue and learning, and vnto the common weale in woldly thinges'.

[6] R. Smyth, *Eivsdem D. Richardi Smythei confvtatio qvorundam articulorum de votis Monasticis Petri Martyris Itali, Oxoniae in Anglia Theologiam proficientis. De votis haec incogitanter, indocte, & impie effutiuit, obnixe contendas illa nuncupare Deo nefas esse homini Christiano, saltem vt sint perpetuo necessaria*, Leuven, 1550¹, G 7 r; for Billick, see A. Postina, *Der Karmelit Eberhard Billick*, Freiburg, 1901.

[7] G. C. Gorham, ed., *Gleanings of a few scattered Ears, during the period of the Reformation in England*, London, 1857, 154; B. Latomus, *Responsio ad epistolam quandam Martini Buceri de dispensatione eucharistiae et invocatione divorum et coelibatu clericorum*, Köln, 1543, in: L. Keil, ed., *Corpus Catholicorum* 8 (1924); in 1543 Gardiner wrote two disapproving letters against Bucer's *Die ander verteydigung und*

ous other such encounters, especially in the German Empire, the Low Countries and Scandinavia.

1. EARLY REFORMATION DEBATES (1521-1541)

The attacks by Josse Clichtove and the Dominican Michael Vehe on Luther's 1521 *Themata de Votis* and his *Iudicium de votis monasticis* were among the first controversial writings.[8] Also among the first-generation defenders of monastic vows was the Franciscan Nikolas Herborn of Köln. In his *Epistola ad Coloniensem felicissimam urbem* against François Lambert, Herborn attacked the abolition of monastic life among the 'religious innovations'. A fervent advocate of monasticism, he devoted parts of his *Enchiridion* and his *Confutatio* to a systematic discussion of celibacy and monastic vows in order to refute 'the heresies of this age'—in particular the rise of Lutheranism.[9]

Another German pioneer, the Augustinian Kilian Leib, began his attacks two years after Clichtove's first refutation. Three years later, he reiterated his positions in a lengthy tract in the vernacular, *Der kyrchen schwert wider Martin Luter*.[10] A proficient defender of celibacy and monastic vows, he contributed four more works to the

---

erklerung der Christlichen Lehr in etlichen fürnehmen Hauptstucken, Bonn, 1543, in which the reformer had confuted Latomus's manifesto on clerical celibacy. Bucer intended to counter Gardiner's attack but was apparently discouraged from doing so.

[8] J. Clichtove, *De laude monasticae religionis opusculum: vnde ipsa ceperit exordium incrementum et stabilimentum diludice declarans, quoniam etiam modo tria praecipua illius vota, obedientia, paupertas & castitas integre observandae sint*, Paris, 1523; M. Vehe, *Assertio sacrorum quorundam axiomatum, quae a nonnullis nostri seculi pseudoprophetis in periculosam rapiuntur controuersiam*, Leipzig, 1535, ch. 4 (celibacy) and ch. 13 (monastic vows).

[9] Cf. F. Lambert, *Commentariorvm Francisci Lamberti Avenionensis Theologi de Sacro Coniugio, & aduersus pollutissimum Regni perditionis caelibatum, Liber*, Strassburg, 1524: 'huius tempore haereses'; N. Herborn, *Epistola fratris Nicolai Herborn Minoritae Guardiani Brulensis, ad Coloniensem felicissimam urbem*, Köln, 1527; idem, *Locorum communiorum adversus huius tempore haereses Enchiridion*, Köln, 1528, loci 30-40; idem, *Confutatio Lutheranismi Danici anno 1530 conscripta a Nicolao Stagefyr seu Herborneo OFM*, Quaracchi, 1902, §§18 and 24-25.

[10] K. Leib, *Der kyrchen schwert wider Martin Luter* in: I. v. Döllinger, ed., *Beiträge zur politischen, kirchlichen und Cultur-Geschichte* 2 (1863), 445-611.

debate.[11] Central to the controversy was the dispute between the Carmelite provincial Eberhard Billick of Köln and Bucer. In many ways, it mirrored the later controversy between Smyth and Vermigli: Billick was both a colleague of Bucer's in Köln, and among his most prominent critics. In his *Iudicium de doctrina Martini Buceri*, he voiced his conviction that Bucer 'mingled truth and falsehood, with the intent to lead astray the simple-minded'.[12] Like Smyth's attack on Martyr six years later, Billick's rejection of Bucer hinged on the fact that the reformer had broken his vow of celibacy by entering into marriage. Bucer's praise of the sale of church property for the relief of the poor in Strassburg was cited as evidence of evangelical appropriation of monastic property. Billick concluded:

> This excellent reformer is most compassionate in teaching theft, robbery and plundering of church property to feed the sick, the poor, the strangers, while in reality those goods are being used to support the debauchery of heretical preachers, apostates, breakers of vows, hypocrites and all those living in illegitimate unions. Is that piety? What would be more godless? If that is reformation, what then is destruction? If all this is permissible, what then is prohibited?[13]

The crisis in Köln escalated when Bartholomaeus Latomus from Trier and Matthias Kraemer, a local lecturer, both independently attacked Bucer's views.[14] Following the publication of a second edition and the translation of Billick's *Iudicium* into German, the reformer published a refutation and instigated an academic debate on the subject.[15] The differences culminated in a confrontation between the conservative cathedral chapter and archbishop Hermann von Wied who, despite severe pressure from the emperor, continued to toe Bucer's line.

---

[11] K. Leib, *Sendbrief zur Beschützung geistlichs Closterstand gegen die Lutherischen*, in: I. v. Döllinger, ed., *Beiträge zur politischen, kirchlichen und Cultur-Geschichte* 2 (1863), 445-611: 'Kilian Leib, Annales Maiores 1524-1548'; Döllinger (1863), 445-611: K. Leib, *De caelibatu atque castimonia epistola, Spiegel der Sponsen Christi*; idem, *Apologia oder verantworttung des Closterstandes*; and his *Resolutio questionis de S. Apostolo* [Paul] *an coniungatus fuerit necne*, Ingolstadt, 1545.
[12] E. Billick, *Iudicium deputatorum et universitatis Coloniensis de doctrina et vocatione Martini Buceri ad Bonnam*, Köln, 1543, 39 v.
[13] Ibid., 36 r.
[14] M. Kraemer, *Christlich Bericht*, Köln, 1543.
[15] Also published in 1543; translated by Caspar von Gennep, 1543.

MONASTIC VOWS

149

Twenty years into the debate, the protestant observers at the council of Trent once again struggled to defend clerical marriage. They argued that to enforce clerical celibacy was demeaning to marriage although, in their view, scripture ranked marriage higher than chastity.[16] Their thesis, 'marriage to a spouse is greater grace than others', was presented to the bishops at Trent together with the assertion that Western clergy should be allowed to marry regardless of canon law or ecclesiastical vows, since celibacy slighted the matrimonial union.[17] Priests who were not conscious of having received the gift of chastity, therefore, ought to be permitted to marry.[18] This opinion was rejected by the council.[19]

The historical understanding of celibacy, or the requirement of a continent life-style for already-married clergy, dated back to the early Fathers. Some arguments encountered in the sixteenth century had already been debated in the patristic period.[20] The Fathers differed widely in their interpretation of scriptural evidence such as 1 Cor 9.4f.[21] They offered opposite views on whether the disciples of Jesus were married and, if so, whether they had been married before, during or after Jesus's call to follow Him. The pericopae used in argument regularly included passages that could be interpreted in favour of married disciples with families

---

[16] A view favoured in Switzerland for instance by Heinrich Bullinger and in England by William Turner, cf. H. Bullinger, *The golde boke of christen matrimonye, newly set forthe in English*, London, 1543, A 2 v, and W. Turner, *The huntyng & fyndyng out of the Romishe fox whiche more then seven yeares hath bene hyd among the bisshoppes of Englong*, Basel [=Bonn], 1543, B 2 r-B 2 v.

[17] In 1563; in: Görres-Gesellschaft, ed., *Concilium Tridentinum*, Freiburg im Breisgau, 1901—, (cited as: CT) Session 24.1809: 'Matrimonium coniugibus maiorem gratiam quam aliis'.

[18] 'You should state that Western priests may contract a marriage, you should not condemn marriage, but allow that everyone who does not feel that they have the gift of chastity can contract a marriage' (Licite contrahere posse matrimonium sacerdotes occidentales, non damnare matrimonium, posseque omnes contrahere matrimonium, qui non sentiunt se habere donum castitatis).

[19] CT 24.1809.

[20] For an extensive discussion of the patristic sources for the canonical requirement of celibacy, see C. Cochini SJ, *Les origines patristiques du célibat sacerdotal*, Paris, 1981, 187-412.

[21] 1 Cor 9.5: 'Do we not have the right to be accompanied by a believing wife, as do the other Apostles and the brothers of the Lord, and Cephas?'

(such as Mt 19.27 and Lk 18.28-30),[22] or scriptural evidence which could be interpreted as referring to non-conjugal relationships, such as 1 Cor 9.5.[23] Other Pauline evidence debated intensely included 1 Tim 3.2-5, 1 Tim 3.12-13, 1 Tim 5.9 and 1 Tim 5.14.[24] The passage from 1 Cor 7, in which Paul discusses the relative merits of matrimony and celibacy, was employed by Smyth to extract an oral *tractatio* on vows from his evangelical successor. Together with Mt 19.12 it featured among the most controversial pericopae.[25]

Rather than retort to the testimony of the council of Nicaea on clerical celibacy, most evangelical propagators of clerical marriage preferred to refer to one particular incident at Nicaea. The intervention of 'bishop Paphnutius' became a hallmark of polemical debate.[26] The Byzantine church-historian Socrates described the incident in his *Ecclesiastical History*:

> It had seemed good to the bishops [of Nicaea] to introduce a new law in the church: consecrated men—I mean bishops, priests and deacons—should not sleep anymore with the wives they had married

---

[22] Mt 19.27: 'Look, we have left everything and followed you'; Lk 18.28-30: '"Look, we have left our homes and followed you". And Jesus said to them, "Truly I tell you, there is no one who has left house or wife or brothers or parents or children, for the sake of the kingdom of God, who will not get back very much more in this age, and in the age to come eternal life" '.

[23] ἀδελφὴν γυναῖκα, 'as with a sister', 'a sister wife' or 'a wife as sister'.

[24] 1 Tim 3.2-5: 'A bishop must be ... married only once. ... He must manage his own household well, keeping his children submissive and respectful in every way—for if someone does not know how to manage his own household, how can he take care of God's church?'; 1 Tim 3.12-13: 'Let deacons be married only once, and let them manage their children and their households well'; 1 Tim 5.9-12: 'Let a widow be put on the list if she is not less than sixty years old and has been married only once. ... But refuse to put younger widows on the list; for when their sensual desires alienate them from Christ, they want to marry, and so they incur condemnation for having violated their first pledge'; 1 Tim 5.14: 'So I would have younger widows marry, bear children, and manage their households, so as to give the adversary no occasion to revile us'.

[25] Mt 19.12: 'There are eunuchs who have made themselves eunuchs for the sake of the kingdom of heaven'.

[26] Both Smyth and Martyr believed in the existence of the bishop of 'upper Thebaid', cf. Smyth (1550[1]), G v r, where he held that the principal question that arose was 'whether the custom of wives be permitted to those priests who married them before being admitted to holy orders, as Paphnutius persuaded that synod' (An sacerdotibus permittendus sit vsus vxorum, quas duxerant antequam sacris erant initiati, quod synodo illi persuasit Paphnutius?) Vermigli argued that 'Catholics of every age deny sacred scripture' (Cum scriptura sacra negant catholici omnis aetatis); Vermigli (1559), 19.

while they were laymen. As the matter was under discussion, Paphnutius stood up in the middle of the episcopal assembly and, with a strong voice, protested that such a heavy yoke should not be imposed on consecrated men. The conjugal bed is honourable, and marriage has no stain, he said. One should fear lest, through an excess of severity, the bishops might bring harm to the church. ... It was by name of chastity that Paphnutius did not hesitate to call a life in common with a legitimate wife. It is quite enough to require of these clerics that they are not to remarry [after ordination], in accordance with the ancient traditions of the church—but let us not separate them from the wives whom, monogamous as they are, they once married when they were laymen.[27]

This claim was frequently cited by evangelicals. Catholic scholars tried very hard to repudiate the incident. In the eighteenth century historical research relegated Paphnutius to the realm of myths, and Robert Bellarmine's interpretation of the concept of perpetual continence was confirmed.[28] Bellarmine maintained that sacerdotal continence had been 'observed by deacons, priests and bishops since the time of the Apostles'.[29] As an apostolic tradition, it was rightly enshrined in canon law as a prerequisite to ordination. Protestant theologians tried to resurrect Paphnutius in the early twentieth-century, but a comprehensive protestant refutation finally ended the debate, five hundred years after Bellarmine's rejection of the existence of the 'bishop of upper Thebaid'.[30]

2. Smyth's 'De Votis Monasticis' (1550)

The intellectual exchange between Smyth and Vermigli not only comprised the first attack in a series of three works directed by Smyth against his evangelical successor and the only direct response Vermigli ever made 'to Richard Smyth's books'.[31] The first

---

[27] Socrates, *Ecclesiastical History*, in: J. P. Migne, ed., *Patrologia cursus completus, series Graeca*, Paris, 1857-1866, (cited as: PG) 67.1016-1046.

[28] J. Stiltinck, 'An verisimile sit, S. Paphnutium se in Concilio Nicaeno opposuisse legi de continentia Sacerdotum et Diaconorum', in: *Acta Sanctorum Septembris*, Venice, 1761, 3.748-87.

[29] Cochini (1981), 214.

[30] P. Nagel, ed., *Probleme der koptischen Literatur*, Institut für Byzantinistik der Martin-Luther-Universität Halle-Wittenberg, 1968, 145-153: F. Winckelmann, 'Paphnutius, der Bekenner und Bischof'.

[31] 'Ad Riccardi Smythaei libellos'.

edition of Smyth's *De coelibatu liber unus* and his *De Votis Monasticis* had been printed in March 1550.[32] Their continuous pagination indicates that the two volumes were sold as one. They had probably been composed before Smyth left England in April 1549. This is indicated by the observation that Martyr was 'now' lecturing on the first epistle to the Corinthians at Oxford, 'that is, in the month of March, in the year of the Lord 1549'.[33] The volume was a direct response to the *tractatio* on monastic vows Smyth had provoked at the Divinity School during Martyr's exposition of 1 Cor 7. The fact that a debate or *tractatio* took place at Oxford was confirmed by Vermigli's testimony.[34]

The book followed scholastic method. Just as in an oral disputation, Smyth cited a passage by Vermigli and commented on the extract. He had gleaned his material from Martyr's lectures on 1 Cor, or from discussions he instigated during those lectures. In Smyth's work this is indicated by the recurrence of a qualifying 'says he' (*inquit*) to introduce Martyr's views. Vermigli must have been aware that those 'opinions of mine' might be used to provide the overarching structure for a polemical publication against him, since he confirmed that

> at about the time of the exposition of the end of chapter seven [of 1 Cor], I thought—in good faith—that I would act as an assurance to my readers. What was rather vainly condemned was what my opponents appear to say.[35]

Vermigli's *Defensio* followed similar lines. He picked examples from Smyth's refutation and proceeded to counter them by adding his own interpretation of the matter. The work was primarily conceived as a defence of his own position; by defending himself he repudiated Smyth's claims. It is a less polemical and much more measured work. Rather than follow scholastic lines of argument, Martyr made use of exegetical methods to prove a point. The

---

[32] Smyth (1550), subscript; A i v.

[33] Smyth (1550), A viij r: 'Peter Martyr ... who is now, that is in March 1549, lecturing at Oxford on the first epistle to the Corinthians' (Petrus Martyr, qui nunc, hoc est Anno D. 1549 mense martio Oxoniae in Anglia enarrat epistolam ad Corinthios Priorem).

[34] Vermigli (1559), introduction 1.

[35] Vermigli (1559), introduction 3: 'meae rationes'; 'Idque in expositione circa finem 7. capitis lectoribus me aliquando praestium ire, bona fide recepi. Deinde otiolum quod damnatus, quae uisa sunt meae sycophantae respondi'.

overall format of the work, however, was dictated by his opponent, to whose *responsiones* he added his own *conclusiones*. Both therefore followed the rules prescribed for an oral scholastic disputation.[36]

As in all polemical works, both opponents accused the other of varying degrees of impure academic method, apostasy (in Vermigli's case), or frequent recantations (in Smyth's case).[37] Smyth did not shrink back from using expletives, nor were the two writers sparing in their use of negative superlatives when referring to the other. Smyth called Vermigli's teaching 'as immoral as it is unlearned' (cum impudenter, tum indocte), prefaced most arguments as 'most false' (falsissimus), and threw in 'impious' (impietas) or 'crimes' (crimina) for good measure.[38] Martyr in turn spoke of the fact that Smyth

> possessed the craft of a smith and sharpened himself against the true Word and, although he was unable to prevail in a fair fight, he still stirred up the weak and strengthened the opposition to the Gospel of Christ, when he could do nothing else, with sticks and reeds. To the strong who have God on their side and are not disturbed by every wind of doctrine his attempts are hardly harmful at all.[39]

This had caused him to reply to 'the impious and superstitious matters in this book, as they are forceful and serious'.[40] Since Smyth had sullied his reputation Martyr emphasised that he wrote in self-defence and had always taken great courage from Mt 5.11:

---

[36] Cf. for instance, S. Gibson, ed., *Statuta antiqua universitatis Oxoniensis*, Oxford, 1931, 128.

[37] Smyth (1550), G i r-G i v frequently accused Vermigli of breaking his vows in order to marry: 'Who was released by breaking his vow (such a man is that Peter, who—they say—took monastic vows in Italy) to consider marriage lawful in his mind and not admit that it was any crime of his' (Qui uoto est astrictus persoluendo, nuptias vt licitas in mentem inducere, nullum sese admississe scaelus). In like vein Vermigli attacked Smyth, for instance in Vermigli (1559), 6.

[38] Smyth (1559), F ii v; for instance F vii v; G vii r.

[39] Vermigli (1559), 2: 'Fabrili uersutia, & ipse contra ueritatem linguam acuit, & quamquam iusto praelio non possit uincere, turbat attamen infirmos, & aduersario Euangelii Christi, quando aliter nequit, uel baculis arundineis confirmat: robustis uerò, qui non ad omnem uentum doctrine, ut paruuli agitantur, Deo propitio, conatus eius minimè nocent'.

[40] Vermigli (1559), 3: 'Impiis & superstitiosis eius libelli, tanquam fortes & graues'.

'Blessed are you when people revile you and persecute you and utter all kinds of evil against you falsely on my account'.[41]

Both rivals clearly believed the dictum that 'truth is often revealed in debate'.[42] Vermigli claimed that Smyth merely repeated arguments and that 'he is unable to present anything new. What he says is merely that which has thus far been said and has been repeated by the other flatterers of the Pope and the henchmen of Antichrist'.[43] Smyth tried to convince his readers 'how foolishly Peter Martyr hallucinates'.[44] The readers, however, had probably made up their minds already: religious conservatives would agree enthusiastically with Smyth and catholic authorities would bestow *imprimatur* and imperial privilege on his books. Evangelical readers supported Vermigli's views and were convinced that nothing but popish abuse came from catholic presses. Evangelical officials, therefore, banned Smyth's writings and intercepted them on their way to England. Books like those published by Smyth and Martyr were intended for a scholarly audience, and each side sifted through the writings of the opposition, only to sharpen their pens in order to refute them.

2.1. *Mt 19.12*

Without so much as an introduction to his work, Smyth leapt into the subject matter and opened his exposition by citing Vermigli's assertion that

> Virginity (he says) or abstention from intercourse with a wife is an open question throughout the Gospel, but whoever has permanently offered his virginity to God in order to preserve it, makes it a requirement and therefore abuses the Gospel against the very principle of the Gospel Christ preached.[45]

---

[41] Vermigli (1559), 3: 'He attacks me, and inveighs ferociously against my name' (meum nomen rabidè proscindat & insectetur).
[42] Vermigli (1559), ibid: 'Veritas altercando saepè admittitur'.
[43] Vermigli (1559), ibid: 'Nihil noui proferre ualuerit. Sed ea tantum habeat, quae ab alii Papae adulatoribus & Antichristi mercenarijs dicta & repetita hactenus fuerunt'.
[44] Smyth (1550), F iv r: 'Quam crasse hallucinatus sit Petrus Martyr'.
[45] Smyth (1550), F i v: 'Virginitas (inquit) aut continentia a concubitu cum vxore est res per euangelium libera, sed quisquis vouet eam Deo, perpetuo, duraturam, facit illam necessariam, ergo contra Christi authoris euangelij institutum, euangelio abutitur'.

This libertarian interpretation the Gospel filled Smyth with dismay, since it did not call into question the permanence of vows, but judged them contrary to the teaching of Christ like many of the rituals of the old Covenent.[46] Since Martyr's arguments were based on scriptural evidence, Smyth chose to counter them on the same terms. In a brief but pithy rejection, Smyth assembled a small collection of Old Testament excerpts (for instance Deut 23.22), as well as some New Testament passages (for instance Ac 5.1-10) relating to vows. In conclusion, he added further patristic testimony and impertinence to his arguments: 'How strangely these false proofs begin and conclude. How on earth do clarity and the obvious manage to escape Peter Maryr's arguments altogether?'[47]

In order to substantiate his assertion that scripture contained evidence endorsing vows, Smyth coupled his opening quotation with a second statement from Martyr's lectures: 'Nothing that refers to vows (he says) can be read in the Gospel'.[48] Both arguments had been held by 'the Lutherans, of whom John Calvin is the dirtiest' long before Martyr.[49] The fact that the council of Trent had recently taught that the Apostles led celibate lives only confirmed Smyth's beliefs that Vermigli merely reproduced the opinions of other heretics.[50] Mt 19.12 established that the Gospels contained examples of vows of celibacy: 'how untrue this is—although it is constantly repeated—... that eunuchs who have castrated themselves for the sake of the kingdom of God, and dedicated their chastity to God, enjoy eternal merit'.[51] He emphasised that those who were celibate for the sake of the kingdom had dedicated themselves to God by living chaste lives by vows of continence and self-castration (*execti sunt testiculi*). They therefore

---

[46] Smyth (1550), F i v: 'Who can restrain himself from laughter, or rather tears, when he observes the man whom many trust?' (Quis potest se hic à risu, imo à lachrimis potius temperare, cum videat illum, à quo nonnullis spes est?)

[47] Smyth (1550), F ii r: 'Quam absurdos inceptosque exitus habent argumenta ex falso petitia, vel hoc Petri Martyris argumento propalam ac perspicuum euadit?'.

[48] Smyth (1550), F ii r: 'In evangelio (inquit) nihil legitur quod ad votum pertinat'.

[49] Smyth (1550), ibid.: 'Lutherani è quorum colluuie est Ioannes Caluinus'.

[50] Council of Trent, Session 24; DS 1807-1809.

[51] Smyth (1550), ibid.: 'Hoc quam sit falsum, ac perperam assertum, ... quod eunuchis qui sese castrauerunt propter regnum Dei, perpetuum profitebantur, ac vouebant deo continentiam'

neither were able nor at liberty to engage in intercourse (*nec libet nec licet*). Consequently, Vermigli's claim that 'nothing ... refers to vows' circumvented the argument, Smyth concluded.[52]

Vermigli's rejection of Smyth's accusations on the basis of Deut 23.22 and Mt 19.12 is divided in two parts, an *assertio* and a *defensio*. He defined his own understanding of a vow: a vow was either a strong wish (*desiderium*) or an ardent prayer, but could also represent a pledge made to God out of a prior obligation.[53] While Martyr acknowledged that anyone who made a religious promise was under the obligation to fulfil his promise, he denied that they constituted the strict and binding vows Smyth sought to defend, since 'by that very promise, we bind ourselves to offer God something in return'.[54] Martyr proceeded to distinguish between simple vows and solemn vows, as well as between public and private vows. Vows were 'holy and free promises' man made to God as a part of his religious beliefs during a communal act.[55] Because they have a binding quality which other human promises did not possess (as explained in Num 30.10-13), they were classified as a vow. He maintained that promises 'freely made' by definition could not be based on legal or canonical obligations, since they contravened the voluntary character of the vow.[56] This undermined any canonical requirements such as pre-ordination vows of chastity. As legal obligations, they could never be classified as 'promises freely made' and did not constitute a vow in the strictest sense of Martyr's definition.[57] He appealed to Lombard who held that 'a vow is testimony of a freely-made promise which, in religious matters, should rightfully be made to God'.[58] In Lombard's opinion therefore vows were not promises, Vermigli pointed out, but only

---

[52] Smyth (1550), F ii r: 'Nihil ... ad votum pertinat'.
[53] Vermigli (1559), 7.
[54] Vermigli (1559), 8: 'De ipsa promissione ... nos obstringimus ad aliquid Deo reddendae'.
[55] Vermigli (1559), ibid.: 'Sanctae & spontaneae promissiones'.
[56] Vermigli (1559), ibid.: 'That promise does not form a basis for a vow' (Illa promissio rationem Voti non habuit).
[57] Vermigli (1559), ibid.: 'spontaneae promissiones'.
[58] Peter Lombard, *Petri Lombardi, Episcopi Parisiensis, Sententiarum Libri IIII*, Venice, 1570, 4, distinctio 38: 'Votum esse testificationem quandam promissionis spontanea, quae Deo & de his quae Dei sunt, propriè fieri debet'.

represented the testimony of a promise, that is the act of making the promise itself.

In his *assertio* Martyr contrasted Smyth's selective Old Testament evidence with scriptural material that enabled him to adopt an even narrower interpretation, excluding a large number of binding promises. By suggesting communal rather than individual acts of covenant, he reduced the spectrum for debate even further. In effect there could be hardly any binding long-term promises freely made by individuals. If these existed at all, then the evidence from scripture as well as tradition suggested a communal act rather than an individual act. In his *defensio* Martyr focussed more closely on evidence from the New Testament. Specifying that Paul principally spoke of vows 'according to Mosaic law' (that is as part of the ritual requirements of the old Covenent superseded by the advent of Christ) he dismissed Smyth's allegorical interpretations altogether.[59]

Martyr chose to concentrate on the specific arguments from Mt 19.12 instead. He explained that the pericope did not substantiate the idea that those who had 'given themselves up for the sake of the kingdom of heaven' had previously agreed to take vows of celibacy. These 'eunuchs' never had the intention

> to make a vow of celibacy, but rather it is shown that several men were found for whom celibacy was a better way of promoting the Gospel, and they willingly abstained from marriage: neither nature, nor human force, prohibited them from having intercourse with women.[60]

In Mt 19.9-10 the Apostles approached Jesus to enquire about the fate of divorcees.[61] Vermigli commented: 'They did not say "does making a vow benefit a man?", but "not getting married"—and Christ did not approve their question—rather, he said that not everyone was to abstain from marriage, but only those to whom it

---

[59] Vermigli (1559), 11: 'de more Mosaico'.

[60] Vermigli (1559), 11: 'Caelibatum uouere, sed ostenditur, nonnullos inueniri qui ad promouendum Euangelium felicius, sponte, ac uolentes à coniugio abstineant: cum neque ab ipsa natura, neque ui hominum prohibiti fuerint, ne mulieribus commisceri possent'.

[61] Mt 19.9-10: 'Jesus said: "And I say to you, whoever divorces his wife, except for unchastity, and marries another commits adultery". His disciples said to Him, "If such is the case of a man with his wife, it is better not to marry".'

is granted'.[62] Jesus had neither spoken about vows nor had He touched upon the fact that 'those who abstain in order to promote the kingdom of heaven were prevented from taking a wife because of the terms of their vow'.[63] He only replied to the question of whether it is lawful for a man not to be married in the first place.

Martyr continued to question his opponent's reading of scripture when he exclaimed: 'Nor is it permitted to a true and serious theologian to reinforce a dogma on the basis of scripture—words which are understood differently in their correct and appropriate context'.[64] Martyr proceeded to accuse his opponent severely of ignoring dominical teaching when claiming that those 'whose testicles are cut off' neither are able nor may engage in intercourse.[65] How could eunuchs have been at liberty to engage in intercourse, if they had been incapable, Vermigli interjected disingenuously before rounding off his argument with a final acerbic rejoinder:

> And so, to say nothing about your papal eunuchs, you should have seen that they were willing and able: able, because the same mud always sticks to them, and willing, because—even if they are given a small handout by their bishops—they go and whore liberally and continually cause great scandal to the church.[66]

Most readers, no doubt, would have interpreted this passage as a direct reference to Smyth who, himself a catholic priest bound by laws of chastity, was routinely portrayed by Vermigli and his friends as causing 'great scandal' by allegedly unchaste behaviour.[67]

---

[62] Vermigli (1559), 11: 'Non dicunt, expedit homini uouere, sed non contrahere matrimonium, quod eorum dictum Christus non approbauit: imò dixit, non omnium esse à matrimonio abstinere, sed eorum quibus est datum'.

[63] Vermigli (1559), 13: 'Qui abstinent à coniugio propter regnum coelorum promouendum, lege uoti prohiberi ne uxorem ducant'.

[64] Vermigli (1559), ibid.: 'Nec licet sano & sobrio theologo dogma confirmare ex uerbis scripturae, quae aliter & quidem uere, atque commode intelligantur'.

[65] Vermigli (1559), ibid.: 'Quibus execti sunt testiculi'.

[66] Vermigli (1559), ibid.: 'Et ut non nihil dicam de tuis Eunuchis papisticis, uidere debueras, illis & libere, & licere. Libet, quia semper in eodem luto haerent: licet etiam, quia data pecuniola suis episcopis, impune, ac magno cum scandalo Ecclesiae perpetuo scortantur'.

[67] Vermigli (1559), ibid.: 'Magno cum scandalo', cf. Gorham (1857), 155, Vermigli to Bucer: '[Smyth] had a manservant who took to himself a wife: he lodged with them and, as is generally reported, they had all things in common. Such are the advocates of the *Celibacy of Clerks and Monks*'.

2.2. *Mt 19.27*

Smyth did not shrink from sharp criticism either. In his introduction to arguments from Mt 19.27, he sketched Martyr as inept, illogical, and the laughing-stock of the Oxford Divinity School:

> It should have been a cause of shame to this man Peter—if he wasn't so bereft of shame—to weave such an inept and inadequate argument in the presence of so many learned men as were at that time assembled in the Oxford Divinity School. They had come to hear him lecture. But whenever he began to speak among them, it was the same shifty and futile 'proof': 'You owe everything to God, so there is nothing you can dedicate to God by way of a vow'. He thought this an irrefutable syllogism, but was clearly inept and stupid.[68]

His ensuing argument hinged once more on the conviction that Martyr misinterpreted the Gospel-message to prove that there was no need to affirm acts of faith by vows. No-one could return anything to the giver of all gifts, since everything was a gift from God. The law of Christ forbade man to do so, Smyth quoted Martyr. In a lengthy exposition, Smyth rejected these opinions and used Mt 19.27 as evidence for the existence of the threefold vow of poverty, chastity and obedience in the apostolic age.[69]

At Oxford Vermigli had asked Smyth 'who would wish to go beyond the rightful promises of the Gospel in order to make a vow to God, when the Gospel urges chastity, poverty and virginity?'[70] When challenged directly with his evidence from Mt 19.12, he had offered an intriguing interpretation: his opponent claimed that the kingdom which those 'eunuchs' sought to attain was not the

---

[68] Smyth (1550), H vij r-H vij v: 'Puduisset ergo Petrum hunc si non omnem pudorem exisset, tam ineptus & imperitum nectere argumentum, coram tanta hominum doctorum contione, quanta tunc Oxoniae in gymnasio theologico, ad eum praelegendum auscultandum erat congregata, Quoties vero inter praelegendum inculcauit, istud futile & elube argumentum: Debes omnia Deo, ergo nihil est quod illi voto dedices—irrefutabilem hunc putat esse syllogismum, eum sit plane ineptus & stupidus'.

[69] Mt 19.27: 'Look, we have left everything and followed you. What then will we have?'; Smyth (1550), H vij r, omitting references to vows of obedience, 'Does Christ not want me to be free from the slavery of chastity and poverty?' (Vult ne Christus si me liberum à seruitute continentiae, & paupertatis?)

[70] Smyth (1550), F viij r: 'Qui fieret, vt ille progredi velle vtra euangelium recte dicatur, qui ex Deo voueat, quae consulit euangelium nempe castitatem, paupertatem, virginitatem'.

same place that was open to all other followers of the Gospel. Rather, Christ had referred to a place 'where Jewish laws are not kept'.[71] Vows belonged to the cultic traditions of the Old Testament which had been superseded by the Gospel. There was no place for vows among those seeking the kingdom of Christ. Anyone making vows was excluded from that kingdom, since he still adhered to the self-imposed religion rejected by Paul in Gal 2.23.[72]

While Smyth conceded that it was possible to live without the rituals of the old Covenent, he held strongly that they could never be disregarded completely. Just as the passover meal foreshadowed the eucharist, or the keeping of sabbath prefigured Christian festivals, so vows also were visible indicators of the age to come and therefore could not be construed as 'detrimental to religion'.[73] Smyth next concentrated on evidence from Mt 19.27. He elaborated that the Apostles strove toward 'celibacy and virginity for the perfection of the Gospel' in order to receive something 'far more excellent ... than the rewards of former generations'.[74] Their statement 'we have left everything and followed you, what then will we have?' not only confirmed their desire to attain perfection, but also their expectation that they would be rewarded. As in his *Diatriba de hominis justificatione*, he elaborated further that the call for supererogatory works, such as vows, could be supported by scriptural evidence, such as 1 Tim 5.18.[75] He felt justified in concluding: 'Now how much more aware of taking on work are those who combat all lust and lead a completely celibate life,

---

[71] Smyth (1550), ibid.: 'Quam Iudaeis non seruantibus ea'.
[72] Col 2.22-23: 'All these regulations refer to things that perish with use; they are simply human commands and teachings. These have indeed an appearance of wisdom in promoting self-imposed piety, humility, and severe treatment of the body, but they are of no value in checking self-indulgence'.
[73] Smyth (1550), H viij v: 'noxius Dei cultus'.
[74] Smyth (1550), G iv r: 'Caelibatum ac virginitatem ad euangelij perfectionem'; 'aliorum priorum praemijs ... longe praestantius'.
[75] For instance, R. Smyth, *Diatriba de hominis justificatione aedita Oxoniae anno 1550 mense februario adversum Petrum Martyrem Vermelium ... nunc apostatam*, Leuven, 1550, 22; see above, chapter III, 138. 1 Tim 5.18: 'The labourer deserves to be paid'. The fact that this pericope is embedded in practical guidelines regarding the treatment of employees and farm-animals, did evidently not deter Smyth from offering an allegorical interpretation, which was rejected by Peter Martyr, cf. Smyth (1550): F viij r.

abstaining from marriage, rather than those who enjoy the embraces of their wife'.[76]

Smyth emphasised that just as the Apostles had given up everything—property and families—in order to proclaim the Gospel, so their successors also were obliged to follow that precept. This was to fulfil the hope they both shared: 'A life more perfect than that of married men'.[77] It was evident that Christ had instructed His disciples to live chaste lives. Vows to that effect were not only permissible but a requirement for all seeking ordination.[78] He launched a final *ad hominem* attack in conclusion, in which he named Martyr a liar and apostate. He concluded: 'As you imitate Calvin and deny that celibacy and a vow of chastity were a vow to them ... you Peter, by your impudence—not to mention malice—are that which may be read above'.[79]

In reply, Martyr's interpretation of Mt 19.27 contextualised the pericope and considered the question of Christian vocation in general. To follow Christ, Martyr emphasised, was open to every Christian. To heed the divine call in order to receive greater merit later was a reasonable prerequisite only when read in conjunction with Mt 19.29, where everything abandoned is contrasted with a rich reward.[80] The disciples had already become recipients of divine munificence, just as the Apostle Paul sustained himself by the charity of his congregations.[81] There was no need to strive beyond the commandments and to wait for reward, he concluded:

---

[76] Smyth (1550), G iv r: 'Iam quid nescit plus laboris insumere qui expugnantes omnem libidinem & paenitus ab officio coniugali abstinentes caelibem degunt vitam, quam qui indulget vxorem amplexibus'.

[77] Smyth (1550), ibid.: 'Perfectionem maiorem quam coniugatorum'; cf. Smyth (1550), G iv r-G v r: 'Surely their life is more perfect?' (Nonne istorum perfectior est vita?); 'Chastity is better for men than marriage' (Melior est autem castitas quam nuptorum). In another allegory Smyth concluded that those living chaste lives should be identified with those numbered in 1 Cor 3.12f. He referred to Augustine, *De fide et operibus S. Avgvstini episcopi Hipponensis liber* [=PL 40.199-223] in support of his interpretation.

[78] Smyth (1550), G v r.

[79] Smyth (1550), G iv r: 'Cum tu Caluinum imitatus negas celibatum & votum continentiae fuisse eis votum ... tu Petre, qua es impudentia ne dicam malitia id prorsus prelegendo'.

[80] Vermigli (1559), 17; Mt 19.29: 'And everyone who has left houses or brothers or sisters or father or mother or children or fields, for my name's sake, will receive a hundred-fold, and will inherit eternal life'.

[81] For instance Lk 5.3-5.10; Phil 4.15-18.

'Therefore, just as the Apostles did not give up their wealth, because they never owned anything in any case, is it similarly improbable that they left their wives'.[82] A married clergyman himself, he rejected the view that married Apostles had abandoned their wives: they would have lent their husbands valuable assistance in spreading the Gospel.[83]

In a brief selection of highlights from conciliar and ecclesiastical history, Martyr explained that there would not have been a single 'obstat' at the Council of Nicaea 'so that the ministers of the church would not rush off to leave their wives; as if Christ merely by calling them separated the Apostles from their wives in a permanent divorce'.[84] 'Bishop Paphnutius' made another appearance and his 'intervention' on behalf of married clergy was again cited as proof that there had been no apostolic principle of celibacy.[85]

Martyr next tackled the problem of the alleged vows of poverty. He explained that it was difficult to comprehend how leaving behind property could presuppose a vow: 'Nor can I understand how to leave behind one's possessions or to own nothing of one's own could construe a vow, as these sophists make out'.[86] He remained unconvinced by his opponent's proposition that the Apostles had taken vows of poverty.[87] The lack of further arguments was probably the reason for another *ad hominem* attack: 'Besides, you left England so that the degree of your treachery should remain concealed. Should I then assume that you made a vow not to return to England?'[88] In dismissing his opponent's conclusion that an accomplished action presupposed a prior vow,

---

[82] Vermigli (1559), 18: 'Vt igitur apostoli non sic abiecerunt pecunias, ut nullas unquam habuerint, ita non est credendum, eos ita reliquisse uxores.'

[83] Vermigli (1559), 19.

[84] Vermigli (1559), 19: 'Ne praeciperetur ministris ecclesiasticis ab uxoribus discedere, si Christus uocando apostolos perpetuo diuortio eos ab uxoribus diuisisset'; he added the example of the Apostle Peter's wife (cf. 1 Cor 9.5) and the exhortation to bishops in 1 Tim 3.

[85] Vermigli (1559), ibid.

[86] Vermigli (1559), ibid.: 'Neque possum intellegere, quomodo sua relinquere, uel, nihil habere proprij significet uouere, quemadmodum hi sophistae uolunt', citing Plato's *Republic*, 3 as further evidence: 'Guards and assistants possess no property of their own' (Custodes & auxiliarij nihil habuerunt proprij).

[87] Vermigli (1559), ibid.

[88] Vermigli (1559), 19: 'Tu praeterea reliquisti Angliam, ne patereris quod tua perfidia commerita fuerat. Ex te scire uelim, an uoueris in Angliam non redire?'

Martyr pointed to Smyth's own biography to illustrate this. If Smyth believed that the Apostles had made a vow of poverty by giving up everything, then he and all others who happened to leave property, preferments or—as it were—homeland, had made the same vow; a clumsy generalisation aimed at the feelings of his opposition.

Martyr did not devote much energy to Smyth's rejection on logical grounds of his claim that man cannot render anything to God.[89] He concluded that 'they consider that they displayed great obedience, having been called by God and leaving all their possessions'.[90] To follow Christ implied living in obedience to one's particular calling. This obedience encompassed a range of expressions, interestingly including giving up property and family ties. The principal consideration was to heed that call.[91] There was no reason to assume that the Apostles had taken vows to relinquish all in order to follow Christ. The apostolate undoubtedly required sacrifices: 'we agree, therefore, that the Apostles were—for some time—without either their wives or their possessions in order to follow Christ and preach. But we will not grant that they renounced all these things by way of a vow'.[92]

Martyr's argument that man cannot make a promise to live up to his calling is as inconsequential as Smyth's claim to the contrary. Martyr's *defensio* from Mt 19.27 was nothing but a fault-finding exercise. He sought to dissect Smyth's logic in order to dismiss the entire argument on the basis of logical errors. This holds true for the remaining *defensiones* in this section. Vermigli employed a standard formula when pointing to three logical errors in Smyth's arguments: (1) no-one knew whether the Apostles left all their belongings behind, therefore it was impossible to infer from Mt 19.27 that they had done so; (2) it was impossible to prove whether or not they had repossessed their belongings after the resurrec-

---

[89] Martyr began his refutation by turning the argument around, and questioned whether it was at all possible to take vows to fulfill duties one was obliged to undertake.

[90] Vermigli (1559), 20: 'Hoc habuerunt quod a Domino uocati sua omnia relinquendo egregiam praestiterunt obedientiam'.

[91] Vermigli (1559), ibid.

[92] Vermigli (1559), 20f.: 'Fatebimur ergo apostolos quandoque fuisse absque uxoribus & suis rebus, ut Christum sequerentur, & praedicarent. Sed quòd istorum omnium usum uoto abdicarent, non dabimus'.

tion; (3) even if they had left 'all behind' and never repossessed their former belongings, no-one can prove that this pattern of life should apply to all Christian ministers, 'even when they have a similar call'.[93] Since it was impossible to prove or dismiss these claims, Smyth's arguments were rejected as illogical. Not only his logic but also his exegetical skills lacked refinement, Martyr pointed out sharply, and concluded:

> You seem to embark on a contradiction, which is called arguing from secondary sources rather than from primary sources. For God does not call us to leave our possessions, except when we either travel the globe to preach or in times of persecution when we should rather renounce our possessions than deny Christ. Therefore, you interpret those words of Christ wrongly as an absolute—that we should in the first place *leave* our possessions.[94]

2.3. *1 Tim 5.11f. and 1 Cor 7*

Both these passages from Paul's letters were central to any debate on clerical celibacy and monastic vows. 1 Tim 5.11f. deals explicitly with the behaviour of ordained clergy and their fellow ministers, such as lay-ministers. 1 Cor 7 is concerned with questions of sexual morality, and culminates in the Pauline injunction 'I wish that all were as I myself am'.[95] Smyth intertwined both arguments and used them for vicious personal attacks on Martyr. 1 Cor 7 lent itself particularly well to question of Martyr's status, an apostate monk who had renounced his vows in order to marry. At the last judgement an apostate would undoubtedly be condemned. He could not claim to be a lay-person who sanctified his desires by marriage (1 Cor 7.9), but would forever remain a fallen monk who had not been able to keep his vows of continence. He quoted Vermigli's assertion that men who had taken vows of chastity should not try to

---

[93] Vermigli (1559), 23: 'Neque cum illis uocationem habeant eiusdem generis'.
[94] Vermigli (1559), ibid.: 'Viderisque paralogismum inducere, quem appellant ad secunda quid ad simpliciter. Non enim uocat Deus ad sua relinquenda, nisi quum uel discurrendum est per orbem ad praedicandum, uel in persecutione, ubi potius debemus abdicare omnibus rebus nostris, quàm Christum negare. Malè itaque abs te uerba Christi accipiuntur, quasi absoluté, ac simpliciter debeamus nostra relinquere'.
[95] 1 Cor 7.7-9.

excel to keep them but rather forsake them entirely to fuel further his rejection of the Italian's apostasy.[96]

2.3.1. *1 Tim 5.11f.*

Smyth began his exposition by amassing evidence from his opposition. He quoted his evangelical successor's reasons for leaving monastic life: 'If you are able to serve chastely, do so, but see that you don't regard yourself as bound by vows to serve because otherwise you will offer yourself to God by vows you may not be able to fulfil'.[97] He also reproduced a corresponding exegetical section from Martyr's lectures. Vermigli distinguished between Paul's personal preferences on celibacy and the dominical precepts. He maintained that to argue for universal clerical chastity and celibacy was erroneous.[98] Smyth used this as basis for another fierce rejection of apostasy and pointed out: 'Don't you see, trusty reader, how untrustworthy that Peter is? He thinks—what a clear disgrace to any thinker—that every writer stands by himself'.[99] Steering clear of the evidence for married clergy in 1 Tim 3.2-4 he proceeded to produce scriptural evidence from 1 Tim 5.11-12 to prove that by his apostasy Martyr had already brought upon himself condemnation. Smyth concluded: 'How, therefore, did you assert, Peter, that nothing was just which the law of God commanded? Indeed, I am ashamed to pen down these trifles, trifles you were not ashamed rashly to bring before an assembly of learned men'.[100]

The sheer length of Vermigli's *defensio* reflects the importance he attributed to these allegations. His method resembles the two *defensiones* from Mt 19. Still, his primary aim was not to identify weaknesses in Smyth's exegesis or logic, but to defend his own

---

[96] Smyth (1550), H iij r; cf. 1 Tim 5.11f.: 'For when their sensual desires alienate them from Christ, they want to marry, and so they incur condemnation for having violated their first pledge'.
[97] Smyth (1550), H iij r: 'Ne putes vi voti astringi ad servandum'.
[98] Smyth (1550), ibid.
[99] Smyth (1550), ibid.: 'Videsne, pie lector, quam indignus sit iste Petrus cui fides habeatur, qui tam dilucide tamque impudenter mentibus, illum scriptorem à se stare'.
[100] Smyth (1550), H viij r: 'Quo itaque ore asserebas Petre, nihil iustum esse, quod non idem lex Dei praeciperet? Certe pudet me has nugas refutare, quas te non puduit coram conserto doctorum virorum confessu temere afferre'.

reputation. His defence takes the form of a brusque denial of Smyth's allegations and a critical exegesis of the passage. Vermigli maintained:

> If there is any passage in the New Testament by which our adversaries think they can prove vows of celibacy, Smyth preaches it as if it were beyond controversy. ... He presented the truth to me as if it were false, yet he will not unravel it because it is too difficult.[101]

Consonant with every single rejection so far, he accused Smyth of mediocre biblical exegesis. The 'pledge' (*promissio, externa pactio*) in 1 Tim 5.11 was a formal promise to undertake a certain ecclesiastical ministry, which required widows not to remarry. Although there was close correlation between the pledge not to remarry and the vow of chastity monks took, Martyr still denied that 1 Tim 5.11 had any bearing on his own situation.

Instead he offered a subtle distinction between a vow (*votum*) and an external binding arrangement (*externa pactio*) which was in itself not a religious promise, despite that the fact that in the case of 1 Tim 5.11 the pledge was prerequisite for the church's ministry. He likened the agreement to the commission of soldiers, who pledged absolute allegiance to their sovereign but did not take vows:

> Just as when soldiers are given authority—by their pledge or an oath of allegiance—and bind themselves either to do, or avoid, such things as will occur in the course of their service, yet, however, they make no vow. This could be the pledge made by widows [1 Tim 5.11] who, not surprisingly, live celibately and chastely in peace while they spend their time in church.[102]

Martyr held with the fervour of a convert that Smyth was wrong when attributing obligatory vows to the ministry of widows: 'He imagines that widows were not admitted unless they had vowed to uphold perpetual widowhood: if, at a later stage, this pledge was

---

[101] Vermigli (1559), 36: 'Si quis est locus in literis noui testamenti, quo putent aduersarij nostri se Votum caelibatus posse conuincere, is citra controuersiam esse praedicatur. ... Smythaeus mihi obijcitur uerum ut sint falsi, ostendere non erit usque adeo difficile'.

[102] Vermigli (1559), ibid.: 'Ut milites cum auctorantur, promissione, uel sacramento militari ad haec, uel illa facienda, uel cauenda sese astringunt, quoad fuerint in ea militia: cum tamen Votum nullum edant. Haec potuit esse fides à uiduis data, nimirum ut dum in Ecclesia uersarentur, caelibes temperatè atque castè, uiuerent'.

not kept and they wished to re-marry, they would have violated their previous vow, and they would, therefore, stand condemned'.[103] Although widows bound themselves to continue to remain unmarried by a solemn promise, this promise had no spiritual component. Neither had the promise to remain celibate any bearing on the private lives of contemporary clergy. There was no ceremony of vows in the Gospels. There was therefore no condemnation of those who chose to marry, since they only followed Paul's advice on the matter (1 Cor 7.9). The pledge they freely chose to make was a human pledge, imposed neither by Christ nor by His Apostles, it was of momentary and not binding character. While Martyr had little choice but to concede that Paul favoured men living celibate lives, he felt fully justified in claiming that '[Paul] does not attribute this simply to a vow of chastity for widows. To forgo marriage is a human invention, against the will of Christ and that of the Apostle [Paul], and God's will is to be preferred to human contrivance'.[104] There were no binding promises enforcing virginity or chastity in the apostolic age. Claims to the contrary were based on scanty exegesis and fictitious evidence.[105]

The arguments from 1 Tim 5.11f. could so easily be interpreted to refer to his own situation. The monk-turned-husband could easily be portrayed as someone who, when his 'sensual desires alienated him from Christ, wanted to marry, and so incur condemnation for having violated his first pledge' (1 Tim 5.11). In his *defensio* from 1 Tim 5.11 the *ad hominem* attacks against Smyth increase in passion, frequency and desperation. Martyr concluded angrily:

> Since Smyth teaches untruths and twice was forced to recant, he now will have to undergo a third ignominy and see his doctrines

---

[103] Vermigli (1559), 42: 'Fingit enim non receptas fuisse uiduas nisi prius uouissent perpetuam uiduitatem: quae fides, quoniam postea non seruabatur, dum uolebant nubere, uiolatrices nuncupati Voti efficiebantur, atque adeo damnationem habebant'.

[104] Vermigli (1559), 46: 'Voto continentiae uidualis tantum tribuere noluit, cum sit res humanitus inuenta, ut matrimonium contra Christi & Apostoli sententiam rescindat, cum uoluntas diuina omnibus humanis inuentionibus praeferenda sit'.

[105] Vermigli (1559), 46: 'Nothing furthers your cause' (Nihilo facere causam tua meliorem).

condemned everywhere. Unable to endure this, he not only left England, but will go after Satan and the Antichrist, to whose tyranny he pledged himself earlier in many ways—or at least thinks he has done so.[106]

2.3.2. *1 Cor 7*

Most disagreement between religious conservatives and evangelicals in the debate about vows and celibacy was based on 1 Cor 7. References to Paul's exhortations pervaded Smyth's work like a red thread and made an appearance both in the small aside and the large excursus. There was no direct *defensio* based on the many allusions to the Pauline text. However, Martyr's commentary on the epistle itself documents the rejection of Smyth's arguments.

In the *Votis*, the first references to Paul's statements on sexual morality are presented in a discussion leading up to the debate outlined above (2.1). Smyth argued that vows were free decisions, like any other agreement. Only the promise of chastity first required a vow. Paul spoke in support of this requirement in 1 Cor 7.8f and 1 Cor 7.25-28. In 'view of the impending crisis' (1 Cor 7.26), it befitted the clergy to imitate the abstinence of John the Baptist rather than indulge in their desires. Smyth cited the example of James of Jerusalem, 'from the womb of the holy Mother', who had adhered to these precepts.[107] Did Martyr believe that 'this holy man was bound to all these precepts without a prior vow?'[108] If James had set himself aside by vows of self-denial, Paul must have had in mind the 'vow of virginity or chastity', when he counselled the Corinthians to keep from defilement of body and spirit (2 Cor 7.1).[109]

Vows existed to restrain human desire, Smyth held in his second argument from 1 Cor 7:

---

[106] Vermigli (1559), 43: 'Quemadmodum Smythaeus, quum erronea docuerit, & ad Palinodiam canendam fuerit bis adactus, ut postremò tertio adigendus, atque uideret dogmata sua passim damnari, hanc non ferens ignominiam, non solum ex Anglia discessit, sed post satanam & Antichristum abijt, cuius nihilominus tyrannidem antea multis modis abiurauerat, uel se abiurasse finxerat'.

[107] Smyth (1550), F iv v: 'ex vtero matris sanctae'.

[108] Smyth (1550), F iv v: 'Astrictus erat vir hic pietissimus omnia haec sine voto?'

[109] Smyth (1550), F iv v: 'Votum virginitatis aut continentiae', cf. 2 Cor 7.1: 'Since we have these promises, beloved, let us cleanse ourselves from every defilement of body and of spirit, making holiness perfect in the fear of God.'

Vermigli, therefore, clearly has evaded the argument—'to vow is not to rely on a divine law opposed by any human tradition'—although that vow-breaker and apostate falsely claims so and, without any shame, foolishly and contrary to religion, lives by this maxim, thereby covering up his whoring (for how else can you describe this abuse of a woman and producing stupid and profane dogmas).[110]

On the basis of 1 Cor 7.8, Vermigli's apostasy was nothing but common prostitution. Still, 'surely a priest or someone under a vow sins less if he goes whoring and fornicating than when he binds himself to a loose woman instead of a wife'.[111] Even the infrequent violation of the vow of chastity was preferable to abjuring a vow. The monk who 'is a law unto himself' and broke his vows—for 'such a man is that Peter who, it is said, made a profession as a monk in Italy'—had not once showed contrition for his sin.[112] On the contrary, he had convinced himself that the church he left was in error. Smyth rounded off his argument: 'They wish to marry and, acting contrary to Christ's ordinance, receive their condemnation: since first of all they renounce their faith and, secondly, do not seek marriage but adultery'.[113] Arguing from 1 Cor 7.8f., he held that to be freed from the ritual Law of Moses did not bring freedom from 'the detestable vow' (obnoxij voto). It only set men free to live chaste lives in accordance with apostolic instruction. Vows were permanent and binding. The person taking them had been joined to Christ in matrimony. When 're-marrying', those who had taken vows of celibacy and had dedicated their lives to Christ not only committed adultery, but rejected the Lord.[114] To use 1 Cor 7 to justify clerical marriage was beyond impudence: 'If a [clergyman] burns with desire and

---

[110] Smyth (1550), G i r: '[Vermigli] euasit satis itaque perspicuum, vouere non esse reniti diuinae legi, quo contra eam statuantur vllae hominum traditiones, tametsi iste votifragus, & apostata id falso impudenter, indocte & impie causetur, quo & ipse habeat quod suae scortationi praetextat (Quid enim aliud est, qua abutitur foemina, atque crassa & impia obtrudat dogmata)'.

[111] Smyth (1550), G i v: 'Num minus peccet sacerdos aut voto obstrictus quispiam cum scortatur aut fornicatur, an quando asciscit sibi in locum vxoris solutam foeminam'.

[112] Smyth (1550), ibid.: 'sui iuris est'; 'Qualis est iste Petrus quem ferunt monachum in Italia professum'.

[113] Smyth (1550), G ii r: 'Se gesserint contra Christum nubere volunt, habentes iudicium, quoniam primam fide reprobauerunt, non nuptias sed adulterium sequentes'.

[114] Smyth (1550), G ii v.

cannot contain himself, is that man free—or, indeed, ordered by the Apostle—to marry?'[115]

While Vermigli's commentary on 1 Cor 7.8f. was diametrically opposed to Smyth's views, it offered no radical theological innovations. He interpreted the Pauline profession of celibacy as a gift rather than a prohibition. Although many of the passages were written with Smyth's accusations in mind, the commentary on 1 Cor formed an independent work.[116] There are no direct responses to Smyth's condemnations. Nonetheless, Martyr elaborated on the question of celibacy and devoted himself to the question of vows at length. Unlike his *Defensio*, his exegetical work concentrated on the theological aspects of the debate.

Vermigli affirmed that man was subject to divine predestination. God had equipped him with appropriate gifts. Rejecting the views of his catholic opponent, he argued that 'it cannot suit everyone to lead a celibate life'.[117] If celibacy had been intended as a way of life for all, then all men could claim it (*omnes illum sibi uendicare possent*) in order to be set apart for prayer and fasting (1 Cor 7.6). Martyr instead pointed to Paul's injunction that those who cannot practise self-control should marry, 'for it is better to marry than to burn'.[118] His conclusion does not follow logically: 'Since, therefore, not everyone possesses that gift, and neither Pope, nor Bishop, nor Abbot can grant it, why do they dare to extort a vow?'[119]

Paul's exhortation in 1 Cor 7.8 did not disturb Martyr, for man was not free to choose his walk of life at all. He was predestined either to receive the gift of matrimony or of celibacy, a view entirely opposite to Smyth's.[120] Since the gift of celibacy was of divine origin, Martyr claimed it could not be transferred simply by the laying on of hands. Only some—'since it is not meant for all'—

---

[115] Smyth (1550), G ii r: 'Estne illi iam liberum aut ab apostolo iussum vt innouet nuptias si se non continet et vrit?'

[116] For a rejection of vows see Vermigli (1551), 158 v-159 r.

[117] Vermigli (1551), 158 v: 'sequitur coelibatum non posse omnibus conuenire'.

[118] 1 Cor 7.9.

[119] Vermigli (1551), ibid.: 'Cum itaque donum istud non omnes habeant, neque Papa, neque episcopus, neque Abbas conferre possit, cur audent uotum extorquere?'

[120] Vermigli (1551), 161 r: celibacy depends on man's election and co-operation (*oportere ut nostra uoluntas & electio*).

were able to submit themselves to the wishes of the Apostle.[121] No additional vows beyond the initial baptismal promises had ever been required. Therefore, no-one could claim chastity by vows unless he had been predestined to receive it as a gift:[122]

> Therefore we should not make vows, since they are not required from everyone. Perhaps you will say: 'Why then do we make vows at baptism, since we are unable by our own strength to live up to that promise?' We shall reply: 'We promise nothing at baptism, except what God requires of all Christians and commands all, and wishes all to live up to'. If, however, there is a vow or promise there, it does not appear as such. Which is why, if we pray to God in faith, we will—without doubt—obtain strength and gifts to endure it.[123]

3. SMYTH AND VERMIGLI IRRECONCILABLE

Theologically, neither Smyth's *Votis* nor Vermigli's *Defensio* startle. Both were polemical works designed to illustrate the opponent's 'heretical' statements and his exegetical incompetence. They verged on the safe side of their respective theological opinions rather than presenting radically new insights. Yet the fact that Vermigli set down his own theology of vows at all is due to Smyth's initiative; there would have been no need to do so otherwise. A written disputation liberally corded with spiteful polemic and stretching over nine years, the two works present a summary of an ongoing contemporary debate.

Martyr's reflections on the subject resulted in an evangelical reinterpretation of the traditional concept of vows. He dismissed

---

[121] Vermigli (1551), 161 r: 'Quia non est omnium'.

[122] Vermigli (1551), ibid.: just as one could not make a vow to live as a prophet, 'because it is not in my hands, nor is it God's command for me. But to vow chastity is almost as if I had vowed to be a prophet' (Quod neque in manu mea est, neque à deo mihi praecipitur. At uouere castitatem coelibatus, perinde est ac si uouerem me fere prophetum).

[123] Vermigli (1551), 158 v-158 r: 'Quamobrem vouere non debemus, quod neque ab omnibus requirit. Dices fortasse: cur vouemus in baptismo, cum ea quae promittibus nostris uiribus praestare non ualeamus? Respondemus: Nos in baptismo nihil promittere, nisi quae deus ab omnibus Christianis requirat, omnibus praecipiat, & omnibus fieri uelit: Si tamen ibi promissio aut uotum sit, quod non expresse apparet. Quare si deum fideliter orauerimus, uires & facultates ad ea praestanda proculdubio impetrabimus'; for his discussion on the subject of election to celibacy, see Vermigli (1551), 159 v-161 r.

vows as a human construct without any spiritual dimension. As such, they only served the purpose of segregating the people of God (*perfectionem praetextunt*). As an alternative, Martyr offered his own theology of predestination: the elect did not stand in need of any exterior works such as vows.[124] They had already been justified and only sought to perform righteous acts as a result of their prior justification.[125] To make a vow, therefore, was not a work of faith that purchased a greater spiritual depth (*largiorem spiritum*). Only divine grace 'or the full remission of sins' could ever grant the gift of a fulfilled spiritual life.[126] Believers were therefore called to live their life in Christ according to their election, whether as celibate men or women, or as married couples: 'to be able to acquire a place among either group—as well as all faith and charity'.[127]

In Martyr's eyes God's election, confirmed by baptism, was universal and open to all 'if they manage to live rightly ... since that is a necessary precondition to salvation'.[128] Through Christ, God had even called eunuchs—infertile men and among the most despised in Israel—to His service.[129] Nothing could force divine election, in return for God's gifts man only had to lead his life in accordance with His commandments. As if suddenly weary of further elucidation, the Italian remarked in conclusion:

> Because it is not necessary to explain the absurdity of all this any further. We recognise always that all men are liars and that only God is ever true. If human works were just and acceptable for holy and righteous living, what need would there be for the Law?[130]

Smyth's understanding of election was fundamentally different to that of Martyr. Anyone who was inspired by divine grace to fulfil the will of God through his actions could cherish the hope of

---

[124] Vermigli (1559), 57.
[125] Vermigli (1559), 65.
[126] Vermigli (1559), 58: 'Vel remissionem peccatorum copiosorem'.
[127] Vermigli (1559), ibid.: 'In utroque illorum posse habere locum, & summam fidem, & summam charitatem'.
[128] Vermigli (1559), 65: 'Si superuixerint, ut recte viuant ... quum id ad salutem consequendam sit necessariam'.
[129] Vermigli (1559), 15; cf. Deut 23.1: 'No-one whose testicles are crushed or whose penis is cut off shall be admitted to the assembly of the Lord.'
[130] Vermigli (1559), 69: 'Quod, ut sit absurdum, pluribus explicare non est necesse. Sit nobis semper ob oculos, omnem hominem mendacem esse, atque Deum vnum ueracem. Si hominum opera iusta & idonea regulae fuissent, ad pie sancteque uiuendum, quid opus erat lege?'

justification. Vows were just a special expression of the human desire to conform more closely to the will of God. They had been defined by apostolic tradition, and confirmed by Fathers and councils. Vows were binding permanent promises which man freely made to God (*votum est testificatio quaedam promissionis spontaneae*).[131] The acts or deeds which a believer pledged were works that went beyond the fulfilment of the commandments. On the basis of his own free will, man was free to express his allegiance by a vow. Once this 'promise ... to the Holy Spirit and God' was made, it could not simply be revoked.[132] Unlike any other free promise, a solemn pledge was permanently binding. For Smyth the fraudulent nullification of a vow meant nothing less than spiritual death (*fraudis sui poenas mortis penderit*).[133]

While vows were strictly speaking based on legal precepts, like other works of supererogation they were inspired by the workings of 'the grace of God ... rather than by faith and Christ's merits, in order to aspire to eternal salvation'.[134] They formed a part of the works of grace which inspired man to devote himself to God by his promise. Vows were not a pact made *ex lege* (that is under the terms of the old Covenant) but *sub lege* (that is an act of faith based on 'the aid of God and the merit of Christ').[135] As such a vow counted toward the building-up of merit and 'is a foundation for the building-up of a spiritual home in the human soul'.[136] Smyth's understanding of the working of divine grace through human co-operation was central to his definition of vows. Vows were not merely an adequate response to the inspiration of divine grace: as supererogatory works they were in themselves an instrument of salvation.

English monastic life may have been suspended in 1536. The theological framework that lay at the heart of religious communities, however, was not dismantled with the same ease as the buildings that used to house monks or nuns. Smyth's defence of

[131] Smyth (1550), F iv r.
[132] Smyth (1550), F iv r: 'promissio ... spiritui sancto & deo'.
[133] Smyth (1550), ibid.
[134] Smyth (1550), F vij r: 'Dei gratia ... citra quam fidem, & Christi meritum adspirare ad aeternam salutem'.
[135] Smyth (1550), F vij v: 'Dei auxilio & Christo merito'.
[136] Smyth (1550), F vij v: 'Fundamentum est extruendi edificij spiritualis in hominis anima'.

monastic vows was by no means only an *ad hominem* campaign fought to expose Martyr as a married apostate. Rather, like his defence of the catholic doctrine of justification and the eucharistic life, it was part of his persistent concern for the spiritual welfare of his homeland. For Smyth, it has been shown repeatedly, England had become corrupted by evangelical doctrines.[137] The discontinuation of monasticism, and the subsequent loss of the 'monasticism of the masses' that went with it—the traditional expressions of piety—were only symptoms of the real struggle that lay at its heart: the departure from the catholic understanding of salvation. Smyth truly believed that, unless he strove 'to reduce the people agayne vnto the catholike fayth' by his fervent defence of catholicism, the soul of the English nation would be lost, and with it his own.[138]

---

[137] Smyth (1554), ¶ vi v.
[138] Ibid.

CHAPTER FIVE

EUCHARISTIC THEOLOGY

From 1546 until his final series of lectures at Douai the eucharist was at the forefront of Smyth's concerns. He produced no less than five works devoted to the defence and elucidation of the theology of the mass, ranging from his first two publications in 1546, to his last, published only a few months before his death in 1563.[1] He launched salvos against particular individuals, such as a sharp attack on archbishop Cranmer's eucharistic doctrine (1550), but also provided more general refutations of evangelical views. His two initial publications (1546) were directed against John Frith and Martin Luther, while his 1562 publication takes on Philipp Melanchthon, John Calvin, Wolfgang Musculus and John Jewel.[2] His extensive output was popular at the time; all works ran through a second edition, some, such as the 1546 edition of *A Defence of the Blessed Masse and the Sacrifice thereof*, and the 1562 edition of *De Missae Sacrificio*, went to a third edition.[3]

In his earliest publications, Smyth spoke about the motives that caused him to add his views to the controversy of the sacrifice of

---

[1] R. Smyth, *A defence of the blessed Masse and the sacrifice thereof, prouynge that it is aualable bothe for the quycke and the dead*, London, 1546¹; idem, *A confutation of a certen booke, called a defence of the true, and Catholike doctrine of the Sacrament, &c., sette fourth in the name of Thomas Archebysshoppe of Canterburye*, Paris, 1551; idem, *Confutatio eorum, quae P. Melanchthon objicit contra missae sacrificium propitiationem. Cui acc. & repulsio calumniarum J. Calvini & Musculi, et J. Juelli, contra Missam, eius canonem et purgatorium, denuo excusa*, Leuven, 1562¹; idem, *Defensio comprehendaria, et orthodoxa, sacri externi, et visibili Iesu Christi sacerdotii. Cui addita est sacratorum catholicae Ecclesiae altarium propugnatio, ac Calvinia altarium propugnatio, ac Calvina communionis succincta refutatio*, Leuven, 1563.

[2] For John Frith, see W. A. Clebsch, *England's earliest Protestants 1520-1535*, New Haven CT, 1964, 78-136 and C. R. Trueman, *Luther's Legacy: Salvation and the English Reformers 1525-1556*, Oxford, 1994, 121-155; for a comprehensive study of the earliest opposition to Martin Luther's sacramental theology, see D. Bagchi, *Luther's earliest Opponents: Catholic Controversialists, 1518-1525*, Minneapolis MN, 1991, 118-141.

[3] R. Smyth, *A Defence of the Sacrifice of the Masse*, London, 1546; *De Missae Sacrificio enarratio, ac brevis repulsio argumentum quae P. Maelanchthon, J. Calvinus, et alii sectarii objecerunt adversus illud, et purgatorium. Acc. Epistola docens quae ecclesia sit nobis tuto sequenda*, Leuven, 1562.

the mass and the real presence.[4] He felt his task was to establish that the contemporary English doctrines were recent innovations and, more importantly, were contrary to the established faith and laws of the realm. The fact that catholic doctrine had been enshrined in law by act of parliament did not safeguard it from the errors of heresy.[5] Smyth lamented that

> even the chiefest and the most weighty matters of our religion and fayth have been called into question, babled, talked, and tangled upon (reason I can not, nor oughte to call it).[6]

He resolved to counter the erosion of the catholic faith in England by addressing all who had strayed from the truth. Smyth felt that it was necessary to make use of plain reasoning to spell out the dangers connected with the reformers' 'pestilous and contagious doctrine'.[7] The rejection of heresy afforded the use of a stronger armoury than the subtle skills of eloquence, he argued in setting out his first of many polemic rejections of evangelical doctrine.[8]

The catholic church had been able to contain attacks on her eucharistic doctrine from medieval dissenters such as Berengar, de Bruys, Hus and Wyclif.[9] Even John Frith's views, which Smyth tackled in an appendix to his second work in defence of the mass, he regarded as merely motivated by 'foly and ignoraunce'.[10] The dissemination of Lutheran doctrine in England, on the other hand, presented genuine spiritual danger. Smyth frequently emphasised that 'Luthers wicked errours and damnable heresies' not only caused the king to write a defence of the catholic doctrine but also forced parliament to ban Lutheran writings alto-

---

[4] Smyth (1546^1), 3 v.
[5] Smyth (1546^1), 14 v; Smyth (1546^2), xi v.
[6] Smyth (1546^1), 2 v.
[7] Smyth (1546^2), xiii v.
[8] Smyth (1546^2), colophon, x v: 'Rudely & grossely set fourth, for the easier vnderstandynge of it'.
[9] Smyth (1546^2), ix v, marginalium; for Berengar of Tours, see A. J. Macdonald, *Berengar and the Reform of Sacramental Doctrine*, London, 1930; J. de Montclos, *Lanfranc et Bérenger: La controverse eucharistique du XIe siècle*, Spicilegium Sacrum Lovaniense 37, Leuven, 1971; H. Chadwick, *Journal for Theological Studies* New Series 40 (1989), 414-445: 'Ego Berengarius'; for Peter de Bruys, see M. D. Lambert, *Medieval Heresy: Popular movements from the Gregorian reform to the Reformation*, Oxford, 1992, 47-50; J. Fearns, *Archiv für Kulturgeschichte* 48 (1966), 311-335: 'Peter von Bruis und die religiöse Bewegung des 12. Jahrhunderts'.
[10] Smyth (1546^1), 90 v.

gether.[11] His two 1546 publications sought to address this danger of theologically reasoned evangelicalism. Both were dedicated to his patron and 'moost godlye and ... vertuous christen prince' Henry VIII, whom he regarded as a worthy champion in the battle over the sacrifice of the mass and real presence.[12]

Towards the end of his academic career, Smyth once more sought the patronage of influential allies in his continued struggle against the evangelical interpretation of the eucharist. He was convinced that the primate of the Low Countries and Flemish privy councillor Cardinal de Granvelle would prove to be another worthy champion.[13] Both Henry VIII and Granvelle provided Smyth with the necessary stipends to fund his doctrinal skirmishes.[14] Fifteen years later, while Smyth's opinions had remained fundamentally the same, he no longer regarded true catholicity a prerogative of crown and parliament but of the Holy See.[15] In his defence of the eucharist Smyth strove to uphold the faith for which he had chosen exile above a life in conformity. While his opponents were representatives of two very different schools of theology—both Lutheran and Reformed—in Smyth's eyes they shared one crucial feature: all had departed from catholic orthodoxy.

1. The Late Medieval Understanding of the Eucharistic Sacrifice

Prior to the council of Trent, the sacrifice of the mass had not been defined formally. Still, from the time of Aquinas' seminal analysis, it had routinely been portrayed as an act in which Christ

---

[11] Smyth (1546²), xi r-v; Henry VIII, *Assertio septem sacramentorum adversus Martinum Lutherum, aedita ab invictissimo Angliae et Franciae rege et domine Hyberniae Henrico eius nominis octavo*, Rome, 1521, in: P. Fraenkel, ed., *Assertio septem sacramentorum adversus Martinum Lutherum*, Corpus Catholicorum (cited as: CC) 43, Münster, 1992.

[12] Smyth (1546¹), 2 r.

[13] Smyth (1562¹), 2 v: Smyth attested that Granvelle fought 'better armed and more surely against the enemies of the Christian faith' (Armatior et tutior adversus christiane fidei hostea).

[14] See above, chapter I, 5.3.

[15] Smyth (1562¹), 7 r.

and His one sacrifice on the cross are truly made present.[16] The sacrament served as an *imago repraesentativa*; a close, realistic representation of the passion of Christ. For Aquinas the eucharist was a dynamic event which effected the participation of believers in the real presence of Christ, and brought to life the very act of redemption on the cross in its daily re-enactment on the altar. Aquinas' interpretation of the strong Augustinian understanding of the representational *imago* as a lively reflection of reality formed the core of the Tridentine definition of the doctrine.[17] According to this understanding, the celebration of the eucharist was nothing but the making present (*repraesentatio*) of the propitiatory sacrifice Christ had made once for the sins of all people on Calvary in the daily life of the Church, following His commandment 'do this in memory of me'.[18] Just as an image made present the person or object depicted, so the body and blood of Christ as well as His sacrifice on Calvary were re-presented in the mass.

As a sacrifice, the offering at mass was the unbloody (*incruentus*) repetition of the bloody (*cruentus*) redemptive sacrifice made once at a certain point in history.[19] The fact that the sacrifice is unbloody, however, does not take from it its efficacy as a perpetual instrument to placate the Father's wrath. Just as the one sacrifice of Christ on Calvary was a singular and effective propitiatory sacrifice for the sins of the world, so the daily sacrifice of the church mirrored the historic sacrifice. Christ is not re-sacrificed, but the officiant and the faithful partake mystically in the sacrifice

---

[16] That is, re-presented, Th. Aquinas, *Summa Theologica*, London, 1963-1966, (cited as: ST) 3a, q. 79, a. 1: 'What is represented by this sacrament ... is Christ's Passion'. In ST 3a, q. 83 Aquinas set out to ask whether Christ is immolated in the sacrament and concluded in ST 3a, q. 83, a. 1: 'The celebration of this sacrament is called a sacrifice for two reasons. First, because, as Augustine says, "the images of things are called by the names of the things whereof they are the images; as when we look upon a picture or a fresco, we say, 'This is Cicero and that is Sallust'." But, as was said above, the celebration of this sacrament is an image representing Christ's Passion, which is His true sacrifice. Accordingly the celebration of this sacrament is called Christ's sacrifice'.

[17] Augustine, *Ad Simplicianum*, in: J. P. Migne, *Patrologia Latina*, Paris, 1844-1890, (cited as: PL) 40.143; cf. Council of Trent, in: H. Denzinger, H. Holping, P. Hünermann, edd., *Enchiridion symbolorum et definitionum de rebus fidei et morum: Kompendium der Glaubensbekenntnisse und kirchlichen Lehrentscheidungen*, Freiburg im Breisgau and Rome, [38]1999, (cited as: DS) 1740.

[18] Mt 26.28.

[19] DS 4599, n. 2.

made on the cross. In the context of the mass, this *repraesentatio* goes far beyond a mere memorial of Christ's passion. It is both a memorial and an application of the fruits of Christ's passion.

1.1. Gabriel Biel (c. 1420-1495)

Both nominalists as well as Thomists acknowledged this insight. The later nominalist school, and in particular the teaching of the German catholic controversialists, had already departed from the views of Duns Scotus on the mass.[20] While Scotus still maintained a difference in the offering of the church from that of Christ, for Biel and his contemporaries there was no longer an essential difference between the historical events on Calvary and those repeated daily on the altars of the church.[21] Biel maintained that the sacraments are the 'testament' Christ left to His Church. For believers to receive Christ's inheritance—the products of His death on Calvary—required the continuous offering of the mass.[22]

---

[20] For 'catholic controversialists' or 'katholische Kontroverstheologen', see Bagchi (1991), 2 n.

[21] J. Duns Scotus, in: L. Wadding OFM, ed. et al., *Quaestiones quodlibetales*, 12.20.22, Lyons, 1639: 'Would it not seem that the celebration of one mass is equal to the passion of Christ, if at that moment the One who offers is the same as One who is made an oblation? But it is certain that a mass is not equal to the passion of Christ'. (Alioquin videretur, quod unius missae celebratio aequivaleret passioni Christi, si idem esset offerens immediate et oblatus. Certus est autem, quod missa non aequivalet passioni Christi). Duns Scotus argued that the sacrifice of the mass was not offered by Christ Himself since, since according to Heb 9.12 He only offered Himself once. The offering of the priest *in persona ecclesiae* was therefore of less value than Christ's; cf. W. Werbeck, *Zeitung für Theologie und Kirche* 69 (1972), 175ff: 'Valor et applicatio Missae. Wert und Zuwendung der Messe im Anschluß an Johannes Duns Scotus'.

[22] G. Biel, *Sacri canonis missae expositio resolutissma*, Basel, 1510, 53 N [=H. A. Oberman, W. J. Courtenay, edd., *Gabrielis Biel Canonis Missae Expositio*, Veröffentlichungen des Instituts für europäische Geschichte Mainz, Wiesbaden, 1965, (cited as: VIEG) 32.2.324-325]: 'Since it is the witness of the final distribution of goods, confirmed by the death of the testator—whether a constitution or tradition made legitimate by the testimony of good ordinances—the New Testament is true faith, and the Law of Christ. In it, Christ distributes, ordains and promises eternal sonship to His brothers and the faithful. This Law is confirmed by the death and passion of Christ, by which His blood was poured out; and this out-pouring is the true attestation and confirmation of this covenant' (Cum testamentum sit ultima distributio bonorum morte testatoris firmata, seu constitutio vel traditio de ordinandis bonis attestatione legitime firmata, recte fides et lex christi est testamentum novum. In illa siquidem christus eternam hereditatem fratribus suis

The daily repetition of the sacrifice of the mass was a representation of the testator's death.[23] It was a tangible reminder of the merits of Christ promised to believers in His *novum testamentum*— the sacraments of the Church. The sacrifice of the mass also ensured a real participation in the corporal presence of Christ in the sacrament. Only the sacrificial commemoration in the course of the eucharist, therefore, enabled man to partake in the one historical sacrifice, as well as to share in the real presence of Christ under the elements of bread and wine.

While the doctrine of transubstantiation had been defined at the fourth Lateran council in 1215, it had been interpreted in various ways.[24] Biel held an Ockhamist view of the real presence. Christ's body was made truly present, but not as a quantifiable entity.[25] He distinguished between the circumscriptive and the definitive presence of Christ: Christ is circumscriptively present in heaven. He leads a quantifiable, physical existence at the right hand of the Father. Yet He is definitively present under the elements of bread and wine on the altar. Biel defined definitive presence in the same terms as he would define the presence of an angel in a room, or the soul in the body. Both are somehow present yet cannot be located by spatial co-ordinates.[26]

---

et fidelibus distribuit, ordinat et promittit. Haec autem lex confirmata est per mortem et passionem christi in qua sanguis eius effusus est, quae effusio est sui testamenti legitime attestatio et confirmatio).

[23] G. Biel, *Sacrosancti canonis missae expositio in Epitomen contracta*, Antwerpen, 1556, 77 r: 'Christ is offered by us not in His death, but in the memorial of His death. For this reason our offering is not a repetition of His offering for punishment, but a representation to call forth in the name of God' (Offertur idem Christus a nobis non in mortem, sed in mortis memoriam. Unde nostra oblatio non est reiteratio suae oblationis in poenam, sed representatio ad provocandam Dei misericordiam), cf. H. A. Oberman, *Spätscholastik und Reformation. Der Herbst der mittelalterlichen Theologie*, Zürich, 1965, 254f.

[24] Fourth Lateran Council, *Constitutio I*, DS 802.

[25] Biel (1510), 39 C [=VIEG 32.2.86]: 'Emulating the most noble Doctor William Ockham in this, I come to the following conclusion: the body of Christ which was borne by the Virgin Mary is truly and really contained under the form of bread and wine' (Imitans in hoc clarissimum doctorem Guilhelmium ockham ... pono hanc conclusionem: corpus christi quod sumptum est de virgine maria ... sub specie panis vere et realiter continetur).

[26] For Biel's understanding of circumscriptive and definitive presence, see Oberman (1965), 257-258. Biel here differs substantially from Aquinas, whose material perception of the definitive presence led him to argue that Christ could not be present definitively on every altar and therefore was neither circumscriptively nor definitively present in the eucharist, cf. ST 3a, q. 76, a. 5.

In his debate on the sacraments this perception of Christ's physical presence became crucial. Biel sought to counter the views held by medieval dissenters such as Berengar or de Bruys that Christ was only ever present *in signo*. According to nominalist thought, sacramental efficacy was endangered by a symbolist reading of the eucharist.[27] In his defence of the unity of sacraments in Christ, Biel rejected altogether the notion of a merely spiritual presence of Christ in the eucharist.[28] Only the shedding of Christ's blood and the promise of his physical presence in bread and wine maintained the validity of Christ's 'testament' to His church, the sacraments.[29]

Like the nominalist school, the Tridentine definition rejected the Scotist view of the eucharistic sacrifice and the sacrifice on Calvary as two separate events. Christ's high-priesthood, the council of Trent argued, prevailed beyond death and ensured the perpetuation of the re-presentation of His historic sacrifice by the church.[30] The sacrificial victim is the same as the one who is offered daily through the ministry of priests:

> In this divine sacrifice which is celebrated in the mass, the same Christ who offered Himself once in a bloody manner on the altar of the cross is contained and is offered in an unbloody manner.[31]

1.2. Luther and his Early Opponents

In 1517 Martin Luther was seeking only to repeal the sale of papal indulgences. The concerns that had motivated his attack on the late medieval penitential system eventually lead to a crucial change of his doctrine of justification, which has been documented elsewhere.[32] The radical, yet logical, second step in Luther's theological breakthrough saw the thorough questioning of other theological concepts. His subsequent evaluation of traditional doctrine involved scripture and the rejection of any human co–

---

[27] Biel (1510), 39 A [=VIEG 32.2.85-86].
[28] Biel (1510), 39 B [=VIEG 32.2.86].
[29] Biel (1510), 53 N [=VIEG 32.2.325].
[30] Council of Trent, DS 1740.
[31] Council of Trent, DS 1743.
[32] Above, chapter III, 114-119; cf. for instance A. E. McGrath, *Luther's Theology of the Cross: Martin Luther's theological breakthrough*, Oxford, 1985.

operation as a necessary precondition for salvation. There was therefore no longer any need to implore a heavenly judge to mediate the merits gained by the crucifixion of His Son to the believer through a repetition of this sacrifice in the context of the mass. On the contrary, by basing his doctrinal understanding entirely on Scripture and the notion of *sola fides*, Luther was forced to reject the doctrine of the sacrifice of the mass not only as unscriptural, but as a doctrine which sought to perpetuate the late medieval system of meritorious justification which he had set out to abolish in the first place.[33]

In their direct debate with Luther, Cochlaeus and Eck therefore strove to prove the unity of the two sacrifices. The sacrifice on the cross was the same as that of the mass, for if the sacrifice of the altar was essentially the same as that on Calvary, then the Lutheran rejection of that doctrine could be proved flawed. Both had finally departed from the Realist opinion reflected in Scotus' *Quaestiones Quodlibetales* and adopted a eucharistic understanding not unlike Biel's.[34] In September 1523 Cochlaeus wrote in direct response to Luther's *Ein Sermon von dem newen Testament*:[35]

> Though Christ was sacrificed only once mortally and visibly on the cross, He is offered daily in the mass immortally and invisibly through His memorial of and meditation on His passion and death and now is a spiritual sacrifice that is made without slaughter.[36]

Eck also took up arguments of his nominalist contemporaries in defence of catholic eucharistic doctrine. Until the publication of his *Enchiridion locorum communium adversus Lutherum* he did not concern himself with the theology of the sacrifice of the mass in

---

[33] R. A. W. Rex, *The Theology of John Fisher*, Cambridge, 1991, 130, summarises Luther's position succinctly: 'The core of his case against the sacrifice of the mass lay in his new theory of sacraments, according to which the essence of a sacrament was a "word of promise" (verbum promissionis) by which Christ assured forgiveness to those who had faith in him and thus in his words and promises'.

[34] Cf. n. 26.

[35] M. Luther, *Ein Sermon von dem newen Testament, das ist von der heyligen Messe*, Nürnberg, 1520, in: idem, *Luthers Werke*, Weimar, 1883—, (cited as: WA) 6.353-78.

[36] J. Cochlaeus, *Glos und Comment Doctor Johannes Dobneck Cochlaeus von Wendelstein uff CLIIII Artikeln gezogen uss einem Sermon Doctor Martini Luters von der heiligen mess und nüem Testament*, Strassburg, 1523, Z ii f.; for Cochlaeus, see R. Bäumer, 'Johannes Cochlaeus', in: E. Iserloh, ed. et al., *Katholische Theologen der Reformationszeit*, Katholisches Leben und Kirchenreform im Zeitalter der Glaubensspaltung (cited as: KLK) 44, Münster 1984, 73-82.

print.[37] Before 1525 he regarded the matter as a pastoral problem, and fought the evolving Lutheran eucharistic doctrine by his sermons. His *Homily on the Fruits of the Blessed Sacrament*, delivered appropriately on Maundy Thursday, is a good example.[38]

Eck's views echo those of Biel and Cochlaeus closely. However, he not only maintained close links with German controversialists, but also with contemporary English thinkers. He made considerable use of the refutations of Luther's *De captivitate Babylonica ecclesiae praeludium* by king Henry VIII and bishop John Fisher.[39] Eck mirrored Henry's clear perception of the integral unity of the sacrifice on Calvary and that of the altar closely, claiming that the historic and the representational sacrifice were one and the same sacrament (*unum sacramentum*) as they both derived from the same institution. During the course of the mass the two became conjoined and reached beyond time and space to form one and the same moment. Eck echoed Biel's and Fisher's perception that the efficacy of the sacrament was entirely dependent on the making present of Christ in the eucharist.[40] The passion on its own was ineffectual unless the merits of Christ were communicated through the *nova oblatio* on the altar.[41] Just like Biel and Fisher, Eck understood the sacraments of the New Covenant to be the 'testa-

---

[37] J. Eck, in: P. Fraenkel, ed., *Enchiridion locorum communium adversus Lutherum et alios hostes ecclesiae (1525-1543)*, CC 34, Münster, 1979.

[38] J. Eck, in: J. Metzler SJ, ed., *Tres orationes in exequiis Joannis Eckii habitae. Accesserunt aliquot epitaphia in Eckii obitum scripta et catalogus locubrationem eiusdem (1543). Nach den Originaldrucken mit biobibliographischer Einleitung, einer Untersuchung der Berichte über Ecks Tod und einem Verzeichnis seiner Schriften*, CC 16, Münster, 1930, CX-CXII, No. 68.

[39] M. Luther, *De captivitate Babylonica ecclesiae praeludium*, Nürnberg, 1520, in: WA 6.497-573. There are eight references to Henry VIII (1992), in Eck's *Ad invictissimum Poloniae regem Sigismundum, de sacrificio missae contra Lutheranos, libri tres*, Augsburg, 1526; cf. E. Iserloh, ed. et al., *Johannes Eck: De Sacrificio Missae libri tres (1526)*, CC 36, Münster, 1982, 7, 111f, 152f, 155, 159, 163-164. Eck also quoted extensively from Fisher's *Sacri sacerdotii defensio* and also made use of his *Assertionis Lutheranae confutatio*; cf. J. Fisher, *Sacri sacerdotii defensio contra Lutherum*, 1525, in idem: *Opera Omnia*, Würzburg, 1597, 1232-1298; idem, *Assertionis Lutheranae confutatio*, in: *Opera Omnia*, 272-745.

[40] Eck (1982), 60; cf. Henry VIII (1992), G iii r-v, H ii v.

[41] Cf. J. Fisher, *Assertionem Regis Angliae de fide Catholica adversus Lutheri Babylonicam captivitatem defensio*, Köln, 1525, in: idem (1597), 223-224.

ment' of Christ.[42] The communication of Christ's merits to the faithful was entirely dependent on the continuous sacrifice of Christ in the mass, Eck argued, in the same way that a testament required the death of its testator.[43] The mass was an instrument of grace: it was essential to communicate the *thesaurus Christi* to the believers but had no independent benefits of its own. Similarly, the sacrifice of Christ would have been consigned firmly to a place in history unless its spiritual benefits were communicated through the *nova oblatio* in the mass.[44]

From Aquinas' first definition of the sacrifice of the mass as a 'making present' of the sacrifice of Christ on Calvary in the daily life of the church to the authoritative definitions of the council of Trent on the subject there was a steady development towards a less commemorative view. Among the German controversialists Biel particularly emphasised the soteriological aspect of the *repraesentatio* of Christ's sacrifice. The sacrificial act on the altar, offered by the priestly minister *in persona Christi*, was an instrument intrinsic to the salvation of man. On the other hand, the chief English propagators of the theology of the sacrifice of the mass, John Fisher, Henry VIII and Thomas More, stressed in particular the interdependence of the historic and present sacrifices.[45] If the mass was indeed a sacrifice—which both Fisher and Henry set out to defend—it was none other than that offered on Calvary. If there was no such deep-rooted union between the first historical sacrifice and the daily repetition of Christ's sacrifice on the altars of the church, then the sacrifice of the mass was fraudulent.

---

[42] Fisher (1597), 188; for a clear distinction between the Lutheran understanding of the eucharist as the 'testament of Christ' and the catholic notion of the 'testament' as Christ's gifts of the new covenant, see Fisher (1597), 183-187; cf. Eck (1982), 59: 'We believe that the institution of the eucharist pertains to the testament' (Institutionem eucharistiae diximus ad testamentum pertinere).

[43] Eck (1982), 59-60: 'But any testament involves the death of the testator, and the death of Jesus the testator was the sacrifice and offering made to God for our sins. Therefore this offering also involved a testament' (Testamentum autem involvit mortem testatoris, mors testatoris Iesu fuit sacrificium et hostia pro peccatis nostris Deo oblata, itaque testamentum, et hanc oblationem involvit).

[44] Cf. Eck (1982), 174f; Cochlaeus (1523), E iii v.

[45] For a thorough analysis of Fisher's position see Rex (1991), 131. Rex overly generalised when he claimed, ibid., 'the identity of the sacrifice of the mass ... had perhaps become obscured in the later middle ages'. For Henry VIII's views see Bagchi (1991), 136.

2. SMYTH'S 1546 PUBLICATIONS AND THEIR SOURCES—
ECK AND FISHER

When Smyth set out to compose his own first two contributions in the debate, the initial storm surrounding the publication of Luther's *De captivitate Babylonica ecclesiae praeludium* and his *Ein Sermon von dem newen Testament* had passed. He could not have possibly expected a response to his works from Luther or Frith.[46] Smyth was not jumping onto the bandwagon towards the end of an ongoing debate but trying to address a particularly English problem, as he made clear in the introduction to his *Assertion and Defence of the Sacrament of the Aultar*.[47] Henrician England had seen the dilution of the catholic doctrine of the sacrifice of the mass in the *Bishops' Book* (1537).[48] This was reversed by the introduction of the *Six Articles of Religion* (1539) with their strong emphasis on catholic doctrinal teaching and, although the *King's Book* (1543) had not touched explicitly on the doctrine of the sacrifice of the mass, it emphasised that priests were called to 'consecrate and offer'.[49]

Smyth's contributions to the debate are not very original. Smyth was a brilliant polemicist but depended substantially on the scholarship of other debaters. He often cited their work tacitly, a common practice in sixteenth-century theological debate. Two earlier works can singled out as the theological basis for Smyth's first two publications: Eck's *De Sacrificio Missae* and Fisher's *De Veritate Corporis et Sanguinis Christi in Eucharistia*. Smyth depended on the scriptural and patristic arguments in defence of the sacri-

---

[46] Frith had been burnt at the stake in 1533. His *A christen sentence and true iudgement of the most honorable Sacrament of Christes body & bloude*, however, was not printed until about 1545.

[47] Smyth (1546²), 3 r.

[48] *The Institution of a Christen man*, in: Ch. Lloyd, ed., *Formularies of faith put forth by authority during the reign of Henry VIII*, Oxford, 1825. There is no mention of the sacrifice of the mass, neither is the priest's authority to offer sacrifice mentioned in the book's discussion of holy orders. As an *ex officio* member of convocation Smyth's name was routinely added to the *Bishops' Book*. He almost certainly held different personal convictions at the time.

[49] H. Gee, W. J. Hardy, *Documents illustrative of English church history*, London, 1896; for the *Six Articles of Religion*, see G. Redworth, *Journal of Ecclesiastical History* 37 (1986), 42-67: 'A Study in the Formulation of Policy: The Genesis and Evolution of the Acts of Six Articles'; Henry VIII, cf. T. A. Lacey, ed., *The King's book; or, A necessary doctrine and erudition for any Christian man, 1543*, London, 1932, 66.

fice of the mass assembled by Eck from late medieval compendia, and on Fisher's patristic scholarship.[50]

2.1. Eck's 'De Sacrificio Missae' and Smyth's 'Defence of the Sacrifice of the Mass'

Any debate about the sacrifice of the mass hinged on the eucharistic pericope in Mt 26.26par. At the last supper, Christ pointed to bread and wine and called them His body and blood. He added that His body was given for His disciples and that His blood was poured out for them, which for catholics underlined the sacrificial character of the eucharist.[51] In the eucharist, therefore, Christ imparted to believers the body that was sacrificed to the Father on the cross, and His blood 'which is poured out for many for the forgiveness of sins'.[52] The dominical commandment 'do this in remembrance of me' emphasised that this sacrificial act should be repeated until the Second Coming.[53] Christ Himself commanded that a *memoria* or *repraesentatio* of His sacrifice be celebrated daily, Eck and his later contemporaries would argue.[54] In his *De Sacrificio Missae* (1523) Eck frequently described this commemoration as a 'memorial of the passion and sacrifice of Christ' or, alternatively, as a 'representative action'.[55] Like Biel, he spoke of the sacrifice of the mass as the 'the representative image of the passion of Christ, who was truly sacrificed'.[56] Smyth resorted to similar terminology and spoke of the 'remembraunce of that hys passion and bloody sacrifice', a commemoration 'but more chiefly, more lyuely and

---

[50] J. Fisher, *De Veritate Corporis et Sanguinis Christi in eucharistia*, Köln, 1527.
[51] Lk 22.19-20.
[52] Mt 26.28.
[53] Lk 22.19.
[54] Cf. Smyth (1546¹), xlix v-r.
[55] Eck (1982), 62: 'The eucharist is offered at the mass and received in memory of the passion and offering of Christ' (Eucharistia in missa offeratur et sumatur in memoriam passionis et oblationis Christi); 'A representative act' (Actio repraesentativa).
[56] Eck (1982), 62: 'But the celebration of the eucharist is a representative reflection of the passion of Christ, which was the true offering' (Celebratio autem eucharistiae est imago quaedam repraesentativa passionis Christi quae fuit vera immolatio).

expressly, by offering of hys verye bodye and blood in sacrifice whiche is done of the preest at his masse'.[57]

Smyth endeavoured to demonstrate that the English evangelical position, which ultimately would propagate the 'one, perfect and sufficient sacrifice, once offered', was untenable without the understanding of the continuous re-presentation of the sacrifice on Calvary. His conviction that priests 'do offere the selfe same sacrifice, which Chryste ones for euer offered by death and bloode shedynge on the crosse' was supported by his references to the dominical commandment to continue the celebration of the eucharist 'in remembrance of me'.[58] Smyth paraphrased Mt 26.26par substantially to confirm his understanding of a sacrifice of the mass. He argued that at the institution of the eucharist Christ Himself had given instruction to offer His body and blood in thanksgiving, and as a propitiatory sacrifice. In an act of quasi–ordination, Christ had authorised and empowered His disciples

> to do the whiche I haue done euen nowe at thys my maundye, that is, take ye breade, geue thankes to god for all his benefites geuen to man, blesse it, consecrate it, turnynge the substaunce of it in to my flesshe, offere it to my father, nat onely to gyue hym thankes for his benefites bestowed on man, but to purchase his grace also.[59]

In his rejection of English evangelical claims that the sacrifice of the mass was a recent invention, Smyth strongly emphasised that a continuous sacrifice of the mass had been instituted directly by Christ, and 'nat by the bysshop of Rome nor of any other bysshoppe or preest'.[60] He made use of a number of Johannes Eck's arguments in order to prove this point.[61] Eck held that just as grace is communicated through the sacraments, so by the act of making Christ's sacrifice present in the mass the benefits of His passion are communicated to the faithful.[62] Smyth adopted the language of representation in his argument: 'the masse therefore is a sacrifice, exercised on the aulter for the continuall

---

[57] Smyth (1546¹), liv r, lxvi r.
[58] Smyth (1546¹), liv r.; cf. Lk 22.19.
[59] Smyth (1546¹), xlix r-v.
[60] Smyth (1546¹), xlix v.
[61] Cf. Eck (1982), 64ff.
[62] Eck (1982), 64: 'The merits and fruits of the Lord's offering are applied to the faithful by an act of representation' (Merita et fructus oblationis dominicae applicantur fidelibus ... per actionem repraesentationis).

remembraunce of christes death and bloody sacrifice ones offred vpon the crosse.'[63] While Christ had bled only once on Calvary, 'the pure hooste or sacrifice [is] offred ... vnbloudye or offred without bloudshedyng'.[64] The effects of Christ's sacrifice on the cross—a unique event in history—are eternal.[65] The parallels with Eck's and Biel's theology of representation cannot be overlooked. While the sacrifice of the mass is not identical to the historical sacrifice on the cross, it is not an act of devotion which merely commemorates the sacrifice on Calvary (unlike the stations of the cross). Eck made clear:

> The offering in which Christ by dying in His own person offered Himself to God the Father for the redemption of the human race is both bodily and real. ... The sacramental offering of Christ in worship is something else by which Christ is offered to God the Father by His bride, the church, not through the bitterness of death as on the cross, nor solely through devout and prolonged meditation, but also by solemn representation ... of the true body of Christ ... under the veil of the venerable sacrament, the eucharist.[66]

Just as in Eck's writings, in Smyth's theology of the sacrifice of the mass Christ is regarded as the true priest at mass, offering sacrifice.[67] Both authors depend on a conservative understanding of the high-priestly office of Christ, the true successor of the king of Salem, Melchizedek, who once offered bread and wine to God.[68] According to patristic tradition, the order of Melchizedek was that of a high-priest who did not offer sacrificial animals and holocaust

---

[63] Smyth (1546^1), lxxi r.
[64] Smyth (1546^1), xl r.
[65] Cf. Eck (1982), 122f.
[66] Eck (1982), 123f: '[Oblatio] una est corporea et realis, qua Christus in persona propria moriendo se obtulit Deo Patri in redemptionem generis humanis. ... Alia est oblatio Christi sacramentalis in mysterio, qua Christus offertur a sua sponsa ecclesia Deo Patri, non per acerbitatem mortis sicut in cruce, nec solum per devotam et iugem meditationem, sed et per repraesentationem solemnem ... veri corporis Christi ... sub velo venerabilis sacramenti eucharistiae'; cf. Smyth (1546^1), lxi r; cf. Smyth (1546^2), 62r-v, no. 62-4.
[67] Smyth (1546^1), xxxi v-r; Eck (1982), 182.
[68] Gen 14.18-20: 'And King Melchizedek of Salem brought out bread and wine; he was priest of God Most High. He blessed Abram and said, "Blessed be Abram by God Most High, maker of heaven and earth; and blessed be God Most High, who has delivered your enemies into your hand!"'; Ps 110.4: 'The Lord has sworn and will not change His mind, "You are a priest forever according to the order of Melchizedek"'.

offerings, but bread and wine.[69] In Heb 5.10, Christ is proclaimed the one true successor of Melchizedek who had become the high priest of the New Covenant sealed by the blood of Christ shed on the cross.[70] This image is taken up in the Roman canon of the Mass.[71] As Christ was the new high priest in the order of Melchizedek, He made a permanent offering of Himself to the Father for the forgiveness of sins. The controversialists held that there must therefore be another sacrifice (*alia sacrificio*) parallel to that on Calvary: 'Christ is both the true priest and the victim'.[72] This sacrifice, offered by the ministry of priests, was the eucharistic sacrifice. There are therefore three distinct yet unified offerings made to the Father, Smyth and Eck maintained.[73] In accordance with 1 Cor 5.7, Christ was once offered metaphorically as the paschal lamb, yet He was also offered sacramentally in the eucharist, as well as 'truly and actually on the cross':[74]

> For thoughe that blessed and immaculate lambe Christ was there offered vpon the crosse, and now dayly and continually is offred in Christes churche, yet the thinge which is offered is not diuerse in substance ... though in the manner of offering and sacrificienge there might be diuersitie.[75]

---

[69] Smyth (1546[1]), xxxv r: 'The whiche only amonge preestes offred bread & wyne'.

[70] Heb 5.6, 10; Heb 9.11f: 'But when Christ came as a high priest of the good things that have come, then through the greater and perfect tent ... He entered once for all into the Holy Place, not with the blood of goats and calves, but with His own blood, thus obtaining eternal redemption'.

[71] *The Weekday Missal*, London, 1982, 1310.

[72] Eck (1982), 182: 'When the true priest and the true offering ... is Christ, at the same time the priest is the offering minister in the person of the church' (Ubi verus sacerdos et vera hostia ... Christus est, sacerdote ministro in persona ecclesia simul offerente); Smyth (1546[1]), xxvii r-v: in Smyth's view, Melchizedek offered a corporal sacrifice of bread and wine, 'so truly [did] first the sauyour and our lord, afterwards the preestes whiche were instituted by hym, exercisyng the spirituall office of preesthode'.

[73] Cf. H. Emser (c. 1477-1527), *Missae Christianorum contra Lutheranum missandi formulam assertio* (1523), in: Th. Freudenberger, ed., *Schriften zur Verteidigung der Messe*, Münster, 1959, CC 28.17, CC 28.20-28; and idem, *Wider der zweier Pröbst zu Nürnberg falschen Grund und Ursachen, warum sie die heilige Meß und andere christliche Stück und Ceremonien geändert und zum Teil abgetan haben* (1525), in: CC 28.35ff, 28.128.

[74] Eck (1982), 160: 'On the cross, in all truth and reality' (In cruce, vere ac realiter); for the incorporation of the threefold sacrifice in the eucharistic doctrine of the council of Trent, see DS 1743.

[75] Smyth (1546[2]), 143 r.

In his *Defence of the Blessed Masse and the Sacrifice thereof* Smyth not only adopted the title of Eck's popular refutation of Luther's eucharistic doctrine, but followed the German controversialist's arguments very closely. Like Eck, Smyth divided his evidence into five distinctive groups of sources, first citing arguments from the Old Testament and the New Testament before proceeding to present arguments from apostolic tradition, the councils and the Fathers.[76] His section on the Fathers bears a close resemblance to Eck's, as do his arguments from the Old Testament.[77] The exegetical method employed by Smyth for his Old Testament sources particularly seems to indicate that they had their origin in Eck's polemic rejection of Lutheran doctrine. Both put great emphasis on Old Testament sources.

J. Eck: 'De Sacrificio Missae'		R. Smyth: 'Defence of the Sacrifice of the Mass'	
Mal 1.11ff	pp. 19-25	Mal 1.11ff	pp. xxxviii v-xlvi r
Mal 3.3ff	pp. 25-28	Mal 3.3ff	pp. xxxviii v-xlvi r
Lev 21.6-8	p. 29	Lev 21.6-8	pp. xxxv r-xxxviii v
Gen 14.18-20	p. 31	Gen 14.18-20	pp. xxi r-xxiv v
Ps 110.4	p. 31	Ps 110.4	pp. xxvi v-xxxv v
Judg 9.13	p. 32	Not used	
Dan 12.9-12	pp. 35-41	Dan 12.9-12	p. xx r
Ps 72	pp. 41-47	Not used	
1 Sam 2.31-36	pp. 48-53	Not used	
Not used		Isa 66.20	p. xxv r
Not used		Ex 29.33-35	p. xxxviii v

Figure 4: Parallel uses of Old Testament evidence in Johannes Eck's *De Sacrificio Missae* and Richard Smyth's *Defence of the Sacrifice of the Mass*.

2.1.1. *Arguments from the Old Testament*

In their reflection on arguments from Genesis and the prophecy of Malachi, both Eck and Smyth quoted the same rabbinical commentaries to establish that there had been a pre-Christian

---

[76] Smyth (1546¹), xii r-xlvi v: Old Testament sources; xlvi v-lxxii r: New Testament sources; lxxii r-lxxix v: Conciliar evidence; lxxx r-lxxxiii v: arguments from apostolic tradition; lxxxiv r-cxxxv: patristic evidence.

[77] Cf. Eck (1982), 89-115.

understanding of the sacrifice of Melchizedek as an early form of the mass.[78] Eck had made use of Porchetus' and Galatinus' talmudic commentaries in his compilations. Smyth did not acknowledge the origin either of his rabbinical or his exegetical sources.[79] He made use of the original texts and added his own interpretation, or of Eck's work and similar sets of commentaries.[80] The omission of references to his German and English sources would have been diplomatic, since the works of Fisher and Eck were still banned in England. Both were considered *personae non gratae* for maintaining papal supremacy in ecclesiastical matters.

Eck and Smyth place a strong emphasis on Mal 1.11ff and Mal 3.3. Eck knew his subject matter well, having lectured on Malachi previously (in 1520 or 1527).[81] He was a good biblical interpreter and frequently quoted from the original Hebrew text. In his more populist writings Smyth hardly ever used Hebrew. Despite the different order of opening texts—Gen 14.18-20 in Smyth's case, and Mal 1.11ff in Eck's—both theologians imitated Reuchlin's false etymology of the Latin *missa*, attributing it to the Hebrew מנחה.[82] Indeed, for Smyth, 'the name of the Masse sheweth that it is a sacrifice'—it therefore was the direct equivalent of the LXX θυσία or the Vulgate *oblatio*.[83] As such, the sacrificial character of the mass had already been prefigured in Old Testament prophe-

---

[78] Gen 14.18, cf. Ps 110 (109).4

[79] Smyth (1546¹), cxi r-cxxii v, cf. Eck (1982), 79-97.

[80] Cf. Eck (1982), 31: 'I found Porchetus and Galatinus' (Inveni Porchetum et Galatinum); cf. S. Porchetus, *Victoria adversus impios Hebraeos ex sacris litteris tum ex dictis Talmud ac Caballistarum et aliorum omnium authorum, quos Hebraei recipiunt monstrantur veritatis catholicae fidei*, Paris, 1520; P. Galatinus OFM, *Opus de arcanis catholicae veritatis, quum ante natum Christum, tum postscriptis, contra obstinatam Iudeorum perfidiam absolutissimus commentarius*, Ortona, 1518. Both Porchetus and Galatinus held that their sources were pre-Christian whereas they were, in fact, written much later, cf. E. Iserloh, *Die Eucharistie in der Darstellung des Johannes Eck. Ein Beitrag zur vortridentinischen Kontroverstheologie über das Messopfer*, Reformationsgeschichtliche Studien und Texte (cited as: RTS) 73, Münster, 1950, 78 and G. Kattermann, *Zentralblatt für Bibliothekswesen* 55 (1938), 42-52: 'Luthers Handexemplar des antijüdischen Porchetus in der Landesbibliothek Karlsruhe'.

[81] The latter date seems more likely since he devoted a series of twenty-five sermons to the prophecy of Malachi in the same year, cf. Iserloh (1950), 60 n; see also J. Eck, B. Walde, ed., *Explanatio Psalmi vigesimi* (1538), CC 13, Münster, 1928, xix, 29 n; and J. Eck, J. Metzler SJ, ed., *Epistola de ratione studiorum* (1538), CC 2, Münster, 1921, 58, 71 n.

[82] Cf. J. Reuchlin, *Rudimenta hebraica*, Pforzheim, 1506, 307.

[83] Smyth (1546¹), xviii v.

cies. While Smyth was content merely to point to the etymological link between the Hebrew word for an oblation and the Latin word *missa*, Eck elaborated that Malachi made use of the word intentionally since, according to Lev 6.14-17, it designated a propitiatory offering of unleavened bread.[84] Both agreed that Mal 1.11 pointed to the sacrifice of the New Covenant: 'the whiche [pure offering] our lorde sayeth by hys prophet shuld be offred to him from the risinge of the sonne to the goyng downe'.[85] Smyth used this brief excursus for one of his polemical attacks on Luther and his followers, 'the messengers of Antichrist', whereas Eck added rabbinical evidence to his cause before turning to the prophecies of Daniel for further evidence.[86]

Smyth followed Eck in his interpretation of Dan 12.9-12, which he conflated with his own attack on Luther. The prophetic vision of Daniel in which the erection of a sanctuary to Antichrist is foretold, lent itself particularly well to the cause of the German controversialists.[87] Smyth followed his continental colleagues in concluding that the continual sacrifice 'can be none other but the sacrifice of the masse'.[88] Those who denied its existence were liked to 'antichrist labouringe al that he can to destroy christes faith'.

---

[84] Eck (1980), 22: There are five forms of offering in Lev, 'The law of this final sacrifice, called מנחה ... was the same as the type of offering which the sacrifice of the church rightly expresses. ... From here, the prophet [Malachi], intending to elucidate the particular sacrifice of the New Testament says קרבן, not עלה, nor זכח, nor שלמים, nor חטאת, nor אשם, which were all the names of sacrifices' (Lex huius ultimi sacrificii, quod מנחה dicitur ... erat similia ... quod genus oblationis recte exprimit sacrificium ecclesiae. ... Hinc propheta, peculiariter sacrificium novi testamenti explicaturus, מנחה dicitur, non קרבן, non עלה, non זכח, non שלמים, non חטאת, non אשם, quae omnia sunt nomina sacrificiorum); cf. Lev 6.14-17: 'This is the ritual of the grain offering: ... It shall be eaten as unleavened cakes in a holy place. ... It shall not be baked with leaven. I have given it as their portion of my offerings by fire; it is most holy, like the sin offering and the guilt offering'.

[85] Smyth (1546¹), xl r; cf. Eck (1982), 22-23.

[86] Smyth (1546¹), xx r.

[87] The controversialists employed the scriptural link between the removal of a 'continuous sacrifice' (Dan 12.11) and the arrival of Antichrist in numerous debates. Eck frequently made use of that argument during his disputation with Oecolampadius in summer 1526 in Baden; for the Baden debate see for instance, I. Backus, *The disputations of Baden, 1526 and Berne, 1528: Neutralizing the early Church*, Princeton NJ, 1993.

[88] Smyth (1546¹), xx r.

Smyth follows Eck closely at this point and his own statements are little more than loose paraphrases of Eck's Latin.[89]

On the other hand, Smyth did deviate both from his German predecessor and from mainstream catholic orthodoxy in his reflection on Gen 14.18. One of the reasons for his later recantation in 1547 was his statement that while the sacrifice of Melchizedek prefigured the institution of the mass and the sacrifice of the altar, it was not related to the historic sacrifice on Calvary.[90] According to Heb 5.10 Christ had been designated a 'high priest according to the order of Melchizedek', a high priest who offered bread and wine to God rather than blood sacrifices. On the cross, Christ had offered His own body and blood to the Father. Smyth now claimed that while there was an intrinsic link between the two sacrifices, there was a clear difference in the way in which they had been offered, since one involved flesh and blood and the other bread and wine.[91] Rather than resort to the explanation that both were different expressions of the same eternal sacrifice offered to the Father, Smyth specified that while the link between the two could not be severed, still

> no man can truely say that christe was a preest after this ordre of Melchizedech when he offred vp himselfe on the crosse to his father for our sinnes, for he did not offre his body vnder the forme of bread & wine, but vnder the forme of fleshe & blode, & therefore he was that time so offering sacrifice a priest after the ordre of Aaron & nat of Melchizedech, ... & the prophecy ... by Dauyd [Ps 110.4] was fulfilled by Christ at his maundy.[92]

In his interpretation of 1 Sam 2.31-36 Eck, on the other hand, emphasised that the high priesthood of the New Covenant had superseded the priesthood of Aaron altogether. The question concerning the origin of Christ's high priesthood at the moment of His death on the cross was related to the complete substitution of Jewish sacrificing priests and levites with the eternal high

---

[89] Smyth (1546¹), ibid.; Eck (1982), 23: 'They are precursors of Antichrist, causing the desolation of the church' (Praecursores sunt Antichristi, facientes desolationem ecclesiae).
[90] Cf. R. Smyth, *A godly and faythfull Retraction made by R. Smyth. Reuokyng certeyn errours in some of hys books*, London, 1547, D i r-D ii v.
[91] For instance Smyth (1546¹), liv r.
[92] Smyth (1546¹), xxvii r-v.

priesthood of Christ, *secundum ordinem Melchizedec*, and not to the different character of the sacrifice.[93]

For Smyth the arguments from the Old Testament were of no further interest beyond their immediate value as scriptural evidence for his doctrinal views. Just as he had argued elsewhere that there had been evidence of a long-standing tradition of vows in certain passages of the Old Testament, here Smyth also made use of the text as a quarry from which he would draw useful material for the erection of his doctrinal fortress.[94] In his argument the Old Testament passages were used as a proof of a culture of divinely–instituted sacrifices in the Jewish world.[95] The rich tradition of Jewish propitiatory sacrifices fitted into Smyth's overall argument, as he was able to maintain that, since God Himself had commanded man to make 'well-pleasing offerings' for the atonement of his sins (for instance Mal 1.10-11), He would still look favourably on the sacrifice offered by the members of the New Covenant, the catholic church. The efficacy of the sacrifice of the mass therefore ought not to be called into question, since it was a 'repaying of all maner of hurt, a purgation or purgynge of al vncleannes ... agaynst al them which denye that the masse is a sacrifice propitiatorye, that is makinge god mercifull to vs, and appeasynge his wrath towarde vs for our synnes'.[96]

A second strand of Smyth's argument was the fact that a continuous sacrifice had always been offered to God, as the evidence from Daniel and Malachi indicated. Once more, he had little actual interest in the text itself (there is no parsing of different Hebrew terms for *oblatio* as in Eck's work). Rather, he rather concentrated on establishing that the Old Testament supported his theories. The passages cited underlined the fact that since time immemorial a worshipping community had offered sacrifices to God, an important argument in Smyth's polemics. Antiquity and immutability for Smyth automatically implied authority and

---

[93] Eck (1982), 52: 'For He is Himself the sacrifice, not according to the order of Aaron, but Melchizedek' (Ipsum enim est sacrificium, non secundum ordinem Aaron sed Melchisedek).

[94] For Smyth's Old Testament arguments on vows, see above, chapter IV, 110-111.

[95] Cf. Smyth (1546¹), xviii v.

[96] Smyth (1546¹), xl v-xli r.

reliability. He not only introduced most of his patristic evidence by emphasising its antiquity, but also stated expressly that the new doctrines debated in his own day were unreliable, simply because they were new. If for more than fifteen hundred years no-one had ever questioned the doctrine of the sacrifice of the mass, 'except one Peter de bruis', the new doctrines could safely be dismissed as innovations.[97] Any doctrine which a theologian 'chose of his owne head' without 'any good authoritie' should be rejected forthwith.[98] In the light of his earlier interpretation of Dan 12.10, the fact that Luther 'first of all men spake against the sacrifice of the holye masse' automatically rendered him 'antichristes messenger'.[99] He had broken a ceaseless strand by removing the continual sacrifice instituted by God and perpetuated by the church. By careful presentation of his scriptural evidence, Smyth painted an image of an uninterrupted tradition of a Jewish custom which, if interpreted in allegorical or Christological terms, prefigured the doctrine he set out to prove in the first place. In his eyes it was impossible for an evangelical hierarchy that valued the ideals of an Old Testament patriarchal society so highly to reject the doctrine of the sacrifice of the mass and to follow 'the deuyls ... sowinge yll seade, of false and erroneous doctrine in the same, by heretiques his ministers'.[100]

2.1.2. *Arguments from the New Testament*

Smyth next turned to the New Testament to elucidate the scriptural nature of the sacrifice of the mass. As in Eck's work, this section is considerably shorter than his compilation of Old Testament passages.[101] The argument centred around the words of institution of the eucharist (Lk 22.19), three Pauline pericopae and an excursus on the idea of Christ as the Lamb of God (Jn 1.29). Of more interest to the debate was Smyth's excursus which clearly mirrored Eck's introduction. Both discuss the nature of the paschal lamb slain for the atonement of sins. The two argued that

---

[97] Smyth (1546¹), ix, marginalium.
[98] Smyth (1546¹), xvii r.
[99] Ibid.
[100] Smyth (1546¹), xv v.
[101] Smyth (1546¹), xliv r-lxxii v (Old Testament: xix v-xliii v); Eck (1982), 53-78 (Old Testament: 19-53).

if Christ was the true paschal lamb, offered in sacrifice according to the ordinances prescribed in Lev 8.18-19; 31, then the manner in which that mystical lamb had been offered needed to correlate with that prescribed for lambs of burnt offering.[102] This presupposed the sacrificial offering of the paschal lamb—Christ—in the daily sacrifice of the mass. Smyth elaborated:

> Christ had offered hys verye body and bloud at his maundye and afterward receued it ... for the Jewes dyd fyrste offre the paschal lambe in sacryfice and afterwarde eate him, as Moyses testifieth. Therefore Christ dydde at hys laste supper offre his bodye in sacrifice to his father, fyrst in a fygure offerynge the paschal lambe, and after that in very dede without a figure.[103]

He concluded the interpretation of Heb 5.1 with a polemical sideswipe at Luther's concept of the priesthood of all believers which mirrors Eck's closely:[104]

> This texte is manifeste agaynst Martin Luthers heresye, whiche is, that all Christen people are preestes and that among christen folke there is none rather a preeste than all other. ... It neyther dothe belonge to the layte to vse that office, nor the office of the preest is onelye to preach as some men vntruely do saye.[105]

---

[102] Lev 8.18-19: 'Then Moses brought forward the lamb of burnt offering. Aaron and his sons laid their hands on the head of the lamb, and it was slaughtered. Moses dashed the blood against all sides of the altar'; Lev 8.31: 'Moses said to Aaron and his sons: "Boil the flesh of the lamb ... and eat it there with the bread that is in the basket of ordination offerings, as I was commanded, Aaron and his sons shall eat it; and what remains of the flesh and the bread you shall burn with fire" '.

[103] Smyth (1546¹), lxi r, cf. Eck (1982), 55: 'Our paschal lamb, therefore, is Christ. The type of lamb that once was associated with a figurative lamb is abolished. It is to be seen as our true lamb, because the former has been fulfilled by them. In the same way that there were two forms in the symbolic lamb—the first was sacrificed and the second eaten—likewise our true and mystic lamb is first offered in the sacrifice of the mass and then the flesh of the paschal lamb consumed in the receiving of communion' (Est ergo agnus noster paschalis Christus, abolito agno typico, quid autem olim agebatur cum agno typico in figura, oportet ut iam agatur cum agno nostro in veritate, quia omnia in figura contingebant illis. Modo in agno typico duo fiebant, nam primo in immolabatur, dein edebatur; sic et de agno nostro vero mystico, qui primo immolabatur in sacrificio missae, dein manducatur caro agni paschalis in sumptione et communione).

[104] Heb 5.1: 'Every high priest chosen from among mortals is put in charge of things pertaining to God on their behalf, to offer gifts and sacrifices for sins'.

[105] Smyth (1546¹), lxix r.

Eck had concluded in 1523: 'Luther professed the priesthood of the entire church, indeed, he counted not only lay-people, but even women among the universal priesthood. It is consequently also necessary of maintaining the priestly sacrifices in the church, which are gifts and sacrifices for their own sins as well as those of their people'.[106] While Eck's exegesis centred on the theological necessity to maintain an offering priesthood, Smyth transformed such statements into polemical attacks on Luther and on those members of the English convocation who were labouring hard to raise the office of 'preaching the Gospel' over and above that of offering the mass. While his attack appeared to be directed against Luther, it was actually directed against the evangelical members of convocation.

Smyth transformed the theological attacks of an earlier generation into polemical instruments to be employed in the ongoing controversy about sacrificing priests in his own day.[107] Although his own theological contributions were not on a par with those of his predecessors they served a different purpose altogether. His concern was to address English lay-people—'the reder which is not of the beste lerned'—rather than enter into an academic debate with Luther. As such, his 'study for the edifieng of the simple & the rude' can certainly not be called a mere reproduction of another, more learned work on the subject.[108] It is rather a reworking of Eck's ideas to suit a distinctive, non-academic audience. No longer forced to battle with Luther, Smyth was able to address himself to his own situation, which he did in lightly veiled asides. While he still beckoned those who had 'ben deceaued by Luther this blynde teacher' to return to the path of orthodoxy, it was

---

[106] Eck (1982), 73: 'Therefore Luther removes the entire priesthood from the church—who holds that not only laymen, but even women are priests in the world—yet he admits that it is necessary to uphold the priestly offices in the church, to offer gifts and sacrifices for their own sins and those of the people' (Ergo Luther auferat omne sacerdotium de ecclesia—qui contra non solum laycos, sed ipsas enim foeminas constitutit in universum sacerdotes—fateatur necesse est et officia sacerdotalia esse in ecclesia, quae sunt offere dona et sacrificia pro peccatis et suis et populi).
[107] Smyth (1546¹), x r-v.
[108] Smyth (1546¹), xviii r.

really the English evangelicals whom he called to turn again to catholicism.[109]

Ultimately, Smyth's exposition of the words of institution does not carry the same conviction as his authoritative interpretation of the Old Testament prophecies. His sources carried much less useful material on the subject.[110] Arguably, there would have been no need to search beyond the commandment 'do this in remembrance of me'. Smyth concentrated on providing evidence for the sacrificial character of the eucharist from scriptural sources other than Mt 26.26par. He elaborated on the exact nature of Christ's institution of the eucharist extensively at a later stage, in his second *Assertion and Defence of the Sacrament of the Aulter* and his *A confutation of a certen booke, called a defence of the true, and Catholike doctrine of the Sacrament, &c., sette fourth in the name of Thomas Archebysshoppe of Canterburye*. Like Eck's selection of New Testament pericopae, Smyth's quotations consisted of a reflection on the high priestly office from the letter to the Hebrews, as well as various other isolated New Testament passages (such as Ac 13.2 and 1 Cor 10.16f). Both authors added a brief interpretation of Heb 13.10 by way of an afterthought which led them back to their initial etymological argument:[111] the apostolic evidence for the existence of an altar (θυσιαστήριον) in the church not only confirmed that every altar in an English parish church was a place 'where sacrifice is offred or kepte', but more so that the mass was the continuation of the Jewish מנחה. It was an essential part of the eternal Covenent between God and His people, a Covenent that had been renewed and re-defined by Christ on the cross. Smyth felt confident to conclude his arguments from scripture by reiterating that 'the masse therefore is a sacrifice, exercised on the aulter for the

---

[109] Smyth (1546[1]), xvi r.
[110] Iserloh (1950), 71: 'Eck's treatment of the words of institution is unsatisfactory. He does concentrate on the essential points of the question, but whoever seeks to get a firmer grip on the argument finds himself drawing a blank' (Die Behandlung des Einsetzungsberichtes durch Eck kann nicht befriedigen. Es werden wohl die entscheidenden Punkte genannt, von denen aus die Frage angefaßt werden kann. Aber wenn man bei Eck genauer zupacken will, dann greift man ins Leere).
[111] Heb 13.10: 'We have an altar from which those who officiate in the tent have no right to eat'; cf. Smyth (1546[1]), lxxi r; Eck (1982), 74f.

continuall remembraunce of christes death and bloody sacrifice ones offred vpon the crosse'.[112]

Smyth's biblical passages were chosen expressly for their argumentative value. As he stated elsewhere, the thought that 'nothynge is to be admytted or allowed, except it be specially and expressly spoken of and touched in scripture' was particularly harmful to theological debate.[113] Erwin Iserloh's evaluation of Eck's use of scripture holds equally true for Smyth's:

> Scripture is ... one large arsenal. Everything is freely at hand to serve as a tool in the polemical skirmishes with the opposition, or to serve as evidence for preconceived concepts.[114]

In his exegesis, Smyth did not so much strive to provide a better understanding of the pericopae in question, as to choose passages to fit his argument. Smyth's rigorous Christological interpretation of Old Testament seeks to 'prove' the pre-existence of a concept of the sacrifice of the mass. The fact that some passages might lend more weight to his cause than others was ignored by Smyth. His main intention was to amass evidence for the existence of the doctrine.[115] As an experienced disputant he adhered to the principle that a broader argument based on more evidence—however shallow—was better than a choice selection of biblical or patristic evidence. Where his predecessors still resorted to the original biblical texts and tried to expound the pericopae by their exegetical skill, Smyth believed that as long as the text could be employed to argue for the existence of the doctrine in question, there was no need for any exegesis beyond the allegorical interpretation of the pericope.

His treatment of Scripture often failed to live up to a critical representation of the biblical text in the context of his own day. Far too often Smyth merely gleaned material from various sources, themselves marginal.[116] The success of Smyth's *Defence of the Blessed Masse and the Sacrifice thereof*, therefore, did not rest on his original

---

[112] Smyth (1546¹), lxxxi r.
[113] Smyth (1546²), 194 v.
[114] Iserloh (1950), 79: 'Die Schrift ist ... ein großes Arsenal! Alles liegt gleich griffbereit und handlich, um als Waffe in dem Wortgefecht mit dem Gegner zu dienen und für ein vorher schon fertiges Begriffsgebäude den Beweis zu liefern'.
[115] Cf. Smyth (1546¹), xxxviii v-xlvi r; xxxviii r.
[116] Cf. similar criticism directed against Eck, Iserloh (1950), 81.

use of primary source material—there was little or no originality to his arguments—but rather his polemical re-interpretation of standard sources to suit the context of a late 1540's English debate. As a forceful contribution to the debate on the nature of the sacramental priesthood, the parish mass and the duties of the clergy, rather than the defence of the sacrifice of the mass against Luther the work makes itself out to be, it was a success.[117]

2.2. FISHER'S 'DE VERITATE CORPORIS ET SANGUINIS CHRISTI IN EUCHARISTIA' AND SMYTH'S 'ASSERTION AND DEFENCE OF THE SACRAMENT OF THE AULTER'

The second 1546 publication in defence of catholic eucharistic doctrine, the *Assertion and Defence* was written with the intention to reconfirm the belief

> that this most holye sacramente of the aulter, ... by our blessed sauiour Christ instituted and ordeyned, hath bene the catholyque faythe and true opinion of all chrysten people.[118]

Taking 'certaine true & vndoubted canons' as his yardstick of orthodoxy, Smyth prepared for another attack on the 'notable errours that haue ben heretofore and also now in our dayes', specifically among them the denial of the real presence.[119] At the end of this work Smyth set out to provide 'a sufficient and good aunswer and solution' to aspects of the eucharistic doctrine currently called into question—once again for the benefit of the 'vnlerned and simple people'.[120]

It is noteworthy that he did not address himself to an academic audience, but rather chose to direct his writings to non-theologians, to call back to the catholic faith all who, 'for lack of wytte, learnyng and grace' had departed from orthodox teaching.[121] The author's strong concern to list and repudiate contemporary eucharistic 'heresies' is another indication that the work served as a form of handbook for local clergy or the informed laity.

---

[117] A second and third edition of the work were published in the same year.
[118] Smyth (1546²), 12 r.
[119] Ibid.
[120] Smyth (1546²), 13 r.
[121] Smyth (1546²), 4 r-v.

Dedicated to his 'deare brethren', they were to provide a 'warrante and a buckler for your defence and for the atteinynge of your saluatyon'.[122] In a passage that bears some resemblance to the first preface of Fisher's *De Veritate*, Smyth compiled a systematic list of prominent eucharistic heresies throughout history.[123] Commencing with the New Testament criticism of the 'Capharnites' (Jn 6.59-63) and early Christian heresies such as Nestorianism, he concluded in his own day and country with the views of Wyclif and Frith.[124] A lengthy systematic repudiation of 'objections' from the works of Frith and other contemporary evangelicals followed his compendium on common eucharistic heresies. The author's pithy arguments, or 'solutions', take up almost a third of the *Assertion and Defence*.[125]

Smyth took great pains not to repeat the mistake of many of his catholic predecessors and sought a way to affirm the royal supremacy over the church while defending catholic doctrine. Echoing the *King's Book*, he reminded his readers that by act of parliament the faith of the church and that of the realm were one and the same, and both still held that

> in the sayde mooste blessed sacrament of the aulter, by the strengthe and efficacye of Christes myghtye worde, it beynge spokenn by the preist, there is presente really vnder the forme of bread and wyne, the naturall body and bloude of our sauiour Jesv christ, conceiued of the vyrgyn Marye, so that after the consecration there remaineth no substaunce of bread and wyne, nor any other substaunce, but onelye the substaunce of christ, god and man.[126]

This statement was programmatic for the composition of his work. The assertion that real presence hinged on the 'efficacy of Christes myghtye worde' through the proclamation—at the moment of consecration—of the words of institution by Christ's ministers, the

---

[122] Smyth (1546^2), 163 r; 247 r.
[123] Cf. Fisher (1527), BB 4 v-BB 5 r.
[124] Smyth (1546^2), 80 r-90 v.
[125] For a thorough study on the life of parochial clergy in early sixteenth-century England, see P. Heath, *The English Parish Clergy on the Eve of the Reformation*, London, 1969; for popular preaching and catechising, see J. W. Blench, *Preaching in England in the late Fifteenth and Sixteenth Centuries*, Oxford, 1964; and J. A. H. Moran, *The Growth of English Schooling: learning, literacy, and laicization in pre-Reformation York diocese*, Princeton NJ, 1985.
[126] Smyth (1546^2), 14 v; cf. Lacey (1932), 50-51; 55.

priests, was a controversial statement in Smyth's day. This traditional understanding of ministerial priesthood clearly set him apart from the evangelical understanding of the *ministerium Christi* as the office of proclaiming the Gospel through preaching.[127] Furthermore, the question of Christ's real presence in the eucharist not only raised questions about the exact mode of that presence—whether Christ could be said to be present locally at various places on earth as well as at the right hand of God in heaven as stated in the creeds—but also the need to reject latent Monophysitism by stating expressly that Christ was truly present in His resurrection body, true man and true God.[128] Smyth had put his finger on three concerns that divided theological opinion in the English church of his day: (1) The exact nature of the office and work of a priest as minister of Christ; (2) the question of the real presence over and above a commemorative re-enactment of the last supper; (3) the question of the mode of Christ's presence in the eucharist.

Smyth's chief concern in the *Assertion and Defence*, however, was neither the priestly office, nor a Christological reflection. The central issue at stake was his assertion

> that the body and blud which christ at his last supper gaue to his apostles vnder the forme of bread & wine (& so in the sacrament, to be received & taken) ... were trulye, & in dede, without any doubt, the very body & bloud of our sayd sauyour Jesus Christ: which is the thinge we go about to persuade in this treatise.[129]

In his initial 'persuasion' Smyth did not linger on the words of institution (Mt 26.26par) and considered only very briefly the three synoptic accounts and the dominical sayings from 1 Cor 11.23f.[130] In a final section of his work, he turned to further biblical evidence and rejected a number of evangelical arguments derived from Scripture.[131] His main concern lay in demonstrating the

---

[127] Smyth (1546²), ibid.; for a study on the evangelical understanding of ministry see for instance R. Stupperich, *Reformatorische Verkündigung und Lebensordnung, Klassiker des Protestantismus III*, Bremen, 1963.

[128] For a succinct introduction to the patristic background of the debate, see J. N. D. Kelly, *Early Creeds and Controversies*, London, ³1993, 331-342.

[129] Smyth (1546²), 16 r.

[130] Smyth (1546²), 14 v-16 r.

[131] His 'objections and solutions', cf. Smyth (1546²), 164 r-189 v.

patristic and conciliar arguments for the real presence of Christ in the eucharist, to which he devoted more than 180 pages.[132]

2.2.1. *Arguments from Patristic and Conciliar Sources*

A large proportion of Smyth's patristic evidence can be traced to the preface of the fourth book of Fisher's *De Veritate*.[133] Just as Eck's books, the work had been banned by royal proclamation because of the author's strong views on the papal supremacy.[134] Smyth's use of Eck's exegetical work resulted in a coherent argument with a distinctive slant (that is the claim that a denial of the sacrifice of the mass by some evangelical members of convocation undermined the nature of the sacramental priesthood). In the case of *De Veritate*, he simply adopted the entire argument, paraphrasing and rearranging Fisher's evidence.

Fisher had built his argument around five groups each spanning roughly three hundred years, ranging back from the 1500s to the days of the first Christian martyrs. While in the first three parts of his argument, moving back from his own day to about the year 400, Fisher was content merely to list the names of outstanding propagators of the real presence, he began to substantiate his arguments with relevant quotations from patristic sources in the second and first parts.[135] His patristic evidence formed the backbone for Smyth's own arguments from the Fathers. In his *Assertion and Defence*, he turned the framework around and began his proof for the real presence by citing the evidence contained in *De Veritate* in chronological order, rather than copying Fisher's retrograde

---

[132] Smyth (1546²), 5 r.

[133] Rex (1991), 140, points out that 'in the fourth preface we are presented with Fisher's patristic scholarship at its best'.

[134] Cf. P. L. Hughes, J. F. Larkin, edd., *Tudor Royal Proclamations*, New Haven CT, 1964-1969; Smyth was in illustrious company, as Rex (1991), 87, has documented. Among the English conservatives who drew on Fisher's works were his contemporaries Stephen Gardiner, Thomas More and fellow-exile Thomas Stapleton as well as a later successor of Smyth's at Oxford, Garcia Villasancta.

[135] Fisher (1527), 'second period': lxxxv r-lxxxvi v; 'first period': lxxxxvi v-lxxxviii v.

pattern.[136] Smyth did not depend exclusively on Fisher's *De Veritate*, but expanded the argument with citations from other conservative sources. A statement from Eusebius Emissenus, for instance, that 'the invisible preist christ, by his word and secret power, dothe turn the visible creatures into the substance of his body and bloud', was gleaned from Henry VIII's work. Some citations from Ambrose derived from Fisher's *Sacri sacerdotii defensio contra Lutherum*.[137] The use of second-hand evidence was common in the sixteenth century, and so when citing the early liturgies of Clement of Rome (and, in Fisher's case, James of Jerusalem) in support of the real presence, both authors derived their evidence from an earlier sermon on the eucharist by Cardinal Bessarion.[138]

In the works of the Fathers, as read through the eyes of John Fisher, Smyth found strong evidence for the special nature of the eucharist over and above other early Christian communal celebrations, such as agape meals.[139] The names given to the eucharist bore witness to its divine origins. He recalled that Pseudo-Dionysius spoke of the 'communion ... that maketh us one with God', that Ignatius called the eucharist 'the medicine of immortalitie' or 'the tryacle or preseruature of life and purgatyue medicine', and that Clement spoke of a 'holy portion and parte'.[140] The eucharist was no ordinary sharing of bread and wine to commemorate Christ's last supper, but rather a meal that enabled man to share in a glimpse of the divine reality. The communion bread was no everyday comestible. It was the 'brede of God, the heauenly brede of life', of which Irenaeus spoke.[141] For at the moment of consecration

---

[136] In both cases, however, the chronology contained a number of deliberate anachronisms, for instance in Smyth (1546²), 16 v-22 v, the works of Gregory Nazianzen, Gregory of Nyssa, Basil the Great and Hilary were quoted alongside the works of Cyprian, Clement of Alexandria, the Latin Fathers and Pseudo-Dionysius; cf. Fisher (1527), lxxxvi v-lxxxviii v.

[137] Smyth (1546²), 22 r; cf. Henry VIII (1992), *De Sacramento Altaris*; Fisher (1525), 48.

[138] Smyth (1546²), 16 v, cf. Bessarion, *Oratio de Sacramento Eucharistiae*, Strassburg, 1513, A 8 v; see especially Rex (1991), 141.

[139] Smyth (1546²), 16 v.

[140] Smyth (1546²), 16 v-17 v, cf. Pseudo-Dionysius, *Hierarchia*; Ignatius, *Ad Ephesiis* 20.2, Clement, *Liturgia*.

[141] Smyth (1546²), 17 v; cf. Irenaeus, *Adversus haereses*, 4.18.4, in: J. P. Migne, *Patrologia cursus completus, series Graeca*, Paris, 1857-1866, (cited as: PG) 7/1.1027f.

> there is made the blessed Sacrament of the bodye and bloude of our Sauioure Chryste of whyche is increased, and doth consyst the substaunce of our flesshe, for membres we be ... of his bodye, and of his flesshe and bones.[142]

In an ensuing elucidation, Smyth stressed the distinction between the ordinary and the divine. He used the difference between the transcendent and the natural to defend the doctrine of real presence of the body and blood of Christ in the eucharist against evangelical claims of symbolism.

In order to repudiate the evangelical reduction of the real presence to a mere symbol, in the *Assertion and Defence*, Smyth sought to demonstrate that the sacrament of the altar consisted of something greater than ordinary bread and wine. This argument required the existence of a reference point beyond the elements themselves. When addressing himself to a number of 'objections' to the real presence from the pen of John Frith, he settled for an interpretation of the sacrament taken from the second preface of Fisher's *De Veritate*, where the Thomist threefold signification of the sacrament represented (1) Christ's real presence; (2) His sacrifice on the cross; (3) a symbol of Christian unity.[143] Like his earlier contemporary, he made use of this distinction to reject the evangelical assertion that an object cannot at once be both signifier and signified. In defence, Smyth demonstrated plausibly that the separation of the elements reflected both the historic sacrifice of Christ on the cross and the spiritual union of the faithful with Christ. Bread and wine did indeed point beyond themselves and therefore required a Realist interpretation of the eucharistic presence.[144] He concluded his refutation of Frith's symbolism:

> There muste be put an other maner difference betwene a figure and a badge, and a sacramente, than this wise wodecocke [Frith] full vnlearned and maliciousely hath here brought in vnto vs.[145]

---

[142] Smyth (1546²), 17 v; cf. Irenaeus, ibid.

[143] Cf. Fisher (1527), xxix r-xxxii v; Smyth (1546²), 190 r-v; for the evolution of Fisher's argument from the threefold signification of Aquinas, see Rex (1991), 138f.

[144] For instance Smyth (1546²), 121 r; 74 r, 20 r; cf. Fisher (1527), xxxii r.

[145] Smyth (1546²), 111 v; he had emphasised earlier (103 v) that Frith had made use of second-hand arguments from Johannes Oecolampadius to make his case, *De Genuina Verborum Domini, Hoc Est Corpus Meum, Expositione Liber*, Hagenau, 1525?, E 4 v.

The difference of which he speaks was the second aspect to the sacrament of the altar, the reality of the body and blood of Christ it contained.

This adoption of the threefold signification of the eucharist also had a distinctive bearing on Smyth's understanding of biblical and patristic evidence. While he admitted that the people of the First Covenant had been justified in interpreting their relationship to God in symbolic terms prior to the incarnation, the advent of Christ made obsolete symbolic or figurative readings of Scripture.[146] His frequent reiteration of the sentiment that while 'the Jewes ... were fedde with figures and shadowes & had not the thinge in dede ... [Christians] are fedde with the body of Christe', emphasises his unwavering persuasion that no-one should claim the right to interpret the offering of Christ in the sacrifice of the mass in the same terms as the sacrifice of the paschal lamb in, say, Ex 12.21-27.[147]

Even if the language of real presence was symbolic, 'it is no good argumente ... to saye that because a thinge is a sygne, ther is nothyng els but a sygne'.[148] Like Fisher, he thought that while the blessed sacrament was a sign, it also contained the essence it represented.[149] Smyth's distinctively Realist way of reading the Fathers is illustrated well in his 'solution' to one of the evangelical objections from Tertullian: Christ 'made [the bread] His body by saying *this is my body*, that is, *a figure of my body*'.[150] This was a favourite evangelical text to exclude any realist interpretation of the eucharistic bread as the body of Christ. Smyth countered the argument by explaining that the sign, that is the bread, also contained the signified and pointed to the body of Christ. The eucharist pointed beyond itself. It represented both the crucified Christ and invisibly contained His true body.[151]

---

[146] For instance Smyth (1546²), 19 r: '[Christ,] being the fulnes or plenitude, did make ful the veritie of the thinge prefigurated'.

[147] Smyth (1546²), 54 v.

[148] Smyth (1546²), 108 r.

[149] Smyth (1546²), 108 r, cf. the discussion in Fisher (1527), xlvi v-xlviii v.

[150] Smyth (1546²), 205 r; cf. Tertullian, *Adversus Marcionem IV* [=PL 2.492]: 'Corpus illum suum fecit: hoc est corpus meum, dicendo, id est, figura corporis mei'.

[151] Smyth (1546²), 206 v; cf. Fisher (1527), xlviii v.

A second concern for Smyth was to demonstrate that by sharing in the blessed sacrament the believer participated directly in the life of God. By eating the eucharistic bread and wine, man not only consumed the body of Christ, but was incorporated into the hypostatic union.[152] Smyth followed Augustine (as read by Fisher) in affirming that man did not consume the substance of the body and blood of Christ, but that he was incorporated into the substance of Christ.[153] He distinguished rigorously between the resurrection body and the spiritual body of Christ, and affirmed that the believer only ever partook of the spiritual body (for like the communion host 'the spyryte ... neyther hathe flesshe, neither boones').[154] The believer was joined to the incarnate Christ not only by the humanity they both shared, but more so—and more effectively—by partaking of the spiritual body of Christ in the eucharist, a physical bond 'by nature of the flesshe and not by coniunction onlye of the wylles'.[155]

Just like Fisher, Smyth rejected the evangelical conviction that a spiritual communion or indeed the inward 'digestion' of the Word of God was sufficient for salvation.[156] While he affirmed that Christians could be nourished spiritually by the Word of God, he added that by partaking of the body of Christ they shared directly in the divine Word, through the hypostatic union.[157] The angels lived by the 'ioye and delectation which they haue of God and of his glory' and therefore had no need of the sacrament, which

---

[152] For instance Smyth (1546²), 53 v, 70 r.

[153] Smyth (1546²), 82 v; 109 v; see especially T i r (pagination duplicated); cf. Fisher (1527), xxx v.

[154] Smyth (1546²), 64 r: 'Where the body of Christ is contained neyther locally, neyther circumscriptively, nor yet definitiuely, but by turnynge and changynge of the bread into Christes said body'; Smyth (1546²), 17 v, cf. Lk 24.39; for Smyth's strong distinction between the physical and the spiritual body see for instance 20 v: 'The bloude conteyned in the said sacrament is not enforced or compelled by strengthe to break forth of the vaynes'.

[155] Smyth (1546²), 20 r: 'Howe then can that person be thought not to abyde naturally in us, which beinge borne man, dyd take the nature of our flesh, whyche nowe to hym is inseparable, and also hath myngled or adioyned the nature of his fleshe, to the nature of the godheade or eternytye, vnder the sacrament of his fleshe to be communicated vnto us?'

[156] Fisher (1527), lxxx v; cf. Rex (1991), 144.

[157] Smyth (1546²), 225 r.

derived from life in the presence of Christ and the full comprehension of the Word Incarnate.[158] He concluded

> they who receyue Christes fleshe and bloud but only spiritually, are not so vnited and incorporated vnto Christes said very naturall body, but onely to his mystical body, that is his church, and his faithfull congregation.[159]

Smyth's Realist interpretation of the Fathers is mirrored by his emphasis on the consecration. In the *Assertion and Defence* Smyth once more put considerable emphasis on the priestly vocation. Unlike his evangelical opponents who maintained that the main task of a *minister Christi* was the communication of the Gospel, he reiterated that priests were called to offer sacrifice and thus bring about Christ's work of redemption—'the handy worke of the greate God'.[160] Priests offered on earth the sacrifice offered in heaven by Christ and, by making the words of Christ at the moment of institution their own, 'turne the visible creatures into the substance of [Christ's] body and bloud'.[161] Partaking of the blessed sacrament was essential to salvation. Everlasting life began with the participation in the eucharist.[162] Since 'none shall be saued but by the vertue of the sacrifice done vpon the crosse', the ministry of the priests as representatives of the risen high priest Christ as sacrificers was crucial to human salvation.[163] To put it crudely: No priests—no sacrament, no sacrament—no salvation.

---

[158] Smyth (1546²), 126 v.
[159] Smyth (1546²), ibid., cf. T ii v (pagination duplicated).
[160] Smyth (1546²), 21 v f.
[161] Smyth (1546²), ibid.: 'And as in the hygh heauens, the depe sees, and the wyde worlde were made euen at his worde, so ... by like power of his worde, is made his bodye and bloude in this mooste blessed sacrament'; while no-one can perceive this change physically, it is known to the believer by an act of faith, cf. 22 v: 'Before the consecration ... it is breade, but after the wordes of consecration it is the body of Christ'.
[162] Smyth (1546²), 71 r.
[163] Smyth (1546²), 50 r; cf. 204 r.

2.3. 'Priest and Prophet'—Smyth's 'A Defence of the Blessed Masse' and his 'Assertion and Defence of the Sacrament of the Aulter'

The strong belief in the real presence of Christ in the eucharistic elements is a key to Smyth's 1546 publications. His firm conviction that human salvation commenced with the participation of the believer in the blessed sacrament led him to assert that, while the faithful might not comprehend the mystery of the consecration of ordinary bread and wine to form the body and blood of Christ,

> yet muste we not therefore leaue and forsake our fayth ... but forsakynge vtterlye the iudgemente of carnall reason. ... We must (knowynge gods wyll and pleasure) assuredlye and constantly sticke to the catholyque faith of Christes churche, wherein we shall not be deceiued.[164]

The eucharistic presence was closely connected with a number of concerns that determined Smyth's entire thinking.

Three distinctive themes can be identified as dominating Smyth's eucharistic theology. The first, his distinctive understanding of the office and work of a priest, had its origins in the order of sacrificing high priests of the Old Testament. From the powerful image of a heavenly liturgy offered for the shortcomings of mankind as laid out in Hebrews flowed the conviction that the ordinary worshipper is called to participate in the life of the divine sacrifice, through the ministry of Christ's representatives on earth, the priests.[165] Every priest shared in Christ's ministry of redemption in the sacrifice of the mass. Their work was not magic but a sign of God's ministry on earth. At mass, the divine creator interacted daily with His human creatures to effect redemption through the ministry of his chosen representatives—'the maruayle is hereby taken away and the thynge credible and true'.[166]

The real presence served as a guarantee that human salvation could be achieved in the present age. At the intersection of the two previous concerns lay the strong conviction that a mere

---

[164] Smyth (1546²), 236 v-r.
[165] Smyth (1546²), 215 v.
[166] Smyth (1546²), 237 r.

symbolic representation of the body of Christ in the blessed sacrament was not sufficient for human salvation:

> If in the Sacrament of thaulter, there were nothynge but very bread & wine for a remembraunce, then there were no nede of any masse or sacrifice at all, seynge that breade and wyne may be had in common places whiche for a remembraunce onelye ... myght serue as well for that purpose, as anye thynge else.[167]

Smyth reiterated again and again that the participation of the believer in the divine economy was dependent on the real, physical presence of Christ in the elements of bread and wine, a concept he gleaned from Augustine and Cyprian.[168] The spiritual, almost intellectual, commemoration of Christ's death propagated by contemporary evangelicals stripped the sacrament of its transcendent nature and made it entirely ineffective.[169]

The urgency of the danger to human salvation through tampering with the eucharist convinced Smyth to respond both by his *Assertion and Defence* and, from exile in Paris, his *Confutation* of the works of Thomas Cranmer. In 1546 and 1551 Smyth sought to warn the English nation that their salvation was endangered unless they turned against evangelical doctrine and returned to the belief of the church. This is the central message of his English publications on the eucharist. It is only fitting that he should conclude his *Assertion and Defence* with the urgent appeal that his readers needed to conform to the catholic faith in order to have 'a warraunte and a buckler for your defence and for the atteinynge of your saluatyon'.[170]

3. 1550 AND 1562—THE 'MANDUCATIO IMPIORUM' AND THE SACRIFICE FOR THE DEAD

In early 1551, Smyth mounted a vehement attack on Thomas Cranmer's *Defence of the true and catholike doctrine of the sacrament of*

---

[167] Smyth (1546²), 59 r.
[168] Smyth (1546²), 139 r-140 r.
[169] Smyth (1546²), 57 r.
[170] Smyth (1546²), 247 r.

the body and bloud of Christ, published the year before in London.[171] His *Confutation of a certen booke, called a defence of the true, and Catholike doctrine of the Sacrament, &c.*, sette fourth in the name of Thomas Archebysshoppe of Canterburye left the press of the Parisian printer Regnault Chaudière in early January 1551. Any follower of Smyth's writings would have noted immediately the close parallels between his two 1546 publications and this work. The *Confutation* made use of the same arguments he had issued as a prophetic warning to his evangelical colleagues in convocation five years previously. This time, however, they were applied to specific 'innovations' regarding the doctrine of the eucharist already enforced by the Edwardian reformers.[172]

For the English council officials who intercepted the 'barrel of Dr Smith's most false and detestable books from Paris' in March 1551, the work in question was merely another diatribe against the establishment from the pen of a controversial author whose works had been prohibited by the archbishop.[173] For the archbishop and the ecclesiastical establishment the work appeared at an inconvenient time, in the middle of the debate about a successor volume to the 1549 *Book of Common Prayer*.[174] The English reformers would have found the book a polemical version of Smyth's earlier

---

[171] Th. Cranmer, *A Defence of the true and catholike doctrine of the sacrament of the body and bloud of Christ*, London, 1550.

[172] Smyth (1551), A iii v.

[173] See Royal Commission on Historical Manuscripts, *Calendar of the Manuscripts of the Most Honourable the Marquis of Salisbury at Hatfield House*, London, 1883—, 1.83, No. 346; and Peter Martyr Vermigli to Martin Bucer, 10 January 1550, in: G. C. Gorham, ed., *Gleanings of a few scattered Ears, during the Period of the Reformation in England*, London, 1857, 154: 'Although [Smyth's] books are not dispersed in England having been prohibited by the order of the Magistrates, and chiefly, as I think, of the Most Reverend of Canterbury, yet since they have been printed at Louvain, they will be universally circulated'.

[174] Despite this prohibition, both Stephen Gardiner's attack on Cranmer's work, *An Explication and assertion of the Catholic Faith touching the most blessed sacrament of the altar*, Rouen?, 1550, and Smyth's work attracted the attention of the English episcopate. Cranmer chose to reject both works in his *An answere of Thomas, Archebyshop of Canterburye vnto a crafty and sophisticall cauillation devised by S. Gardiner, late Byshop of Winchester, agaynst the trewe and godly doctrine of the moste holye Sacrament ... wherin is also ... answered ... the booke of R. Smyth*, London, 1551; cf. D. MacCulloch, *Cranmer: A Life*, New Haven CT and London, 1996, 485-490; for a concise introduction to the 1551 debate about the Second Prayer Book, see for instance C. Haigh, *English Reformations—Religion, Politics and Society under the Tudors*, Oxford, 1993, 179-181.

views. While the book ostensibly sought to attack Cranmer's work, its real addressee was the life-long object of Smyth's antagonism, Peter Martyr Vermigli, whom he called Cranmer's 'great god'.[175] He had long suspected that 'the mutable teacher' Vermigli had influenced the archbishop's views for 'advantage and profite'.[176] During his exile Smyth had sought every opportunity to denounce the Italian's work. It is possible that he believed that Vermigli had managed to have his own opinions published 'in the name of Thomas Archebysshoppe of Canterburye'. Cranmer rose to Smyth's bait immediately and rushed to Vermigli's defence. Smyth could exult at the discomfort his Parisian prodding had caused Canterbury:

> And if D. Smith understood him [Vermigli] otherwise in ... the beginning, it was for lack of knowledge, for that then D. Smith understood not the matter, nor yet doth not, as it appeareth by this foolish and unlearned book, which he had now set out.[177]

3.1. The 'Manducatio Impiorum'

When Smyth left England, parliament had just introduced a number of far-reaching changes to the eucharistic doctrine of the church in England which practically erased the doctrine of transubstantiation. The debates about the real presence that preceded the introduction of the Act of Uniformity in January 1549 had been dominated by a memorandum in favour of evangelical eucharistic doctrine, issued by protector Somerset but essentially drawn up by Peter Martyr.[178] In his memorandum, Vermigli not

---

[175] Smyth (1551), K iiij r.
[176] Smyth (1551), B i r. In A viij v-B i r he alleged that Vermigli used to hold Lutheran views on first coming to Oxford, 'but when he came ones to the court, and sawe that that doctrine mystyfied them, that myght do hym hurt yn his lyuinge, he anon after turned his tipped, and sange an other songe', a view shared by Nicholas Parsons, *A treatise of three conuersions of England from Paganisme to Christian Religion*, St Omer, 1603-1605, 350f.
[177] J. E. Cox, ed., *Miscellaneous writings and letters of Thomas Cranmer*, Parker Society, Cambridge, 1846, 1.374.
[178] British Library, Royal MS 17C v, Of the Sacrament of Thanksgiving: A Short Treatise of Peter Martyr's making; see M. Dewar, *Sir Thomas Smith—A Tudor Intellectual in Office*, London, 1964, 39 n, suggests that the manuscript was not prepared for a formal Lords' debate but proposes that it may have been used at preliminary discussions with bishops; see MacCulloch (1996), 403.

only destroyed any remaining notion of the real presence but also introduced a strictly reformed understanding of the presence of Christ in the eucharist—that of the *manducatio impiorum*.[179] The idea of the *manducatio impiorum* was based on the Pauline conviction that 'whoever eats the bread or drinks the cup of the Lord in an unworthy manner will be answerable for the body and blood of the Lord'.[180] None who stood without salvific faith received the body of Christ at communion. The eucharist was reduced to an individual, spiritual signification rather a communal, corporeal participation. Christ was spiritually present in the eucharist only by the faith of the believers. In the treatise drawn up for parliament Peter Martyr explained that

> the presence of Christ ... doth belong more rightly and properly to the receivers than to the tokens ... [that is] of those receivers that do rightly and faithfully come to the communion.[181]

While this doctrine had not yet made its way into the *Book of Common Prayer* of 1549, it was definitely reflected in the pages of Cranmer's *Defence* a year later.[182]

Smyth devoted the fourth book of his *Confutation* to the refutation of the reformed understanding that the physical presence of Christ in the eucharist was dependent on the faith of its recipients.[183] MacCulloch's point that 'anyone who believed that only the faithful consume the body of Christ had clearly left behind any notion of real or corporeal presence' is pertinent to Cranmer's printed statement that 'synners eate not christes very body with

---

[179] For Martyr's doctrine of the *manducatio impiorum*, see A. Schindler, ed. et al., *Die Zürcher Reformation: Ausstrahlungen und Rückwirkungen*, Bern, 2000, 317-326: J. A. Löwe, 'The bodie and bloud of Christ is not carnallie and corporallie in the bread and wine: The Oxford Disputation revisited—Zwinglian traits in the Eucharistic Theology of Pietro Martire Vermigli'.
[180] 1 Cor 11.27-30.
[181] F. A. Gasquet and E. Bishop, *Edward VI and the Book of Common Prayer*, London, 1928, 159: The House of Lords adopted the doctrine of the *manducatio impiorum* and decided that 'Christ is in the Holy Supper to them that do come to his table, and he doth verilie feed the faithful with his body and blood. There is no transubstantiation'.
[182] Cranmer (1550), 90.
[183] Smyth (1551), R i v-T ii r.

214 CHAPTER FIVE

their mouthes, nor drinke his bloud in the sacrament, but only bread and wyne'.[184]

In rejecting the archbishop's convictions, Smyth argued from Scripture, interspersing his explanation with some patristic evidence. His argument essentially hinged on an alternative reading of 1 Cor 11.27, in which he pointed out that while Paul had indeed stated that all those who consumed the sacrament 'in an unworthy manner will be answerable for the body and blood of the Lord', he had not claimed that they would receive anything other than the body of Christ. Rather, Paul implied that only those who received the body of Christ faithfully would receive the body of Christ to their salvation.[185]

> The vngodly men & women do eate and drinke christes flesh & bloud in receauing of the holi sacrament, althoughe they haue not euerlasting lyf as the godly only haue, but euerlastinge damnation.[186]

They 'eat and drink judgement against themselves' (1 Cor 11.29). Smyth argued that the Apostle expressly spoke of the unrighteous becoming guilty of the body of the Lord, and not of mere material bread.[187] Paul had left no doubt that the unrighteous 'eateth & drinketh not material bread, & wyne of the grape, but christes very body & bloud which he called bread & wyne'.[188]

When confronted with the example of Judas Iscariot (who, in medieval depictions, was frequently seated apart from the remaining eleven, suggesting that he did not share in their table-fellowship), Smyth upheld his strict views that everybody received the physical body of Christ:

> The other apostles did eate christes body both bodyly with their mouthes, and also spiritually with a perfect fayth and a pure conscience, but Iudas did eate it only bodyly with his mouth. ...

---

[184] MacCulloch (1996), 405; Cranmer (1550), ibid., based on Jn 6.51: 'I am the living bread that came down from heaven. Whoever eats of this bread will live forever; and the bread that I will give for the life of the world is my flesh'; cf. op. cit. 98, 3.
[185] Smyth (1551), R iij v.
[186] Smyth (1551), R v r.
[187] Smyth (1551), S iv r.
[188] Smyth (1551), S iij r.

Only good men do eate christes flesh vnto their profite and saluation.[189]

Smyth's perception of the eucharist as a communion at which sinners and righteous alike partook of the 'foode of mans soul' is maintained in Roman Catholic eucharistic doctrine.[190] It was the responsibility of the individual to nurture a 'lyvuely wourkinge faith' that ensured him of the spiritual benefits associated with the partaking of the body of Christ.[191]

The eucharist could not be reduced to a communion in which some partook of the body of Christ and others received ordinary bread, Smyth emphasised. If Christ was truly present in the eucharistic gifts as He promised, then He would not restrict His physical presence in bread and wine to the act of faith of a particular individual. Believers and unbelievers could not be distinguished by whether they did or did not receive the physical body of Christ in the eucharist as Cranmer suggested, but only by the merits associated with that participation.[192] Whether a communicant received these merits was dependent on his faith, and his good works. Smyth elaborated this view in the concluding section of book four of the *Confutation*, in which he held strongly that the reliance on the working of the Holy Spirit in the individual alone was not sufficient to attain the necessary precondition for this disposition of faith.[193] Only the collaboration of divine grace with human 'faith, hope, fear, repentance, prayer, almes, dedes, fastinge, charitie and receuinge of the holy sacramentes' made a believer worthy of the merits of Christ.[194] The concept that only the faithful receive the body of Christ was therefore untenable, and 'my lords exposition of saint paules wordes is vayne, & false'.[195]

---

[189] Smyth (1551), R viij r.
[190] Cf. for instance *Catechism of the Catholic Church*, London, 1994, 313, §1385-1387.
[191] Smyth (1551), S iv r: 'The thynge of the sacrament is christes body and bloud therin conteyned and encrease of goddes grace with other benefites of god, which only the good men receaue'.
[192] Smyth (1551), R iv v-R v r.
[193] Smyth (1551), S i v-S ii r.
[194] Smyth (1551), V i r-v, cf. above, chapter III, 2.1.3., 131f.; and for instance *Corpus Iuris Canonici auctoritate Ioannis Pauli PP. II promulgatus*, Città del Vaticano, 1983, § 919.
[195] Smyth (1551), S iv r.

216   CHAPTER FIVE

3.2. THE SACRIFICE FOR THE DEAD

The Tudor reformation also challenged the idea of a eucharistic sacrifice that encompassed both the living and departed. In 1546, 1550 and 1562 Smyth devoted his attention to these issues. In the final book of the *Confutation*, and in the concluding section of the *Defence of the blessed Masse* he confirmed that the sacrifice of the mass was 'auayleable and profitable to them which are departed from this lyfe'.[196] In the last years of his life, the subject of purgatory and the benefit of prayers for the departed offered at mass once more preoccupied Smyth. While his 1562 *De Missae Sacrificio* was primarily based on arguments used in his 1546 publication, his attack on the evangelical rejection of purgatory and the efficacy of prayers at mass for the departed should not be excluded from a survey of Smyth's eucharistic doctrine. It represented a last attempt to remind the English of the dangers of Elizabethan doctrine.

In his 1562 compendium, Smyth reiterated the 'statements of the ancient doctors of the catholic church regarding the sacrifice of the mass, and purgatory' in order to contrast them with the recently adopted Anglican eucharistic doctrine as set out in Jewel's *Apologia Ecclesiae Anglicanae*.[197] He had replied to the eucharistic passages of Jewel's book almost immediately. His *De Missae Sacrificio* formed the vanguard of a conservative reaction against the *Apologia*.[198]

Smyth only sought to document the dissent of his opposition and rarely cited their opinions. He derived his own confident approach to the doctrine from the writings of 'most ancient ecclesiastical writers' and adopted three axioms (questioned by

---

[196] Smyth (1546¹), cxxv v; cf. Smyth (1551), X ii r ff.

[197] Smyth (1562¹), 19 r: 'The opinions of the ancient doctors of the catholic church concerning the sacrifice of the most holy mass and purgatory' (Veterum ecclesiae catholicae doctorum sententiae de sacrosanctae missae sacrificio, ac purgatorio); the author commends his work for the perusal of the 'candidate of theology' (Theologiae candidatus). For the *Apology* see J. Jewel, *Apologia Ecclesiae Anglicanae*, Oxford, 1639; cf. J. E. Booty, *John Jewel as apologist of the Church of England*, London, 1963.

[198] Later exiles at Leuven, such as Thomas Harding, Thomas Dorman, John Rastell, Nicholas Sander and Thomas Stapleton, continued the attack on Jewel a few years later.

current evangelical doctrine) as the basis for his own views:[199] (1) The existence of purgatory (a concept first defined at the council of Florence mainly on the basis of pericopae from 1 Cor 3.15 and 1 Pet 1.5 as well as the affirmation, by Gregory, that 'for lesser faults, we must believe that, before the final judgement, there is a purifying fire');[200] (2) the existence of a sacrifice of the mass, which not only recalled Christ's death on the cross for the sins of the world, but also imparted the merits of His death to believers; (3) the application of those benefits to the faithful departed in purgatory.[201]

In an opinion confirmed by the council of Trent in September 1562, Smyth had argued in August that the concept of purgatory was based on apostolic tradition and had been upheld by many 'men erudite in matters theological'.[202] Its basis was the eschatological concept of heaven, hell and purification by fire outlined by Augustine.[203] Heaven (the Kingdom of God) was a place where the church triumphant worshipped God face to face. Its direct opposite, hell, was a place where 'every apostate, or stranger to the faith of Christ, will endure eternal torments'.[204] The third place, a place of purification, was the only hope remaining for the faithful who did not join the communion of saints straightaway. To take away this halfway house was to expose those faithful to hell and deprive them of eternal salvation, Smyth maintained.[205]

---

[199] Smyth (1562¹), 19 r: 'vetustissimi scriptores'.

[200] Gregory, *Dialogus*, 4, 39 [=PL 77.396].

[201] Cf. the contemporary ruling of the council of Trent, DS 1743: 'Which is why it is offered not only for the sins, punishment and other needs of the faithful living, but also for the dead in Christ who are not yet fully through purgatory' (Quare non solum pro fidelium vivorum peccatis, poenis, satisfactionibus et aliis necessaribus, sed et pro defunctis in Christo, nondum ad plenum purgatis ... offertur).

[202] Smyth (1562¹), 19 v: 'in re theologia eruditis viris'.

[203] Smyth (1546¹), cxxvi r reflected the first generation debate: 'The grekes ... dyd deny vtterly that there was any meane place between heauen and hell, wherein mannes soule shulde be deteined for a tyme, tyll it myght please god to deliver him from thence, to his glorious sighte. The whiche errour ... Johan Wycleffe, Martin Luther & Johan Frith dyd mayntayne and defende'.

[204] Smyth (1562¹), 19 v: 'Omnis apostata, vel à Christi fide alienus, aeterna supplicia experientur'.

[205] Smyth (1562¹), 20 r: for Smyth the hope of all departed was 'a third place which will exist after the day of the final judgement when all will either stand at the right hand of Christ to go with Him into eternal life and seek the heavenly kingdom, or on His left, to be forced down from there with the devil to the hell of

In his general and cursory rejection of protestant eschatological doctrine, Smyth in turn attacked the works of Johannes Brenz, Wolfgang Musculus, Thomas Cranmer and Philipp Melanchthon without really entering into debate with any of the authors.[206] A poignant marginal note in which he characterised Thomas Cranmer as a 'heretic who was burnt in England', emphasises that by the time Smyth was composing his attack on their doctrine, most of his opposition had died.[207] In his wholesale rejection of the protestant opposition Smyth particularly defended the opinions of Augustine and Ambrose on purgatory, since both had maintained that 'sacrifices benefited the condemned to alleviate the pains of hell'.[208] Just as he had done sixteen years earlier, in his *Defence of the blessed masse and the sacrifice therof*, Smyth countered the argument by referring the reader to Augustine, who offered mass regularly for the intention of his departed mother:[209] 'It cannot be denied that the souls of the departed may be relieved by the prayers of their living relatives, or that they may receive mercy when the sacrifice of the Mediator is offered for them', Smyth affirmed.[210]

4. Seeking to Restore the Eucharistic Life

Smyth was moved to compose his polemical works primarily by the desire to restore the catholic tradition in his homeland. His polemics were as much affected by a deep repugnance of the 'innovations' that had shaken England, as by a genuine concern

---

eternal fire' (Quem tertium locum, qui futurus esse post diem extremi iudicij, quando omnes aut stabunt à Christi dextera, ituri cum eo in vitam aeternam, regnumque petituri coeleste, aut à sinistra, detruendi hinc cum diabolo in gehennam aeterni ignis).

[206] Smyth clearly confused Wittenberg and Württemberg, and erroneously referred to Brenz's *Confessio Wittenbergensis*; cf. J. Brenz, E. Bizer, ed., *Confessio Virtembergica: Das Württembergische Bekenntnis von 1551*, Stuttgart, 1952; Ph. Melanchthon, J. A. O. Preus, ed., *Loci Communes 1543*, St Louis MO, 1992.

[207] Smyth (1562¹), 21 v: 'Thomas Cranmerus hereticus in Anglia combustus'.

[208] Smyth (1562¹), 22 r: 'Sacrificia prodesse damnatis, ad persoluendas gehennae poenas'.

[209] Smyth (1562¹), 21 v, cf. Smyth (1546¹), cxxviii r and Augustine, *Confessiones* 9.12-13 [= PL 32.776-780].

[210] Smyth (1562¹), 21 v: 'Neque negandum est defunctorum animas pietate suorum viuentium releuari, quum pro illis sacrificium mediatoris offertur, vel eleemosynae fiunt'.

for the people of England. In the four books examined, those two concerns went hand in hand: Smyth was convinced that by abandoning tradition the souls of the faithful both living and departed were gravely endangered. Those who held false doctrines and encouraged others to adopt them had not only excommunicated themselves automatically from the church universal but put innocent souls at risk.[211] By breaking the continuum of eucharistic offerings dating back beyond the days of the Apostles to the time of propitiatory offerings to God, English evangelicals had not only abandoned the belief of the one church but were revealed clearly as a 'sectarian brood'.[212]

However, by 1562, Smyth's crusade against evangelical eucharistic doctrine in England had become futile. His last work on the eucharist did not even attract sufficient attention to warrant a reply from Jewel. While Smyth's last works certainly served as an example to his fellow-exiles who continued the polemic tradition in their own attacks on protestant doctrine, in the long run the reformation in England could no longer be fought by writings issued from abroad. Different ways of aiding the embattled English catholic community had to be explored.

It is at this point that a central aspect of Smyth's eucharistic theology suddenly emerged as paramount, rising beyond the pages of his polemical publications. Smyth had always emphasised the role of the ministerial priesthood in the life of the church as a eucharistic community. His strong convictions that individual salvation and union with Christ were mediated locally by Christ's ministers, the priests, ran throughout his works on the eucharist. Rather than declare Smyth's work not sufficiently persuasive to halt the ongoing religious changes in his homeland, it should be regarded as a summons and challenge to his contemporaries in exile. The need to train men as catholic underground clergy in the

---

[211] Smyth (1562¹), 24 r: 'Lutherans, Zwinglians, and Calvinists now teach as a true dogma what the whole church—Greek and Latin—1,200 years previously condemned as heresy, and they falsely claim for themselves the church of Christ, when they are outside it; rather than at the heart of it' (Lutheranos, Swinglianos, & Caluinianos docere iam pro vero dogmate, quod ante 1200 annos tota Christi ecclesia, Graeca, & Latina, pro haeresi condemnauit, ac illos falso vendicare sibi ecclesiam Christi, vt extra quam penitus sint).

[212] Smyth (1562¹), 23 v: 'The gathering of sects is not the church' (Sectarum coetus non sunt ecclesia).

reformed kingdom became evident during the last years of Smyth's life.[213] His fervour in fostering the vocations of his students at Douai to a sacrificing priesthood has been documented above.[214] His defence of that priesthood, faithfully bound to the Roman church by vows of celibacy and obedience, against the Edwardian and Elizabethan English church was another strand of his polemic work.[215] Perhaps his role in preparing the way for the establishment of a place of learning to train exiled catholics for the English mission ultimately was a more lasting memorial to his eucharistic theology than his writings ever could have been.

---

[213] See above, chapter I, 71-74; see also P. Guilday, *The English Catholic Refugees on the Continent, 1558-1795*, London, 1914, 11-13; C. Haigh, *The English Reformation Revisited*, Cambridge, 1987: 'The Continuation of Catholicism in the English Reformation', 176-208.
[214] See above, chapter II.
[215] See above, chapter IV.

CONCLUSION

'A BOUCLIER OF THE CATHOLIKE FAYTH'

Richard Smyth was primarily a polemicist rather than a theologian. Motivated by his traditional doctrine and the conviction that he must strive to live up to the potential that God had granted him, he felt compelled to make use of his theological acumen to uphold and teach the catholic faith.[1] While he probably published his early tracts on the eucharist to consolidate his national reputation as a leading conservative theologian, from the time of his first exile (1549) his works strike a more belligerent and defensive note.[2] They are more the writings of an impassioned defender of the catholic faith than those of a successful academic. Furthermore, during his periods of continental exile, career ambitions took a secondary role, even though Smyth still displayed uncanny talent in enlisting the support of his superiors for his polemical skirmishes.[3]

Smyth's urge to counter the doctrinal innovations of his generation stems from his desire to uphold catholic orthodoxy. First conveyed to him by Worcestershire monks in the 1510s, the catholic faith was the basis of his livelihood as a theologian and, in his view, the key to his own salvation.[4] Smyth's conviction that human justification was dependent on the faith of the Roman church has been documented above.[5] This belief is demonstrated as early as 1550, when in his *De coelibatu liber unus*, he convinced himself of Peter Martyr's spiritual death on the basis of his apostasy.[6] At the end of his life, his fervour had not diminished. In 1562, Smyth summed up his firm trust in the tradition:

---

[1] Cf. R. Smyth, *The second parte of the booke called a Buckler of the Catholyke fayeth ... made by Richard Smith*, London, 1555, ¶ vi v-¶ vi r.
[2] See above, chapter I, 1.2.2.
[3] See above, chapter I, 64-65, and chapter III, 119.
[4] See above, chapter I, 17-18.
[5] See above, chapter III, 108-109.
[6] R. Smyth, *Celeberrimi sacrae theologiae professoris D. Richardi Smythaei, in Achademia Oxoniensi sacris Literas profitentis de Coelibatu Sacerdotum Liber vnus*, Leuven, 1550¹, F 4 r.

>The preaching of the church of the same opinion is ensured by the order of succession handed down by the Apostles. It remains in the churches right up to the present. This truth only is to be given credence, it differs in no way from the tradition of the church.[7]

1. SMYTH AS A POLEMICIST

In his recent analysis of evangelical reformation polemics, Peter Matheson suggested that the sixteenth-century passion for defending a personal credo almost invariably resulted in polemic battles of an eschatological urgency:

>Opponents were viewed within the apocalyptic categories by which the *causa reformationis* itself was interpreted. The struggles on earth are but a dim reflection of the battles being waged on a heavenly sphere.[8]

Smyth did not become a polemicist through exile. His fervour for upholding his beliefs by his writings was only accentuated by the experience of exile. The writings published in England in 1546 already display a distinctively polemical style. They are clearly rooted in the meta-language of the late scholastic debate. Smyth holds, as it were, a conversation in literary form. He addresses the reader, calls upon the Fathers to come to his defence, anticipates the objections of his opponents and submerges them under barrages of questions. So for instance he exhorted the 'good christen reader' to 'beware of his [Luther's] pestilous, and contagious doctrine'; asked his readership whether they would 'nat rather beleue thys holye father and aunciente clerke then Martyn Luther'; and maintained that if John Frith's beliefs 'here made were true (as it is not) then myghte I lykewyse allege for truthe that which is false in dede'.[9]

---

[7] R. Smyth, *De Missae Sacrificio ... enarratio, ac brevis repulsio ... argumentum quae P. Maelanchthon, J. Calvinus, et alii sectarii objecerunt adversus illud, et purgatorium. ... Acc. Epistola ... docens quae ecclesia sit nobis tuto sequenda*, Leuven, 1562, 4 r: 'Hae eiusdem sententiae verò ecclesiastica praedicatio, per successionis ordinem ab apostolis tradita, & vsque ad praesens in ecclesijs permanens. Illa sola credenda est veritas, quae in nullo ab ecclesiastica traditione discordat'.

[8] P. Matheson, *The Rhetoric of the Reformation*, Edinburgh, 1998, 187.

[9] R. Smyth, *A defence of the blessed Masse and the sacrifice thereof*, London, 1546[1], xiii v; xxviii r; idem, *Assertion and Defence of the Sacrament of the Aulter*, London, 1546[2], 97 v.

Like earlier English writers, such as Thomas More, he interspersed his theological arguments with frequent *ad hominem* attacks on the opposition and made use of distortion and sarcasm to characterise them, for instance in his sweeping dismissal of Luther as 'antichristes messanger' and 'a blynde doctour' who 'witched you not to obeye the truth'.[10] Among the more conventional but no less polemical characteristics of his rhetoric are regular references to the authority of the church, his persistent repetition of arguments, his attempts to denigrate his opponents, or the *reductio ad absurdum* of their arguments.[11] Another trademark of his first English publications is his application of past theological debates (such as the disputes between Luther and Eck on the eucharistic sacrifice) to his own struggle with contemporary evangelicalism. Smyth often cloaked himself with the controversies of earlier generations to confute his opposition. In the *Assertion and Defence*, his attacks on Luther and Frith often are barely veiled criticisms of modern evangelical practice.[12] Yet, despite this accomplished use of rhetoric, he was not a rhetorician:[13]

> I wolde nat, yf I coulde neuer so well, paynt this my boke with many termes of Rhetoricke or of any other straunge spech, wher by the mater ... might be the more obscure & darke to the reder.[14]

---

[10] Smyth (1546¹), ix v, marginalium; xii r; xii v; Smyth (1562), 6 r: 'Beware, O Sectarian, of holding your triumphal march before the end of the battle' (Hic caue, ô secta, triumphum agas ante victoriam); for More's use of polemic, see for instance, R. Pineas, *Thomas More and Tudor Polemics*, Bloomington IN, 1968, 103-115.

[11] For instance Smyth (1546²), 4 v; 177 v-178 r; 181 v; for More's polemic use of arguments from tradition, see Pineas (1968), 99; for Fisher's, see B. Bradshaw, E. Duffy, edd. et al., *Humanism, Reform and the Reformation: The Career of Bishop John Fisher*, Cambridge, 1989, 109-130: R. A. W. Rex, 'The Polemical Theologian', 124; for a more general introduction, see J. K. Lowers, *Mirrors for Rebels*, Berkeley CA, 1959, 74.

[12] See above, chapter V, 184-185.

[13] For one of the first analyses of English rhetoric, see G. Puttenham, *The arte of English poesie, contriued into three bookes: the first of poets and poesie, the second of proportion, the third of ornament*, London, 1589.

[14] Smyth (1546¹), xxviii r-v.

His aptitude at polemic was recognised by his contemporaries at an early stage.[15] His ability is particularly evident in his two 1547 recantations, probably the two most polemical works he ever wrote.[16] In these two short statements Smyth made expert use of polemic tropes to defend his cause. He employed the argument from tradition ('Shall I now be ashamed to acknowledge my self to haue ben deceyued in my Booke of Traditions? ... Wil ye not beleue S. Austen in other poyntes of our Religion because he erred?'); made use of exaggerations ('every man is a liar [*omnis homo mendax*] ... theldest & best writers in the Christen Church, doo euidently declare, because they all haue erred in their bookes'); and employed repetitions and *variationes* to assure the audience of his good intentions ('I wyt not to nor entent to defende nor auere').[17] A master craftsman of words, Smyth revoked a number of his former beliefs in strings of alliterations as 'a vayne, vnlawfull, vniust and vnportable burden to Christen consciences'.[18] The recantations, two works in which every single word is weighed carefully, display his accomplished use of language particularly well.

His Latin works are no less polemic than his writings in the vernacular. While making use of the same underlying methodology, they adopt a more sophisticated style of *ad hominem* attack. In his *Confvtatio qvorundam articulorum de votis Monasticis Petri Martyris*, Smyth put himself in the role of both prosecutor and judge, not only accusing his opponent of lax morals or heterodox beliefs, but also passing sentence on him.[19] He charged Peter Martyr with

---

[15] For instance by Stephen Gardiner, see J. Foxe, *Actes and Monumentes of these latter and perillous dayes ... newly recognised and inlarged by the Authour*, London, 1583, 753-736 [=J. Foxe, *The Acts and monuments of John Foxe. New and complete edition, with a preliminary dissertation by G. Townsend. Edited by S. R. Cattley*, London, 1837-1841, 6.35].

[16] R. Smyth, *A godly and faythfull Retraction made by R. Smyth. Reuokyng certeyn errors in some of hys books*, London, 1547¹; R. Smyth, *A playne declaration made at Oxford the 24. Daye of July, by Mayster Richarde Smyth upon his Retraction*, London, 1547².

[17] Smyth (1547¹), A ii r; B ii v.

[18] Smyth (1547¹), B ii v.

[19] Compared to other sixteenth-century polemicists Smyth was moderate in his accusations; cf. Matheson (1998), 191: 'Memorable images branded one as thief or murderer, a spreader of plague, poison, filth, sexual deformity, corruption and death'; see also, J. Loach, *Bulletin of the Institute for Historical Research* 48 (1975), 31-44: 'Pamphlets and Politics, 1553-1558', 31: 'The work of Catholic apologists such

apostasy, whoring and corrupting the young, and at last numbered him among those condemned to hellfire.[20] Martyr did not only pervert the youth by his heretical views. While Smyth was convinced that 'these are suitable listeners who should not be taught by such a *praelector*, who catches us by admiration and drags us into his web—which is a maze of many heresies', he was certain that the evangelical had also contaminated the English episcopate.[21] When directing an attack against Thomas Cranmer in 1551, he suggested that the archbishop had been misled by Peter Martyr.[22] In this written trial, Smyth sought to provide his readers with extensive evidence for the theological crimes of his evangelical opposition. His readership constituted the jury and were called upon again and again to endorse his judgement: 'Now, discern carefully, reverent reader, whether this area persuades you of what Peter claims he does not acknowledge'.[23]

In his attack on Thomas Cranmer's eucharistic theology, published in Paris 1551, Smyth is less thunderous than in his works against Peter Martyr. Nonetheless, the work is littered with polemical tropes. The argument from tradition features prominently ('hou then could she [the church] erre so shamefullie these M ccccc yeres?'); as do his frequent parallelisms and *variationes* ('false ... & vtterly improued'; 'not catholike, nor godly'; 'to heale & cure'); alliterations ('reforme and restore'); and his use of hyper-

---

as Richard Smith ... is markedly pallid and pedantic compared with the writings of men like John Bale and Bartholomew Traheron'.

[20] R. Smyth, *Eivsdem D. Richardi Smythei confvtatio qvorundam articulorum de votis Monasticis Petri Martyris Itali, Oxoniae in Anglia Theologiam profientis. De votis haec incogitanter, indocte, & impie effutiuit, obnixe contendas illa nuncupare Deo nefas esse homini Christiano, saltem vt sint perpetuo necessaria*, Leuven, 1550, K 1 v: 'He wounds himself daily with hidden spears, while he whores every day and gives in to his libido behind the appearance of concern and self-control' (Quotidie occultis sauciari iaculis, dum scortatur quotidie, ac exercet libidinem sub solicitudinis ac continentiae specie); cf. F iv r.

[21] Smyth (1550), K 1 v: 'Hi sunt idonei ausculatores, quam a tali erudiantur praelectore, nos in admirationem rapit in sua trahit nassam, hoc est, labyrinthum multarum haeresum'.

[22] R. Smyth, *A Confutation of a certen booke, called á defence of the true, and Catholike doctrine of the sacrament, &c. sette fourth of late in the name of Thomas Archebysshoppe of Canterburye. By Richarde Smyth, Docter of diuinite, and some tyme reader of the same in Oxforde*, Paris, 1551, L v v: 'Were ye not then, my lord, fowly disceaued when ye, folowinge peter Martir, rehersed this place for your purpose?'

[23] Smyth (1550[1]), G 6 r: 'Dispice iam sedulo pie lector, num hic locus persuadeat quod Petrus hic ait se non admittere', cf. G 3 r; L 1 r, etc.

bole ('inuention of Antichrist').[24] Despite the more civil style and his obvious respect for Cranmer's episcopal office, Smyth's polemic remains hard-hitting; for instance when accusing the archbishop of rejecting apostolic tradition wilfully: 'Do ye despise al godly ordre, and the fathers doctrine, and yet saye that your boke is approued of the old doctours?'[25]

On return to England in 1553 the emphasis in Smyth's writings shifted considerably. Rather than condemn and reprimand, he saw his task to call back evangelicals to the catholic faith and to re-educate the wavering.[26] A concern shared by many Marian catholic writers, the mid-1550s saw an exceptional rise in the publication of such catechetical works and primers.[27] Eamon Duffy explains:

> The Marian authorities, in addition to the perennial task of teaching the fundamentals of the faith, were alert to the need for a programme of doctrinal instruction designed to combat heresy, to quicken zeal for the sacraments and to encourage loyalty to the Church and its traditions and rites.[28]

Smyth's Marian writings are a good example of this genre. When composing the *Bouclier of the Catholike Fayth* he employed his polemic aptitude

> to teach the vnlearned, to stay and establish the waueryng, to assure and certify the doubtfull of the trouth, to bryng them agayne vnto the trouth of the catholyke churche.[29]

In this apology for the catholic faith, Smyth once more draws on a well-stocked polemical arsenal: arguments from tradition, the repetition of evidence, rhetorical questions and the resolute condemnation of his opposition. He claims that 'the olde beliefe (which hath been euer in this realm sence it was last conuerted to the fayth) is the very true belief, because it hath been at all tymes folowed of good christen people, and not only of vs English men';

---

[24] Smyth (1551), B ii r-v; B vij v; D vi v; D ii r; C vij r; E v v; A i v.
[25] Smyth (1551), D iiij v.
[26] Smyth (1555), ¶ vi r.
[27] So for instance bishop Bonner's *An honestly godlye instruction, and information for bringinge up of children*, London, 1555, or *The Primer in Englishe with many godly and devoute prayers ... Wherunto is added a plaine and godly treatise concerninge the Masse ... for the instruccyon of the unlearned and symple people*, London, 1555.
[28] E. Duffy, *The Stripping of the Altars: Traditional Religion in England 1400-1580*, New Haven CT, 1992, 543.
[29] Smyth (1555), ¶ vii r.

confutes a number of 'abominable errour[s] of Peter Martyrs setting furth'; and finally charges his readers to determine the fate of his erstwhile opponents:

> Were it lawefull so to abuse theyr owne herytage agaynste the order of charytye? Dooe they thynke neuer to make an acconmpte to GOD, for thys theyr dooynge?[30]

To the end of his life, Smyth's polemical fervour remained undiminished. While he no longer shouldered evangelical criticism effortlessly, he confided to archbishop Granvelle that he took consolation from the Sermon on the Mount: 'But your grace, noblest cardinal, I know you are hardly forgetful of the saying ... *Blessed are you, when men revile you*'.[31] Yet he continued to wage war on the English evangelical establishment. By 1562, Smyth's opponents had changed. Martyr's disciple and close friend John Jewel had replaced the aged Italian.[32] So Smyth directed his polemics against the bishop of Salisbury instead:

> Do you not see, Jewel, that here we must return to the origin of truth, which is the principal question. We must keep the doctrine of Christ, the Lord of Heaven, so that heresies and schisms will be avoided. Why have you closed your eyes to these matters?[33]

In 1562, his personal credo was still sharp, as in his first published works sixteen years earlier. Smyth was more convinced than ever that no-one would attain salvation *extra ecclesiam* and published his cutting missives to recall English schismatics to the catholic faith. He presented them at length with the consequences of their schism:

---

[30] Smyth (1555), ¶ iv v; C iv r.

[31] Smyth (1562), 4 r: 'At celsitudinem tuam eximiam, cardinalis amplissime, haud immemorem esse sat scio ... Beati estis, cum male dixerint homines'; cf. Mt 5.11.

[32] Martyr had left England for Strassburg in 1553, and ultimately settled in Zürich in 1556. Apart from the publication of his *Defensio* (1559), the main part of his remaining theological debates were restricted to the Württemberg reformer Johannes Brenz, cf. P. M. Vermigli, J. P. Donnelly SJ, tr. and ed., *Dialogue on the Two Natures in Christ*, Kirksville MO, 1995, xv-xx.

[33] Smyth (1562), 4 v: 'Videsne hic Iuelle, ad quam veritatis originem nobis sit redeundum, quod caput quaerendum, & quae magistri caelestis est, Christi, doctrina sit nobis seruanda, vt haereses vitentur, & schismata? Cur ad ista clausisti oculos?'

The Pope is the successor of Saint Peter in Rome, and he (at the instigation of Christ Himself) has joined the ranks of the throne of Peter. He knows that on this Rock the church of Christ was founded. Only the very foolish approve anyone outside this church ... ultimately, the man who was not in this Ark, that is the Roman Church, will despair of its foundations, at the time of the last judgement.[34]

Until his death in 1563 Smyth remained a polemicist. Neither his principal concerns, nor his methodology changed much from his first defence of the eucharist in 1546 to his rejection of Melanchthon's theology of justification in 1563.[35] His works are rooted firmly in the meta-language of orthodoxy, linking the writer with his predecessors in the battle against evangelicalism. While he was not innovative as a theologian, his lasting accomplishment as a polemical writer is undeniable.

2. SMYTH'S POLEMICAL ACHIEVEMENT

Smyth's achievement as a writer is mirrored by the literary success of his works. His earliest English writings in defence of the eucharist both ran through two editions within the first year of their release.[36] His defence of priestly celibacy and monastic vows against Peter Martyr, published in Leuven 1550, was reprinted in Paris the following year.[37] His *Bouclier*, printed in London 1554, was followed

---

[34] Smyth (1562), 7 r: 'Romani Pontificem esse diui Petri successorem, illum vel Christo ipse authore, se Cathedrae Petri communione, veluti socium adiunxisse, se quoque scisse super eam Petram Christi ecclesiam fuisse extructam, propuanum hominem esse, quisque extra eam ecclesiam commenderet ... denique illum desperaturum esse funditus, tempore iudicij extremi, qui non fuerit in ea arca, hoc est, Ecclesia Romana'.

[35] For Smyth's *Assertion and Defence*, see above chapter IV, for his *Refvtatio*, see above, chapter III.

[36] R. Smyth, *Assertion and Defence of the Sacrament of the Aulter*, London, [1]1546; and idem, *A Defence of the Sacrifice of the Masse*, London, [2]1546; idem, *A defence of the blessed Masse and the sacrifice thereof, prouynge that it is aualable bothe for the quycke and the dead*, London, [1+2]1546.

[37] R. Smyth, *De coelibatu liber unus. De votis monasticis liber alter ... (confutatio quorundam articulorum de votis monasticis P. Martyris)*, Leuven, [1]1550; idem, *Defensio sacri episcoporum et sacerdotum Coelibatus, contra impias et indoctas Petri Martyris Vermelii nugas ... nunc vero Lutetiae Parisiorum Theologiam profitentem*, Paris, [2]1551.

by a companion volume the next year.[38] His last publication, a rejection of Melanchthon's doctrine of justification published in Douai 1563, went through three print-runs within the year.[39] Particularly during the course of his two continental exiles when he was probably unable to fund the cost of publishing his work by private means, printers took on his works trusting that they would be a financial success.[40] They were not disappointed. In 1562, his printed output was greater than that of any other author in Leuven.[41] One of his works, the *Refutatio luculenza crassae et exitiosae haeresis*, was even taken on by two Leuven printers at once; Johannes Bogardus and Valerius Stephanus.[42]

Smyth consistently wrote for entirely different audiences. He moved between languages with ease, yet the underlying methodology remained the same. His works in the vernacular were aimed chiefly at 'those that be of the symple and unlearned sort', as he pointed out in his *Assertion and Defence*.[43] He explained to his readers that the book was 'a warraunte and a buckler for your defence and for the atteinynge of your saluatyon'.[44] The second 1546 publication, the *Defence of the blessed Masse*, was aimed primarily at the church establishment. The author was convinced that it was

> worthy not to be redde onely of all learned men, and especially of bysshoppes, but to be also diligently noted, printed in memory, & folowed of them, that they beynge thereby instructed do not let for

---

[38] R. Smyth, *A Bouclier of the Catholike Fayth of Christes Church, conteynyng diuers matters now of late called into controversy, by the newe gospellers. Made by R. Smith*, London, 1554; idem, *The second parte of the booke called a Buckler of the Catholyke fayeth … made by Richard Smith*, London, 1555; idem, *Confutatio eorum, quae P. Melanchthon objicit contra missae sacrificium propitiationem … Cui acc. & repulsio calumniarum J. Calvini & Musculi, et J. Juelli, contra Missam, eius canonem et purgatorium, denuo excusa*, Leuven, [1+2]1562.

[39] R. Smyth, *Refutatio locorum communiorum theologicorum Philippi Melanchthonis Germani, M. Lutheri discipuli primarii*, Douai, [1-3]1563.

[40] Loades (1975), 36: 'Pamphlets were financed, quite prosaically, by their sale'.

[41] See above, chapter I, n. 266.

[42] R. Smyth, *Refutatio luculenza crassae et exitiosae haeresis Johannis Calvini et Christop. Carlili Angli, qua astruunt Christum non descendisse ad inferos alios, quam ad infernum infirmum*, Leuven, 1562^2; cf. I. Cockx-Indestege, ed. et al., *Belgica Typographica 1540-1600. Catalogus Librorum impressorum ab Anno MDXLI ad annum MDC in regionibus quae nunc Regni Belgarum partes sunt*, Brussel, 1968, 573.

[43] Smyth (1546^2), 5 v.

[44] Smyth (1546^2), 247 r.

any mans frendshyppe or for any benefites offered to them, to stand stoutely, and manly in defense of the true doctryne of Christe and his churche.[45]

Although he addressed himself to the English episcopate in his *Defence*, Smyth's concern for the 'unlearned' prevailed in his later vernacular writings. The *Bouclier* was a catechetical work composed for the benefit of literate lay-people.[46] It was an unsophisticated work, Smyth told his readers, and contained 'the trouth playnely and rudelye taught for the edifying of the symple and rude people'.[47]

His Latin works, on the other hand, were composed for the benefit of his academic colleagues, as his 1550 *Diatriba* demonstrates: 'I, this little book, note your name here, which is equal to me in its love and regard for you, if nothing else, consult it as an indication and proof of what is good and just'.[48] They were polemical refutations of evangelical doctrines for the use of theological students ('A compendium ... explaining its content in few words, by which the theological student may see more clearly'); and served as tokens of the author's gratitude towards his patrons ('greatest benefactor and patron').[49] They were written to display the author's erudition and orthodoxy, in the hope of attracting financial support and academic preferment. So, in 1550 Smyth took pains to reflect on his past achievements:

> I first applied my mind to writing and, among other works which have still not been circulated, I wrote about the eucharist, about the sacrifice of the mass and about the traditions of the church; three

---

[45] Smyth (1546¹), vii r-vii v.

[46] For the religious instruction of literate lay-people in the reformation, see especially L. Grenzmann and K. Stackmann, edd. et al., *Literatur und Laienbildung im Spätmittelalter und in der Reformationszeit*, Germanistische Symposien V, Stuttgart, 1984.

[47] Smyth (1555), ¶ vii v.

[48] R. Smyth, *Diatriba de hominis ivstificatione aedita Oxoniae in Anglia, anno à natiuitate Domini nostri Iesu Christi. 1550. Mense Februario aduersus Petrum Martyrem Vermelium, olim Cartusianum Lucensem in Italia, nunc apostata in Anglia Oxoniae, acerrimum improborum dogmatum assertorem, sed imperitum, & impudentem cum primis*, Leuven, 1550², A iii r: 'Libellus hic tui nomen auspicio, quem veluti mei in te amoris & obseruantiae, si nihil aliud, significationem ac testationem quandem aequi bonique consulito'.

[49] Smyth (1562), 18 r: 'Compendiarium ... summam illius paucis explicans, quo Theologiae candidatus, ... clarè perspiciat'; 2 v: 'maximus ... Maecaenas, & patronus'.

books which strongly criticised the propagators of new and irreligious dogmas and the proponents of heresy.[50]

Written in the *lingua franca* of academics, his Latin works were available to a wide European readership, and were easily distributed in the Habsburg empire.[51]

Smyth continued to publish for an English readership from abroad, as his vernacular confutation of Thomas Cranmer's eucharistic theology demonstrates.[52] The arrest of William Seth, one of bishop Bonner's servants, and the discovery in his luggage of a hundred copies of Smyth's *Confutation of a certen booke* and a hundred copies of his *Defensio sacri episcoporum et sacerdotum Coelibatus* not only sheds some light on the approximate size of a print-run, but also indicates their means of distribution in England.[53] The books were smuggled in barrels and passed on to trusted middlemen. The clerk to the privy council noted:

> Examinate brought a letter and a book to one Baldwin Watton, of London, and another letter and a book to one Walter Hopton, of Oxford ... besides a great number appointed and named by Dr Smith to receive of his books.[54]

Seth's examination confirms the existence of 'a well-organised smuggling business', as Loades rightly points out.[55] During the Edwardian reformation English catholics clearly had access to Smyth's writings. The demand for his orthodox polemics warranted the risk of having his books smuggled into the country in order to distribute them secretly. There is no reason to doubt that

---

[50] Smyth (1550²), A iii v: 'Applicui protinus animam ad scribendum, ac inter alia, quae adhuc non sunt inuulgata, scripsi de eucharistia, de missae sacrificio, ac de ecclesiae traditionibus tres libellos, qui nouorum ac impiorum dogmatum promachis, accorypheis assertoribus vehementer displicuerunt'.

[51] For sixteenth-century distribution of books on the continent, see for instance B. Tiemann, *Buchkultur im fünfzehnten und sechzehnten Jahrhundert*, Hamburg, 1995.

[52] Smyth (1551).

[53] *Acts of the Privy Council, 1500-1552*, 232; cf. Loach (1975), 34; 36: 'Even a small edition was expected to have a considerable impact'.

[54] *Acts of the Privy Council, 1500-1552*, 232: 'One Seth, servant to Bonner, late Bishop of London, taken with bringing a barrel of Dr Smith's most false and detestable books from Paris. Examinate received of the said Dr Smith 200 of his books to bring into England, 100 in English and 100 in Latin'.

[55] D. Loades, *Politics, Censorship and the English Reformation*, London, 1991, 102.

similar channels were used during the early Elizabethan reign to distribute Smyth's works.[56]

While Smyth's Latin works probably had only a small English readership, they proved very popular on the continent. Copies of his books were distributed throughout central Europe, read avidly by catholics, and quoted by his academic colleagues.[57] Smyth's principal target, Peter Martyr, recognised this danger at an early stage in their debate: 'Although his books are not dispersed in England ... yet since they have been printed at Louvain, they will be universally circulated'.[58] Similarly, his later works, published in 1562 and 1563, were received as those of an eminent local theologian and were reprinted in Leuven, Douai, and Paris.[59]

These works were not only commercial successes. The reaction displayed by the targets of Smyth's polemics suggests that they were effective exercises in their genre. The irritation Smyth's *Confutation of a certen booke* caused archbishop Thomas Cranmer has been documented above, as has the effect of Smyth's *De votis monasticis liber alter* on Peter Martyr Vermigli.[60] However, the lasting influence of Smyth's polemic is best reflected by the aftermath of the 1549 Oxford disputation on the eucharist.[61] Despite the fact that Smyth had already fled the country and left the actual confrontation in the hands of his friends William Tresham and

---

[56] This view is shared by C. Haigh, in: idem, ed. et al., *The English Reformation Revised*, Cambridge, 1987, 176-208: 'The continuity of catholicism in the English reformation', 204-205.

[57] For instance by Ruard Tapper, *Rvardi Tapperi ab Enchvsia, Ecclesiae Collegiatae S. Petri Lovanienis Decani, et eivsdem florentissimae academiae cancellarii, omnia, qvae heberi potvervnt Opera*, Köln, 1582, 2.78 a.; see above, chapter III, 108, n. 6; for their circulation see J. Pits, *Relationum historicarum de rebus Anglicis tomus primus*, Paris, 1619, 761: 'And I saw many of these in the library of the canons at Kleef, in the southern gateway of the church. Likewise at Dieulouard in Lorraine in the library of the English Benedictines' (Atque haec pleraque vidi Clivis in Bibliotheca Canonicorum in Ecclesiae porticu meridionali. Item Delowariae in Lotharingia in Bibliotheca Benedictorum Anglorum).

[58] P. M. Vermigli, to M. Bucer, 1550, in: G. C. Gorham, ed., *Gleanings of a few scattered Ears, during the period of the Reformation in England*, London, 1857, 155.

[59] Smyth's 1562 *Confutatio eorum, quae P. Melanchthon objicit contra missae sacrificium propitiationem ... Cui acc. & repulsio calumniarum J. Calvini & Musculi, et J. Juelli, contra Missam, eius canonem et purgatorium, denuo excusa* was reprinted in Paris, for second editions in Leuven and Douai, see above, n. 33, 34.

[60] For Cranmer's reaction, see above, chapter V, 210-214; for Vermigli's, see above, chapter I, 45-46.

[61] See above, chapter I, 40-43.

William Chedsey, his earlier accusations against Martyr's evangelical doctrine as well as his first Leuven publication caused sustained damage. Martyr later observed:

> But what the impudencie of some hath spred abroad, as concerning the disputation had by me at Oxford the summer last past, and how they slandered me to all sorts of men, both princes, noblemen, commonaltie, citizens, and countrie men, I will not saie: for they haue doone nothing in secret, but euerie corner, street, house, shop, and tauerne doo still sound of their lieng, triumphs, and victories.[62]

The attacks on Martyr's home in late spring 1549 and the ensuing Oxfordshire uprisings were, to a limited extent, related to Smyth's polemic stirrings.[63] By his Oxford pamphlets and his written works from abroad, Smyth was continually passing judgement on the evangelical's life and morals. His sentence was executed by locals, and is captured well in an anonymous contemporary Oxford doggerel:[64]

> [Richard Cox] wrought by his holpe stynkeinge Martyr
> Peter, that Paule his breath could not abyde
> (for that, like Sathans true knyght of the Gartyr
> His holye doctryne he heere falcyfide)
> that whoe (of Preeists) in maryage was not tyde,
> he was afflicted, tirmoyled and toste,
> to lots of lyinge or some other coste.[65]

---

[62] P. M. Vermigli, *The common places of ... P. Martyr ... with a large addition of manie theologicall ... discources*, translated by A. Marten, London, 1583, 172.

[63] For attacks on Martyr's home, see A. à Wood, P. Bliss, ed., *Athenae Oxonienses: An exact History of all the Writers and Bishops who have had their Education in the University of Oxford*, London, 1813-1820, 327; for the Oxfordshire uprising, see J. Cornwall, *Revolt of the Peasantry 1549*, London, 1977, 128; P. Caraman, *The Western Rising 1549: The Prayer Book Rebellion*, Tiverton, 1994, 80 asserts: 'The Italian Reformer Pietro Martire Vermiglio [sic], ... had been propagating his teachings at Oxford. ... His lectures on the Eucharist, in which he had rejected the doctrine of the real presence and the notion of the sacrifice of the Mass, had caused a stir in the Colleges, which spilled over into the countryside. The whole of Oxfordshire was in turmoil'.

[64] For Smyth's Oxford pamphlets against Martyr, see above, chapter I, 64.

[65] A. à Wood, *The History and Antiquity of the Colleges and halls in the University of Oxford*, Oxford, 1786, 116, for Richard Cox, chancellor of Oxford University and tutor of Edward VI, see D. MacCulloch, *Cranmer: A Life*, New Haven CT and London, 1996, 325-326, 337.

Smyth's ceaseless apologetics for the catholic faith were not always as effectual as in the case of Peter Martyr, where two antagonists were connected by their life-long personal antipathy. His debates with Thomas Cranmer may have had a similar background. MacCulloch suggests that Smyth 'clearly inspired Cranmer with contemptuous anger'.[66] At the outset of the Edwardian reformation, the archbishop still felt obliged to counter Smyth's skirmishes by writings of his own.[67] Numerous reformers, however, ignored Smyth's polemics altogether. Among the English reformers, the 1562 attack on John Jewel remained unanswered; among the continental reformers, the work against John Calvin and Wolfgang Musculus never provoked a response.[68] Like earlier patristic apologists, however, Smyth was not overly concerned whether his work received an answer or not. Martin Luther and John Frith, for instance, both targets of his earliest two works on the eucharist were dead at the time of publication, 1546.[69] Similarly, the target of his 1562 *Refvtatio*, Philipp Melanchthon, was dead by the time the book had reached the Douai press.[70] Like many other catholic polemicists of his age, Smyth was not primarily interested in entering into sustained written academic debates with his opposition.[71] He rather sought to affirm the traditional tenets of his belief by rooting out contemporary doctrinal deviation, regardless of whether his opponents were able or willing to counter his work.[72]

---

[66] MacCulloch (1996), 489.

[67] For Cranmer's response to Smyth's *Confutation*, see Th. Cranmer, *An answere of Thomas, Archebyshop of Canterburye vnto a crafty and sophisticall cauillation devised by S. Gardiner, late Byshop of Winchester, agaynst the trewe and godly doctrine of the moste holye Sacrament ... wherin is also ... answered ... the booke of R. Smyth*, London, 1551.

[68] It highly unlikely that Calvin and Musculus ever received Smyth's *Confutatio eorum, quae P. Melanchthon objicit contra missae sacrificium propitiationem. ... Cui acc. & repulsio calumniarum J. Calvini & Musculi, et J. Juelli, contra Missam, eius canonem et purgatorium, denuo excusa*, Leuven, 1562; for Musculus, see R. Dellsperger, R. Freudenberger and W. Weber, edd. et al., *Wolfgang Musculus (1497-1563) und die oberdeutsche Reformation*, Colloquia Augustana 6, Berlin, 1997.

[69] See above, chapter V, 184, n. 46; Frith was burnt at the stake in 1533, Luther died in 1546.

[70] Melanchthon died in 1560.

[71] For a dated but useful overview of contemporary catholic polemicists, see T. H. Clancy, *Papist Pamphleteers*, Chicago IL, 1964.

[72] Cf. for instance the work of the *Louvainists*, above, chapter I, 71-74.

3. The Purpose of Sixteenth-Century Polemicism

In his recent study of martyrdom in early modern Europe, Brad Gregory calls for a new and more sensitive reading of polemical writings. He argues: 'It is gravely misguided to consign the era's writings of religious controversy to the dustbin of "polemics"'.[73] It can be tempting to dismiss sixteenth-century polemical writings as superfluous on the basis of their volume, their antagonistic rhetoric, and their ostensible irrelevance to modern theological debate. Yet the apologetic writings of the sixteenth century are more than reflections of bygone narrow-minded dogmatic debates. Most theological issues considered in this study—the subject of fervent debate in Smyth's age—persist to preoccupy a largely divided Christian church today.[74]

Richard Smyth and his fellow apologists were painfully aware of the divisions contemporary doctrinal changes caused.[75] Sixteenth-century polemical authors, regardless of their religious persuasion, took to writing in order to encourage others to stand firm in their convictions and to call those who had fallen away from their faith to return.[76] Matheson points out that it is 'a category mistake to see the literature of this period as propaganda'.[77] The polemical language used by the English apologists should not distract the reader from their genuine concern for the spiritual welfare of the English people. Stripped of their polemicism, they reveal a genuine concern for the maintenance of orthodoxy. Smyth confessed in 1555:

> I, remembering ... how the people of this our contrey are infected, and poysoned in theyr soules, by the new preachers euil sermons, and wicked bookes, and that as yet few bookes haue been set foorth for the confutation of them, to reduce the people agayne vnto the

---

[73] B. S. Gregory, *Salvation at Stake: Christian Martyrdom in Early Modern Europe*, Harvard Historical Studies 134, Cambridge MA, 1999, 12.

[74] In 1995, for instance, John Paul II declared that the Roman Catholic church should not gloss over the doctrinal differences that continued to divide denominations: 'Our faith requires us to avoid both false irenicism and indifference to the church's ordinances'; see J. G. Donders, ed., *John Paul II: The Encyclicals*, Maryknoll NY, 1997, 291-324: 'Ut unum sint', 316.

[75] See for instance Smyth (1555), ¶¶ i r and Smyth (1562), 7 r.

[76] For instance Smyth (1555), ¶ vii r; cf. Loach (1975), 38.

[77] Matheson (1998), 248.

catholike fayth, dyd thynke it my duetie to trauayle and labour therin.[78]

Smyth was convinced that man would suffer the consequences for his schism by eternal damnation: 'no manne, nor woman ... as a Schismatike, can be saued from the perill of that death both of body and soule which shall neuer haue ende'.[79] He made use of his polemical aptitude not only to persuade others of the truth of his beliefs; Smyth also sought to repay God for His gifts, since he believed strongly that

> he that hath encreased those giftes by godly usyng of them shall receiue a reward of god accordyng to his doynges, and he whiche hath not so done, shall be punished therefore.[80]

For Smyth and his contemporaries the fear of punishment was genuine. The sixteenth-century Christian lived his earthly life on a precarious path between heaven and hell. As Oberman reminds the modern reader, in the sixteenth century 'man is the battlefield between God and the Devil'.[81] In the context of this cosmic battle between the church militant and the demon heresy, apologists felt justified in abandoning sophistication and civility and instead reaching out for the blunt weapons of polemic.[82]

Immersed in a personal struggle for the salvation of souls it is not surprising that, as in the case of Smyth's encounters with Peter Martyr, sixteenth-century apologists regarded their opposition in the narrow terms of this eschatological battle. Since they viewed their opponents as diametrically opposed to the way of salvation there was little room for objectivity in their debates. There was no time for relaxed reflection on a rival treatise or the 'humane' treatment of an antagonist if the opponent was seen as leading innocent souls to their certain damnation. The battle for salvation called for a forceful response to religious dissent. The skirmishes between Martyr and Smyth show that the step from a defensive rebuttal to the condemnation of the other as 'belonging to the

---

[78] Smyth (1555), ¶ vi v.
[79] Smyth (1555), ¶¶ i r.
[80] Smyth (1555), ¶ vi v-¶ vii r; cf. Smyth (1546^2), 4 r.
[81] H. A. Oberman, *Luther: Man between God and the Devil*, London, 1993, 219.
[82] Cf. Gregory (1999), 14; Matheson (1998), 185.

henchmen of Antichrist' is small.[83] Matheson is right when he suggests that 'once the "other" has been demonised there is no room for ... careful differentiation'.[84]

In the past, readers of sixteenth-century polemics have viewed them as little more than the malignant censure of past doctrinal or political struggles at best, and as irrelevant personal battles at worst. However, to apply a reading that sets out to relativise the polemic nature of early modern religious debates is to ignore their basic concerns. Gregory supports this view:

> It is entirely misleading to put terms like 'heresy' and 'superstition' in quotation marks ...—implying that Protestants were not really heretics, Catholics were not really superstitious. The point is to capture the contemporary character of the denunciations, to see what they meant in context.[85]

The work of Richard Smyth demonstrates clearly that it is impossible to divorce the theological views of the sixteenth-century apologists from their polemical presentation. Stripped of its polemicism, Smyth's work reflects the language of mid-Tudor catholicism—a meta-language of orthodoxy that sought to demonstrate the continuity of the catholic faith by the use of late-scholastic methodology. Smyth's work remains that of an average theologian. Only when seen in the context of its debates does it display the polemical brilliance that made it so popular, and the underlying language that gave it its importance.

---

[83] Above, chapter V; see for instance, P. M. Vermigli, *Defensio D. Petri Martyris Vermilii Florentini diuinarum literarum in schola Tigurina professoris, ad Riccardi Smythaei Angli, olim theologiae professoris Oxoniensis duos libellos de caelibatu sacerdotum, & votis monasticis, nunc primùm in luce edita*, Basel, 1559, 3: 'Antichristi mercenarij'.

[84] Matheson (1998), 185.

[85] Gregory (1999), 13.

BIBLIOGRAPHY

1. MANUSCRIPT SOURCES

ARCHIVES MUNICIPALES DE LA VILLE DE DOUAI, MS BB2, Délibérations des Consaulx
——, Lettres de Vidimus Données des Eschevins de La Ville de Doüay des Lettres Patentes du Roy d'Espagne en forme de convention des Droits & Privileges de l'Universite de Doüay, Layette 172
——, Memoir concernant les retenus, Layette 174, no. 66
——, Comptes, MS CC19
——, Comptes, Liasse 102
DE BAR, F., Bibliothèque municipale de Doaui MS 57, Pavli Apostoli Epistolae
DE FRANCE, J., Bibliothèque municipale de Doaui MS 1304, Discovrs de la Povrsvite et Erection De L'Vniuersité De Douay
BODLEIAN LIBRARY, MS DD
BRITISH LIBRARY, Royal MS 17C V, Of the Sacrament of Thanksgiving: A Short Treatise of Peter Martyrs making
CHRIST CHURCH COLLEGE OXFORD ARCHIVES, MS x (1) c.6, Battels Books
——, MS Estates 13, Estates Book
——, MS D.c.i.b.1, Cathedral Chapter Books
COMPANY OF MERCERS ARCHIVES, Acts of Court
——, Renterwardens' Account Book
CORPUS CHRISTI COLLEGE CAMBRIDGE ARCHIVES, MS 119, Epistolas Virorum Illustrorum
FOPPENS, J. F., Bibliothèque Royale Brussel MS, Doctores sacrae theologiae ac juris utriusque qui hunc titulum adepti sunt Lovanii
——, Bibliothèque Nationale Paris MS, Fasti doctorales universitates Lovaniensis
HEREFORD AND WORCESTER COUNTY COUNCIL ARCHIVES, Registrum Ghinucci (II)
MERTON COLLEGE OXFORD ARCHIVES, Collegii Mertonensis Registrum Vetus (I)
OXFORD UNIVERSITY ARCHIVES, Registrum Actae Congregationis
——, Registrum Cancellarii Ꮄ
——, Register H
PARSONS, N., Bibliothèque Municipale de Douai MS, A Memorial for the Reformation of England
WORCESTERSHIRE RECORD OFFICE, Episcopal Registers, Register 9 (i)

2. PRIMARY SOURCES AND CONTEMPORARY SOURCES IN PRINT

ALLEN, P. S. (ed.), *Opus Epistolarum Desideri Erasmi Roterodami* (Oxford, 1906-1958)

ALLEN, W., *An Apologie and True Declaration of the Institution and Endeavour of the Two English Colleges* (Reims, 1581)
ANDERSON, J. M., *Early Records of the University of St Andrews. The Graduation Roll, 1413-1579, and the Matriculation Roll, 1473-1579* (Edinburgh: Scottish Historical Society, 1926)
ANDERSON, P. J., *Records of the Scots College at Douai, Rome, Madrid, Valladolid and Ratisbon* (I: Register of Students; Aberdeen: New Spalding Club 30, 1906)
AQUINAS, Th., *Summa Theologica* (London, 1963-1966)
——, *Diui Thomae Aquinatis in omnes beati Pauli Apostoli epistolas commentaria* (Paris, 1541)
AYSCOUGH, S. (ed.), *Catalogue of the Manuscripts preserved in the British Museum* (London, 1721)
BALE, J., *The First Examinacyon of the worthy servant of God, Mistress Anne Askewe, lately martyred in Smythfelde* (Marburg, 1546)
——, *The Lattre Examinacyon of Anne Askewe* (Marburg, 1547)
BELLARMINE, R., SOMMERVOGEL, C. (ed.), *Disputationes des Controversiis Christianae Fidei adversus huius temporis* (Bibl. de la Comp. de Jésus 1: 1890; 8: 1898)
BESSARION, *Oratio de Sacramento Eucharistiae* (Strassburg, 1513)
BIEL, G., *Epitome et collectionem ex Occamo circa quattuor sententiarum libros* (Basel, 1508)
——, *Sacri canonis missae expositio resolutissima* (Basel, 1510)
——, *Sermones de festivitatibus Christi* (Hagenau, 1510)
——, *Sacrosancti canonis missae expositio in Epitomen contracta* (Antwerpen, 1556)
——, OBERMAN, H. A., COURTENAY, W. J. (edd.), *Gabrielis Biel Canonis Missae Expositio* (Wiesbaden: Veröffentlichungen des Instituts für europäische Geschichte Mainz, 1965)
BILLICK, E., *Iudicium deputatorum et universitatis Coloniensis de doctrina et vocatione Martini Buceri ad Bonnam* (Köln, 1543)
BOASE, C. W. (ed.), *Register of the University of Oxford, 1449-63, 1505-1571* (Oxford: Oxford Historical Society, 1885
BONAVENTURE, *Sancti Bonaventurae Opera Omnia* (Quaracchi, 1882-1902)
BREF RECUEIL *et recit de la Solemnité faicte à l'entree et Consecreation de l'Viniversité faicte et erigée en la Ville de Douay, en Flandre. Par le tres catholique et tres vertueux Prince Philippe, Roi Despaigne, Conte de Flandre, etc., le v doctobre l'an M.ccccc.lxij* (Douai, 1563)
BRENZ, J., BIZER, E. (ed.), *Confessio Virtembergica: Das Württembergische Bekenntnis von 1551* (Stuttgart, 1952)
BREWER, J. S., GAIRDNER, J. (edd. et al.), *Letters and Papers, foreign and domestic of the reign of Henry VIII, preserved in the Public Record Office, the British Museum, and elsewhere in England* (London, 1862-1932)
BUCER, M., *Die ander verteydigung und erklerung der Christlichen Lehr in etlichen fürnehmen Hauptstucken* (Bonn, 1543)
BULLINGER, H., *The golde boke of christen matrimonye, newly set forthe in English* (London, 1543)
——, *In omnes Apostolicas Epistolas, divi vidilicet Pauli XIIII et VII Canonicas, Commentarii Heinrychi Bullingeri* (Zürich, 1558)

CAJETAN, Th. de Vio, *Evangelia cum Commentariis Reverendissimi Domini Thomae de Vio Cajetani, Cardinalis Sancti Xisti, in quartour Evangelia et Acta Apostolorum ad Graecorum codicum veritatem castigata, ad sensum quem vocant literalem Commentarij* (Paris, 1532)
——, *Opera omnia quotquod in Sacrae Scripturae expositionem reperiuntur, cura atque industria insignis Collegii S. Thomae Complutensis OP* (Lyon, 1639)
CHAMBERS, R., *Biographical Dictionary of Eminent Scotsmen* (London, 1868)
CLARENDON HISTORICAL SOCIETY, *The Journal of King Edward's reign, written with his own hand* (London, 1884)
CLARKE, A. W. H., *The registers of St Dunstan in the East, London, 1558-1766* (London, 1939-1958)
CLICHTHOVE, J., *De laude monasticae religionis opusculum: vnde ipsa ceperit exordium incrementum et stabilimentum diludiuce declarans, quoniam etiam modo tria praecioua illius vota, obedientia, paupertas & castitas integre observanade sint* (Paris, 1523)
COCHLAEUS, J., *Glos und Comment Doc. Johannes Dobneck Cochlaeus von Wendelstein uff cliiii Artikeln gezogen uss einem Sermon Doc. Martin Luterrs von der heiligen mess und nüem Testament* (Strassburg, 1523)
——, *De gratia sacramentorum liber unus aduersus assertionem M. Lutheri* (Strassburg, 1522)
——, *De sanctorum invocatione et intercessione dequm imaginibus & reliquiis eorum pie ritequm colendis. Liber unus. Ioannis Cochlei Germani, adversus Henricum Bullingerum Heluetium* (Ingolstadt, 1544)
——, SCHWEIZER, J. (ed.), *Adversus cucullatum Minotaurum Wittenbergensem. De sacramentorum gratia iterum (1523)* (Münster: Corpus Christianorum 3, 1920)
——, KEEN, R.(ed.), *Philippicae I-VII* (Nieuwkoop, 1995-1996)
CRANMER, Th., *An answere of Thomas, Archebyshop of Canterburye vnto a crafty and sophisticall cauillation devised by S. Gardiner, late Byshop of Winchester, agaynst the trewe and godly doctrine of the moste holye Sacrament ... wherin is also ... answered ... the booke of R. Smyth* (London, 1551)
——, *A defence of the true and catholike doctrine of the sacrament of the body and bloud of Christ* (London, 1550)
——, *An answere against the false calumnacion of D. Richard Smyth, who hath taken upon hym to confute the Defence* (London, 1551)
——, *A confutation of vnwritten verities, both bi the holye Scriptures and moste auncient autors* (Wesel, 1556)
COX, J. E. (ed.), *Miscellaneous writings and Letters of Thomas Cranmer* (Cambridge: Parker Society, 1846)
——, *Concordia Triglotta: Libri symbolici Ecclesiae Lutheranae Germanice, Latine, Anglice* (St Louis MO, 1921)
DENIFLE, H. S., *Chartularium Universitatis Parisiensis ... ex diversis bibliothecis tabularisque collegit et cum authenticis chartis contulit* (Paris, 1889-1897)
——, *Auctarium Chartularii Universitatis Parisiensis* (Paris, 1935—)
DENZINGER, H. & SCHÖNMETZER, K. (edd.), *Enchiridion symbolorum et definitionum de rebus fidei et morum: Kompendium der Glaubensbekenntnisse und kirchlichen Lehrentscheidungen* (Freiburg im Breisgau and Rome, [38]1999)

ECK, J., *Homiliarum doctissimi viri J. D. Joannis Eckij, unicae hoc seculo Christianissimi adversum quoscumque haereticorum insultus calumnae* (Köln, 1538)
——, *De poenitentia & confessione sereta semper in Ecclesia Dei observata contra Lutherum* (No place, 1522)
——, *De Satisficatione et aliis penitentie annexis* (Rome, 1523)
——, Metzler, J., SJ (ed.), *Epistola de ratione studiorum (1538)* (Münster: Corpus Christianorum 2, 1921)
——, Walde, B. (ed.), *Explanatio Psalmi vigesimi (1538)* (Münster: Corpus Christianorum 13, 1921)
——, METZLER, J., SJ (ed.), *Tres orationes in exequiis Joannis Eckii habitae. Accesserunt aliquot epitaphia in Eckii obitum scripta et catalogus locubrationem eiusdem (1543). Nach den Originaldrucken mit biobibliographischer Einleitung, einer Untersuchung der Berichte über Ecks Tod und einem Verzeichnis seiner Schriften* (Münster: Corpus Christianorum 16, 1930)
——, FRAENKEL, P. (ed.), *Enchiridion locorum communiorum adversus Lutherum et alios hostes ecclesiae (1525-1543)*, Corpus Christianorum 34, Münster, 1979
——, ISERLOH, E., (ed. et al.), *De sacrificio missae libri tres (1526)* (Münster: Corpus Christianorum 36, 1982)
EMDEN, A. B., *A Biographical Register of the University of Oxford, 1501-1540* (Oxford, 1974)
EMSER, H., FREUDENBERGER, Th. (ed.), *Missae Christianorum contra Lutheranum missandi formulam assertio. Schriften zur Verteidigung der Messe* (Münster: Corpus Christianorum 28, 1959)
——, *Wider der zweier Pröbst zu Nürnberg falschen Grund und Ursachen, warum sie die heilige Meß und andere christliche Stück und Ceremonien geändert und zum Teil abgetan haben* (Münster: Corpus Christianorum 28, 1959)
ERASMUS, D., *In Novvm Testamentvm ab Annotationes: ingenti nuper accessione per auctorem locupletatae* (Basel, 1519)
——, LECLERC, J. (ed.), *Desiderii Erasmi Roterodami omnia opera* (Leiden, 1703-1706)
FISHER, J., *Sacri sacerdotii defensio contra Lutherum* (Würzburg, 1597)
——, *Assertionis Lutheranae Confutatio* (Antwerpen, 1523)
——, *Assertionem Regis Angliae de fide Catholica adversus Lutheri Babylonicam captivitatem defensio* (Köln, 1525)
——, *De Veritate Corporis et Sanguinis Christi in Eucharistia* (Köln, 1527)
——, HALLET, P. E. (tr.), *The Defence of the Priesthood* (London, 1935)
FITCH, M., *Index to testamentary records in the Comissary Court of London* (London, 1969—)
FOPPENS, J. F., *Bibliotheca Belgica, sive virorum in Belgio vita, scriptisque illustrium catalogus, librorumque nomenclatura, continens scriptores a Valerio Andrea aliisque, recensitos usque ad anno M.D.C.L.XXX* (Brussel, 1739)
FÖRSTERMANN, K. E. (ed.), *Urkundenbuch zu der Geschichte des Reichstages zu Augsburg im Jahre 1530* (Halle, 1833-1835)
FOSTER, J., *Alumni Oxoniensis. The matriculation registers of the University arranged, revised and annotated* (Oxford: Oxford Historical Society Old Series, 1887-1888)

FOXE, J. (ed.), *The Whole workes of W. Tyndall, Iohn Frith, and Doct. Barnes, three worthy Martyrs, collected and compiled in one Tome togither* (London, 1573)
FROEHLICH, K., GIBSON, M. T. (edd.), *Glossa ordinaria editio princeps* (Turnholt, 1992)
GALATINUS, P., OFM, *Opus de arcanis catholicae veritatis, quum ante natum Christum, tum postscriptis, contra obstinatam Iudeorum perfidiam absolitissimus commentarius* (Ortona, 1518)
GARDINER, S., *An Explication and assertion of the Catholic Faith touching the most blessed sacrament of the Altar* (Rouen?, 1550)
GEE, H. and HARDY, W. J. (edd.), *Documents illustrative of English church history* (London, 1896)
GIBSON, E. C. S. (ed.), *The Thirty-Nine Articles of the Church of England* (London, 1896)
GIBSON, S., *Statuta antiqua universitatis Oxoniensis* (Oxford, 1931)
GÖRRES-GESELLSCHAFT (ed.), *Concilium Tridentinum* (Freiburg im Breisgau, 1901–)
GORHAM, G. C. (ed.), *Gleanings of a few scattered Ears, during the Period of the Reformation in England* (London, 1857)
GRAMAYE, J. B., *Rerum Duacensium libri tres ex archivis publicis collecti* (Leuven, 1618)
HAEGHEN, F. F. E. van der, *Bibliotheca Belgica, bibliographie générale des Pays-Bays, par le bibliothécaire-en-chef et les conservateurs de la bibliothèque de l'Université de Gand* (Gent, 1880-1967)
HAMILTON, W. D. (ed.), *Charles Wriothesley: A Chronicle of the England during the reign of the Tudors, from AD 1485-1559* (London, 1875-1877)
HANNAY, R. K. (ed.), *Rentale Sancti Andree, being the Chamberlain and Granitar Accounts of the Archbishopric in the time of Cardinal Betoun, 1538-1546* (Edinburgh, 1913)
HAWS, Ch. H., *Scottish parish clergy at the Reformation 1540-74* (Edinburgh: Scottish Record Society New Series 3, 1972)
HENRY VIII, LACEY, T. A. (ed.), *The king's book; or, A necessary doctrine and erudition for any Christian man 1543* (London, 1932)
HENRY VIII, FRAENKEL, P. (ed.), *Assertio septem sacramentorum adversus Martinum Lutherum, aedita ab invictissimo Angliae et Franciae rege et domine Hybernicae Henrico eius nomen octavo* (Münster: Corpus Christianorum 43, 1992)
HENNESSEY, G. L., *Novum Repertorium Parochiale Londinense* (London, 1889)
HERBORN, N., OFM, *Epistola fratris Nicolai Herborn Minoritae Guardiani Brulensis, ad Coloniensem felicissimam urbem* (Köln, 1527)
——, *Locorum communiorum aduersus huius tempore haereses Enchiridion* (Köln, 1528)
——, *Confutatio Lutheranismi Danici anno 1530 conscripta a Nicolao Stagefyr seu Herboneo OFM* (Quaracchi, 1902)
HESSELS, J., *Tractatus pro invocatione Sanctorum contra Joannem Monneminem* (Leuven, 1562)
HUGHES, P. L. and LARKIN, J. F. (edd.), *Tudor Royal Proclamations* (New Haven CT, 1964-1969)
JEWEL, J., *Apologia Ecclesiae Anglicanae* (Oxford, 1639)

JOSEPH, R., PANTIN, W. A. (ed.), *The letter book of Robert Joseph, monk-scholar of Evesham and Gloucester College, Oxford, 1530-1533* (Oxford: Oxford Historical Society New Series 19, 1967)

KINDLER, E. & HAENDLER, K. (edd.), *Lutherisches Bekenntnis: Eine Auswahl aus den Bekenntnisschriften der evangelisch-lutherischen Kirche* (Berlin and Hamburg, 1962)

KNIGHTON, Ch. S. (ed.), *Acts of the Dean and Chapter of Westminster 1543-1609* (I: The First Collegiate Church 1543-1556, Woodbridge and Rochester NY, 1997)

KNIGHTON, Ch. S. (ed.), *Calendar of State Papers, Domestic Series, of the Reign of Edward VI, 1547-1553* (London, 1992)

KNOX, Th. F., *The first and second diaries of the English College, Douay, and an appendix of unpublished documents edited by the Fathers of the Congregation of the London Oratory, Records of the English Catholics under the Penal Laws 1* (London, 1878)

———, *Cardinal Allen's Letters and Memorials, 1532-1594* (London, 1878-1882)

KRAEMER, M., *Christlich Bericht* (Köln, 1543)

LAMBERT, F., *Commentariorvm Francisci Lamberti Avenionensis Theologi de Sacro Coniugio, & aduersus pollutissimum Regni perditionis caelibatum, Liber* (Strassburg, 1524)

LATOMUS, B., KEIL, L. (ed.), *Responsio ad epistolam quandam Martini Buceri de dispensatione eucharistiae et invocatione divorum et coelibatu clericorum* (Münster: Corpus Christianorum 8, 1924)

LETTRES DE VIDIMUS *Données des Eschevins de la Ville de Doüay des Lettres Patentes du Roy d'Espagne en forme de convention des Droits & Privileges de l'Vniversité de Doüay en 1561* (Douai, 1717)

LEIB, K., *De caelibatu atque castimonia epistola* (Ingolstadt, 1545)

———, *Spiegel der Sponsen Christi* (Ingolstadt, 1542)

———, *Resolutio questionis de S. Apostolo an coniugatus fuerit necne* (Ingolstadt, 1545)

LEIB, K., DÖLLINGER, I. von (ed.), *Sendbrief zur Beschützung geistlichs Closterstand gegen die Lutherischen* (Beiträge zur politischen, kirchlichen und Cultur-Geschichte 2, 1863)

———, *Der kyrchen schwert wider Martin Luter* (Beiträge zur politischen, kirchlichen und Cultur-Geschichte 2, 1863)

LIBRERIA EDITRICE VATICANA (ed.), *The Weekday Missal* (London, 1982)

———, *Corpus Iuris Canonici auctoritate Ioannis Pauli PP. II promulgatus* (Città del Vaticano, 1983)

———, *Catechism of the Catholic Church* (London, 1994)

LLOYD, Ch. (ed.), *Formularies of faith put forth by authority during the reign of Henry VIII* (Oxford, 1825)

LOMBARD, P., *Petri Lombardus, Episcopi Parisiensis, Sententiarum Libri IIII* (Venezia, 1570)

LUTHER, M., *Werke. Kritische Gesamtausgabe* (Weimar, 1883—)

LYELL, L. (ed.), *Acts of Court of the Mercers' Company, 1453-1527* (Cambridge, 1936)

MACLURE, M., *Register of Sermons preached at Paul's Cross, 1534-1642* (Ottawa ON, 1989)

MACRAY, W. D., *Register of the members of St Mary Magdalen College, Oxford* (London, 1894-1915)
MELANCHTHON, Ph., PREUS, J. A. O. (ed.), *Loci Communes 1543* (St Louis MO, 1992)
MITCHELL, W. T. (ed.), *Epistolae Academicae, 1508-1596* (Oxford: Oxford Historical Society New Series 26, 1980)
MOLANUS, J., RAM, P. F. X. de (ed.), *Les quartorze livres sur l'histoire de la ville de Louvain du docteur Jean Molanus* (Brussel, 1861)
MORRIS, Th., *The Provosts of Methven* (Edinburgh, 1875)
MOSELLANUS, P., *Tabvlae de Schematibvs Petri Mosellani, à pluribus mendis quam diligentissime repurgatae* (Köln, 1541)
NICHOLS, J. G. (ed.), *The Diary of Henry Machyn, Citizen and Merchant-Taylor of London, From AD 1550-1563* (London: Camden Society, 1886)
OCKHAM, W., GÁL, G., OFM (ed. et al.), *Opera Philosophica et Theologica* (St Bonaventure NY, 1967)
OECOLAMPADIUS, J., *De Genuina Verborum Domini, Hoc Est Corpus Meum, Expositione Liber* (Hagenau, 1525?)
PARKER, M., *De Antiquitate Britannicae Ecclesiae & Privilegiis ecclesiae Cantuarensis* (Lambeth, 1572)
PIGHIUS (PIGGE), A., *De Libera Hominis arbitrio, & diuina gratia* (Köln, 1542)
PILATE-PRÉVOST, H. J., *Table chronologique et analytique des archives de la mairie de Douai, depuis le onzième siècle jusqu'a dix-huitième* (Douai, 1842)
PLANTIJN, Ch., *Afgheworpen brieuen van den Cardinael van Granvelle ende anderen. Ouergheset inde Nederduytsche spraecke uit de originale copijen* (Antwerpen, 1582)
PLATO, *The Republic* (Harmondsworth, 1987)
PÖHLMANN, H. G. (ed.), *Die Bekenntnisschriften der evangelisch-lutherischen Kirche* (Gütersloh, 1987)
PORCHETUS, S., *Victoria adversus imios Hebraeos ex sacris litteris tum ex Talmud ac Caballistarum et aliorum omnium authorum, quos Hebraei recipiunt monstrantur veritatis catholicae fidei* (Paris, 1520)
POULLET, E., *Correspondance du Cardinal de Granvelle* (Brussel, 1877-1896)
PROFESSORES SOCIETATIS *Nominis Iesv, Lectori Salutem* (Tournai, 1562)
PUTTENHAM, G., *The arte of English poesie, contriued into three bookes: the first of poets and poesie, the second of proportion, the third of ornament* (London, 1589)
RAM, P. F. X. de, *Analectes pour servir à l'histoire de l'Université de Louvain* (Leuven, 1839-1859)
REUCHLIN, J., *De Rudimentis Hebraicis* (Pforzheim, 1506)
REUSENS, E., Van HOVE, A. (edd.), *Actes in procès verbaux des séances tenues par le conseil de l'Université de Louvain* (Brussel, 1903)
——, *Documents relatifs à l'histoire de l'Université de Louvain, 1425-1797, table des notices consacrées aux membres de l'Université* (Leuven, 1977)
REUSENS, E., SCHILLINGS, A. (edd.), *Matricule de l'Université de Louvain (IV: Février 1528-Février 1569)* (Brussel, 1903-1961)
RICHARDOT, F., *Les deux sermons Francois et Latin faicts ... a la solemnité celebrée au dict lieu pour le commencement de la nouelle Université* (Cambray, 1552)
——, *Orationes* (Douai, 1608)

RIVIÈRE, B., *Catalogue des manuscrits de la bibliothèque communale de Douai* (Paris, 1902)
——, *Catalogue méthodique des imprimés de la bibliothèque de Douai* (Douai, 1897-1911)
ROBINSON, H. (ed.), *The Zurich letters, comprising the correspondence of several English bishops and others, with some of the Helvetian reformers, during the reign of queen Elizabeth* (Cambridge: Parker Society, 1842-1845)
——, *Original Letters relative to the English Reformation, written during the reigns of king Henry viii., king Edward vi., and queen Mary: chiefly from the archives of Zurich. With Epistolæ Tigurinæ conscriptæ A.D. 1531-1559* (Cambridge: Parker Society, 1846-1848)
ROGERS, E. F. (ed.), *Sir John Hackett, The Letters, 1526-1534* (Morgantown VA, 1971)
ROYAL COMMISSION ON HISTORICAL MANUSCRIPTS, *Calendar of the Manuscripts of the Most Honourable the Marquis of Salisbury at Hatfield House* (London, 1883)
SALTERS H. E., *Registrum Annalium Collegii Mertonensis, 1483-1521* (Oxford: Oxford Historical Society, 1921)
SANDERUS, A., *Bibliotheca Belgica manuscripta, siue, Elenchus vniuersalis mss in celeberrimis Belgij coenobijs, ecclesij, vrbium, ac priuatorum nominum bibliothecis adhuc latentium* (Insulis [Lille], 1641-1644)
SCHATZGEYER, K., OFM, ISERLOH, E. (ed. et al.), *Schriften zur Verteidigung der Messe* (Münster: Corpus Christianorum 37, 1984)
SCHOTT, F. (ed.), *Reverendissimi et Eloquentissimi Viri D. Francisci Richardoti Atrebatensium Episcopi Orationes ad Noblissimus & Amplissimum virum Dominum Ioannem Richardotvm Equitem Auratum Dominum de Barly &c.* (Douai, 1608)
SCOTT, H., *Fasti Ecclesiae Scoticanae, The Succession of Ministers in the Church of Scotland from the Reformation* (Edinburgh, 1915)
SCOTUS, J. D., WADDING, L. (ed.), *Quaestiones quodlibetales* (Lyon, 1639)
SELWYN, D. (ed.), *A Catechism set forth by Thomas Cranmer from the Nuremberg Catechism translated into Latin by Justus Jonas* (Appleford, 1978)
SHARPE, R. R., *Calendar of Wills proved and enrolled in the Court of Husting London, 1258-1688* (London, 1889)
SMYTH, R., *Assertion and Defence of the Sacrament of the Aulter* (London, 1546)
——, *A defence of the blessed Masse and the sacrifice thereof, prouynge that it is aualable bothe for the quycke and the dead* (London, 1546)
——, *A Defence of the Sacrifice of the Masse* (London, 1546)
——, *A brief treatyse settynge forth diuers truthes necessary both to be beleued of chrysten people, & kepte also, whiche are not expressed in the scripture but left to ye church by the apostles tradition* (London, 1547)
——, *A godly and faythfull Retraction made by R. Smyth. Reuokyng certeyn errors in some of hys books* (London, 1547)
——, *A playne declaration made at Oxford the 24. Daye of July, by Mayster Richarde Smyth ... upon his Retraction* (London, 1547)
——, *De coelibatu liber unus. De votis monasticis liber alter ... (confutatio quorundam articulorum de votis monasticis P. Martyris ...)* (Leuven, 1550)
——, *Diatriba de hominis justificatione aedita Oxoniae anno 1550 mense februario adversum Petrum Martyrem Vermelium ... nunc apostatam* (Leuven, 1550)

——, *A confutation of a certen booke, called a defence of the true, and Catholike doctrine of the Sacrament, &c., sette fourth in the name of Thomas Archebysshoppe of Canterburye* (Paris, 1551)
——, *Defensio sacri episcoporum et sacerdotum Coelibatus, contra impias et indoctas Petri Martyris Vermelii nugas ... nunc vero Lutetiae Parisiorum Theologiam profitentem* (Paris, 1551)
——, *A Bouclier of the Catholike Fayth of Christes Church, conteynyng diuers matters now of late called into controversy, by the newe gospellers. Made by R. Smith* (London, 1554)
——, *The second parte of the booke called a Buckler of the Catholyke fayeth ... made by Richard Smith* (London, 1555)
——, *Refutatio luculenza crassae et exitiosae haeresis Johannis Calvini et Christop. Carlili Angli, qua astruunt Christum non descendisse ad inferos alios, quam ad infernum infirmum* (Leuven, 1562)
——, *Confutatio eorum, quae P. Melanchthon objicit contra missae sacrificium propitiationem ... Cui acc. & repulsio calumniarum J. Calvini & Musculi, et J. Juelli, contra Missam, eius canonem et purgatorium, denuo excusa* (Paris, [1+2]1562)
——, *De infantium baptismo, contra J. Calvinum, ac de operibus supererogationis, et merito mortis Christi, adversus eundem Calvinum et eius discipulos* (Leuven, 1562)
——, *De Missae Sacrificio ... ennaratio, ac brevis repulsio ... argumentum quae P. Maelanchthon, J. Calvinus, et alii sectarii objecerunt adversus illud, et purgatorium ... Acc. Epistola ... docens quae ecclesia sit nobis tuto sequenda* (Leuven, 1562)
——, *Defensio comprehendaria, et orthodoxa, sacri externi, et visibili Iesu Christi sacerdotii. Cui addita est sacratorum catholicae Ecclesiae altarium propugnatio, ac Calvinia altarium propugnatio, ac Calvina communionis succincta refutatio* (Leuven, 1562)
——, *De libero hominis arbitrio adversus Joannem Calvinum, et quotquod impie ... Lutherum imitati* (Leuven, 1563)
——, *Refutatio locorum communiorum theologicorum Philippi Melanchthonis Germani, M. Lutheri discipuli primarii* (Douai, [1-3]1563)
STANIHURST, R., *De rebus Hibernia gestis* (Leiden, 1583)
STAPLETON, T., *Orationes sex, tres funebres, dogmaticae tres* (Antwerpen, 1576)
SYLVIUS (DUBOIS), J., *Nascentis Academiae Duacensis eiusdemque illustrium Professorum Encomium* (Douai, 1563)
——, *Academiae Duacensis, eiusdem Illustrium Professorum, Encomium, Anno M.D.L.XII. Tert. Non. Octobris Dvaci* (Douai, 1563)
TAPPER, R., *Rvardi Tapperi ab Enchvsia, Ecclesiae Collegiatae S. Petri Lovaniensis Decani, et eiusdem florentissimae academiae cancellarii, omnia, qvae heberi potvervnt Opera*, (Köln, 1582)
THE STATUTES *of the Realm 1235-1713: printed by command of His Majesty King George the Third ... from original records and authentic manuscripts* (London, 1810-1822)
TITELMANS, F., OFM, *Collationes qvinqve svper Epistolam ad Romanos beati Pauli Apostoli* (Antwerpen, 1529)
——, *In Omnes Epistolas Apostolicas Elucidatio* (Antwerpen, 1540)
TRACY, R., *The Profe and Declaration of thys Proposition: Faythe only Justifieth* (London, 1543?)
TURNBULL, W. B. (ed.), *Calendar of State Papers, foreign series, of the reign of Edward VI, 1547-1553, preserved in the Public Record Office* (London, 1861)

TURNER, W., *The huntyng & fyndyng out of the Romishe fox whiche more then seven yeares hath bene hyd among the bisshoppes of Englong* (Basel [i.e. Bonn], 1543)
VALOR ECCLESIASTICUS *Tempore Henrici VIIIo auctoritate Regia institutus, printed by command of His Majesty George III* (London, 1814)
VALLA, L., PEROSA, A. (ed.), *Collatio Novi Testamenti* (Firenze, 1970)
VALERIUS ANDREAS, D., *Fasti academici Lovaniensis* (Leuven, 1650)
——, *Collegii trilinguis Buslidiani, in Academia Lovaniensi, exordia ac progressus, et linguae Hebraicae encomium. Vitae ac scripta professorum Collegii trilinguis Buslidiani, breviter commemorata* (Leuven, 1614)
——, *Valerii Andreae ... Bibliotheca Beligica: in quae Belgicae seu Germaniae inferioris provinciae urbesque viri item in Belgio vita scriptisque clari et librorum nomenclatura* (Leuven, 1623)
VEHE, M., *Assertio sacrorum quorundarum axiomatum, quae a nonnullis nostri seculi pseudoprophetis in periculosam rapiuntur controversiam* (Leipzig, 1535)
VERMIGLI, P. M., *In selectissimam D. Pauli Priorem ad Corinthios Epistolam, D. Petri Martyris commentarii doctissimi* (Zürich, 1551)
——, *Defensio D. Petri Martyris Vermilii Florentini diuinarum literarum in schola Tigurina professoris, ad Riccardi Smythaei Angli, olim theologiae professoris Oxoniensis duos libellos de caelibatu sacerdotum, & votis monasticis, nunc primùm in luce edita* (Basel, 1559)
——, *Dialogus de vtraqve in Christo natvra, qvomodo coeant in unam Christi personam inseparabilem: ... illustratur & Coenae dominicae negotium, perspicuisque scripturae & Patrum testimonijs demonstrantur, Corpus Christi non esse ubique, authore D. Petro Martyre Vermelio Florentino* (Zürich, 1561)
——, *Defensio doctrinae veteris & apostolicae de Sacrosancto Eucharistiae Sacramento, D. Petri Martyris Vermilij, ... aduersus Stephani Gardineri, quondam Vintonensis Episcopi. Cui accesserat antea quidem de eodem Eucharistia Sacramento disputatio: nunc verò de votis monasticis & coelibatu aduersus Richardum Smythæum Anglum elegantissima tractatio* (Basel, 1581)
——, *The common places of ... P. Martyr ... with a large addition of manie theologicall ... discources, translated by A. Marten* (London, 1583)
——, DONNELLY, J. P., SJ (tr. and ed.), *Dialogue on the Two Natures in Christ* (Kirksville MO, 1995)
VIVESIUS, A., *Alfonsi Vivesii Canarien. Episcopi Philippicae disputationes uiginti aduersus Lutheranae dogmata, per Philippum Melanchthonem defensa, complectens summarium disputationes nuper Augustae ac deinde Ratsiponae habitas* (Köln, 1542)
VOCHT, H. de, *Inventaire des archives de l'Université de Louvain, 1426-1797, aux archives générales du Royaume à Bruxelles* (Leuven, 1927)
WATT, D. E. R., *Fasti Ecclesiae Scoticanie Medii Aevi ad annum 1638* (Edinburgh: Scottish Record Society, 1969)
——, *Series episcoporum Ecclesiae Catholicae occidentalis: ab initio usque ad annum MCXCVIII* (Stuttgart, 1991)
WEISS, Ch. (ed.), *Papiers d'état du Cardinal de Granvelle d'après les Manuscripts de la Bibliothèque de Besançon* (Paris, 1841-1852)

WILKINS, D. (ed.), *Concilia Magnae Britanniae et Hiberniae: a Synodo Verolamiensi A.D. CCCC XLVI. ad Londinensem A.D. M DCCXVII. Accedunt constitutiones et alia ad historiam Ecclesiae Anglicanae spectantia* (London, 1737)
WOODRUFF, C. W. & CHURCHILL, I. J. (edd.), *Calendar of Institutions by the Chapter of Canterbury 'sede vacante'* (London: Kent Archaeological Society, Records Branch 7, 1923)
ZWINGLI, H., *Von Clarheit vnnt gewüsse oder vnbetrogliche des wort gottes* (Zürich, 1524)
——, *A short pathwaye to the ryghte and true vnderstanding of the holye and sacred Scriptures set fourth by that moste famous Clerke, Huldrich Zwinglius* (Worcester, 1550)

3.1. SECONDARY LITERATURE

ALEXANDER, G., *The Life and Career of Edmund Bonner, Bishop of London* (Unpublished Ph.D. dissertation: University of London, 1960)
ANDERSON, M. W., *Peter Martyr: A Reformer in Exile (1542-1562)* (Nieuwkoop, 1975)
ASTON, T. H. (ed. in chief), *The History of the University of Oxford* (Oxford, 1986—)
BACKUS, I., *The disputations of Baden, 1526 and Berne, 1528: Neutralizing the early Church* (Princeton NJ, 1993)
——, (ed. et al.), *The Reception of the Church Fathers in the West from the Carolingians to the Maurists* (Leiden, 1997)
BAGCHI, D. V. N., *Luther's earliest opponents: Catholic controversialists, 1518-1525* (Minneapolis MN, 1991)
BALE, J., *Illustrium majoris Britanniae scriptorum summarium* (Wesel, 1548)
BARRET, C. K., *The Gospel according to St John: An introduction with Commentary and Notes on the Greek Text* (London, ²1996)
BARRON, C. (ed. et al.), *England and the Low Countries in the Late Middle Ages* (Stroud, 1995)
BASKERVILLE, E. J., *A Chronological Bibliography of Propaganda and Polemic published in English between 1553 and 1558* (Phliadelphia PA, 1979)
BASSE, M., *Certitudo Spei: Thomas von Aquins Begründung der Hoffnungsgewißheit und ihre Rezeption bis zum Konzil von Trient als ein Beitrag zur Verhältnisbestimmung von Eschatologie und Rechtfertigungslehre* (Göttingen: Forschungen zur systematischen und ökumenischen Theologie 69, 1993)
BÄUMER, R., *Johannes Cochlaeus (1479-1552): Leben und Werk im theologischen Dienst* (Münster, 1980)
BÉDOUELLE, G., *Lefèvre d'Etaples et l'Intelligence des Ecritures* (Genève, 1976)
——, and GAL, P. le (ed. et al.), *Le 'Divorce' du Roi Henry VIII: Etudes et Documents* (Genève, 1987)
BEUZART, P., *Les heresies pendant le Moyen Age et la Réform jusqu'a la mort de Philippe II, 1598, dans la région de Douai, d'Arras et au pays de l'Allen* (Paris, 1912)
BLENCH, J. W., *Preaching in England in the late Fifteenth and Sixteenth Centuries* (Oxford, 1964)
BOOTY, J. E., *John Jewel as Apologist of the Church of England* (London, 1963)

———, *An Apology of the Church of England* (Charlottesville VA, 1974)
BOWKER, M., *The Henrician Reformation: The Diocese of Lincoln under John Longland, 1521-1547* (Cambridge, 1981)
BRAUNISCH, R., *Die Theologie der Rechtfertigung im 'Enchiridion' (1538) des Johannes Gropper. Sein kritischer Dialog mit Philipp Melanchthon* (Münster: Religionsgeschichtliche Studien und Texte 109, 1974)
BRECHT, M., *Martin Luther. I: Sein Weg zur Reformation, 1483-1521* (Stuttgart, 1990)
BRESIN, L., MANNIER, E. (edd.), *Chroniques de Flandre, et d'Artois* (Paris, 1880)
BRIGDEN, S., *London and the Reformation* (Oxford, ²1991)
BRODRICK, G. C., *Memorials of Merton College* (Oxford, 1885)
BUCQUET, L., *Villes meurtries de France: Villes du Nord: Lille, Douai etc.* (Brussel, 1918)
BURNET, G., *A history of the reformation of the Church of England* (London, 1679-1715)
CARAMAN, P., *The Western Rising 1549: The Prayer Book Rebellion* (Tiverton, 1994)
CARDON, G., *La Fondation de l'Université de Douai* (Paris, 1892)
CARLSON, E. J. (ed.), *Religion and the English People, 1500—1640* (Kirksville, MO, 1998)
CHIBY, A. A., *Henry VIII's conservative scholar: Bishop John Stokesley and the divorce, royal supremacy and doctrinal reform* (Bern, 1997)
CLARK, F., *Eucharistic Sacrifice and the Reformation* (London, 1967)
CLEBSCH, W. A., *England's earliest Protestants 1520-1535* (New Haven CT, 1964)
CHARTIER, R. (ed.), *The Culture of Print: Power and the Uses of Print in Early Modern Europe* (Cambridge, 1989)
CHOLIJ, R., *Clerical Celibacy in East and West* (Leominster, 1989)
CLANCY, T. H., *Papist Pamphleteers* (Chicago IL, 1964)
COCHINI, Ch., SJ, *Les origines patristiques du célibat sacerdotal* (Paris, 1981)
COCKX-INDESTEGE, I. (ed. et al.), *Belgica Typographica 1540-1600. Catalogus Librorum impressorum ab Anno MDXLI ad annum MDC in regionibus quae nunc Regni Belgarum partes sunt* (Brussel, 1968)
COLINET, P., *L'ancienne faculté de droit de Douai (1562-1793)* (Lille, 1900)
CORNWALL, J., *Revolt of the Peasantry 1549* (London, 1977)
DANKBAAR, W. F., *Martin Bucers Beziehungen zu den Niederlanden* (Den Haag, 1961)
DECAREK, J., *De Dageraad van de Reformatie in Vlaanderen* (Brussel, 1973)
DELLSPERGER, R., FREUDENBERGER, R., WEBER, W. (edd. et al.), *Wolfgang Musculus (1497-1563) und die oberdeutsche Reformation* (Berlin: Colloquia Augustana 6, 1997)
DERASIÈRE, M. J., *Recuil de pièces mémoires &c. pour servir à l'histoire particulière de la ville de Douai* (Douai, 1855)
DESHAINES, C., *Catalogue des Manuscripts de la Bibliothèque de Douai* (Paris, 1878)
DETTLOFF, W., *Die Entwicklung der Akzeptations- und Verdienstlehre von Duns Scotus bis Luther* (Münster, 1963)
DEWAR, M., *Sir Thomas Smith—A Tudor Intellectual in Office* (London, 1964)
DIERICKX, M., *Documents inédits sur l'érection des nouveaux diocèses aux Pays-Bas (1521-1570)* (Brussel, 1960)
DOBSCHÜTZ, E. von, *Zum vierfachen Schriftsinn. Die Geschichte einer Theorie* (Berlin, 1921)
DONDERS, J. G. (ed.), *John Paul II: The Encyclicals* (Maryknoll NY, 1997)

DOWLING, M., *Fisher of Men: The Life of John Fisher, 1496-1535* (Basingstoke, 1999)
DUFFY, E., *The Stripping of the Altars: Traditional Religion in England c.1400-c.1580* (New Haven CT, 1992)
DUFFY, E., BRADSHAW, B., (edd. et al.), *Humanism, Reform and the Reformation: The Career of Bishop John Fisher* (Cambridge, 1989)
DUKE, A. C., *Reformation and Revolt in the Low Countries* (London, 1990)
DUPLESSIS, R. St-C, *Urban Stability in the Netherlands Revolution: a comparative study of Lille and Douai* (Unpublished Ph.D. dissertation: Columbia University New York NY, 1974)
DURME, M. van, *Antoon Perrenot: Bisschop van Atrecht, Kardinaal van Granvelle, Minister van Karel V en van Filips II (1517-1586)* (Brussel, 1953)
DUTHILLŒUL, H. R. J., *Bibliographie douaisienne* (Paris, 1835)
——, *Galerie douaissinne, ou Biographie des hommes remarquables de la ville de Douai* (Douai, 1844)
——, *Catalogue descriptif et raissoné des manuscrits de la bibliothèque [municipale] de Douai* (Douai, 1846)
——, *Histoire ecclésiastique et monastique de Douai* (Douai, 1861)
EISENSTEIN, E., *The Printing Press as an Agent of Change: Communications and Cultural Transformations in Early Modern Europe* (Cambridge, 1979)
EIJL, E. J. M. van, *Facultas S. Theologiae Lovaniensis 1432-1797: Bijdragen tot haar geschiedenis* (Leuven, 1977)
ESCALLIER, E. A., *L'Abbaye d'Anchin, 1079-1792* (Lille, 1852)
ESPINAS, G., *Les finances de la commune de Douai des origine Xème siècle* (Paris, 1902)
ESSEN, L. van der, *De Universiteit te Leuven, haar ontstaan, haar geschiedenis, haar organisatie, 1425-1953* (Brussel, 1955)
ETIENNE, J., *Ruard Tapper, interprete catholique de la pensée protestante sur le Sacrement de penitence* (Leuven, 1954)
FOXE, J., *Actes and Monumentes. Newly revised and recognised* (London, 1583)
——, TOWNSEND, G. and CATTLEY, S. R. (edd.), *The Actes and Monumentes of John Foxe* (London, 1837-1841)
FULLER, Th., *The History of the University of Cambridge, and of Waltham Abbey* (London, 1840)
——, *The Church-History of Britain untill the year M.DC.XLVII* (London, 1655)
——, *The History of the Worthies of England* (London, 1662)
GACHARD, L. P., *Correspondance de Marguerite d'Autriche* (Brussel, 1881)
GASQUET, F. A. and BISHOP, E. (edd.), *Edward VI and the Book of Common Prayer* (London, 1928)
GELDEREN, M. van, *The Political Thought of the Dutch Revolt 1555-1590* (Cambridge, 1992)
GERARDS, H., *Die Entwicklung des Problems der Willensfreiheit bei Philipp Melanchthon* (Unpublished Dr. phil. Dissertation: University of Bonn, 1955)
GERZAGUET, J.-P., *L'Abbaye d'Anchin de sa fondation (1079) au XIVème siècle* (Lille/Arras, 1997)
GRABES, H., *Das englische Pamphlet: Politische und religiöse Polemik am Beginn der Neuzeit (1521-1640)* (Tübingen, 1990)

GREGORY, B. S., *Salvation at Stake: Christian Martyrdom in Early Modern Europe* (Cambridge MA: Harvard Historical Studies 134, 1999)

GRENZMANN, L. and STACKMANN, K. (edd. et al.), *Literatur und Laienbildung im Spätmittelalter und in der Reformationszeit* (Stuttgart: Germanistische Symposien V, 1984)

GUILDAY, P., *The English Catholic refugees on the continent, 1558-1795, Récueil de traveaux, 1ère série 39* (Leuven, 1914)

HAIGH, C., *English Reformations—Religion, Politics and Society under the Tudors* (Oxford, 1993)

———, (ed. et al.), *The English Reformation revised* (Cambridge, 1987)

HARDWICK, C. (ed.), *A History of the Articles of Religion* (London, 1851)

HARVEY, B. F., *Westminster Abbey and its Estates in the Middle Ages* (Oxford, 1977)

HASE, K. von, *Handbuch der protestantischen Polemik gegen die römisch-katholische Kirche,* (Leipzig, [5]1890)

HAYNES, S., *A collection of State Papers, relating to the affairs in the reigns of King Henry VIII, King Edward VI, Queen Mary, and Queen Elizabeth, from the year 1542 to 1570* (London, 1740)

HEATH, P., *The English Parish Clergy on the Eve of the Reformation* (London, 1969)

HEBERDEN, C. B. (ed.), *Brasenose College Register, 1509-1909* (Oxford: Oxford Historical Society Old Series 55, 1909)

HENHOVE, K. de le, *Relations politiques des Pays-Bas et de l'Angleterre sous le règne de Philippe II* (Brussel, 1882-1900)

HEINZ, J., *Justification and Merit: Luther versus Catholicism* (Berrien Springs MI, 1984)

HENNESSY, G. L., *Novum Repertorium Parochiale Londinense* (London, 1889)

HERMESDORF, B. H. D., *Wigle van Aytta van Zwichem. Hoogeleraar en rechtsgeleerd schrijver* (Leiden, 1949)

HOLISHED, R., *Chronicles of England, Scotland and Ireland* (London, 1807-1808)

HSIA, R. P.-Ch., *The World of Catholic Renewal 1540-1770* (Cambridge, 1998)

HUMPHREY, L., *J. Juelli Episcopi Sarisb. vita et mors, ejusque verae doctrinae defensio* (London, 1573)

IMRAY, J., *The Charity of Richard Whittington* (London, 1968)

———, *The Mercers' Hall* (London, 1991)

ISERLOH, E., *Die Eucharistie in der Darstellung des Johannes Eck* (Münster: Religionsgeschichtliche Studien und Texte 73, 1950)

———, *Gnade und Eucharistie in der philosophischen Theologie des Wilhelm von Ockham* (Wiesbaden, 1956)

ISERLOH, E. (ed. et al.), *Katholische Theologen der Reformationszeit I-IV* (Münster, 1984-1987)

ISRAEL, J. I., *The Dutch Republic, 1477-1808* (Oxford, 1995)

JAPPE ALBERTS, W., *Geschiedenis van de beiden Limburgen* (Assen, 1964)

JEDIN, H., *Des Johannes Cochläus Streitschrift De libero arbitrio hominis (1525)* (Breslau, 1927)

JONGH, H. de, *L'ancienne faculté de theologie de Louvain au premier siècle de son existence (1432-1540): ses debuts, son organisation, son ensignement, sa lutte contre Ersame et Luther, avec des documents inédits* (Utrecht, 1980)

JUNGMANN, E., *Die politische Rhetorik in der englischen Renaissance* (Hamburg, 1960)

KELLY, J. N. D., *Jerome: His Life, Writings and Controversies* (London, 1975)
——, *Early Christian Doctrines* (London, ³1993)
KLAIBER, W. (ed.), *Katholische Kontroverstheologen und Reformer des 16. Jahrhunderts: Ein Werkverzeichnis* (Münster: Reformationsgeschichtliche Studien und Texte 116, 1978)
KNIGHTON, Ch. S., *Collegiate Foundations 1540-1570, with special reference to St Peter in Westminster* (Unpublished Ph.D. dissertation: University of Cambridge, 1975)
KOK, J. A. de, *Nederland op de brenklijn Rome-Reformatie* (Assen, 1964)
KRIEGER, C, and LIENHARD, M. (edd. et al.), *Martin Bucer and Sixteenth-Century Europe: Actes du colloque de Strasbourg (28-31 août 1991)* (Leiden: Brill Studies in Medieval and Reformation Thought 52-53, 1993)
KUNZLER, M., *Die Eucharistietheologie des Hadamarer Pfarrers und Humanisten Gehard Lorich* (Münster, 1981)
LAMBERT, M. D., *Medieval Heresy: popular movements from the Gregorian Reform to the Reformation* (Oxford, 1992)
LAMBERTS, E. (ed.), *De Universiteit te Leuven 1425-1985* (Leuven, 1988)
LANGE, D. (ed. et al.), *Überholte Verurteilungen? Die Gegensätze in der Lehre von Rechtfertigung, Abendmahl und Amt zwischen dem Konzil von Trient und der Reformation* (Göttingen, 1991)
LEA, H. Ch., *History of Sacerdotal Celibacy* (New York NY, 1966)
LECHAT, R., *Les refugiés anglais dans le Pays-Bas espagnols durant le règne d'Elisabeth, 1558-1613* (Leuven, 1914)
LITZENBERGER, C. J., *The English Reformation and the laity: Gloucestershire, 1540-1580* (Cambridge, 1997)
LOADES, D., *Politics, Censorship and the English Reformation* (London, 1991)
LOWERS, J. K., *Mirrors for Rebels: A Study of Polemical Literature* (Berkeley and Los Angeles CA, 1953)
MACDONALD, A. J., *Berengar and the Reform of Sacramental Doctrine* (London, 1930)
MACCULLOCH, D., *Thomas Cranmer: A Life* (New Haven CT and London, 1996)
——, *Tudor Church Militant: Edward VI and the Protestant Reformation* (London, 1999)
——, (ed.), *The reign of Henry VIII: politics, policy and piety* (Basingstoke, 1995)
MCGRATH, A. E., *Iustitia Dei: A history of the Christian doctrine of Justification – The Beginnings to the Reformation* (Cambridge, 1993)
——, *Luther's Theology of the Cross. Martin Luther's theological breakthrough* (Oxford, 1993)
MCLELLAND, J. C., *The Visible Words of God* (Edinburgh and London, 1957)
MCROBERTS, D., *Essays on the Scottish Reformation 1513-1625* (Glasgow, 1962)
MACEK, E. A., *The Loyal Opposition: Tudor Traditionalist Polemics, 1535-1558* (New York NY: Peter Lang Studies in Church History 7, 1996)
——, *The Nature of English Catholicism 1535-1558: A Study of the Intellectual and Theological Basis of the Catholic Position on the Sacrament and Justification* (Unpublished Ph.D. dissertation: University of Nebraska, Lincoln NE, 1980)
MACK, P., *Renaissance argument: Valla and Agricola in the traditions of rhetoric and dialectic* (Leiden: Brill Studies in Intellectual History 43, 1993)

MARNEF, G., *Antwerpen in de tijd van de Reformatie: Ondergronds protestantisme in een handelsmetropool 1550-1577* (Amsterdam, 1996)
MATHESON, P., *The Rhetoric of Reformation* (Edinburgh, 1998)
MAYER, Th. F., *Reginald Pole: Prince and Prophet* (Cambridge, 2000)
METZGER, B., *The Text of the New Testament: Its Transmission, Corruption and Restoration* (Oxford, 1968)
MONTCLOS, J. de, *Lanfranc et Bérenger: La controverse eucharistique du XIème siècle*, (Leuven: Spicilegium Sacrum Lovaniense 37, 1971)
MORAN, J. A. H., *The Growth of English Schooling: learning, literacy, and laicization in pre-Reformation York diocese* (Princeton NJ, 1985)
MÜLLER, J., *Martin Bucers Hermeneutik* (Gütersloh, 1965)
MULLETT, M.A., *Catholics in Britain and Ireland, 1558-1829* (Basingstoke, 1998)
MURPHY, J. J. (ed.), *Renaissance Eloquence* (Berkeley CA, 1984)
NEWCOURT, R., *Repertorium ecclesiasticum parochiale Londinense: An ecclesiastical parochial history of the Diocese of London* (London, 1708)
OBERMAN, H. A., *Archbishop Thomas Bradwardine* (Utrecht, 1957)
——, *Spätscholastik und Reformation: Der Herbst der mittelalterlichen Theologie* (Zürich, 1965)
——, *Masters of the Reformation: The Emergence of a New Intellectual Climate in Europe* (Cambridge, 1981)
——, (ed. et al.), *Luther and the Dawn of the Modern Era* (Leiden: Brill Studies in the History of Christian Thought, 1974)
——, JAMES, F. A. (edd. et al.), *Via Augustini: Augustine in the later Middle Ages, Renaissance, and Reformation: Essays in honor of Damasus Trapp* (Leiden: Brill Studies in Medieval and Reformation Thought, 1991)
O'DAY, M. R. & HEAL, F. M. (edd.), *Continuity and Change: Personnel and Administration of the Church in England, 1500-1642* (Leicester, 1976)
OEDINGER, F. W., *Über die Bildung der Geistlichen im späten Mittelalter* (Leiden, 1953)
ORMEROD, G., *The History of the County Palatinate and City of Chester* (London, 1819)
ONG, W. J., SJ, *Ramus: Method and the Decay of the Dialogue* (Cambridge MA, 1958)
PARKER, G., *The Grand Strategy of Philip II* (New Haven CT, 1998)
PARKER, T. H. L., *Commentaries on the Epistle to the Romans, 1532-1542* (Edinburgh, 1986)
PARSONS, R., *A treatise of three conuersions of England from Paganisme to Christian Religion* (St Omer, 1603-1604)
PAQUET, J. N., *Fasti academici Lovaniensi, Analectes pour servir à l'histoire ecclésiastique de la Belgique* (Leuven, 1881)
PÉRINELLE, J., OP, *L'Attrition d'après le Concile de Trente et d'après Saint Thomas d'Aquin* (Paris, 1927)
PESCH, O. H., *Theologie der Rechtfertigung bei Martin Luther und Thomas von Aquin* (Mainz, 1967)
PETER, V. J., *The doctrine of Ruard Tapper (1487-1559) regarding original sin and justification* (Unpublished Ph.D. dissertation: Pontificia Studiorum Universitas a S. Thoma Aquino in urbe, Rome, 1965)
PETTEGREE, A., *Calvinism in Europe, 1540-1620* (Cambridge, 1996)

PFNÜR, V., *Einig in der Rechtfertigungslehre? Die Rechtfertigungslehre der Confessio Augustana (1530) und die Stellungnahme der katholischen Kontroverstheologen zwischen 1530 und 1535* (Wiesbaden, 1970)

PHILIPS, G., *L'Union personelle avec le Dieu vivant: Essai sur l'origine et le sens de la grâce créée* (Leuven: Bibliotheca Ephemeridum Theologicarum Lovaniensium 36, 1989)

PIETRI, Ch. (et al.); TRENAR, L. (ed. in chief), *Histoire des Pays-Bas français: Flandres, Artois, Hainaut, Boulannais, Cambrésis* (Toulons, 1984)

PINEAS, R., *Thomas More and Tudor Polemics* (Bloomington IN, 1968)

PITTS, J., *Ioannis Pitsei Relationum historianum de rebus anglicis* (Paris, 1619)

PLETT, H. F. (ed. et al.), *Renaissance-Rhetorik* (Berlin, 1993)

PONCHEVILLE, A. M. de, *Les vieilles provinces de France: Histoire d'Artois* (Paris, 1935)

POSTINA, A., *Der Karmelit Eberhard Billick* (Freiburg, 1901)

POSTMA, F., *Viglius van Aytta als humanist en diplomaat 1507-1549* (Zutphen, 1983)

——, *Viglius van Aytta. De jaren met Granvelle 1549-1564* (Zutphen, 2000)

RAM, P. F. X. de, *De laudibus quibus veteres Lovaniensium Theologi efferi possunt* (Leuven, 1848)

——, *Mémoire sur la part que le clergé de Belgique, et spécialement les docteurs de l'université de Louvain, ont prise au Concile de Trente* (Brussel: Nouveaux mémoires de l'Académie royale 14/17, 1841)

RAUSCH, G., *Douai: Kultur- und kunstgeschichtliche Studien in Nordfrankreich* (Heidelberg, 1917)

REGINALDUS, A., *De mente sancti Concilii Tridentini circa gratiam se ipsa efficacem, opus posthumus. Accesserunt animadversiones in XXV propositiones P. Ludovici Molinae, auctore Jacobo Le Bossu, et alternae epistolae Petri Soto, Ruardi Tapperi et Judoci Ravestein de gratiae et liberi arbitrii concordia* (Antwerpen, 1706)

REX, R. A. W., *The Theology of John Fisher* (Cambridge, 1991)

——, *Henry VIII and the English Reformation* (Basingstoke, 1993)

RODRÍGUEZ-SALGADO, J. H. (ed.), *The changing face of empire: Charles V, Philip II and Habsburg authority, 1551-1559* (Cambridge, 1988)

ROSSMANN, J. & RATZINGER, J. (edd.), *Mysterium der Gnade* (Regensburg, 1975)

RÖSSNER, M. B., *Konrad Braun—ein katholischer Jurist, Politiker, Kontroverstheologe und Kirchenreformer im konfessionellen Zeitalter* (Münster, 1991)

ROUCHE, M. (ed.), *Histoire de Douai* (Condé-sur-l'Escaut, 1998)

RUMMEL, E., *Erasmus' 'Annotations' on the New Testament: From Philologist to Theologian* (Toronto ON, 1986)

RYDER, A., SCJ, *The Eucharistic Doctrine of Richard Smith: Excerpta ex dissertatione ad Lauream in Facultate Theologiae Pontificiae Universitatis Gregorianae* (Unpublished Ph.D. dissertation: Pontificia Università Gregoriana, Rome, 1970)

SAMUEL-SCHEYDER, M., *Johannes Cochlaeus: Humaniste et Adversaire de Luther* (Nancy, 1993)

SÁNCHEZ, J. (ed.), *For Love alone: Reflections on priestly celibacy* (Maynooth, 1993)

SANDER, N., *The rise and growth of the Anglican Schism* (London, 1877)

SANDERSON, M. H. R., *Cardinal of Scotland, David Beaton, c. 1494-1546* (Edinburgh, 1986)

SCARISBRICK, J. J., *The conservative Episcopate in England, 1529-1535* (Unpublished Ph.D. dissertation: University of Cambridge)
——, *Henry VIII* (New Haven CT, ²1997)
SCHÖFFER, I. (ed.), *De lage landen van 1500 tot 1780* (Amsterdam, 1978)
SPARKS, H. F. D. (ed.), *Novum Testamentum secundum editionem s. Hieronymi I-III* (Oxford, 1889-1959)
STARKEY, D. R., *The Reign of Henry VIII: Personalities and Politics* (London, 1985)
STEPHENS, W. P., *The Theology of Huldrych Zwingli* (Oxford, 1986)
——, *The Holy Spirit in the theology of Martin Bucer* (Cambridge, 1970)
STOW, J, MORLEY, H. (ed.), *A Survey of London written in the year 1598 by John Stow, citizen of London* (Stroud, 1999)
STUIJVENBERG, J. H. van (ed.), *De economische geschiedenis van Nederland* (Groningen, 1977)
STUPPERICH, R., *Reformatorische Verkündigung und Lebensordnung, Klassiker des Protestantismus III* (Bremen, 1963)
STURM, K., *Die Theologie Peter Martyr Vermiglis während seines ersten Aufenthalts in Straßburg 1542-1547* (Neukirchen, 1971)
STRYPE, J., *Memorials of Archbishop Cranmer* (London, 1649)
——, *Ecclesiastical Memoirs relating chiefly to religion, and the reformation of it* (Oxford, 1822)
——, *Annals of the Reformation and Establishment of Religion* (Oxford, 1820-1840)
TIEMANN, B., *Buchkultur im fünfzehnten und sechzehnten Jahrhundert* (Hamburg, 1995)
TINDALE, W. (ed.), *The history and antiquities of the abbey and borough of Evesham: Compiled chiefly from MSS. in the British Museum* (London, 1794)
TRENARD, L., *De Douai à Lille: Une Université et son Histoire* (Lille, 1978)
TRUEMAN, C. R., *Luther's Legacy: Salvation and the English Reformers 1525-1556* (Oxford, 1994)
USSHER, J., *Ignatii epistolae atque martyria. Quibus praefata est de Polycarpi et Ignatij suipsis Usserij dissertatio* (Oxford, 1643)
VAN DER VELDE, J. F., *Recherches historiques sur l'érection, constitution, droits et privilèges de l'Université de Louvain* (No Place, 1788-1789)
VAN UYTEN, R. (ed.), *Leuven 'de beste stad van Brabant'. Geschiedenis van het stadsgewest Leuven tot omstreeks 1600* (Leuven, 1980)
VERHOPSTAD, K. J. W., *De regering der Nederlanden in de jaren 1555-1559* (Nijmegen, 1937)
VERNULAEUS, N., LANGENDONCK, Ch. Van (ed.), *Academia Lovaniensis libri III. Eius origo, incrementum, forma, magistratus, privilegia, scholae, viri illustres, res gestae* (Leuven, 1667)
VIVES, WATSON, F., (tr.), *Vives: On Education* (Cambridge, 1913)
WATNEY, J., *Some account of the hospital of St Thomas of Acorn, in the Cheap, London, and of the Mercers' Company* (London, 1892)
WICKS, J., SJ (ed.), *Cajetan responds. A reader in Reformation Controversy* (Washington DC, 1978)
WIEDERMANN, G., *Der Reformator Alexander Alesius als Ausleger der Psalmen* (Dr. theol. Dissertation: Universität Erlangen-Nürnberg, Erlangen, 1988)

WILS, J. (et al.), *Le cinquième centenaire de la Faculté de Théologie de l'Universié de Louvain (1432-1932)* (Brugge, 1932)

WOOD, A. à, *Athenae Oxonienses: An exact History of all the Writers and Bishops who have had their Education in the University of Oxford* (Oxford, 1813-1820)

———, *The History and Antiquity of the Colleges and halls in the University of Oxford* (Oxford, 1786)

———, BLISS, P. (ed.), *Fasti Oxonienses* (London, 1815-1820)

WIERINGA, F. (ed.), *Republiek tussen vorsten* (Zutphen, 1984)

3.2. SECONDARY LITERATURE: ARTICLES

ALEXANDER, G., 'Bonner and the Marian persecutions', in HAIGH, C. (ed. et al.), *The English Reformation revised* (Cambridge, 1987) 157-175

ALLGEIER, A., OP, 'Les commentaires de Cajétan sur les Psaumes. Contribution à l'histoire de l'exégèse avant le Concile de Trente', *Revue Thomiste* 39 (1934-1935), 410-443

BACKUS, I., 'Renaissance Attitude to New Testament Apocryphal Writings: Jacques Lefèvre d'Etaples and his Epigones', *Renaissance Quarterly* 51 (1998), 1169-1198

———, 'Martin Bucer and the Patristic Tradition', in KRIEGER, C. and LIENHARD, M. (edd. et al.), *Martin Bucer and Sixteenth-Century Europe: Actes du colloque de Strasbourg (28-31 août 1991)* (Leiden: Brill Studies in Medieval and Reformation Thought 52-53, Leiden, 1993), 1.55-69

BÄUMER, R., 'Johannes Cochlaeus und die Reform der Kirche', in BÄUMER, R. (ed. et al.), *Reformatio Ecclesiae: Beiträge zu kirchlichen Reformbemühungen von der alten Kirche bis zur Neuzeit* (Paderborn, 1980), 333-354

BOSSY, J., 'The Counter-Reformation and the People of Catholic Europe', *Past & Present* 47 (1970), 52-67

BRECHT, M., 'Der rechtfertigende Glaube an das Evangelium von Jesus Christus als Mitte von Luthers Theologie', *Zeitschrift für Kirchengeschichte* 89 (1978), 45-77

CAPLAN, H., 'The Four Senses of Scriptural Interpretation', *Speculum* 4 (1929), 282-90; 1-13

CHADWICK, H., 'Ego Berengarius', *Journal for Theological Studies New Series* 40 (1989), 414-445

COLLINS, T. A., 'Cardinal Cajetan's Fundamental Biblical Principles', *Catholic Biblical Quarterly* 17 (1955), 363-378

COOPER, Th., 'Smith, Richard, DD. 1500-1563', in *Dictionary of National Biography* (Oxford, 1897), 53.101

CHRISMAN, M., 'From Polemic to Propaganda: The Development of Mass Persuasion in the Late Sixteenth Century', *Archive for Reformation History* 73 (1982), 175-195

DASCAL, M., 'Types of Polemics and Types of Polemical Moves', in CMEJRKOVÁ, S. (ed. et al.), *Dialoganalyse VI/1* (Tübingen: Beiträge zur Dialogforschung 16, 1998), 15-33

FEARNS, J., 'Peter von Bruis und die religiöse Bewegung des 12. Jahrhunderts', *Archiv für Kulturgeschichte* 48 (1996), 331-335

FLETCHER, J. M., 'The Faculty of Arts', in CATTO, J. I. (ed. et al.), *The History of the University of Oxford: The Early Oxford Schools* (Oxford, 1984), 367-399

GIBSON, M. T., 'The place of the Glossa ordinaria in medieval Exegesis', in JORDAN, M. D. and EMERY, K. (edd. et al.), *Ad Litteram: Authoritative Texts and their medieval Readers* (Notre Dame IN, 1992), 5-27

GUILDAY, P., 'The English Catholic refugees at Louvain, 1559-1575—Vatican Library, MS Regina 2020, fol. 445-446', in *Mélanges Ch. Moeller* (Leuven-Paris, 1914), 2.175-189

HÉLIOT, P., 'Quelques moments disparus de la Flandre wallone: l'Abbaye d'Anchin, les Collégiales Saint-Pierre et Saint Amé de Douai', *Revue Belge d'Archéologie et d'Histoire* 28, (1959), 129-173

HORST, U., OP, 'Der Streit um die Heilige Schrift zwischen Kardinal Cajetan und Ambrosius Catharinus', in SCHEFFCZYK, L., (ed. et al.), *Wahrheit und Verkündigung* (München, 1967), 1.551-1.577

ISERLOH, E., 'Der tridentinische Meßopferdekret in seinen Beziehungen zu der Kontroverstheologie der Zeit', in *Il Concilio di Trento e la Riforma tridentina: atti del Convegno storico internazionale, Trento—2-6 settembre 1963* (Rome, 1965), 401-439

ISRAEL, J. I., 'Spanje en de Nederlandse opstand', in WIERINGA, F. (ed. et al.), *Republiek tussen vorsten* (Zutphen, 1984), 51-60

JEDIN, H., 'Wo sah die vortridentinische Kirche die Lehrdifferenzen zu Luther?', *Catholica* 21 (1967), 85-100

——, 'An welchen Gegensätzen sind die vortridentinischen Religionsgespräche zwischen Katholiken und Protestanten gescheitert?' *Theologie und Glaube* 48 (1958), 50-55

JONGE, H. J. de, 'Novum Testamentum a nobis versum: The Essence of Erasmus' edition of the New Testament', *Journal of Theological Studies* 35 (1984), 394-400

KATTERMANN, G., 'Luthers Handexemplar des antijüdischen Porchetus in der Landesbibliothek Karlsruhe',. *Zentralblatt für Bibliothekswesen* 55 (1938), 42-52

KEEN, R., 'The Arguments and Audiences of Cochlaeus's Philippica VII', *Catholic Historical Review* 78 (1992), 371-391

——, 'Political Authority and Ecclesiology in Melanchthon's *De Ecclesiae Authoritate*', *Church History* 65 (1996)

LAGRANGE, M.-J., OP, 'La Critique Textuelle avant le Concile de Trente', *Revue Thomiste* 39 (1934), 400-409

LEURIDAN, Th .II. J., 'Richard Smith', in *Les théologiens de Douai XI, Extrait de la revue des Sciences Ecclésiastiques* 1904

LEADER, D. R., 'Teaching in Tudor Cambridge', *History of Education* 13 (1984), 215-231

LOACH, J., 'Pamphlets and Politics, 1553-1558', *Bulletin of the Institute for Historical Research* 48 (1975), 31-44

——, 'Reformation Controversies', in MCCONICA, J. (ed.), *The History of the University of Oxford: The Collegiate University* (Oxford, 1986), 363-396

——, 'The function of ceremonial in the reign of Henry VIII', *Past & Present* 142 (1994), 43-68
LOGAN, D. F., 'The Origins of the so-called Regius Professorships: An Aspect of the Renaissance in Oxford and Cambridge', in BAKER, D. (ed.), *Studies in Church History XIV: Renaissance and Renewal in Christian History* (Oxford, 1977, 271-278)
LÖWE, J. A., 'Richard Smyth and the Foundation of the University of Douai', *Nederlands Archief voor Kerkgeschiedenis/Dutch Review of Church History* 79 II (1999), 142-169
——, '"The bodie and bloud of Christ is not carnallie and corporallie in the bread and wine": The Oxford Disputation revisited—Zwinglian traits in the Eucharistic Theology of Pietro Martire Vermigli', in SCHINDLER, A. (ed. et al.), *Die Zürcher Reformation: Ausstrahlungen und Rückwirkungen* (Bern, 2000), 317-326
——, 'Smyth (Smythaeus, Smythus), Richard (1499-1563)', *New Dictionary of National Biography* (Oxford, 2004 [forthcoming])
MACEK, E. A., 'Richard Smith: Tudor Cleric in Defense of Traditional Belief and Practice', *Catholic Historical Review* 72 (1986), 383-402
MCSORLEY, 'Was Gabriel Biel a semi-Pelagian?', in H. J., SCHEFFCZYK, L. (ed. et al.), *Wahrheit und Verkündigung* (München, 1967), 2.1109-2.1120
MARSHALL, P., 'The Debate over 'Unwritten Verities' in Early Reformation England', in GORDON, B. (ed. et al.), *Protestant History and Identity in Sixteenth-Century Europe: The Medieval Identity* (Aldershot, 1996), 1.60-1.77
MEERHOFF, K., 'The Significance of Philip Melanchthon's Rhetoric in the Renaissance', in MACK, P. (ed.), *Renaissance Rhetoric* (Basingstoke, 1994), 46-62
NUFFEL, E. van, 'Leuven en Douai. De "splitsing" van 1562', *Wetenschappelijke Tijdingen* 24 (1964-1965), 473-480
OBERMAN, H. A., 'Facientibus quod in se est Deus non denegat gratiam', *Harvard Theological Review* 55 (1962), 317-42
——, '"Iustitia Christi" and "Iustitia Dei". Luther and the Scholastic Doctrines of Justification', *Harvard Theological Review* 55 (1966), 1-26
——, 'Das tridentinische Rechtfertigungsdekret im Lichte der spätmittelalterlichen Theologie', *Zeitschrift für Theologie und Kirche* 61 (1964), 251-282
——, 'Wittenbergs Zweifrontenkrieg gegen Prierias und Eck. Hintergrund und Entscheidungen des Jahres 1518', *Zeitschrift für Kirchengeschichte* 80 (1969), 331-358
——, 'Headwaters of the Reformation: Initia Lutheri—Initia Reformationis', in OBERMAN, H. A. (ed. et al.), *Luther and the Dawn of the Modern Era* (Leiden: Brill Studies in the History of Christian Thought, 1974), 40-88
PARISH, H., '"Beastly is their living and their doctrine": Celibacy and Theological Corruption in English Reformation Polemic', in GORDON, B. (ed. et al.), *Protestant History and Identity in Sixteenth-Century Europe: The Medieval Identity* (Aldershot, 1996), 1.138-1.152

PESCH, O. H., 'Die Lehre vom 'Verdienst' als Problem für Theologie und Verkündigung', in SCHEFFCZYK, L. (ed. et al.), *Wahrheit und Verkündigung* (München, 1967), 2.1898

PINEAS, R., 'Polemical Technique in Thomas More's "The Answere to ... the Poynesened Booke"', in MURPHY, C. M., GIBEAUD, H., DI CESARE, M. A. (edd. et al.), *Miscellanea Moreana: Essays for Germain Marc'hadour* (Binghampton NY, 1989), 385-393

PFNÜR, V., 'Zur Verurteilung der reformatorischen Rechtfertigungslehre auf dem Konzil von Trient', *Annuarium historicae conciliorum* 8 (1976), 407-428

POSTMA, F., 'Viglius van Ayttas kirchenpolitische Haltung in den Niederlanden unter Maria von Ungarn und in der Frühzeit Philipps II. (bis 1566)', in SICKEN, B. (ed. et al.), *Herrschaft und Verfassungsstrukturen im Nordwesten des Reiches. Beiträge zum Zeitalter Karls V.* (Köln, 1994), 179-204

REDWORTH, G., 'A Study in the Formulation of Policy: The Genesis and Evaluation of the Acts of Six Articles', *Journal of Ecclesiastical History* 37 (1986), 42-67

REUSENS, E., 'Statuts primitifs de la Faculté de theologie', *Annuaire de l'Université Catholique de Louvain*, 1881, 380

——, 'Calendrier de la faculté de theologie de notre ancienne université, datant de l'origine même de la faculté (1435 environ)', *Annuaire de l'Université Catholique de Louvain*, 1881, 461

REIFFENBERG, K. de, 'Mémoires sur les deux premiers siècles de l'Université de Louvain', *Nouveau mémorires de l'Academie des sciences et belles lettres de Bruxelles*, V (1829), 44; VII (1832), 43; X (1837), 27

REX, R. A. W., 'The Polemical Theologian', in DUFFY, E., BRADSHAW, B. (edd. et al.), *Humanism, Reform and the Reformation: The Career of Bishop John Fisher* (Cambridge, 1989), 109-130

SAMUEL-SCHEYDER, M., 'Johannes Cochlaeus et Martin Bucer itinéraires croisés et controverse religieuse', *Etudes Germaniques* 50 (1995), 467-490

SCHULZE, M., 'Martin Luther and the Church Fathers', in BACKUS, I. (ed.et al.), *The Reception of the Church Fathers in the West from the Carolingians to the Maurists* (Leiden, 1997), 2.573-626

SMALLEY, B., 'Stephen Langton and the Four Senses of Scripture', *Speculum* 6 (1931), 60-76

STIERLE, B., 'Schriftauslegung der Reformationszeit', *Verkündigung und Forschung* 16 (1971), 55-88

STILTINCK, J., 'An verisimile sit, S. Paphnutium se in Concilio Nicaeno opposuisse legi de continentia Sacerdotum et Diaconorum', in *Acta Sanctorum Septembris* (Venice, 1761)

SYPHER, G. W., '"Faisant ce qu'il leur vient à plaisir": The Image of Protestantism in French Catholic Polemic on the Eve of the Religious Wars', *Sixteenth Century Journal* 11 (1980), 59-84

TAYLOR, L. J., 'The Influence of Humanism on Post-Reformation Catholic preachers in France', *Renaissance Quarterly* 50 (1997), 119-135

VACCARI, A., SJ, 'Cardinalis Cajetanus Sacrarum Litterarum studiosum', *Verbum Domini* 14 (1934), 321-472

VOSTÉ, I.-M., OP, 'Cardinalis Caietanus Sacrae Scripturae interpres', *Angelicum* 11 (1934), 446-513

——, 'Cardinalis Caietanus in VT praecipue in Hexamaëron', *Angelicum* 12 (1935), 305-332

VICKERS, B., 'Some reflections on the Rhetoric Textbook', in MACK, P. (ed.), *Renaissance Rhetoric* (Basingstoke, 1994), 81-102

WABUDA, S., 'Fruitful preaching in the diocese of Worcester: Bishop Hugh Latimer and his influence, 1535—1539', in CARLSON, E. J. (ed.), *Religion and the English People, 1500—1640* (Kirksville, MO, 1998), 49-74

WERBECK, W., 'Valor et applicatio missae. Wert und Zuwendung der Messe im Anschluß an Johannes Duns Scotus', *Zeitschrift für Theologie und Kirche* 69 (1972), 175

WINCKELMANN, F., 'Paphnutius, der Bekenner und Bischof', in NAGEL, P. (ed. et al.), *Probleme der koptischen Literatur* (Halle-Wittenberg, 1968), 145-153

ZUMKELLER, A, OSA, 'Konrad Treger's Disputation Theses of 1521', in OBERMAN, H. A., JAMES, F. (edd. et al.), *Via Augustini: Augustine in the later Middle Ages, Renaissance, and Reformation: Essays in honor of Damasus Trapp* (Leiden: Brill Studies in Medieval and Reformation Thought, 1991), 130-141

INDICES

NAME INDEX

a Pictavia, Guilelmus, *see*: Poitiers, Guillaume de
Aaron 35n, 38, 105n, 193, 196n
ab Ulmis, Johannes 41n
Abraham (Abram) 188n
Adam 110-111
Agricola, Rudolph 85, 107
Alesius, Alexander, *see*: Allan, Alexander
Allan, Alexander 23
Allen, William Cardinal, *Protector of the English Mission* 74-75
Ambrose of Milan 126n, 140n, 204, 218
Andreas, Valerius 44
Antichrist 154, 192n, 193n, 226, 237
Aquinas, Thomas 11, 97-98, 100-102, 104-105, 110n, 111, 113, 116, 123, 176-178, 180n, 184, 205n
Aragon, Katherine of, *see*: Katherine of Aragon
Aristotle 85
Armstrong, Colin xi
Askew, Anne 33-34
Augustine of Hippo (Austen) 37, 110, 126, 131, 135-136, 140n, 161n, 178, 207, 210, 217-218, 224
Ayris, Paul xii
Aytta, Viglius van, *see*: Viglius van Aytta
Babington, Francis 67
Bale, John 225n
Bar, François de, OSB, *Grand Prior of Anchin Abbey* 79, 81-85, 89-90, 96, 101, 104-107
Barron, Caroline xi
Basil the Great 204n
Baumann, Michael xi
Beaton, David Cardinal, *Archbishop of St Andrew's* 49
Bellarmine, Robert, SJ 151
Berengar of Tours 176, 181
Bessarion, Cardinal 204
Bessemer, Adriaan, *Lecturer of Theology, Douai University* 79, 82

Bewliam, Thomas 28
Beza, Theodore, *see*: Bèze, Theodore de
Bèze, Theodore de 86n
Biel, Gabriel 8, 11, 90n, 114-115, 124n, 125n, 132, 176, 180, 182-183, 186, 188
Billick, Eberhard, OCC, *German Provincial Carmelite Order* 146, 148
Boacher, Joan 35n
Bogardus, Johannes, *Leuven printer* 67n, 229
Bonaventure 112-113
Bonmarcheit, Jacques de, *see*: de Bonmarcheit, Jacques
Bonner, Edmund, *Bishop of London* 5-6, 26, 30, 33-34, 45, 52-54, 226n, 231
Bornstra, Wilbrand, *Lecturer of Classics, Douai University* 69-70
Bouche, Jean, *Lecturer of Theology, Douai University* 79, 82
Brenz, Johannes 218, 227n
Bretton, Henry 49
Bruys, Peter de, *see*: Peter de Bruys
Bucer, Martin 10, 40, 45-46, 48, 75n, 148, 158n, 211n
Bullinger, Heinrich 41n, 47, 87n, 88, 149
Byrne, Lavinia xi
Cajetan, Thomas de Vio Cardinal 82-83, 91-92, 94, 101-103, 105, 107, 120n
Calvin, John 155, 161, 175, 219, 234
Campi, Emidio xi
Cannell, Gill xii
Cano, Melchior 85
Canterbury, Archbishops of, *see*: Cranmer, Thomas; Grindal, Edmund; Parker, Matthew; Pole, Reginald Cardinal
Carlile, Christopher
Cartwright, Nicholas 22n
Castello, Albert de 93n

Catharinus, Ambrosius 97
Cawson, Thomas 53
Chadwick, Owen xi
Charles V, *Holy Roman Emperor* 60
Chaudière, Regnault, *Paris Printer* 211
Chedsey, William, *President of Corpus Christi College Oxford* 21, 43, 233
Chrysostom 88
Cicero 76, 178
Clement of Alexandria 204n
Clement of Rome 204
Clement VII (Guilio de' Medici), *Pope* 97
Clichtovaeus, Jodocus, *see*: Clichtove, Josse
Clichtove, Josse (Joost), *Professor of Divinity, Sorbonne* 120n, 147
Clopton, Hugh, *Alderman and Master Mercer* 25
Cochlaeus (Dobeneck), Johannes 8, 120n, 139, 140n, 142, 182-183, 184n
Cole, Arthur, *President of Magdalen College Oxford* 43n
Cole, Henry, *Provost of Eton College* 55
Company of Mercers 24-26, 32
Cooper, Thomson 13-15, 17
Cornwels, Hugh (Hugo), *Leuven Printer* 45
Cospeau, Louis, *Lecturer of Classics, Douai University* 70
Cotes, George, *Master of Balliol College Oxford* 22n, 29
Courthop, James, *Canon of Christ Church Cathedral* 43n
Cox, Richard, *Chancellor of Oxford University* 41, 52, 233
Cranmer, Thomas, *Archbishop of Canterbury* 2, 43n, 45, 47-50, 54-56, 175, 198, 210-213, 214n, 215, 217, 225-226, 231-232, 234
Cromwell, Thomas, *16th Earl of Essex* 28, 84
Cyprian 131, 204n, 210
d'Etaples, Jacques Lefèvre 93n, 94n, 97n
Daniel 192, 194
David, *King* 38n, 193
de Bar, François, *see*: Bar, François de
de Bonmarcheit, Jacques 62n

de Castello, Albert, *see*: Castello, Albert de
de France, Jérôme, *Conseilleur pensionnaire* 62, 67-68
de Taylour, Philip and Sabina, *see*: Taylor, Philip and Sabina
de Vendeville, Jean, *Professor of Theology, Douai University* 75
Dietenberger, Johannes, *Professor of Divinity, Mainz University* 120n
Dobeneck, Johannes, *see*: Cochlaeus, Johannes
Döllinger, Ignatz von 147n, 148n
Dorman, Thomas 216n
Dubois, Jean 77n, 80
Dubuisson, Jean, *Principal of the Collège du Roi, Douai* 69
Duffy, Eamon xi, 226
Duns Scotus, John, *see*: Scotus, John Duns
Eck, Johannes 8, 127, 182-183, 185-199, 203, 223
Edward III, *King of England* 24n
Edward VI, *King of England* 34, 41, 44
Elizabeth I, *Queen of England* 7, 57, 74
Engammare, Max xii
England, Kings of, *see*: Edward III; Edward VI; Henry IV, Henry VIII; Philip II; Richard II
England, Queens of, *see*: Elizabeth I; Jane Seymour; Katherine of Aragon; Mary I
Enoch 92
Epo, Boetois, *Lecturer in Canon Law, Douai University* 68n
Erasmus of Rotterdam, *see*: Erasmus, Desiderus
Erasmus, Desiderus 9, 44, 82, 91n, 93-94, 97, 101
Eusebius Emissenus 204
Feckenham, John, *Dean of St Paul's, Abbot of Westminster* 53
Ferrarius, Johannes, *Lecturer of Classics, Douai University* 69
Field, Edward, *Master of Whittington College* 24
Fisher, John, *Bishop of Rochester* 8, 11, 32, 85n, 99, 118n, 122n, 125n, 127, 132, 133n, 142, 183-186, 200-201, 203-207

NAME INDEX

Foxe, John 29, 31, 55
Foxe, Edward, *Provost of King's College* 4n
France, Jérôme de, *see* de France, Jérôme
Fraternitas Sanctae Sophiae 26
Frith, John 175-176, 185, 201, 205, 217, 222-223, 234
Galatinus, Petrus, OFM 191
Gardiner, Stephen, *Bishop of Winchester* 4-6, 34, 36, 49, 146, 203n, 211n, 224n, 234n
Ghinucci, Geronimo, *Bishop of Worcester* 18
Granvelle, Antoine Perrenot Cardinal de, *Archbishop of Mechelen* 63, 66, 176, 227
Gravius, Bartholomaeus, *Leuven printer* 67n, 81n
Greengrass, Mark xii
Gregory Nazianzen 204n
Gregory of Nyssa 204n
Gregory the Great 217
Gregory, Brad 235, 237
Grindal, Edmund, *Archbishop of Canterbury* 57n
Gruisbeck, Gerard, *Dean of Liège and coadjutor to the Prince-Bishop of Liège* 66
Gutenberg, Johannes, *Mainz printer* 92
Hackett, John, *Bishop of Lichfield* 97
Haigh, Christopher 73
Haliburton, David, *Provost of Methven* 48-49
Hamilton, John, *Archbishop of St Andrew's* 49
Harding, Thomas 73, 216n
Harpsfield, Nicholas, *Vicar-General of London* 53-54
Hastings, John 22n
Heinz, Johann 114
Henrici, Johannes, *see* Mensing, Johann
Henry IV, *King of England* 24n
Henry VIII, *King of England* 2-7, 22-23, 28, 33-34, 65n, 176, 183-184, 185n, 204
Henshaw, Henry 73
Herborn, Nikolaus, OFM 147
Hessels, Jan, *Professor of Theology, Leuven University* 67n

Heydok, Gilbert 26
Highbe, Thomas 53
Hilary 204n
Hodgekynne, John, *Suffragan bishop of London* 32, 34
Hondt, Philip Nicholai de 63
Hopton, Walter 231
Hosdein, Philip van, *see* van Hosdein, Philip
Hugh of Saint-Victor 112
Hurnonsey, John 22n
Hus, Jan 176
Hussgen, Johannes, *see* Oecolampadius, Johannes
Ignatius 204
Irenaeus 204, 205n
Iscariot, Judas 214
Iserloh, Erwin 199
Isidore 82n
James of Jerusalem 168
Jane Seymour, *Queen of England* 28
Janse, Wim xi
Jedin, Hubert 117
Jerome (Hieronymus) 81, 91, 93, 140n
Jewel, John, *Bishop of Salisbury* 65, 75-76, 175, 216, 219, 227, 234
Joan of Kent, *see* Boacher, Joan
John Paul II, *Pope* 215n, 235n
John the Baptist 139
Joseph, Robert 19n
Katherine of Aragon, *Queen of England* 3, 23
Knox, Thomas 14
Kraemer, Matthias 148
Lambert, François 147
Lange, Dietrich 119-120
Latimer, Hugh, *Bishop of Worcester* 28, 29n, 55-56
Latomus (Le Masson), Bartholomaeus Henrici Arlunensis 146, 148
Le Masson, Bartolomé, *see* Latomus, Bartolomaeus Henrici Arlunensis
Leib, Kilian, OSA, *Prior of Rebdorf* 147
Leuridan, Canon Théodore 14
Lewis, Owen 74
Loades, David 231
Lombard, Peter 42n, 134n, 156
London, Bishops of, *see* Bonner, Edmund; Ridley, Nicholas; Stokesley, John

Luther, Martin 2, 8, 23, 97n, 110, 115-116, 118-121, 136, 155, 175-176, 181-183, 185, 190, 192, 195, 196-197, 217, 219, 222-223, 234
MacCulloch, Diarmaid 76, 213, 234
Macek, Ellen 15-16, 76, 137
Malachi 190-192, 194
Malary, Thomas 30-31
Mallebranque, Pierre 62n
Margaret, Duchess of Parma, *illegitimate daughter of Charles V, royal regent in the Netherlands* 61, 63, 66, 71, 74, 76, 95
Marnef, Guido xi
Marshal, John 74
Martyr, Peter, *see:* Vermigli, Pietro Martire
Mary I, *Queen of England* 2-3, 51-52, 65n
Mary, Blessed Virgin 77, 168, 180n, 201
Masone, Sir John 48
Matheson, Peter 222, 235
Melanchthon, Philipp 6, 23, 85, 109-110, 119, 121, 123-125, 130-131, 138, 140, 175, 218, 228-229, 234
Melchizedek, *King of Salem* 35, 38, 188-189, 193-194
Mensing (Henrici), Johann, OP, *Suffragan bishop of Halberstadt* 120n
Middleton, Richard of, *see:* Richard of Middleton
Montois, Jean Cospcau, *Professor of Classics, Douai University* 69
More, Thomas 184, 203n, 223
Mosellanus, Petrus (Peter) 86n, 107
Moses 133, 169, 196
Musculus, Wolfgang 175, 218, 234
Nestorius 201
Noah 51
Oberman, Heiko Augustinus 236
Ochino, Bernardino 40
Ockham, William 130n, 180
Oecolampadius (Hussgen), Johannes 192n, 205n
Oglethorpe, Owen, *President of Magdalen College Oxford* 22n, 34, 43n
Origen 131
Oostrel, Dom, OSB, *Prior of Anchin Abbey* 79, 82
Paphnutius, *'Bishop of Upper Thebaid'* 150-151, 162

Parker, Matthew, *Archbishop of Canterbury* 57-59
Parsons, Nicholas 212n
Pelagius (Pelagianism, Semi-Pelagianism) 111, 117, 119, 129, 137
Peter de Bruys 176, 181, 195
Petreius, Jean, *Professor of Classics, Douai University* 69
Pfnür, Vinzenz 123
Philip II, *King of Spain and England* 52, 61-62, 65n, 71, 76, 78, 95
Philips, Gérard 113
Philips, Morgan 73
Pictavia, Guillaume, *see:* Poitiers, Guillaume de
Pius IV (Giovanni Pietro Caraffa), *Pope* 67
Plato 162n
Poitiers, Guillaume de, *Provost of Furnes, Archdeacon of Famenne and Campine* 66
Pole, Reginald Cardinal, *Archbishop of Canterbury* 2, 52
Popes, *see:* Clement VII, Pius IV, John Paul II
Porchetus, Salvagus, Ord.Cart. (Porchetto de Salvatici, Victor) 190
Pseudo-Dionysius 204
Puessius, Adriaan, *Professor of Law, Douai University* 69
Purcell, John, *Bishop of Ferns* 18
Pye, William 97n
Rastell, John 216n
Rauch, Petrus von Ansbach, OP, *Suffragan bishop of Bamberg* 120n
Ravesteyn, Josse, *Censor of Leuven University* 65
Raynolds, Thomas 22n
Reuchlin, Johannes 190
Rex, Richard xi
Richard II, *King of England* 24n
Richard of Middleton 114
Richardot, François, *Bishop of Arras* 62, 65n, 69, 71, 78, 82
Ridley, Nicholas, *Bishop of London* 55-56
Rome, Bishops of, *see:* Clement VII, Pius IV, John Paul II
Rubus, Joannes, *see:* Dubuisson, Jean
Ryder, Andrew xi, 14-16

NAME INDEX

Saint-Victor, Hugh of, *see* Hugh of Saint-Victor
Sallust 176
Sander, Nicholas 73, 216n
Sanderson, Margaret 49
Satan 117, 233
Scotus, John Duns 114, 124n, 125n, 128n, 132, 179, 181-182
Seth, William 45, 231
Seton, Alexander 30, 108
Seymour, Edward, *8th Earl of Hertford, 5th Duke of Somerset* 34, 36, 212
Seymour, Jane, *see* Jane Seymour
Sigismund I, *Duke of Silesia, King of Poland*
Smyth, Richard, see Subject Index
Socrates (Scholasticus) 150
Somerset, Duke of, *see* Seymour, Edward
St Andrew's, Archbishops of, *see* Beaton, David Cardinal; Hamilton, John
Standish, Henry, *Bishop of St Davids* 32n
Standish, John, *Fellow of Whittington College* 32
Stanihurst, Richard 18n
Stapleton, Thomas 69, 74, 203n, 217n
Stapulensis, Jacobus Faber, *see* d'Etaples, Jacques Lefèvre
Stephanus, Valerius, *Leuven printer* 67n, 229
Stokesley, John, *Bishop of London* 27n
Strelley, Sir Nicholas, *Knight Commander of Berwick* 50-51
Strype, John 15, 38
Sutton, Anne xi
Syddall, Henry, *Canon of Christ Church Cathedral* 43n
Sylvius, Joannes, *see* Dubois, Jean
Tapper, Ruard, *Chancellor of Leuven University and Inquisitor-General of the Low Countries* 67n, 109n, 120n, 121, 232n
Taylor, Philip and Sabina 24n
Tertullian 110n, 131, 136n, 206n
Theophilus 88
Thomson, Ian xi
Tiletanus, Iudocus, *see* Ravesteyn, Josse
Titelmans, Frans, OFM, *Professor of Theology, Leuven University* 84n, 88, 97-98, 100, 102, 105
Tours, Berengar of, *see* Berengar of Tours
Tracy, Sir Richard, *County-Sheriff of Worcestershire* 27
Traheron, Bartholomew 225n
Tresham, William, *Canon of Christ Church Cathedral* 21, 43, 57, 232-233
Turner, William, *Dean of Wells* 149n
Ulmis, Johannes ab, *see* Ulmis, ab Johannes
Underwood, Edward, *Master of Whittington College* 26
Ussher, James, *Archbishop of Armagh* 17-18
Valla, Lorenzo 85n, 93
van Hosdein, Philip, *Abbot of St Gertrudis Leuven* 66
Vehe, Michael, OP 120n, 147
Vendeville, Jean de, *see* de Vendeville, Jean
Vercammen, Joris xi
Vermigli, Peter Martyr (Pietro Martire), *see also Subject Index*, 10-12, 21, 29n, 40-41, 42-47, 50n, 73, 75, 84n, 88, 108-109, 132, 138, 145n, 146, 150-159, 160n, 161-172, 174, 211n, 212-213, 221, 224-225, 227-228, 232-234, 236
Viglius van Aytta, *Jurist and senior official of Philip II* 62, 70
Villasancta, Garcia, *Lecturer in Divinity, Oxford University* 203n
Volgaia, Philip Nicholai, *see* Hondt, Philip Nicholai de
Waldeshef, William and Joan 24n
Watton, Baldwin 231
Weston, Hugh, *Prolocutor of Convocation* 55-56
Whittington, Alice 24
Whittington, Richard, *Lord Mayor of London* 24-26, 52
Wied, Hermann von, *Prince Archbishop of Köln* 148
Wilson, Nicholas, *Archdeacon of Oxford* 32
Wood, Anthony à 44
Wooding, Lucy 5, 8
Worcester, Bishops of, *see* Ghinucci, Geronimo; Latimer, Hugh

Worsley, Christopher, *Vicar of St Lawrence Jewry* 32
Wriothesley, Charles 35
Wyclif, John 176, 201, 217
Wyttaff, Matthew 22n
Zeghers, Nicholas, OFM, *Lecturer of Theology, Douai University* 79, 83
Zwingli, Huldrych 2, 87n, 219

PLACE NAME INDEX

Anchin Abbey 79-81
Antwerpen, Universitaire Faculteiten Sint Ignatius xi
Arras Diocese 62, 69
Artois 61n
Augsburg 3, 124n
Avignon 147n
Baden 192n
Basel 40n
Berkshire xii
Berwick 50
Brabant 72, 75
Bruges Diocese, *see* Brugge Diocese
Brugge Diocese 66
Brussel (Brussels, Bruxelles) 12, 62
Brussels, Bruxelles, *see* Brussel
Calvary 182-184, 187
Cambridge University xi, 7, 22-23, 40, 73, 146
    University Library 16n, 97
Campine, Archdeaconry 66
Canterbury Cathedral 25
Carthage 111n
Cologne, *see* Köln
Cuxham, Oxfordshire 21
Dieulouard 232n
Doornik, *see* Tournai
Douai 6, 14, 17, 65n, 67, 68-69, 74, 80, 95, 110, 220, 229, 232
    Collégiale Saint-Amé 17, 70-71
    Collégiale Saint-Pierre 17n, 70-71, 77
    English College 14, 72, 74-75
    Market Square 71
    Municipal Archives xii
    Municipal Library 11, 81
    St Catherine's Chapel 79
Douai University 13n, 60, 62, 71-73, 77, 79, 83, 85, 96, 103, 105-107, 176, 234
    Collège d'Anchin 79
    Collège du Roi 79
Escorial 71
Essex 53
Eton College 55
Evesham Abbey 18, 28

Evesham, St Lawrence's Church 18, 27
Exeter 68
Famenne, Archdeaconry 66
Ferns Diocese 18
Flanders, *see* Low Countries
Frodsham, Cheshire, St Lawrence's Church 52
Furnes, Collégiale Sainte-Walburge 66
Geneva 6
Gethsemane, Garden of 98
Goes 63
Habsburg Empire 231
Hainaut 61
Holy See, *see* Rome
Kleef (Cleves, Clivis, Kleve) 232n
Köln 12, 147-148
Leiden University xi
Leuven, St Gertrudis (Geertruiabdij) 66
Leuven University 13, 44, 46, 60, 62-66, 68-70, 72, 76, 79-80, 82-83, 87, 94, 97n, 101, 107, 121, 229
    College of the Crutched Friars (Kruisheren) 63
    College of the Friars Minor 64
    Faculty of Divinity 60n, 73
    Study Houses 'Oxford' and 'Cambridge' 73
Leuven, Collegium Trilinguarum 98
    Printing Presses 44, 47, 67n, 81, 228-229, 232-233
Lichfield Diocese 97
Liège Principality and Diocese 66
Liège, Collégiale Saint-Lambert 66
Lille 60
Lincoln Diocese 21, 56
London Diocese 30, 52
London, Hospital and Church of St Thomas Acon 32
    House of Lords 213n
    Institute for Historical Research xi
    Lambeth Palace 40, 57-58
    Printing Presses 228
    St Anthony's Budge Row 30, 108

St Dunstan's-in-the-East 52
St Lawrence Jewry 32
St Michael's-Paternoster Royal 24-25, 27, 30
St Paul's Cathedral 53
St Paul's Cross 30, 32, 38-39
Westminster Abbey 53
Whittington College 24-27, 35, 52
Louvain, *see*: Leuven
Low Countries 1, 17, 41, 44, 60-61, 63-64, 66, 72-73, 75-76, 95, 121, 147, 177, *see also*: Walloon Low Countries
Luik, Lüttich, *see*: Liège
Maubeuge 60
Mechelen (Malines) 63, 69
Methven 48
Namur 63
Netherlands, *see*: Low Countries
Nicaea 131, 140
Niniveh 127
Oxford 18, 28, 32, 34-35, 38-39, 42-46, 50-51, 54, 77, 233
Oxford University 7, 13, 14n, 19-20, 22, 24-27, 40-41, 54, 57, 71n, 73, 76, 88, 138, 233n
    Augustinian Study House 19
    Balliol College 56
    Brasenose College 29
    Christ Church College 22, 27, 40, 43n, 52, *see also*: Oxford University, King Henry VIII's College
    Corpus Christi College 32
    Divinity School 10, 23, 29, 43, 57, 83, 108-109, 132, 152, 159
    King Henry VIII's College (Christ Church College) 22, 27, 40, 43n, 52
    Magdalen College 21, 43n
    Merton College 19-23
    New College 73
    St Alban's Hall 22n
    St Mary's Hall 74
    University Church of St Mary-the-Virgin 22n, 30-31
Paris 45n, 47, 210-212, 225

University, *see*: Sorbonne
Printing Presses 45n, 47-48, 211, 228, 232
Racmacneia, *see*: Rosslare
Rochester Diocese 142n
Rome 3-4, 31, 36, 61, 67, 177, 228
    St John Lateran Basilica 180
Rosslare 18n
St Omer Diocese 66
Salem 188
Salisbury Diocese 227
Scotland 44, 49, 57, *see also*: Methven, St Andrew's
Slough xii
Sorbonne 93, 97
St Andrews 13n, 43-44, 48, 50
    University 48-49
    St Mary's College 48
St Davids 32n
Strassburg 2, 12, 40
Switzerland 149n
Thame, Oxfordshire, Abbey Church
Thebaid, Upper 150n, 151
Thérouanne Diocese 66
Tournai (Doornik) 60n, 61
    Collegium Linguarum
Trent 67, 91-92, 94n, 115, 149, 177, 181, 217
Trier 148
Utrecht University xi
Wales 76
Walloon Low Countries (Wallonie, Flandre wallone) 61-62
Wendelstein 182
Wexford 18n
Whittington College, *see*: London, Whittington College
Winchester Diocese 4, 36
Windsor Castle 2, 34
Wittenberg 6, 23, 218n
Worcester, Worcestershire (Vigornia, Worcestria) 17-19, 27
Württemberg 218n
Zürich xi, 2, 6

SUBJECT INDEX

Agricola, Rudolph, hermeneutics 85, 107
   eucharistic doctrine 177-178, 184
   theology of justification 112-113, 116, 123
Bar, François de, appointment as Grand Prior of Anchin 80
   lecture notes 11, 79, 96, 105, 107
Bible, Gutenberg edition 92
   Vulgate 80, 92-94
      revisions 92-94
      use at Douai University 80
Biel, Gabriel, eucharistic doctrine 179-181, 183
   theology of justification 114-115
Cajetan, Thomas de Vio Cardinal, censure of 97-98
Cambridge University, Lutheran influences 23
   royal lectureships, creation of 22-23
Charles V, desire to establish a Francophone university 60
Christ Church College, Oxford, *see*: King Henry VIII's College Oxford
Clergy marriage 145-151
   patristic sources 150-151, 155
   scriptural sources 149-150, 155
Cochlaeus (Dobeneck), Johannes, debates with Luther 182-183
Company of Mercers, Whittington College, establishment of 24
Confessio Augustana 110, 119-120
Council of Florence (1438-1445), definition of purgatory 217-218
Council of Trent (1545-1563), definition of purgatory 217
Cranmer, Thomas, heresy trial 54-56
Douai University, appointment of first lecturers 69-70
   Douai University, appointment of theology lecturers 67-69
   first conception of 60-61
   inaugural lecture 71
   letters patent 62

   New Testament lectures 78-84
      Comma Iohanneum 82
   selection of teaching staff 62-63
   Smyth, appointment as premier lecteur 68
   Vulgate, use at 80
Douai, appointment of provost, Collégiale Saint-Pierre 70-71
   Collège d'Anchin, establishment 79
   English College, foundation 72-75, 220
   evangelical teaching, reactions to 61
   Municipal Library, Destruction of Manuscripts 81
   Study Bible Manuscript 80
Eck, Johannes, debates with Luther 182-183
Elizabeth I, accession 57
Eucharist, corporeal presence 101-103, 181, 183-184
   medieval dissenters 176-177, 181, 195, 205
   Ockhamist understanding 180
   sacrifice of the Mass, benefits for souls in purgatory 218
   sacrifice of the Mass, *repraesentatio* 178-179, 183-184, 186-187, 199, 206
   Scotist understanding 179-180, 182
   testamentum Christi 180-181, 187-188
   thesaurus Christi 184, 187-188
   Thomist understanding 177-178, 205
   transubstantiation 180-181
Forty Articles of Religion (1550) 49
Forty Two Articles of Religion (1553) 121, 138
Granvelle, Antoine Perrenot Cardinal de, Smyth's patron 66, 227
Haliburton, David, friendship with Smyth 48
Henry VIII, divorce from Katherine of Aragon 23
   King's College, Oxford, *see*: King Henry VIII's College, Oxford

SUBJECT INDEX

royal lectureships 22-23
Indulgences 146, 181
Indwelling (μένειν; *mansio*) 134-135
Jewel, John, *Apologia Ecclesiae Anglicanae* 216
Jewel, John, polemical attacks on Smyth 75-76, 216
Justification, *fides formata* 112, 121
    human co-operation 111-112, 121
    original sin 110-111
    preconditions of grace 115
    Scholastic understanding 113-114, 131
    Scotist understanding 114, 132
    Thomist understanding 112-113, 116, 123
King Henry VIII's College, Oxford 22, 27
Language, meta-language 1-2, 9-11, 228, 235-237
Latimer, Hugh, burning of 56
Latin, use of 1, 9-10, 16, 224-225, 231-232
Louvain School of Apologetics, *see*: Louvainists
Louvainists 73-74
Luther, Martin, debates with Cochlaeus and Eck 182-183
    early understanding of justification 115-116
    eucharistic doctrine 181-182, 196-198
    iustificatio extranea 116
    justification by faith alone 116-119, 121, 123
Manducatio impiorum *42n, 212-215*
Margaret, Duchess of Parma, opinion of Smyth 67, 74, 95
Melanchthon, Philipp, *Apologia Confessionis Augustanae* 123, 130-131
Melchizedek, priestly order of 35, 188-189, 191, 193-194
Merton College, Oxford, fellowship of 21
Monasteries, dissolution of 145, 173-174
Ochino, Bernardino, invitation to teach in England 40
Oxford disputation on the eucharist (1549) 43, 232

Oxford University, Biblical exegesis 83
    Christ Church College, *see*: King Henry VIII's College, Oxford, *and* Smyth, Richard
    Faculty of Divinity, change of curriculum 83-84
    King Henry VIII's College, *see*: King Henry VIII's College, Oxford, *and* Smyth, Richard
    Merton College, *see*: Merton College, Oxford, *and* Smyth, Richard
    royal commission on Henry VIII's divorce (1530) 23
    royal lectureships, creation of 22-23
    scribe 20
    Whittington College, London, links with 26
Parker, Matthew, and Richard Smyth 57-59
Perspicuitas scripturae 84, 86-89
Polemical writings, eschatological urgency 221-222, 235-237
    smuggling of works into England 45, 211, 231
Purgatory 146, 216-218
    definition of, Council of Florence (1438-1445) 217-218
    Council of Trent (1545-1563) 217
    patristic 216-218
    sacrifice of the Mass, benefits 217-218
Richardot, François, appointment at Douai University 69
    inaugural lecture at Douai 71
    lectures on 1 Timothy 78
Ridley, Nicholas, burning of 56
Romans, letter to the, obscurity 84, 86-89
Royal Supremacy 5-6
Smyth, Richard, academic disputations 11, 19-21, 153-154
    adroitness for biblical exegesis 80
    attacks by prominent evangelicals 27-30, 75-76, 153-154, 158
    attacks on Cranmer 47-50, 175, 210-216, 225-226, 232, 234, *see also*: publications, *Confutation of a certen booke*
    attacks on Seton 30, 108
    bibliographical sources 13-17

SUBJECT INDEX 273

Smyth, Richard
 biographical research on 13-17
 Bishops' Book, signatory 27
 burning of Latimer and Ridley,
  preaches at 56
 contemporary reputation 67, 74, 76-
  77, 95-96
 convocation, representative at 27
 Council of Trent, invitation 67
 Covenent, theology of 98, 198
 David Haliburton, friendship with
  48
 Douai University, inaugural lecture
  71
  premier lecteur 68
 Douai, Collégiale Saint-Pierre,
  provost 70-71
 early education 18-19, 221
 early eucharistic doctrine 33, 193
 early life 17-18
 ecclesiastical livings, Christ Church
  Oxford, canon 52
  Cuxham, Oxfordshire 21
  St Dunstan's-in-the-East 52
  St Lawrence's, Frodsham,
   Cheshire 52
  St Michael's Paternoster Royal 26
 eucharist, corporeal presence 101-
  103, 200-210
 eucharist, corporeal presence,
  participation 207-208
 eucharist, corporeal presence,
  patristic sources 203-208
 eucharist, heresies, attack on 176-
  177, 181, 195, 201-203, 205, 218-
  220
 eucharist, mediation of grace 99-
  100, 187-188, 194, 209-212
 eucharist, ministry *in persona Christi*
  99-100, 104, 201-202, 204, 208-209
 eucharist, Pauline tradition 100-101
 eucharist, priesthood 104, 106-108,
  187-188, 196-197, 201-202, 204,
  208-209, 218, 220
 eucharist, sacrifice of the Mass 186-
  200
 eucharist, sacrifice of the Mass, New
  Testament sources 195-200
 eucharist, sacrifice of the Mass, Old
  Testament sources 188-195

heresy trials, Askew 34
heresy trials, Cranmer 54-56
heresy trials, London 53
justification 30, 39, 84, 120-142, 228,
 234
 accusation of semi-Pelagianism
  137-138
 approbatio 136
 attrition 125n
 certitudo 121, 124
 charitas 132-138
 defence of supererogatory works
  110, 121, 138-142, 145
 facienti quod in se est 142-144, 222
 fiducia 121-124, 126
 first justification 132-134
 merit 121, 129-132
 New Testament sources 125-127,
  133-135
 Old Testament sources 127, 132-
  133, 140
 patristic sources 109, 126, 131,
  136, 140, 221
 rejection of Melanchthon 6, 109-
  110, 123-125, 130-131, 136,
  140, 228, 234
 works of charity 12, 121, 132-138
Lambeth, house arrest at 57
lecturing, Biblical Canon 90-92
 definition of *modi canonici* 91-92
 Douai notes, *see*: Bar, François de,
  lecture notes
 Douai University, inaugural 71
 exegetical method 101-103
 Romans 78-79, 84, 109
 sensus of Scripture 94-96
 teaching methods 85-86, 105
Leuven University, enrolments 44,
 60
Leuven, sojourn at Kruisheren 63-64
Melanchthon *Loci Communes*, refutation of 6, 109-110, 174, 228
Merton College, dean 20-21
 junior fellowship 19
ordination 21
Oxford University, attendance at
 Vermigli's lectures 41
 Bachelor of Arts 19
 Master of Arts 19
 royal *praelector* 23

Smyth, Richard
    royal *praelector*, dismissal 40
    scribe 20
  patrons, loyalty 27, 64-65, 177
  perspicuitas scripturae, rejection of 84, 86-89
  polemicist 218-219, 222-237
    orthodoxy 95-96, 228, 235-237
    preaching 30-32, 56, 108
    techniques 223-228
  publications, *A defence of the blessed Masse* 33, 185-210, 216n, 228-230
    Bouclier of the Catholike Fayeth 51, 53-54, 109, 138-141, 145, 226, 228, 230
    Confutation of a certen booke 47-48, 175, 210-216, 232
    Confvtatio 65, 224
    De libero hominis arbitrio 73n, 84n
    De Missae Sacrificio 65, 216-220
    De Votis Monasticis 45, 151-174, 228n, 232
    Defensio Coelibatus 48, 221, 231-232
    Defensio compendaria 65-66
    Diatriba de hominis justificatione 47-48, 108, 120-142, 228, 230
    Refutatio luculenza 65, 229, 234
    Refvtatio locorum communiorum 72n, 138, 142
    The Assertion and Defence 8, 33n, 185-210, 223, 228-229
  recantations, St Paul's Cross, 34, 36-37, 108
    Oxford, 38-40
  royal pardon 51
  smuggling of works into England 45, 211, 231
solifidianism, opposition 6, 84, 108-110, 123-125, 130-131, 136, 140, 228, 234
St Andrew's, exiles in 43-44, 49-51
vows, New Testament sources 149-150, 156-157, 160-161, 164, 168-170
    Old Testament sources 155-156
  Whittington College, master 26
  Stephen Gardiner, response to Smyth's recantation 36
Tapper, Ruard, theology of justification 120n, 121
Tournai College, curriculum 60n
Vermigli, Peter Martyr, invitation to teach in England 40
  justification, rejection of works 132
  lecture on 1 Cor 40-41
  oral *tractatio* with Smyth 41-42, 152
  physical attacks on 233
  polemical attacks on 41, 44-47, 146, 153-154, 159, 164-165, 174, 224-225, 227, 232, 235-236
  polemical attacks on Smyth 75-76, 153-154, 158, 162-164, 166-168, 235-236
  publications, *Defensio* 152-174
  reformed eucharistic doctrine 41-42
Vernacular, use of the 1, 9-10, 15-17, 222-227
Whittington College London, first dissolution (1548) 26
  links with Oxford University 26
  patronage 25
  statutes 24

STUDIES IN MEDIEVAL AND REFORMATION THOUGHT

FOUNDED BY HEIKO A. OBERMAN †
EDITED BY ANDREW COLIN GOW

36. MEERHOFF, K. *Rhétorique et poétique au XVIe siècle en France.* 1986
37. GERRITS, G. H. *Inter timorem et spem.* Gerard Zerbolt of Zutphen. 1986
38. ANGELO POLIZIANO. *Lamia.* Ed. by A. Wesseling. 1986
39. BRAW, C. *Bücher im Staube.* Die Theologie Johann Arndts in ihrem Verhältnis zur Mystik. 1986
40. BUCER, Martin. *Opera Latina.* Vol. II. Enarratio in Evangelion Iohannis (1528, 1530, 1536). Publié par I. Backus. 1988
41. BUCER, Martin. *Opera Latina.* Vol. III. Martin Bucer and Matthew Parker: Florilegium Patristicum. Edition critique. Publié par P. Fraenkel. 1988
42. BUCER, Martin. *Opera Latina.* Vol. IV. Consilium Theologicum Privatim Conscriptum. Publié par P. Fraenkel. 1988
43. BUCER, Martin. *Correspondance.* Tome II (1524-1526). Publié par J. Rott. 1989
44. RASMUSSEN, T. *Inimici Ecclesiae.* Das ekklesiologische Feindbild in Luthers "Dictata super Psalterium" (1513-1515) im Horizont der theologischen Tradition. 1989
45. POLLET, J. *Julius Pflug et la crise religieuse dans l'Allemagne du XVIe siècle.* Essai de synthèse biographique et théologique. 1990
46. BUBENHEIMER, U. *Thomas Müntzer.* Herkunft und Bildung. 1989
47. BAUMAN, C. *The Spiritual Legacy of Hans Denck.* Interpretation and Translation of Key Texts. 1991
48. OBERMAN, H. A. and JAMES, F. A., III (eds.). in cooperation with SAAK, E. L. *Via Augustini.* Augustine in the Later Middle Ages, Renaissance and Reformation: Essays in Honor of Damasus Trapp. 1991 *out of print*
49. SEIDEL MENCHI, S. *Erasmus als Ketzer.* Reformation und Inquisition im Italien des 16. Jahrhunderts. 1993
50. SCHILLING, H. *Religion, Political Culture, and the Emergence of Early Modern Society.* Essays in German and Dutch History. 1992
51. DYKEMA, P. A. and OBERMAN, H. A. (eds.). *Anticlericalism in Late Medieval and Early Modern Europe.* 2nd ed. 1994
52. 53. KRIEGER, Chr. and LIENHARD, M. (eds.). *Martin Bucer and Sixteenth Century Europe.* Actes du colloque de Strasbourg (28-31 août 1991). 1993
54. SCREECH, M. A. *Clément Marot: A Renaissance Poet discovers the World.* Lutheranism, Fabrism and Calvinism in the Royal Courts of France and of Navarre and in the Ducal Court of Ferrara. 1994
55. GOW, A. C. *The Red Jews: Antisemitism in an Apocalyptic Age, 1200-1600.* 1995
56. BUCER, Martin. *Correspondance.* Tome III (1527-1529). Publié par Chr. Krieger et J. Rott. 1989
57. SPIJKER, W. VAN 'T. *The Ecclesiastical Offices in the Thought of Martin Bucer.* Translated by J. Vriend (text) and L.D. Bierma (notes). 1996
58. GRAHAM, M.F. *The Uses of Reform.* 'Godly Discipline' and Popular Behavior in Scotland and Beyond, 1560-1610. 1996
59. AUGUSTIJN, C. *Erasmus.* Der Humanist als Theologe und Kirchenreformer. 1996
60. McCOOG S J, T. M. *The Society of Jesus in Ireland, Scotland, and England 1541-1588.* 'Our Way of Proceeding?' 1996
61. FISCHER, N. und KOBELT-GROCH, M. (Hrsg.). *Außenseiter zwischen Mittelalter und Neuzeit.* Festschrift für Hans-Jürgen Goertz zum 60. Geburtstag. 1997
62. NIEDEN, M. *Organum Deitatis.* Die Christologie des Thomas de Vio Cajetan. 1997
63. BAST, R.J. *Honor Your Fathers.* Catechisms and the Emergence of a Patriarchal Ideology in Germany, 1400-1600. 1997

64. ROBBINS, K.C. *City on the Ocean Sea: La Rochelle, 1530-1650*. Urban Society, Religion, and Politics on the French Atlantic Frontier. 1997
65. BLICKLE, P. *From the Communal Reformation to the Revolution of the Common Man.* 1998
66. FELMBERG, B. A. R. *Die Ablaßtheorie Kardinal Cajetans (1469-1534).* 1998
67. CUNEO, P. F. *Art and Politics in Early Modern Germany.* Jörg Breu the Elder and the Fashioning of Political Identity, ca. 1475-1536. 1998
68. BRADY, Jr., Th. A. *Communities, Politics, and Reformation in Early Modern Europe.* 1998
69. McKEE, E. A. *The Writings of Katharina Schütz Zell.* 1. The Life and Thought of a Sixteenth-Century Reformer. 2. A Critical Edition. 1998
70. BOSTICK, C. V. *The Antichrist and the Lollards.* Apocalyticism in Late Medieval and Reformation England. 1998
71. BOYLE, M. O'ROURKE. *Senses of Touch.* Human Dignity and Deformity from Michelangelo to Calvin. 1998
72. TYLER, J.J. *Lord of the Sacred City.* The *Episcopus Exclusus* in Late Medieval and Early Modern Germany. 1999
74. WITT, R.G. *'In the Footsteps of the Ancients'.* The Origins of Humanism from Lovato to Bruni. 2000
77. TAYLOR, L.J. *Heresy and Orthodoxy in Sixteenth-Century Paris.* François le Picart and the Beginnings of the Catholic Reformation. 1999
78. BUCER, Martin. *Briefwechsel/Correspondance.* Band IV (Januar-September 1530). Herausgegeben und bearbeitet von R. Friedrich, B. Hamm und A. Puchta. 2000
79. MANETSCH, S.M. *Theodore Beza and the Quest for Peace in France, 1572-1598.* 2000
80. GODMAN, P. *The Saint as Censor.* Robert Bellarmine between Inquisition and Index. 2000
81. SCRIBNER, R.W. *Religion and Culture in Germany (1400-1800).* Ed. L. Roper. 2001
82. KOOI, C. *Liberty and Religion.* Church and State in Leiden's Reformation, 1572-1620. 2000
83. BUCER, Martin. *Opera Latina.* Vol. V. Defensio adversus axioma catholicum id est criminationem R.P. Roberti Episcopi Abrincensis (1534). Ed. W.I.P. Hazlett. 2000
84. BOER, W. de. *The Conquest of the Soul.* Confession, Discipline, and Public Order in Counter-Reformation Milan. 2001
85. EHRSTINE, G. *Theater, culture, and community in Reformation Bern, 1523-1555.* 2001
86. CATTERALL, D. *Community Without Borders.* Scot Migrants and the Changing Face of Power in the Dutch Republic, c. 1600-1700. 2002
87. BOWD, S.D. *Reform Before the Reformation.* Vincenzo Querini and the Religious Renaissance in Italy. 2002
88. PELC, M. *Illustrium Imagines.* Das Porträtbuch der Renaissance. 2002
89. SAAK, E.L. *High Way to Heaven.* The Augustinian Platform between Reform and Reformation, 1292-1524. 2002
90. WITTNEBEN, E.L. *Bonagratia von Bergamo*, Franziskanerjurist und Wortführer seines Ordens im Streit mit Papst Johannes XXII. 2003
91. ZIKA, C. *Exorcising our Demons,* Magic, Witchcraft and Visual Culture in Early Modern Europe. 2002
92. MATTOX, M.L. *"Defender of the Most Holy Matriarchs"*, Martin Luther's Interpretation of the Women of Genesis in the *Enarrationes in Genesin*, 1535-45. 2003
93. LANGHOLM, O. *The Merchant in the Confessional,* Trade and Price in the Pre-Reformation Penitential Handbooks. 2003
94. BACKUS, I. *Historical Method and Confessional Identity in the Era of the Reformation (1378-1615).* 2003
95. FOGGIE, J.P. *Renaissance Religion in Urban Scotland.* The Dominican Order, 1450-1560. 2003.
96. LÖWE, J.A. *Richard Smyth and the Language of Orthodoxy.* Re-imagining Tudor Catholic Polemicism. 2003.